LANDMARKS OF CONTEMPORARY POLITICAL THOUGHT

Christopher C. DeMuth, series editor

HERE THE PEOPLE RULE
SELECTED ESSAYS: SECOND EDITION
Edward C. Banfield

AS FAR AS REPUBLICAN PRINCIPLES WILL ADMIT
Essays by Martin Diamond

BLACKS, WOMEN, AND JEWS ARE NOT MENTIONED IN THE
CONSTITUTION, AND OTHER UNORTHODOX VIEWS
Robert A. Goldwin

TOWARD A MORE PERFECT UNION
Writings of Herbert J. Storing

ON CHARACTER
Essays by James Q. Wilson

Toward a
Perfect U

W

Toward a More Perfect Union

Writings of Herbert J. Storing

Edited by
Joseph M. Bessette

The AEI Press

Publisher for the American Enterprise Institute
WASHINGTON, D.C.

1995

The editor gratefully thanks Mrs. Kathryn Storing, Joseph Cropsey, and Gary Schmitt for helping to make this volume possible.

Library of Congress Cataloging-in-Publication Data

Storing, Herbert J., 1928–1977
  Toward a more perfect Union / writings of Herbert J. Storing.
    p. cm.
  Includes bibliographical references and index.
  ISBN 0-8447-3841-7. — ISBN 0-8447-3840-9 (pbk.)
    1. United States—Politics and government.   2. United States-
  -Constitutional history.   3. Political science—United States.
  I. Title.
  E183.S784   1995
  320.973—dc20   94-22771
                                                          CIP

THE AEI PRESS
Publisher for the American Enterprise Institute
1150 17th Street, N.W., Washington, D.C. 20036

Distributed in Europe, the Middle East, Africa, and selected territories outside the United States by Eurospan. For more information, contact Eurospan, 3 Henrietta Street, London WC2E 8LU, England.

Printed in the United States of America

Contents

Foreword

Herbert J. Storing was a graduate of the Political Science Department of the University of Chicago. He served on the faculty of that department from 1957 to 1976 and, as he was about to take up new tasks at the University of Virginia, died very suddenly on September 9, 1977, at the age of forty-nine.

Storing had been taught by C. Herman Pritchett and Leo Strauss. He devoted himself unreservedly to constitutional law and public administration, but no reader of what is contained in this book will fail to see the influence of political philosophy on his writing and thinking. A stern reasoner with an appetite for the heart of the matter, he strove to keep in sight the human meaning of the issues that he handled. A man and scholar of the strictest rectitude, incorruptibly just, his writings on the position of blacks in this country are a model of intelligent sympathy, of courageous and unsentimental generosity of spirit. His work on the American founding contains an unprejudged juxtaposing of the constitutional principles that won out and those that were rejected when the nation was being designed. The attention that he gave to the political wisdom latent in American literary writings has borne fruit in the work of his former students.

Storing was a powerful, extremely influential teacher. The forthrightness and uprightness of the scholar in his writing were forcefully manifest in the man as a presence. His logic straightened his thought without hardening his heart; his students learned from his example the difference between sentiment and sentimentality. As the years have proved, his learning, his fairness, and his intelligence left such an impression on his students that this book can be understood as a material reminiscence of their teacher and friend. Eventually, it will serve as a monument.

JOSEPH CROPSEY

Toward a More Perfect Union

1
Editor's Introduction

Joseph M. Bessette

This volume brings together major essays and other writings of Herbert J. Storing, written over a decade and a half between the early 1960s and his death in 1977. Many of his widely read and highly influential writings on the American founding, race relations, bureaucracy and public administration, and statesmanship have since fallen out of print, thus limiting access to a body of profound instruction on the nature and enduring importance of America's deepest political principles.

Overview

Of the twenty-four selections included here, fourteen were originally written and published as separate essays. One could not improve on Ralph Lerner's description of these essays as "powerful, lucid, [and] direct" and as "models of clarity, integrity, and judgment."[1] In the present volume, these essays are joined by ten other writings, five of which have not been published before. These previously unpublished selections include two major addresses delivered to academic audiences—one on big government (chapter 17) and the other on the presidency and the Constitution (chapter 19); one piece on liberal education written for an academic conference (chapter 23); two sketches (joined here) of plans for studying the American presidency (chapter 20), written in the last years of Storing's life; and remarks Storing addressed to incoming graduate students at the University of Chicago (chapter 24).

Four selections here are from longer works. One (chapter 3) is drawn from the introductory essay to Storing's monumental seven-volume edition of Anti-Federalist writings, the publication of which was described by Leonard Levy as "a civic event of enduring importance."[2] The entire essay, "What the Anti-Federalists Were *For*," is

---

1. *PS*, vol. XI, no. 1 (Winter 1978), p. 113.
2. *New York Times*, February 21, 1982, sec. 7, p. 24.

also available as a separate publication through the University of Chicago Press. Another selection (chapter 9) is the preface and introduction to Storing's edited collection of writings of black Americans, *What Country Have I?* A third (chapter 12) is a brief excerpt on the public interest from Storing's first book-length publication, *The State and the Farmer*, written with Peter Self. Also included is Storing's introduction to the reissue of Charles C. Thach's *The Creation of the Presidency* (chapter 18). Finally, one selection (chapter 21) is Storing's testimony in 1977 to a Senate committee defending the electoral college against proposals before the committee to replace it with direct popular election.

In any project of this sort space limitations dictate that judgments must be made about what to include and exclude. At the end of this volume the reader will find a chronological bibliography, indicating which of Storing's writings are not included in the present volume or appear only in part. One large project not represented here is Storing's detailed analysis and critique of the administrative writings of Herbert Simon, which was published in the volume Storing edited, *Essays on the Scientific Study of Politics*. Also missing are Storing's reply to a review of this book in the *American Political Science Review*; two essays cowritten with Peter Self (derived from their joint project on British agriculture policy); forewords he wrote to books by former students; his eulogy to Martin Diamond, which appeared in *PS*, a publication of the American Political Science Association; and several book reviews. My rationale concerning inclusion or exclusion has been to bring together Storing's major essays, excerpts from longer works, and significant unpublished writings across the range of issues that focused his scholarship and teaching during his highly productive, though unfortunately truncated, academic career.

A word more, however, should be said about the selection of unpublished writings. Given Storing's own particularly high publication standards, a case could be made that nothing should be included here that he had previously decided, for one reason or another, not to publish. Yet this principle must be balanced against the accident of his untimely death and the realization that whatever is not included in this volume, no matter how valuable, will likely be lost forever to those who did not hear his arguments firsthand in the classroom or in other academic settings. Thus, I have taken a kind of middle ground, including a few particularly substantial essays or addresses and other shorter writings that are not duplicated in the published corpus and that elucidate major themes in Storing's understanding of American political principles.

The Founding Fathers

The writings collected here are organized into six groups. The first, on the constitutional foundations of American government and politics, informs all that follows, as is made explicit in many of the later selections. Storing believed and demonstrated through his writings and teaching that modern Americans had much to learn from a recovery of the thought of the nation's leading Founding Fathers, and especially of those who were principally responsible for drafting and ratifying the Constitution of 1787. He rejected the all-too-common assumption that the deepest kind of political understanding necessarily progresses with the passage of time. If we begin with such an assumption, we foreclose any possibility of learning from those who came before, thereby begging the question whether the architects of our political order—or any other American statesmen or thinkers—have anything important to teach us today.

Storing confronted this issue of the relevance of the thought of the past to our present concerns in his essay on the great black educator, Booker T. Washington (chapter 8). Some would dismiss Washington as merely a "man of his times" who accepted "current notions of Negro education (and even Negro inferiority) . . . [and was] moved by the fashionable currents of Social Darwinism and the Gospel of Wealth." This kind of approach, Storing argues, attempts to explain "what is reasonably clear—what Washington said and did—by viewing it as reflection of what is cloudy and vague—the 'times' in which he lived." It also ignores that these times were indeed "formed out of the ideas of men, men like Washington." Finally, "if we are to presume of Washington that he is merely a 'man of his times' (and treat him with the patronizing tolerance he would then deserve), are we not to presume (and to treat) similarly Washington's opponents and their successors? And have we not therefore cut away any ground upon which we might stand in addressing ourselves, as all of these men thought to address themselves, to questions about the 'times' in which we live?"

In his analysis of the arguments of American political thinkers, Storing found some persuasive and others wanting, but in every case he did his best to understand the thinker as he would have understood himself. He took all his subjects seriously, presuming that they had something important to say and that what they did say should be evaluated on its own terms. To begin with the assumption that we know more because we came later, that the arguments of earlier thinkers were either historically determined or of no value outside the historical epoch that produced them, or that such arguments

3

merely reflect underlying interests or prejudices is to consign our own thought and arguments to the same indictments some years hence and thus to undermine political thought itself.

As is also clear from these writings, Storing's investigation and analysis of the political thought that animated the nation's founders were not exercises in the sociology of knowledge or even intellectual history as conventionally understood. He rejected the notion that one could learn as much about the nation's founding principles from the second-rate thinker as from the first-rate. The major political actors of the era were not all equally penetrating in their understanding of republican government and what would be necessary to ensure its success. Indeed, as Storing noted in his review of more than a hundred essays and pamphlets written in defense of the Constitution during the ratification struggle of 1787–1788 (chapter 4), these "other" Federalist writings, "taken as a whole, . . . tend to be rather shallow and routine" in comparison with the much more famous *Federalist Papers* written by Alexander Hamilton, James Madison, and John Jay. Storing found "nothing in [these] Federalist writings comparable to the range and depth of *The Federalist*." Consequently, the reader will find much more analysis in the present volume of the thought of Hamilton and Madison than of their lesser contemporaries.

What, then, of the Anti-Federalists, those who opposed the adoption of the plan of government recommended by the Constitutional Convention? That Storing devoted much of his scholarly efforts over a decade to the preparation of the first complete edition of Anti-Federalist thought is testimony enough to the value he placed on recovering the principles of this side of the debate as well. While it is true that Storing's own mature conclusion after years of close study was that "the Anti-Federalists lost the debate over the Constitution . . . because they had the weaker argument," he also came to believe that the deepest of the opponents of the Constitution rightly understood the necessary dependence of any popular government on republican virtue. The Anti-Federalists were reasonably fearful that the new governmental scheme did not make adequate provision for inculcating and promoting such virtue (chapter 3). Indeed, "will not the constitutional regime, the Anti-Federalists asked, with its emphasis on private, self-seeking, commercial activities, release and foster a certain type of human being who will be likely to destroy that very regime?" At their best, "the Anti-Federalists saw . . . the insufficiency of a community of mere interest. They saw that the American polity had to be a moral community if it was to be anything, and they saw that the seat of that community must be the hearts of the people."

Although the Federalists did not deny the importance of virtue, they did express reservations about its sufficiency in preventing interested majorities or factious leaders from violating private rights or the public good. Madison, in particular, had written that "neither moral nor religious motives can be relied on as an adequate control" (*Federalist* 10). More so than their opponents, the leading Federalists emphasized the importance of effective government as "the key to the attachment of the people and to civic virtue itself. A government that can actually accomplish its resolves, that can keep the peace, protect property, and promote the prosperity of the country, will be a government respected and obeyed by its citizens. It will, moreover, promote private and public morality by providing them with effective protection." Effective government, in turn, meant "wise deliberation and vigorous execution." And these required a well-designed bicameral legislative body and a unified executive promoting a system of sound administration.

Thus, at bottom the founding debate was a great contest over how to achieve the ends of liberty and self-government to which both sides were thoroughly committed. As Storing notes in the lead essay to this volume and elsewhere, to see the creation of and contest over the Constitution as merely the result of a clash of interests—"the large and small state interests; the commercial and landed interests; [and] the northern and southern interests"—is to miss an essential dynamic of the founding process and to do an enormous disservice to those responsible for fashioning the American political order (chapter 2). For what divided the delegates to the Constitutional Convention, as well as Federalists and Anti-Federalists more generally, were not merely interests but also "certain broad principles of free government."

These principles included: the necessity of a strong Union versus the virtue of small political units; the need for energetic administration of government versus the importance of republican spirit in promoting law-abidingness; the importance of institutions for moderating and refining public opinion versus the need for republican government to remain true to the interests and reasonable desires of the citizenry; and the reliance on self-interest in counteracting tyranny from popular majorities or governmental institutions versus the ultimate grounding of republican institutions on civic virtue. It is perhaps not an overstatement to say that understanding and explicating these great founding principles were the core of Storing's scholarly efforts.

Much of the rest of Storing's corpus, then, is best understood in light of its relationship to the American founding and to the debate over the principles of free government that animated the epochal political events of the founding period. No issue, of course, raises deeper questions about the founders' commitment to liberty and self-government than does slavery. Critics of the Founding Fathers ask how we can take seriously anything said by Jefferson, Madison, and their contemporaries on the subject of liberty and democracy, when these men and many of their countrymen were denying liberty and self-government to some hundreds of thousands of black Americans.

Race Relations

Common today is the view that "the founders excluded the Negroes from the 'rights of man' expressed in the Declaration of Independence and sanctioned slavery and Negro inferiority in the Constitution" (chapter 6). As Storing shows, this critique of the Founding Fathers embraces both the radical Abolitionists' view that the Constitution, in protecting and furthering the slave interest, was a "compact with the devil"; and the view of mid-nineteenth century slavery defenders, who held either that the principle of human equality in the Declaration of Independence was a "self-evident lie" or that the founders could not possibly have meant to include blacks among the "all men" who "are created equal."

Yet these interpretations of the founders' approach to slavery were rejected by no less a person than Frederick Douglass, former slave and the most prominent and gifted black orator and spokesman during the decades surrounding the Civil War. Storing reminds us that in the middle of that conflict Douglass proclaimed that "the federal government was never, in its essence, anything but an anti-slavery government. . . . It was purposely . . . framed so as to give no claim, no sanction to the claim, of property in man." Storing's close analysis of the constitutional provisions related to slavery and of judicial and political practice and opinion in the nation's first decades is a masterful defense of Douglass's view—one also shared by Abraham Lincoln and other leaders of the Republican party, if now all but forgotten and little taught.

The Civil War ended slavery in the United States, but in so doing it precipitated a challenge of perhaps equal difficulty: bringing the two races, for decades consigned by positive law into a master-slave relationship, together onto a plane of social and political equality. Storing shows that leading American statesmen such as Jefferson and Lincoln had entertained grave doubts as to whether white prejudice and black resentment for past wrongs would allow the creation of a peaceful biracial democratic society. He speculates, writing in the mid-1970s, that a thoughtful Founding Father reviewing present-day circumstances might well "be amazed at the degree to which blacks and whites have progressed in making a civil society together. I think he would frankly admit that he would never have expected anything like the degree of harmony, mutual trust and toleration, and opportunity for blacks that have been achieved in the United States."

Yet as Storing notes, race relations remain a serious problem for American democracy. Where is one to look—where in particular ought black Americans to look—for insight and guidance as to how the two races can be brought together into a genuine community of citizens? Storing points the way to recovering the thought and contributions of two towering black Americans: Frederick Douglass and Booker T. Washington. He contrasts these teachings with those of W. E. B. Du Bois, one of the founders of the National Association for the Advancement of Colored People (NAACP), and a man whose writings were the inspiration for much black political thought in the United States in the early and mid-twentieth century.

In the final selection in this section, the preface and introduction to his one-volume edition of black political thought, Storing shows how black American thinkers address not only the needs of their race but also "perennial questions of political life," including the issue of individual responsibility, the nature of prejudice, the relation between the political whole and its parts, and the relation between law and justice (chapter 9). It is through reflection on these perennial issues, as well as on the specific problem of race relations in the United States, that thoughtful Americans will learn much from black American political thought and from Storing's perceptive analysis.

The Public Interest

The next section brings together several somewhat disparate writings that address the relationship of rights, the rule of law, and the public interest. The first is a summary of the political thought of the British lawyer and jurist, William Blackstone (chapter 10). It elucidates an issue that occupied much of Storing's attention in both his writings and the classroom: the difficulty in maintaining the rule of law, of conventional authority, in a governmental system devoted to securing natural rights and, therefore, self-interested ends. Just what specific civil rights and duties flow from government's origin in natural rights is by no means obvious and thus defines much of the task of both lawmakers and jurists in a liberal political order. Moreover, natural rights remain a standard to which aggrieved parties or critics of the law can recur, denying authority to conventional laws and perhaps undermining the disposition to law-abidingness essential to civil society.

This last point is addressed by Storing at some length in his case against civil disobedience (chapter 11). Although the argument here is framed by the civil rights struggles of the 1950s and 1960s, neither the case for civil disobedience (made most famously by Martin Luther King in his "Letter from a Birmingham Jail") nor Storing's critique of it are contingent upon the specific types of grievances that prompted civil rights leaders to violate local and state laws. Recurring to a natural standard against which to measure conventional laws, King categorized laws into two types: just laws and unjust laws. As citizens we owe obedience to the former but not the latter. We have a right, even an obligation, to disobey unjust laws, but the transgressor ought willingly to accept the punishment.

In his analysis of what may well be the most distinctive contribution of the civil rights movement to American political thought, Storing asks searching questions about the practical consequences of a doctrine that encourages individuals to break laws that violate their personal sense of justice, as well as the principled justification for such actions in any fundamentally just regime. For the unjust regime, Storing argues, the proper stance is not civil disobedience but revolution. But in the fundamentally just regime, civil disobedience endangers the habituation to law-abidingness that is essential if "the liberal regime [is to perform] one of its most admired functions, to provide the basis for political deliberation and political education." In the decades since Storing's essay was written, we have witnessed other episodes in which Americans—some even in government service—have claimed a right to violate democratically enacted laws in the name of justice or a higher good. In evaluating the soundness of such claims, one can do no better than to enter into the debate between Storing and the civil rights movement's leading activist and theoretician.

Both sides in the civil disobedience debate link their arguments to views about the public interest. The proponents maintain that the public interest is better served if unjust laws are publicly disobeyed, so as to call attention to the need for reform. Opponents force us to think about the dangers to civil order in the just regime if the citizenry is not habituated to law-abidingness. Indeed, it may not be too strong to say that all substantial political debate is an argument about the public interest. This simple fact is recognized, almost without reflection, by both political leaders and the citizenry. Yet the very question whether there is such a thing as the public interest has been a troublesome one for modern scholars of government and politics. The last two selections in this section address this issue.

In the first of these, Storing and coauthor Peter Self elucidate the deficiencies of the critique of the concept of a public interest that emerges from the school of thought known as pluralism, or the group theory of politics. As they show in their analysis of the place of the agricultural interest in British politics, interest groups themselves recognize that "they are parts of some whole, and their conception and promotion of their own interest must be based on *some* view of that whole" (chapter 12). Moreover, whether and how political decision makers respond to group claims will depend not simply on the political strength of those making the claim, but also on the persuasiveness of the case they make, connecting their partial interest to the well-being of the whole. And to those who maintain that group interests are clear and objective while the public interest is abstract and undefinable, Storing and Self show that "the public interest is often . . . as clear as that of any special interest."

"In British political life," they write, "nobody doubts the existence of a public interest in such matters as physical security, foreign trade, financial solvency, economic growth, and other matters. This point would hardly need making, were it not that some writers on the political process, influenced by American group theory, seem to forget that public interests, although much broader, are fully as 'objective' and discernible as those of special groups." Indeed, the very concept of statesmanship presumes a good of the whole that is not simply the summation of the claims of the parts. Storing applied this notion to the contribution of Frederick Douglass: "In Frederick Douglass we find a deep understanding of the dependence of the partial good, the good of blacks, on the good of the whole American community. It is well that there are leaders who take upon themselves the duty of promoting the good of the part, but that duty includes a recognition of and participation in a higher statesmanship" (chapter 7).

In the second essay on the public interest, Storing examines the "three major parts of the criticism of the meaningfulness and usefulness of 'public interest': that the idea is undemocratic, that it is vague, and that it is unscientific" (chapter 13). In each case he shows that the critique is not persuasive. It is also inconsistent with the principles that underlay the American founding. Hamilton distinguished between the "interests" and the "inclinations" of the people: their interests were seen as connected to the broader public good in a way that their mere inclinations could not be. Similarly, Madison called for a governmental system that would promote "the permanent and aggregate interests of the community."

Public Administration

In their rejection of the feeble, state-centered Articles of Confederation in favor of a genuine national government resting on a broad, popular foundation, the founders embraced energetic government capable of enforcing its mandates over a vast territory and a growing population. This gave sound and efficient administration an importance for the success of popular government not found in the earlier theories of republican government; for at the time of the American founding, it was widely accepted that republics had to be small enough that citizens would identify their private interest with the public good and would willingly carry out the laws with little need for governmental compulsion or force. Small republics meant small governments and little formal distinction between the government itself and the citizenry, as in ancient Athens, where many offices simply rotated among the citizens. In the writings brought together in the fourth part of this volume, Storing explores the implications for American democracy of the founders' original choice for a large republic and therefore big government.

One of those implications is the growth over time of a large federal bureaucracy that, according to critics, is unresponsive to public interests and desires and is therefore, in some fundamental respects, undemocratic. Yet as any student of the *Federalist Papers* knows, the government fashioned by the Constitution of 1787 was not designed to be simply responsive to public opinion. Madison, for example, had written of the need for representatives to "refine" and "enlarge" the public views. Here the Senate, with its election by state legislatures and six-year terms, was to play a larger role than the House, with its direct popular election and two-year terms. Storing asks whether today's Senate, now popularly elected and much more subject to external influences, continues to moderate and elevate public opinion. He finds instead that the modern Senate is "but a faint reflection of its former self . . . far more popular, far more susceptible to the passing fancies of the people, than the founders intended" (chapter 14). Does any other institution in the national government, then, fill the role of the original Senate? Storing's provocative answer is that the national bureaucracy at its best infuses certain "senatorial" qualities into American popular government. Such qualities include a commitment to orderly administration and procedural fairness; a "cautious prudence"; a disposition to follow precedents and, more generally, to preserve the rule of law; a "degree of insulation from shifting political breezes"; and a capacity to bring "the accumulated wisdom of the past to bear upon political decisions" (chapter 15).

Statesmanship

Paralleling the growth of a large federal bureaucracy in the United States in the twentieth century has been the development of a science of administration that seeks both to understand and to guide what civil servants and their agencies do. As both student and critic of the new science, Storing challenged the soundness of its fundamental premise: the radical disjunction between deciding what to do (*politics* determining the ends) and actually carrying it out (*administration* fixing the means). In the end, Storing argued, there is no getting around the fact that civil servants must exercise discretion, often in large amounts, in carrying out their responsibilities. In so doing, they will necessarily be guided more by reasoning about ends and principles—the essence of political reasoning—than by the instrumental reasoning of one who merely serves the will of another. "In the most crucial sense," Storing held, "it can be said that, for the founders, the problem of government is a matter of administration" (chapter 22). Yet such administration cannot be understood as a merely instrumental art, divorced from the kinds of reasoning that lie at the heart of practical wisdom, of what used to be called prudence.

This means that good administration necessarily points toward statesmanship, a task that in our political system seems to fall more often to presidents than to other public officials. In the selections that constitute the fifth part of this collection, Storing sketches the essential elements of democratic statesmanship and their grounding in the American constitutional order. He particularly faults the common view that "the presidency is or ought to be simply democratic" (chapter 20). Some framers, such as James Wilson, saw "that the president would have to be the 'man of the people,' . . . but they also saw that the president would have to be a major element in government capable of restraining, checking, and guiding the people. It is this combination that makes the politics of the presidency so fascinating and difficult." This problematic nature of the president's relationship to the people and their wants forms the basis of Storing's delineation of the president's three great constitutional tasks: to administer effectively the laws passed by Congress, to check and balance the will of the legislature (and thus at times the will of the people), and, at least occasionally, to guide and instruct public

11

opinion. The first two of these tasks, Storing maintains, were quite consciously built into the constitutional structure. But the last was only hinted at by some framers and opposed by others, who feared that popular rhetorical leadership would of necessity decay into demagoguery. In devising their carefully crafted institutions, "what some of the founders neglected is that in a popular government . . . the people have to be reasoned with by their statesmen. This means reasoning not only at the level of specific policies but also at the level of constitutional principle" (chapter 22). And here the argument comes full circle, for it was the opponents of the Constitution of 1787, more than its creators and defenders, who anticipated the need in this or any other republican government for popular or moral leadership to enlighten understanding and to form character.

Storing's fullest account of statesmanship, from which several of the above quotations are drawn, is contained in the essay "American Statesmanship: Old and New," left unfinished at the time of his death (chapter 22). Here Storing identifies the "strong tendency" in American politics "to resolve the role of the public official into two simple elements: populism, or radical democracy, and scientific management." Neither element alone nor the combination of the two encompasses the heart of statesmanship as traditionally understood. Our modern doctrines of leadership—a term much more common now than statesmanship—represent a decay from the founding generation, when it was understood that at least occasionally one needed in public life "an extraordinary (and perhaps ultimately inexplicable) devotion to public duty and an understanding of the principles of governmental structure and operation of the broadest and deepest kind." At the end of this essay, Storing sketches the key elements of the "essence of statesmanship." These include an understanding of the ends of an organization or political community, moral stature and the grasp of "the moral side of public decision making," sound practical reason (what used to be called "prudence," or practical wisdom), and decisiveness.

Liberal Education

As the reader of this volume will readily discover, Herbert Storing was a dedicated teacher of the great principles of republican government. He taught black Americans the principles of Frederick Douglass and Booker T. Washington; he taught political leaders that statesmanship worthy of the name must rise above the mere service of popular desires; and he taught all his countrymen the profound insights of the Founding Fathers into the challenge of establishing and preserving republican government. This is liberal education and education for citizenship at its best, the specific subject of the final part of this collection. The volume ends appropriately with Storing's reflections on the contribution of his own teacher, the political philosopher Leo Strauss, to the discipline of political science and to our recovery of the wisdom of the past.

The great themes of Storing's scholarship were the great themes of the political discourse of the nation's founding. Although one can find much variety and disagreement in the political thought of the founders, most agreed on certain fundamental points: that the people's inclinations are not always the same as their interests; that statesmanship requires moderating and guiding public opinion; that the public interest is a meaningful concept and is not simply reducible to the interests of the parts; and that republican government will not be successful without promoting qualities of sound citizenship. It is striking how little our contemporary leaders, as well as modern scholarship on government and politics, have to say on these matters. Those who decry the impoverishment of American political discourse over the past two centuries will find their concerns confirmed by Storing's careful exposition of the founders' thought. But they will also find here the insights and interpretation requisite for a rejuvenation of our public discourse, and for a renewed and deepened understanding of the nature and necessary supports of just republican government.

There is perhaps no fitter end to this essay and no fitter introduction to these writings than another aspect of Storing's speculation as to how a particularly thoughtful founder might reflect on modern American government and politics: "I think he would concede, finally, that while in his heart of hearts he had thought that he and his generation had finished in its essentials the task of making the American polity, there is after all work still to be done" (chapter 6).

PART ONE
Constitutional Foundations

2
The Constitutional Convention: Toward a More Perfect Union

In these days of new nations, the "founding" of nations is something that goes on literally all the time. As citizens of the first major "made" nation in modern times, we Americans may be expected to have special sympathy for and understanding of the problems of nation making. Moreover, our founders set a fashion in written constitutions, so that such a constitution as that of Britain—whose source is both lost in remote antiquity and as fresh as yesterday's Act of Parliament—is today the exception rather than the rule.

The American founders expected, or at least hoped, that they would provide an example for the rest of mankind. But that example is not to be found merely in the fact of a written constitution, or even in the substantive provisions of this particular constitution. To avoid what we may call the "blueprint fallacy" we must look more deeply into the founders' doings. James Madison was so keenly aware of the example being set by the Constitutional Convention of 1787 that he put himself to the task of transcribing the debates as accurately and fully as he could. In an unfinished preface to the debates, Madison said:

> The curiosity I had felt during my researches into the History of the most distinguished Confederacies, . . . and the deficiency I found in the means of satisfying it more especially in what related to the process, the principles—the reasons, & the anticipations, which prevailed in the formation of them, determined me to preserve as far as I could an exact account of what might pass in the Convention. . . . I was [impressed] with the gratification promised to future

---

This essay, unpublished at the time of Storing's death, appeared in Morton J. Frisch and Richard G. Stevens, eds., *American Political Thought: The Philosophic Dimension of American Statesmanship*, 2nd ed. (Itasca, Ill.: F. E. Peacock Publishers, Inc., 1983). It was edited by Murray Dry and is reprinted with permission from Peacock Publishers.

curiosity by an authentic exhibition of the objects, the opinions & the reasonings from which the new System of Govt. was to receive its peculiar structure & organization. Nor was I unaware of the value of such a contribution to the fund of materials for the History of a Constitution on which would be staked the happiness of a young people great even in its infancy, and possibly the cause of Liberty through[out] the world.[1]

Each day Madison took notes on the speeches, and he was seldom absent except for very short periods; most nights he spent writing up his notes. It is interesting to speculate whether, in addition to the cost in labor and health, Madison also sacrificed some part of his influence on the deliberations by undertaking this toil on behalf of posterity. What is important for our purposes is Madison's judgment that future generations of Americans, and constitution makers elsewhere, would find instruction in a report of the proceedings of the convention. For the present, it will be enough to try to catch a glimpse of this lesson ourselves, without going on to consider how it might be applied to the new nations of today.

The now familiar distinction between an unwritten and a written constitution was thought by the founders to be only a manifestation of the much more fundamental distinction between a constitution instituted mainly by chance and one instituted by design. Previously, they thought, governments had been the product of tradition, or accident, or force. At best a people, out of desperation or by some other chance, had agreed to accept a system of laws designed by a single man. Here in the United States in 1787 was the first case of a whole people, through their representatives, deliberately constituting themselves into a political community. This great act of constitution contained two distinct steps: first, there were the deliberations of the men at Philadelphia which resulted in the act of proposing a constitution; second, there were the deliberations in the several state conventions and in the country at large resulting in the act of accepting the constitution.

We shall consider here the former of these two steps, relying mainly on Madison's notes. More particularly, we shall be concerned with the discussion leading up to the "Great Compromise" which established the different principles of representation in the Senate and the House of Representatives. It will be helpful first to recall some superficial things which indicate the character of the work of

---

1. Max Farrand, ed., *Records of the Federal Convention of 1787* (New Haven, Conn., 1966), vol. 3, p. 550.

the convention. Although the convention undertook to act on behalf of the whole people of the United States—although it engaged in an act of the greatest possible *public* significance—its deliberations were secret; and that secrecy was remarkably well preserved. Madison went so far as to refuse to allow the publication of his notes until after his death. This secrecy meant that the delegates were freer than they otherwise would have been to range widely in their consideration of what was the best government for the United States. They could not, and did not, ever forget that they had to make proposals which would have some chance of being accepted; but they did not have their constituents constantly breathing down their necks.

The flexibility of the rules of procedure also fostered this freedom of deliberation. Questions once decided were very often taken up again. It was recognized that a delegate might put forward proposals or pursue arguments tentatively, that he might test his ideas by offering them to others. It was recognized that a delegate might change his mind and that the other delegates would at least be moderate in scoring the debating points that can so readily be made against a man who opens his mind to the inspection of others. It was recognized finally that there would have to be compromise, and that the spirit of the debate, while not inhibiting serious and strenuous argument, should be such as to maintain the conditions of compromise.

When we read the notes of the convention debates, then, we have before us neither treatise nor tract, but the record of deliberations aimed at decision. We cannot enter into these deliberations as fully as we can enter into a treatise on political philosophy or a polemical discourse on the Constitution such as the *Federalist Papers*. And we could not do so even if we had available an exact transcript of the proceedings. We can never entirely reconstruct the complex and unique interplay of many different men, opinions, and interests. We can never fully recapture that practical experience of the whole situation which was available to the actors, and out of which the Constitution arose. We can, however, approximate such direct experience. We can study the men involved, paying attention not only to words but to character, idiosyncrasy, even appearance. It is certainly relevant to know that the extraordinary ability and patriotism of this group of men were almost universally recognized, at the time of the Philadelphia meeting and later. Thus one of the major Anti-Federalists (Richard Henry Lee), in the course of attacking the Constitution, acknowledged that "America probably never will see an assembly of men of a like number more respectable."[2]

---

2. *Observations of the Federal Farmer* V, in Herbert J. Storing, ed., *The Complete Anti-Federalist*, 7 vols. (Chicago: University of Chicago Press, 1981),

We need to know, too, that this was an unusually young group of men. The average age was forty-three; and more than a third of the fifty-five delegates were in their thirties, including James Madison, Alexander Hamilton, Gouverneur Morris, and Edmund Randolph. Four of our Founding Fathers, including Charles Pinckney, were not yet thirty years of age. We can try to find out who was respected and who failed, perhaps unaccountably, to strike fire. We can go some distance in understanding the subtle and complex ways in which these characters played upon one another, and the impression each of them made on the body as a whole. We can learn something about the silent part of the debate—not only the important discussions outside Independence Hall, but significant glances, smiles, and frowns, during the debates themselves. Washington, for example, as president of the convention, did not say a word in debate until the last day; but he allowed his countenance to speak for him, and it is said to have spoken eloquently and to great effect. It is relevant to know the physical surroundings and when it was hot and when cool, when the delegates were tired and when fresh. Gradually we might be able to sense for ourselves something of the shifting, elusive "mood of the House."

Finally, we need to be alert to an element of the whole situation which is always of enormous practical importance, and that is *time*. Knowing where the discussion is, from day to day and even from moment to moment, is decisive both to the political actor and to the student of practical politics. Madison's notes, especially at first reading, often make it seem that the debates were without any order at all, but there is an order. It is not the kind of order one finds in a systematic exposition of general principles, but rather the rhythm of sustained, high-level political debate. The metronome is the need for a decision and consequently the probable need for compromise.

Compromise

At last, it may be said, we are getting to the heart of the matter. This is certainly the central theme of many interpretations of the convention; and the Constitution itself has been characterized as a "bundle of compromises." According to one view, the actors in this drama at Philadelphia are "interests": the large and small state interests, the commercial and landed interests; the northern and southern interests; as well as the narrower personal and "group"

---

vol. 2, p. 254. Editor's note: see Storing's discussion of the dispute regarding Lee's authorship of *The Federal Farmer*, pp. 215–16.

interests of the different delegates. These interests clash, fall back and reform, clash again. Alliances are made, tested, remade. Demands are put forward, considerations proffered and rejected or accepted. Slowly, sometimes imperceptibly, progress is made toward the accommodation of the major interests, with the minor ones falling into their proper places behind. Overall hangs a blue haze of argument and rationalization, interesting as surface coloring and sometimes useful as a means of identifying the interests at work, but as little a part of what is really going on as the smoke in the smoke-filled room.[3]

This view of the convention and of the Constitution is by no means simply wrong, but it is flat, lacking in perspective. Of course, the delegates recognized that clashes of interest were involved; but they also saw beyond that. We might say, for example, that the "interest" of the small states was to maintain a degree of influence in the affairs of the Union disproportionate to the number of people they contained; and that the "interest" of the large states was to use their greater population to dominate the Union. The delegates were sufficiently realistic to recognize these narrow interests; but they were also keen enough to see that these narrow interests were defensible only insofar as they were the carriers of certain broad principles of free government in the United States. The large states stood, not just for the large states, but for certain principles associated with *Union;* the small states stood, not just for small states, but for certain principles associated with *states* as such. It is significant that the amount of direct discussion of interest increases substantially in the later part of the debate. More specifically, the great division of *interests,* as Madison pointed out, did not lie between large states and small ones but between North and South. Yet that latter division was scarcely touched during the first half of the debate. The differences of interest between North and South only came to occupy a major share of the convention's attention after compromise had been reached on the question of *principle* involved in the controversy between the large and small states.[4]

As a result of the Great Compromise of the convention, it was agreed that each state should have an equal vote in the second branch of the legislature (representation in the first branch according to

---

3. See John Roche, "The Founding Fathers: A Reform Caucus in Action," *American Political Science Review* (December 1964), pp. 799–816.

4. See Hamilton's statement in the New York Ratification Convention on the main differences of interest, in Farrand, *Records of the Federal Convention,* vol. 3, pp. 332–33.

population having been decided earlier). There were other elements in this compromise—which was really a series of compromises—but our chief concern is with the debate leading to the recognition of different principles of representation in the two branches. We shall be interested in the *question* of principle, the *answer* in practice, and the way great politicians move from the one to the other.

Reference was made earlier to the work of the convention as the making of a nation, but of course no founder begins afresh, unless he contents himself with a wholly imaginary nation. He has been given materials to work with: a particular people at a particular time and place. His materials will be pliable in some respects, brittle in others; they invite certain kinds of nation making and foreclose others. This is all connected with the practical character of the founder's doings. While there was some discussion at Philadelphia, for example, of limited monarchy, and not a little indication that many of the delegates thought this the best form of government, there was no serious thought of instituting a limited monarchy in the United States. It was simply not a practical possibility then and there. Thus it was not necessary—indeed it would have been improper—to consider its claims at any great length.

In the American case, not only did the founders have to work with given materials, but those materials had been subjected to law and formed into a political community. The United States already had a legal identity, a constitution; and it was to improve that constitution that the delegates met. The old constitution had two major features which provided the founders with their central problem. The parties to the Articles of Confederation were *states* which explicitly retained their sovereignty, freedom, and independence; but at the same time those states explicitly bound themselves together in a perpetual *Union* or league of friendship. The full title is the Articles of Confederation and Perpetual Union. Moreover, the articles specifically named the kind of political association which they instituted. The first article says: "The Stile of this *confederacy* shall be 'The United States of America.' " In the Constitution of 1787, on the other hand, there is no such naming, although the first words—"We the people of the United States . . ."—clearly indicate that the confederacy was reconstituted into some other kind of political association. Neither is there any reference in the Constitution to either "sovereignty" or "perpetual union." These very silences are part of the practical answer to the great theoretical question which the founders inherited.

The convention met continuously for almost four months, from May 25 through September 17, 1787. It began its substantive business on May 29 when Governor Edmund Randolph of Virginia outlined what he thought were the defects of the Confederation and proposed a series of resolutions, known as the Virginia Plan, to remedy them. Although presented as amendments to the Articles of Confederation, Randolph's plan amounted to a substitution of a strong national government for the old "league of friendship." It proposed to substitute for the Congress of states a bicameral legislature, in which representation would be according to numbers of financial contribution, and a national executive and judiciary. The new Congress was "to legislate in all cases to which the separate states are incompetent, or in which the harmony of the United States may be interrupted by the exercise of individual legislation"; it was also to have the power to veto state laws, and to call forth the force of the Union against any delinquent state.[5]

The convention resolved itself into a committee of the whole house, and during the next two weeks, the Virginia Plan swept almost all opposition aside. By June 13, the Virginia proposals had been substantially accepted. Indeed, Randolph's first proposal, which referred to the enlargement and correction of the Articles of Confederation, was replaced by a more emphatic proposal "that a *national* government ought to be established consisting of a *Supreme* Legislative, Judiciary, and Executive."[6]

Randolph's second proposal was that "the right of suffrage in the National Legislature ought to be proportioned to the Quotas of contribution, or to the number of free inhabitants. . . ." This was taken up on the second day of the debate and (according to Madison), "being generally relished, would have been agreed to," when George Read from Delaware moved its postponement. He explained that the Delaware delegation was instructed not to agree to any change in the rule of suffrage under the articles, and might therefore be forced to leave the convention if such a change were agreed upon. Though this very early threat of a boycott was resented by some (especially since it was known that Read had been partly responsible for this instruction), it was successful and the question was postponed.[7] When it was taken up later, on June 9, the number of delegates from the small states had increased, and they were beginning to rally in

---

5. *Records of the Federal Convention*, vol. 1, p. 21 (May 29).

6. *Records of the Federal Convention*, vol. 1, p. 39 (May 30) (Storing's emphasis).

7. *Records of the Federal Convention*, vol. 1, pp. 35–38 (May 30). For Delaware's instructions and a letter from Read to Dickinson suggesting the suffrage restriction, see *Records of the Federal Convention*, vol. 3, pp. 574–76.

the face of the nationalists' initiative. The small-state group failed to retain the equality of representation among the states, but so far as the *second* branch was concerned, they failed by only one vote, following an assertion by Roger Sherman that "the smaller states would never agree to the plan on any other principle than an equality of suffrage in this branch."[8]

This vote was taken on Monday, June 11; on Wednesday the committee of the whole reported the Randolph proposals, as amended. On Friday, William Paterson of New Jersey presented an alternative plan, known as the New Jersey Plan. Under this, the Congress was to be given power to lay a duty on imported goods, thus meeting one of the most obvious deficiencies of the articles by providing the general government with a source of income independent of requisitions on the states. Supplementary requisitions would still be necessary, but Congress was to have the power to make the collections itself in those states that did not comply voluntarily. Finally, Paterson proposed the establishment of a plural executive and a national judiciary.[9]

These amendments would have very considerably increased the power and altered the organization of the general government, but they would have left untouched the basic principle of the Articles of Confederation, the equality of the states.[10] Defending his proposals the next day, Paterson argued that they were both within the powers of the convention and consistent with the sentiments of the people. He contended that the Virginia Plan, in contrast, asked the convention to overreach itself legally and practically. "Our object is not such a Government as may be best in itself, but such a one as our Constituents have authorized us to prepare, and as they will approve."[11] This is a constant theme throughout the debate—and in the debate over ratification later. It should be observed, however, that it is a negative theme, because it begins with the *limitations* on the convention rather than with the *aim*. It seems to allow the other side

---

8. *Records of the Federal Convention*, vol. 1, p. 201 (June 11).

9. For the Paterson plan, see *Records of the Federal Convention*, vol. 1, pp. 242–45 (June 15).

10. In addition, Paterson's plan did not provide for a bicameral legislature. See his explanation on June 16 (*Records of the Federal Convention*, vol. 1, p. 251), and see Madison's basic argument against the plan on June 19 (*Records of the Federal Convention*, vol. 1, pp. 314–22).

11. *Records of the Federal Convention*, vol. 1, p. 250 (June 16). "We must follow the people; the people will not follow us," Paterson had said (June 9) in the last stage of consideration of the Virginia Resolutions. *Records of the Federal Convention*, vol. 1, p. 178.

to take the higher ground. Partly this may have been in the nature of the respective cases—that is, it may have been the expression of a flaw in the principle for which the small states contended. But this willingness to abandon the higher ground must also have reflected the view of Paterson and his friends that they occupied a very strong position lower down. The heart of Paterson's argument was as follows:

> If we argue the matter on the supposition that no Confederacy at present exists, it can not be denied that all States stand on the footing of equal sovereignty. All therefore must concur before any can be bound. . . . If we argue on the fact that a federal compact actually exists, and consult the articles of it we shall find an equal Sovereignty to be the basis of it.[12]

This was the dilemma which the representatives of the small states challenged their opponents to resolve. Within the articles or outside, the states stood on a footing of sovereign equality. That equality could be relinquished only with the consent of the states concerned, a consent which the states were under absolutely no obligation of any kind to give, and which the small states did not propose to give.

On the next working day Alexander Hamilton made his first speech before the convention—and one might almost add figuratively, his last speech. He did not resolve the dilemma Paterson had set, but he pointed to the resolution in his remark that "the *states* sent us here to provide for the exigencies of the *union*." The old constitution was *based* on sovereign states, but it was *aimed* at perpetual union. Hamilton vigorously attacked the Paterson plan and the whole principle of divided sovereignty; he doubted that even the Virginia Plan went far enough. Praising the British government, he confessed his doubt that "anything short of it would do in America." Finally he proposed a "strong, well-mounted" government which would include an executive and senate elected for life.[13] His speech almost certainly deprived him of whatever influence he might have had in the convention, and it was one of the grounds of the charge of "monarchist" that was to plague him during the rest of his career. Following immediately upon Paterson's proposals, however, it is almost equally certain that it helped to maintain the central place of the Virginia proposals. Before Hamilton's speech, the convention had

---

12. *Records of the Federal Convention,* vol. 1, p. 250 (June 16).

13. *Records of the Federal Convention,* vol. 1, pp. 283 (Storing's emphasis), 288 (June 18); letter to Washington, July 3, 1787, in *Records of the Federal Convention,* vol. 3, p. 53.

two plans before it. That from Virginia had the present advantage, having been on the floor first and having apparently gained majority acceptance. But it was clear that the deliberations were not over, and that the more modest and "legal" New Jersey Plan might well attract the moderates. After Hamilton's speech the position was changed. There were now three plans on the floor, and that from Virginia was back solidly in the center, New Jersey's having been pushed to one extreme by Hamilton's vigorous presentation of the opposite extreme.

Hamilton's speech attracted very little explicit notice, however, and the convention returned to Paterson's proposals and arguments. With respect to the sentiments of the people, the representatives of the large states contended throughout that these could not be known precisely. Moreover, they argued, we do not take such a low view of the people's judgment as to think that they will prefer a worse government to a better one. This argument again enabled the large-state man to take the higher ground. James Wilson of Pennsylvania used it effectively both in the convention and later in defending the Constitution before the Pennsylvania ratifying convention. Paterson's legal argument, however, was much more difficult to refute. Dealing with the question of the authority of the convention, Wilson contended that, while they were empowered to *conclude* nothing, they were free to *propose* anything.[14] This would certainly have been unexceptionable had the delegates been merely private men, but they were delegates of the states, sent to Philadelphia "for the sole and express purpose of revising the Articles of Confederation."

Governor Randolph came closer to the only argument that could refute Paterson on this point, when he said that "there are certainly reasons of a peculiar nature where the ordinary cautions must be dispensed with; and this is certainly one of them." He was not scrupulous on the point of power, "when the salvation of the Republic was at stake."[15] But the whole question was whether there was "*the* Republic," whose salvation was at stake, or whether there were several republics whose "league of friendship" was at stake; and Randolph's argument is only tenable on the former ground.

Paterson's main contention—that under either of the only two admissible assumptions, a confederation or no confederation, the states were on a footing of equality—had not been disposed of, or even directly attacked, when the New Jersey Plan was voted down and the convention turned to a reconsideration of the Virginia resolu-

---

14. *Records of the Federal Convention*, vol. 1, p. 253 (June 16).
15. *Records of the Federal Convention*, vol. 1, p. 255 (June 16).

tions as reported by the committee of the whole. Paterson's argument was, however, taken up in the discussion of the first proposition reported: that a national government ought to be established consisting of a supreme legislative, executive, and judiciary. After a long speech by Madison, Rufus King of Massachusetts sought to show that the term "sovereign," as used in the Articles of Confederation, was a misnomer, that under the articles the states retained none of the essential attributes of sovereignty, that they could in no way treat with foreign sovereigns, that if they formed a confederation in some respects, they formed a nation in others, and that therefore Paterson's logic was grounded on a false assumption.[16]

This began to expose a serious weakness in Paterson's argument, and Luther Martin of Maryland (later a vigorous Anti-Federalist) immediately sought to remove the discussion to deeper ground. He supported the Paterson position by contending that the separation from Great Britain had placed the thirteen states in a state of nature toward each other, and that they would have thus remained except for the Articles of Confederation which the states entered on a footing of equality. It was the states, Martin argued, to which the people look "for the security of their lives, liberties and properties." The federal government was formed for the limited purpose of defending the whole against foreign enemies and the smaller states against the greater. This was denied by James Wilson, who read to the convention the language of the Declaration of Independence: "That these *United* Colonies are and of right ought to be Free and Independent states." This language is not unambiguous, but Wilson inferred that the states were independent, not individually but unitedly, and that therefore, they had never been independent *of one another*.[17]

Here, then, was a fundamental disagreement about the true origin of the American Union, which reflected a disagreement about its true character or constitution. According to Martin and his friends, the only relations between the states had been those of free and equal sovereigns, whether at the time of the Revolution or under the Articles of Confederation. As Martin said later in the debates, "the language of the States being Sovereign and independent, was once familiar and understood; though it seemed now so strange and obscure."[18] The states were the only real governments, and the Union

---

16. *Records of the Federal Convention,* vol. 1, pp. 323–24 (June 19).

17. For Martin's remarks, see *Records of the Federal Convention,* vol. 1, pp. 324 (June 19) and 340–41 (June 20). Wilson's response is to Martin's first speech, also at p. 324.

18. *Records of the Federal Convention,* vol. 1, p. 468 (June 29) (emphasis in the original).

was their creature. It was the states to which the people looked for the preservation of their cherished rights.

Wilson and his friends, on the other hand, argued that the states had never been independent sovereigns. The American Union was forged during the War of Independence and was constituted by the Declaration of Independence. The articles, far from creating the Union, were only a temporary instrument of a preexisting union. This instrument was defective in many respects, the most important being the admission of all states to equal suffrage. Wilson had stated the grounds of this argument early in the debates:

> Among the first sentiments expressed in the first Congress one was that Virginia is no more, that Massachusetts is no [more], that Pennsylvania is no more, etc. We are now one nation of brethren. We must bury all local interests and distinctions. This language continued for some time. The tables at length began to turn. No sooner were the State Governments formed [note the suggestion that the national government preceded the states] than their jealousy and ambition began to display themselves. Each endeavored to cut a slice from the common loaf, to add to its own morsel, till at length the confederation became frittered down to the impotent condition in which it now stands. . . . To correct its vices is the business of this convention. One of its vices is the want of an effectual control in the whole over its parts. What danger is there that the whole will unnecessarily sacrifice a part? But reverse the case, and leave the whole at the mercy of each part, and will not the general interest be continually sacrificed to local interests?[19]

This disagreement rested, as is clear even from this sketch, on a deeper stratum of agreement—as any disagreement which can be compromised must. The basic understanding of government and individual rights expressed in the Declaration of Independence was taken for granted—and for our present purposes we can also take it for granted. But different conclusions were drawn.[20] On the one hand it could be said, with Wilson, that these are the principles which we announced as a united people; they are the bond of brotherhood between us. It was from this viewpoint that Wilson could refer to the *artificial* system of states, in implicit contrast to the *natural* character

---

19. *Records of the Federal Convention*, vol. 1, pp. 166–67 (June 8).

20. As Roger Sherman (a compromiser) said: "The question is not what rights naturally belong to men; but how they may be most equally and effectually guarded in Society." *Records of the Federal Convention*, vol. 1, p. 450 (June 28).

of the Union. On the other hand, it could be argued that the maintenance of the principles enunciated in the Declaration demands (at least under present circumstances) modest republican governments, close to the people, and supported by a degree of public spiritedness which cannot be achieved under a government covering such an extent as the whole of the United States. In this view, the Union is the artificiality; it exists for the sake of the states which are the political units of truly human dimensions.

In *Federalist* 10 and in a briefer version of the same argument early in the convention, Madison sought to resolve this difference on a theoretical level. He rested the argument for the primacy of the Union, not on any notion of a band of brothers or popular patriotism and self-restraint, but on self-interest and private passion, properly regulated. Whatever the theoretical adequacy of this argument, it may have served both to strengthen the nationalist cause and to prepare the way for compromise by blunting the differences in principle as they were generally seen. Indeed one might argue that as a practical matter Madison's *Federalist* 10 represented the highest ground of Union available at that time. But that would be a separate subject.

The exchanges between Wilson and Martin which led to this consideration of the difference in principle occurred on June 19 and 20. By June 27, the convention reached the proposition relating specifically to the rules of suffrage in the two branches of the legislature: the lines of disagreement were becoming sharper and there was a growing feeling that the fate of the convention itself was at stake. Martin again made a long speech, covering the better part of two days, in which he repeated his former arguments. Significantly, however, he added two new points. First, he contended that the people had no *right* to dissolve the Articles of Confederation without the consent of the state governments. Second, in warning of the danger of dissolution of the Union if the proponents of the Virginia Plan persisted, he concluded "that he had rather see partial Confederacies take place, than the plan on the table"[21]—the first indication that the maintenance of the Union might under some circumstances be undesirable. This time it was Madison who replied. He tried to show that the interests of the small states were really best served by the large-state proposal *because* the alternative was the breaking up of the Union, which would be more to the disadvantage of the small

---

21. *Records of the Federal Convention*, vol. 1, p. 445 (June 28). Martin had made the first of these points on June 20 (p. 341), but it is more emphatic here.

states than of the large ones. "In a word; the two extremes before us are a perfect separation & a perfect incorporation, of the 13 States."[22]

The convention had now been sitting, six days a week, for four and a half weeks. Many subjects had been discussed and difficulties encountered. The weather was hot and tempers frayed—Martin's long speeches had contributed to that. What seemed to be irreconcilable differences of principle threatened to destroy the convention.[23] At this point, on June 28, Benjamin Franklin intervened with a proposal for daily prayer. Franklin pointed to the small progress made and the closeness of votes, which he thought provided "a melancholy proof of the imperfection of the Human Understanding." He sought to elevate the delegates' thoughts. "In this situation of this Assembly, groping as it were in the dark to find political truth, and scarce able to distinguish it when presented to us, how has it happened, Sir, that we have not hitherto once thought of humbly applying to the Father of lights to illuminate our understandings?" Franklin turned the attention of the delegates to the War of Independence by recalling that during that war there was "daily prayer in this room for the divine protection." He reminded them of the "frequent instances of a Superintending providence in our favor" and chided them for now forgetting or imagining that they no longer needed the assistance of "that powerful friend."

> . . . without his concurring aid we shall succeed in this political building no better than the Builders of Babel: We shall be divided by our little partial local interests; our projects will be confounded, and we ourselves shall become a reproach and bye word down to future ages. And what is worse, mankind may hereafter from this unfortunate instance, despair of establishing Governments by Human Wisdom and leave it to chance, war and conquest.[24]

Franklin's specific proposal was itself the subject of considerable controversy. Hamilton and others thought it introduced another subject of possible discord and that the public might conclude that the convention had been driven to this expedient by severe dissensions.

---

22. *Records of the Federal Convention*, vol. 1, p. 449 (June 28).

23. See Caleb Strong's remark in the Massachusetts Ratification Convention, that a committee (discussed below) was appointed "because the small States were jealous of the large ones; and the Convention was nigh breaking up but for this." *Records of the Federal Convention*, vol. 3, p. 262. See also William Few on the state of matters at this time. *Records of the Federal Convention*, vol. 3, p. 423.

24. *Records of the Federal Convention*, vol. 1, pp. 451–52.

Randolph proposed that a sermon be preached on July 4 at the request of the convention and that prayer be offered at the sessions thereafter, but the House adjourned without taking action. Human wisdom proceeded unassisted.

Both in his recollection of the great *act* of the American Union, the War of Independence, and in his reference to "our little partial local interests," Franklin assisted the Madison and Wilson party, without, however, becoming a member of it. He assisted that party by transcending it. In such a debate as this, there are men who take responsibility for the parts—as such men as Madison and Wilson and Paterson and Martin did. So also there must be a smaller number of men who take a special responsibility for the whole. This is what Franklin sought to do here, and in most of his relatively infrequent interventions in debate. Whether Franklin here was concerned with the propitiation of "our powerful friend," or whether he was calling "divine providence" to the service of "human wisdom," is not our present concern. There can be no question, however, that he sought to restore the sense of proportion and of the obligations of statesmanship which the convention seemed in danger of losing.[25] Incidentally, Franklin was, at eighty-one, the oldest member of the convention.

The first speech on the following day was given by sixty-year-old William Johnson from Connecticut, in which the proposal was explicitly made which became the central element of the Great Compromise. The proposal for different principles of representation in the two houses of the legislature had been suggested tentatively several times before. In particular, it had been twice put forward by Johnson's fellow delegate from Connecticut, Roger Sherman, who is generally given major credit for what is sometimes called the Connecticut Compromise in recognition of the role played by the Connecticut delegation in compromising the differences of the large and small states. Sherman, at sixty-six, was the oldest member of the convention except for Franklin; he was incidentally the only man to sign the Declaration of Independence, the Articles of Confederation, and the Constitution.

Johnson's speech was the perfect counterpart to Franklin's. As Franklin sought to restore proportion by turning the delegates' minds to the fallibility of human reason, to the War of Independence, and to divine providence, so Johnson sought it by turning their minds to

---

25. "The concurring aid which Franklin evoked implied a purification from the domain of selfish interests. In the next meeting the members were less absorbed by inferior motives." George Bancroft, *History of the Formation of the Constitution of the United States*, 2 vols. (New York, 1882), vol. 2, p. 59.

a very matter of fact statement of the problem and a very matter of fact solution of it. "The controversy must be endless," Johnson began, "whilst Gentlemen differ in the grounds of their arguments; Those on one side considering the States as districts of people composing one political Society; those on the other considering them as so many political societies." The fact is that there is a little of both. "On the whole he thought that as in some respects the States are to be considered in their political capacity, and in others as districts of individual citizens, the two ideas embraced on different sides, instead of being opposed to each other, ought to be combined; that in *one* branch the *people* ought to be represented; in the *other* the *States*."[26]

Each of the major delegates now restated his position—but the character of the debate was now governed by the broad-mindedness and good sense of Franklin and Johnson, and also by the knowledge that the time for decision was fast approaching. Madison was perhaps the most successful in avoiding extremes while sticking emphatically to his principle. He agreed with Johnson "that the mixed nature of the Government ought to be kept in view; but thought too much stress was laid on the rank of the States as political societies." "He entreated the gentlemen representing the small States to renounce a principle which was confessedly unjust, which could never be admitted, and if admitted must infuse mortality into a Constitution which we wished to last forever. He prayed them to ponder well the consequences of suffering the Confederacy to go to pieces."[27]

Elbridge Gerry of Massachusetts sought to restate the fundamental grounds of the nationalist position, arguing, as Wilson and King had earlier, "that we never were independent States, were not such now, and never could be even on the principles of the Confederation. . . . He lamented that instead of coming here like a band of brothers, belonging to the same family, we seemed to have brought with us the spirit of political negotiators."[28] Again Gerry was echoing Wilson, but he was also echoing the spirit of Franklin.

Following another, and somewhat petulant, plea for state sovereignty by Martin, the convention decided that the rule of suffrage in the first branch should not be that of the Articles of Confederation. Whereupon Ellsworth of Connecticut, seizing upon the compromise suggested by his colleague, moved that the rule of suffrage in the second branch should be the same as under the articles, frankly

---

26. *Records of the Federal Convention*, vol. 1, pp. 461–62 (June 29) (emphasis in the original).

27. *Records of the Federal Convention*, vol. 1, pp. 463–64 (June 29).

28. *Records of the Federal Convention*, vol. 1, p. 467 (June 29).

defending this proposal as a compromise.[29] The spirit of compromise was gaining. Wilson offered one, Franklin another, remarking that "a joiner, when he wants to fit two boards," takes a little from both.[30] But the spirit of partisanship was also growing. There was to be one more flicker of extreme partiality, brighter than anything that had gone before. Gunning Bedford of Delaware delivered a bitter polemic against the large state representatives, contending that the large states were "seeking to aggrandize themselves at the expense of the small" and directly asserting that "interest had blinded their eyes" to the right. Warming to his subject, Bedford displayed his resentment at the implied threats of the large state representatives when they argued that the small states depended more on Union than the large.

> The little States are willing to observe their engagements, but will meet the large ones on no ground but that of the Confederation. We have been told (with a dictatorial air) that this is the last moment for a fair trial in favor of a good Government. It will be the last indeed if the propositions reported from the Committee go forth to the people. He was under no apprehensions. The Large States dare not dissolve the confederation. If they do the small ones will find some foreign ally of more honor and good faith, who will take them by the hand and do them justice.[31]

Bedford's speech was the nadir of the debate. Everyone knew, of course, that what he threatened was a possibility, but no one had so far pressed his argument with this open recklessness and disregard of consequences. Bedford's isolation is an indication of the quality of these debates. Indeed it is probable that, in his extreme imprudence, Bedford strengthened Franklin's argument, for he stood as a powerful reminder of the imperfection of human reason and the danger that awaited the Union if the delegates could not moderate their different demands.

On the next working day, July 2, a vote was taken on the motion to allow each state an equal vote in the second branch.[32] The result seems to suggest that Franklin's prayer for divine providence was not altogether fruitless, though human reason also played its part. The

---

29. *Records of the Federal Convention,* vol. 1, p. 468 (June 29). The real division of interests, North versus South, was explicitly mentioned on the 29th and the 30th. See Hamilton and Madison, in *Records of the Federal Convention,* vol. 1, pp. 466, 486.

30. *Records of the Federal Convention,* vol. 1, p. 499 (Yates, June 30).

31. *Records of the Federal Convention,* vol. 1, pp. 491–92 (June 30).

32. *Records of the Federal Convention,* vol. 1, p. 510.

Maryland delegation was divided on this question, Daniel Jenifer being opposed to equal representation and Luther Martin in favor of it. Providentially, Jenifer was late in taking his seat that morning and Martin was thus able to cast the vote of Maryland in favor of the motion. The consequence of this was that when Georgia, the last state to be polled, was reached, instead of the question having been decided in the negative, five states had voted in favor of the motion and five against. Ordinarily the whole of the four-man Georgia delegation would have voted against equal representation, but it happened that two of the members were absent. One of the remaining Georgians was Abraham Baldwin, who was a native of Connecticut and was supposed to have come under the moderating influence of the Connecticut delegation. In any case, Baldwin apparently feared that the convention would break up unless a concession was made to the small states. By chance or providence, the absence of two of his colleagues put in his hands the power perhaps to determine whether there was to be a Union or not. Voting, contrary to his convictions, in favor of equal representation in the second branch, Baldwin divided Georgia's vote, maintained the tie, and kept open the way for compromise.

A committee was appointed to make proposals, and the convention adjourned to give it time to do so. This was on July 2. Thus by coincidence, the compromise which settled the question of representation in the legislature was worked out over Independence Day. On the basis of a motion made by Franklin this committee proposed that each state should have an equal vote in the second branch but that, in return, all money bills should originate in the first branch (where the large states would have representation in proportion to their population) and should not be subject to amendment by the second branch. To this was added, after many days of discussion and more referrals to committees, the provision that both representation in the first branch and direct taxes should be apportioned according to the number of inhabitants, counting slaves as three fifths.

On July 16, the Great Compromise was accepted by the convention, and the crisis had passed.[33] Although many more important issues were considered and the terms of the compromise were amended, the subsequent debate became increasingly detailed and concrete and complex. The level of principle was never abandoned, but the discussion was limited by compromises already agreed, and by the necessity for accommodation. It is significant that almost all of the major theoretical arguments occurred relatively early in the de-

---

33. *Records of the Federal Convention*, vol. 2, pp. 15–16.

bates, and that Madison took less full notes towards the end. Like most political discussions, the convention debates began on relatively high ground. The different sides had yet to coalesce, and while demands were put forward to their maximum extent, there was at the same time a considerable willingness to entertain and pursue questions of principle. As the time for decision approached, the lines of division became clearer and the debates warmer; the willingness to engage in wide-ranging deliberation declined. Each side became more engrossed in the approaching decision, preparing the ground for it, and defending its flanks. There was, in a word, less enthusiasm for the abstract *question* and a more sober and cautious concern with the practical *answer* that was to be given.

It has been suggested that the men at Philadelphia had more opportunity for free deliberation about good government than usually offers itself to political men. There are even serious references to the question of what is the best government simply. But the delegates were not engaged in political speculation for its own sake. They regarded themselves as, above all, practical politicians, and most of them were impatient with speculations about government that were unconnected with a particular time and place. Madison himself, perhaps the most theoretically minded of the group, had little but scorn for what he called "mere closet philosophy."[34] The delegates were met to adopt, as Rufus King said, "no idle experiment, no romantic speculation," but "a measure of Decision"[35] about the future government of the United States: if possible, the best decision; if possible, a theoretically clear and consistent decision—but, in any case, a decision that could be lived with. It is this need for decision even where there is lack of entire agreement on principle that gives rise to compromise. And it is because of the primary place of decision that compromise is intrinsic to political action, as it is not intrinsic to political speculation. Herein lies the highest task of the political craftsman, and to this task Franklin again turned the delegates' minds on the last day of the convention when he urged them to join him in sacrificing to the public good their opinions about the defects of the Constitution. "Within these walls they were born, and here

---

34. *Records of the Federal Convention*, vol. 1, p. 332 (June 19).

35. While the precise source for the Madison reference has not been found, see "Madison to Philip Mazzei, October 8, 1788," *The Papers of James Madison*, eds. W. T. Hutchinson, W. M. E. Rachal, C. F. Hobson, R. Rutland, 13 vols. (Chicago, Charlottesville, 1962–1981), vol. II, pp. 278–79. The reference to philosophy in the letter is complimentary, whereas the "closet philosophy" is not.

they shall die—."[36] Not all of the delegates were able or willing to make this sacrifice, but most of them did so, including most of the delegates from the small states.

The Constitution was, in fact if not in name, national, but the delegates from the small states succeeded in having incorporated into that government something of the principle for which they contended. They succeeded in securing a place in the national government for the states as such, and therewith a formal position from which they could continue to press their principle. The weakness of the small-state position was that, while they argued that union was not the essential feature of the American governments, they could scarcely deny that it was a necessary feature. Their opponents, on the other hand, could and did argue, not only that union was essential, but that the states were dispensable. That the proponents of national government did not make more of the latter argument, however, suggests the weakness of their position. They denied the legal or moral authority of the principle of state sovereignty in the Articles of Confederation, and consequently they denied the principle that unanimous agreement was requisite to constitutional change. Nevertheless, in practice they needed something close to unanimity, in order to establish the principle for which they contended, which was, after all, *union*. Any unyielding pursuit of their principle would, almost certainly, have resulted in the irretrievable loss of that very principle. The two sides found the grounds of compromise in their common desire to "form a more perfect union," though their ideas of a perfect union differed. The debates leading up to the Great Compromise yield insight into a great question of principle lying at the heart of the American political order. They also yielded an example of how such questions are properly approached in political life.

---

36. *Records of the Federal Convention*, vol. 2, p. 643 (September 17).

3
Federalists and Anti-Federalists: The Ratification Debate

The Small Republic

The Anti-Federalists' defense of federalism and of the primacy of the states rested on their belief that there was an inherent connection between the states and the preservation of individual liberty, which is the end of any legitimate government. Robert Whitehill of Pennsylvania, for example, feared that the proposed Constitution would be "the means of annihilating the constitutions of the several States, and consequently the liberties of the people."[1] "We are come hither," Patrick Henry urged his fellow Virginians, "to preserve the poor Commonwealth of Virginia, if it can be possibly done; Something must be done to preserve your liberty and mine."[2] The states have to be preserved because they are the natural homes of individual liberty. As Luther Martin had argued in Philadelphia:

> At the separation from the British Empire, the people of America preferred the Establishment of themselves into thirteen separate sovereignties instead of incorporating them-

---

This material originally appeared in Herbert J. Storing, "What the Anti-Federalists Were *For*," sections 3, 5, and 9, in Storing, ed., *The Complete Anti-Federalist*, 7 volumes (Chicago: University of Chicago Press, 1981), volume 1, pp. 15–23, 38–47, 71–76. It is reprinted with permission from the University of Chicago Press. Storing's essay on the Anti-Federalists was also published as a separate volume, *What the Anti-Federalists Were For* (Chicago: University of Chicago Press, 1981).

References to *The Complete Anti-Federalist* (for example, Henry 5.16.2) are by volume, position of an essay or series of essays in the volume, and paragraph.

1. *Pennsylvania and the Federal Constitution, 1787–1788,* John Bach McMaster and Frederick D. Stone, eds. (published for the subscribers by the Historical Society of Pennsylvania, 1888).

2. Henry 5.16.2.

selves into one: to these they look up for the security of their lives, liberties, & properties: to these they must look up—The federal Govt. they formed, to defend the whole agst. foreign nations, in case of war, and to defend the lesser States agst. the ambition of the larger.[3]

The governments instituted to secure the rights spoken of by the Declaration of Independence are the state governments. They do the primary business that governments are supposed to do. The government of the Union supplements the state governments, especially by giving them an external strength that none of them could manage on its own. But in principle the general government is subordinate to the state governments.

Why must the essential business of government be done by governmental units like the states? Primarily this was, in the Anti-Federalist view, a question of size. It was thought to have been demonstrated, historically and theoretically, that free, republican governments could extend only over a relatively small territory with a homogeneous population.[4] Even among the states this rule was evident, for "the largest States are the Worst Governed."[5] One problem is that in large, diverse states many significant differences in condition, interest, and habit have to be ignored for the sake of uniform administration. Yet no genuine equality of government is possible in such a large state. The capital city, to take the prime example, will be close to some parts of the large state, but it will be remote, in every relevant sense, from the extremities.[6] A national government would be compelled to impose a crude uniform rule on American diversity, which would in fact result in hardship and inequity for many parts of the country.

---

3. *The Records of the Federal Convention of 1787,* Max Farrand, ed. (New Haven: Yale University Press, 1937) I, 340–41 (20 June) (hereafter cited as Farrand); see Brutus VII, 2.9.87.

4. Hamilton himself confessed that "the extent of the Country to be governed, discouraged him." Farrand I, 287 (18 June); see also Wilson's account, *Pennsylvania and the Federal Constitution,* 220ff. For arguments in defense of the small republic, see Yates and Lansing 2.3.7; Brutus I, 2.9.11; Federal Farmer I, 2.8.14; IV, 2.8.75; XVII, 2.8.208; Sidney 6.8.1–2; Cato Uticensis 5.7.6; [Maryland] Farmer III, 5.1.52–53; Pennsylvania Convention Minority 3.11.16; Old Whig IV, 3.3.20; Monroe 5.21.13; Cato III, 2.6.12–13; Agrippa XII, 4.6.48; Albany Anti-Federal Committee 6.10.2; Centinel I, 2.7.19; V, 2.7.94; Martin 2.4.44; [Pennsylvania] Farmer 3.14.7, 9; Columbian Patriot 4.28.4; Warren 6.14.5; Smith 6.12.19–20; Henry 5.16.2; Clinton 6.13.13; etc.

5. Ellsworth, Farrand I, 406 (25 June); see Martin, Farrand II, 4 (14 July).

6. Federal Farmer II, 2.8.17; XII, 2.8.158; Cato III, 2.6.16; Impartial Examiner 5.14.6.

Behind the administrative defects of a large republic lie three fundamental considerations, bearing on the kind of government needed in a free society. Only a small republic can enjoy a voluntary attachment of the people to the government and a voluntary obedience to the laws. Only a small republic can secure a genuine responsibility of the government to the people. Only a small republic can form the kind of citizens who will maintain republican government. These claims are central to the Anti-Federalist position.[7]

It should be noted at the outset that there is a complication in the practical conclusions drawn from these considerations. Assuming the soundness of the case for the small republic and assuming that nothing but republican government is to be seriously considered for the United States, the obvious conclusion is that no attempt should be made to extend a single republican government over the whole United States. But if one republican government over the whole United States should nevertheless be unavoidable, despite serious disadvantages, then the Anti-Federalist arguments for the small republic serve the practical purpose of revealing and helping to minimize these disadvantages. Cognizance of the advantages of the small republic may be helpful in avoiding the worst disadvantages of a large one. In the discussion that follows we shall be meeting both kinds of arguments. Some defend the idea of the small republic

---

7. In Gordon Wood's view, the Anti-Federalists became fervent defenders "of the traditional assumption that the state was a cohesive organic entity with a single homogeneous interest at the very time they were denying the consequences of this assumption." Wood understands this traditional view, the "republicanism" of the Revolution, to be a secularized Puritanism aimed at securing a sacrifice of individual interest to the common good. *The Creation of the American Republic, 1776–1787* (Chapel Hill, N.C.: University of North Carolina Press, 1969, pp. 499, 418, and ch. 2. One of my own reasons for turning to the study of the Anti-Federalists was the expectation that they defended some such tradition; the Anti-Federalists seemed to be of interest as defenders of at least residual principles of premodern, preindustrial, preliberal worlds. Yet, without here taking up the more complex question of how far such principles may in fact have been involved in Revolutionary republicanism, they are strikingly absent from the Anti-Federalist thought. The Anti-Federalists are liberals—reluctant and traditional, indeed—in the decisive sense that they see the end of government as the security of individual liberty, not the promotion of virtue or the fostering of some organic common good. The security of liberty does require, in the Anti-Federalist view, the promotion of civic virtue and the subordination (not, in the usual case, "sacrifice") of individual interest to common good; but virtue and the common good are instrumental to individual liberty, and the resemblance to preliberal thought is superficial.

simply; others (drawn from the same theoretical source) aim to improve or mitigate the dangers of the large republic that American circumstances seemed to require. The different kinds of arguments will be clear enough as we go along, but both the distinction and the common source should be kept in mind.

The dependence of any republican government on the confidence of the people was one of the reasons given by the nationalists in the Constitutional Convention, notably James Wilson, for resting the general government directly on the people. Wilson "was for raising the federal pyramid to a considerable altitude, and for that reason wished to give it as broad a basis as possible. No government could long subsist without the confidence of the people. In a republican Government this confidence was peculiarly essential."[8] The Anti-Federalists emphatically endorsed this principle. "The great object of a free people," *The Federal Farmer* argued, "must be so to form their government and laws, and so to administer them, as to create a confidence in, and respect for the laws; and thereby induce the sensible and virtuous part of the community to declare in favor of the laws, and to support them without an expensive military force."[9] But the Anti-Federalists denied that the simple expedient of having the people elect federal representatives was enough to secure their attachment. In a large republic the people "will have no confidence in their legislature, suspect them of ambitious views, be jealous of every measure they adopt, and will not support the laws they pass."[10] Both reason and experience prove, Richard Henry Lee wrote, that so extensive and various a territory as the United States "cannot be governed in freedom" except in a confederation of states. Within each state, "opinion founded on the knowledge of those who govern, procures obedience without force. But remove the opinion, which must fall with a knowledge of characters in so widely extended a country, and force then becomes necessary to secure the purposes of civil government." The general rule is that government must exist, if not by persuasion, then by force.[11] In a large empire standing armies

---

8. Farrand I, 49 (31 May).

9. Federal Farmer III, 2.8.24. Agrippa XII, 4.6.50, referred to our present government, which "is respected from principles of affection and obeyed with alacrity." See Mason, Farrand I, 112 (4 June); Smith 6.12.10; Henry 5.16.17; Clinton 6.13.13.

10. Brutus I, 2.9.18.

11. Richard Henry Lee, letter to ——, 28 April 1788, in *The Letters of Richard Henry Lee*, James Curtis Ballagh, ed., 2 vols. (New York: MacMillan, 1911–1914), vol. II, p. 464; Federal Farmer III, 2.8.24; VII, 2.8.93. One of the arguments for leaving the states to decide how they would raise the money needed by the general government was this need for popular confidence.

are necessary "to cure the defect of the laws" and to take the place of popular confidence in and respect for the government.[12]

The second characteristic of the small republic is its capacity to ensure a strict responsibility of the government to the people. In a direct democracy, responsibility is ensured by the absence of much differentiation between the people and their government. However, most of the Anti-Federalists admitted the need, under American conditions at least, for a system of representation as a substitute for the meeting together of all the citizens.[13] The problem, then, was to keep the representatives responsible, in the rather narrow meaning of that term, that is, directly answerable to and dependent on their constituents.[14] This is the reason for the concern with short terms of office, frequent rotation, and a numerous representation.[15] The Anti-Federalists understood, however, that such devices are insufficient. Effective and thoroughgoing responsibility is to be found only in a likeness between the representative body and the citizens at large.

"Because *each* being thus accommodated, and participating [in] the advantages of union,—*none* subjected to any inconvenience thereby,—all will consequently concur in nourishing an affection for the government, that so cemented them." Impartial Examiner 5.14.6.

12. Agrippa XII, 4.6.48. See Cato III, 2.6.16; Pennsylvania Convention Minority 3.11.51; Brutus IX, 2.9.105–10; Candidus 4.9.23. If this thought seems utterly archaic, the modern reader may grasp it better by substituting "bureaucracy" for "standing army." The Anti-Federalists were not so much worried about military coups or about "militarism" in the popular sense, as about rigid rule of a large and varied republic by the force of government, of which the standing army is the ultimate expression. Consider Cato's challenge: "will you submit to be numbered like the slaves of an arbitrary despot; and what will be your reflections when the taxmaster thunders at your door for the duty on that light which is the bounty of heaven." VI, 2.6.41.

13. Cf. Brutus I, 2.9.14ff; IV, 2.9.45ff; [Maryland] Farmer VII, 5.1.98. Cf. James Wilson's remarks in the Constitutional Convention on representation with those in the Pennsylvania ratifying convention. Farrand I, 132–33 (6 June); *Pennsylvania and the Federal Constitution,* pp. 221ff. See Montesquieu, *The Spirit of Laws* XI, ch. 6.

14. Cf. Federal Farmer I, 2.8.4–6; VIII, 2.8.108; *The Federalist,* Jacob E. Cooke, ed. (Cleveland: World Publishing Co., 1961), no. 63; no. 74, p. 500; no. 76, pp. 510–12; no. 79, p. 532.

15. Columbian Patriot 4.28.4; Pennsylvania Convention Minority 3.11.33–37; Tamony 5.11.7; Warren 6.14.8, 47; Symmes 4.5.7; Smith 6.12.9; Federal Farmer XIV, 2.8.178. Rotation was thought to serve not only as an instrument of responsibility but also as training in public service, thus contributing to the attachment of the citizens to their community. Smith 6.12.27–28.

Thus "a full and equal representation is that which possesses the same interests, feelings, opinions, and views the people themselves would were they all assembled. . . ." According to Melancton Smith, representatives "should be a true picture of the people; possess the knowledge of their circumstances and their wants; sympathize in all their distresses, and be disposed to seek their true interests."[16] This describes the state legislatures reasonably well, it was claimed, but the federal legislature could not even come close to being representative in this genuine sense, at least not without a sharp increase in its number. Federal elections will present the voters with a choice among representatives of the well-known few, or the "natural aristocracy" as the Anti-Federalists often called them.[17] "It is deceiving a people to tell them they are electors, and can chuse their legislators, if they cannot, in the nature of things, chuse men from among themselves, and genuinely like themselves."[18]

What is wanted in a representative system is not "brilliant talents" but "a sameness, as to residence and interests, between the representative and his constituents." No great talents are necessary for government, and the men of great abilities are, on the whole, a danger rather than a benefit to a republic.[19] If, however, the Anti-Federalists distrusted "great abilities," they were willing to admit that "sameness" in a representative body is not literally possible. Every representative body is more aristocratic than the body of the people by whom it is chosen,[20] and any representative body covering

---

16. Federal Farmer II, 2.8.15; Smith 6.12.15. See Brutus I, 2.9.14; III, 2.9.42; and *passim*; Pennsylvania Convention Minority 3.11.4–5; Martin 2.4.42; Clinton 6.13.35.

17. The state legislatures "are so numerous as almost to be the people themselves. . . ." Federal Farmer XII, 2.8.163. See ibid. 2.8.155; VIII, 2.8.106; IX, 2.8.113; Smith 6.12.15, 22; Henry, *The Debates of the State Conventions on the Adoption of the Federal Constitution*, 2d ed., Jonathan Elliot, ed., 5 vols. (Philadelphia: Lippincott, 1896), vol. 3, p. 322 (hereafter cited as Elliot); Lee 5.6.2.

18. Federal Farmer VII, 2.8.97.

19. Federal Farmer XII, 2.8.158; see Centinel I, 2.7.3; VI, 2.7.106–10; IX, 2.7.129. "There are no such mighty talents necessary for government as some who pretend to them, without possessing them, would make us believe. Honest affections, and common qualifications, are sufficient. . . . Great abilities have generally, if not always, been employed to mislead the honest unwary multitude, and draw them out of the plain paths of public virtue and public good." [Trenchard], *Cato's Letters* I, 177–78, quoted by Friend to the Republic 4.23.8.

20. Federal Farmer IX, 2.8.113.

the whole United States would inevitably be highly selective. Here the argument shifts from the desirability of the small republic to the mitigation of the evils of the large one.[21] Given the need, especially in the general government, for some considerable compromise of the principle of sameness, the Anti-Federalists' secondary, more practical goal was a representation large enough to secure a substantial (if not proportionate) representation of the middling classes, in particular the sturdy yeomanry. This view was based not on a presumption of intrinsic superiority in the yeoman but on the political consequences of his peculiar situation. Melancton Smith gave the Anti-Federalist argument in his classic confrontation with Alexander Hamilton on the subject of representation.

> The same passions and prejudices govern all men. The circumstances in which men are placed in a great measure give a cast to the human character. Those in middling circumstances, have less temptation—they are inclined by habit and the company with whom they associate, to set bounds to their passions and appetites—if this is not sufficient, the want of means to gratify them will be a restraint— they are obliged to employ their time in their respective callings—hence the substantial yeomanry of the country are more temperate, of better morals, and less ambitious than the great. . . . When . . . this class in society pursue their own interest, they promote that of the public, for it is involved in it.[22]

All are agreed, Sydney argued, "that the rights and liberties of a country were ever in danger from the rich and poor, and their safety in the middle sort or yeomanry of the country. . . ."[23] An adequate representation of the middling classes serves, then, as a practical and effective substitute for a full representation of the people; for it does not require an excessively large body, and yet in pursuing their own interests the middling classes tend to pursue the interests of the public at large. However, the proposed House of Representatives

---

21. There is a continuity in the argument, since the principle of representation, which is the cause of the difficulty, is generally admitted by the Anti-Federalists even in the small republic. Many of them did think that there is a quantitative limit to the reach of the representative principle, that that limit was exceeded by the dimensions of the United States, and that therefore any representative body covering the whole United States must be inherently inadequate and untrustworthy. See Federal Farmer VI, 2.8.75; VII, 2.8.99; Smith 6.12.9.

22. Smith 6.12.17–18; cf. Hamilton, Elliot II, 254–57.

23. Sydney 6.9.19. See [Maryland] Farmer III, 5.1.56–58.

failed not only the strict test of sameness but the looser test of adequate representation of the middling classes. Given the number of representatives and the proportion of representatives and people, few if any of the members of this class could expect to be elected.[24] The Anti-Federalists generally saw this as an inherent deficiency of any nationwide government, yet, as we shall see, they accepted the need for such a government. If this was a contradiction it was not, they thought, due to any deficiency in their reasoning, for it lay at the heart of the American situation. The prudent course was to confine the contradiction to the narrowest possible scope by, on the one hand, making the representation in the first branch of the national legislature as full as circumstances permitted and, on the other hand, leaving as much of the power as possible in the states, where genuine responsibility could exist.

A related aspect of the question of responsibility concerned the much-discussed issue of jury trial, which it was alleged the Constitution would weaken or destroy. There is no need to go into detail, but the crux of the objection lay in the political significance of the jury trial. While an adequate representation in at least one branch of the legislature was indispensable at the top, law-making, level, the jury trial provided the people's safeguard at the bottom, administrative, level. "Juries are constantly and frequently drawn from the body of the people, and freemen of the country; and by holding the jury's right to return a general verdict in all cases sacred, we secure to the people at large, their just and rightful controul in the judicial department."[25] A [Maryland] Farmer argued, indeed, that the jury trial is more important than representation in the legislature, because "those usurpations, which silently undermine the spirit of liberty, under the sanction of law, are more dangerous than direct and open legislative attacks. . . ."[26] The main point, however, is that the democratic branch of the legislature and the jury trial are the means of effective and lawful popular control. They "are the means by which the people are let into the knowledge of public affairs—are

---

24. See below, pp. 56–64. In addition, because of the dispersed circumstances of the landed interest it would not be equally represented under the new system, which would tend to follow the lead of the commercial interests. Cornelius 4.10.11.

25. Federal Farmer XV, 2.8.190. A general verdict is one in which the jury finds either for the plaintiff or for the defendant in general terms, judging both law and fact, as opposed to a special verdict, in which a particular finding of fact is made by the jury, leaving to the court the application of the law to the facts thus found.

26. [Maryland] Farmer IV, 5.1.65; see generally ibid. 5.1.61ff.

enabled to stand as the guardians of each others rights, and to restrain, by regular and legal measures, those who otherwise might infringe upon them." The often extreme and apparently unfounded claims by the Anti-Federalists that the proposed Constitution would destroy the trial by jury should be seen against this background. The question was not fundamentally whether the lack of adequate provision for jury trial would weaken a traditional bulwark of individual rights (although that was also involved) but whether it would fatally weaken the role of the people in the *administration* of government.[27]

The third part of the Anti-Federalist defense of the small republic concerned the kind of citizens a free republic needs. The Anti-Federalists emphasized repeatedly that the character of a people is affected by government and laws, but that that relation had been dangerously ignored in the framing of the proposed Constitution. In the words of Melancton Smith, "Government operates upon the spirit of the people, as well as the spirit of the people operates upon it—and if they are not conformable to each other, the one or the other will prevail. . . . Our duty is to frame a government friendly to liberty and the rights of mankind, which will tend to cherish and cultivate a love of liberty among our citizens." "If there are advantages," the Federal Farmer argued, "in the equal division of our lands, and the strong and manly habits of our people, we ought to establish governments calculated to give duration to them, and not governments which never can work naturally, till that equality of property, and those free and manly habits shall be destroyed; these evidently are not the natural basis of the proposed constitution."[28]

---

27. Federal Farmer XV, 2.8.190. Noah Webster argued, for example, that the trial of the vicinage was no longer necessary to do justice in individual cases. *Pamphlets on the Constitution of the United States*, Paul Leicester Ford, ed. (Brooklyn, N.Y.: 1888), p. 53. However, the Federal Farmer made it clear that for him that was not the main concern.

28. Smith 6.12.20; Federal Farmer V, 2.8.59. See [Maryland] Farmer III, 5.1.52; Turner in Massachusetts ratifying convention, Elliot II, 31; Smith 6.12.9; Agrippa XII, 4.6.48. While the Federalist writers were less concerned with this question, see A Federalist, *Boston Gazette and Country Journal* 3 December 1787, who denied an Anti-Federalist argument that a constitution maker should adapt the constitution to the pre-civil habits of the people: ". . . his object would be, to introduce a code of laws that would *induce* those habits of civilization and order, which must result *from* good government. The truth of the case is, that as a people, we are destitute of *Federal Features* and *Habits*—the several *State Constitutions* are local, partial, and selfish; they are not calculated in their construction to form *national views*. . . ."

A republican citizenry must be free and independent-minded, but it must also be homogeneous. "In a republic, the manners, sentiments, and interests of the people should be similar. If this be not the case, there will be a constant clashing of opinions; and the representatives of one part will be continually striving against those of the other. This will retard the operations of government, and prevent such conclusions as will promote the public good." Only within the relatively small communities formed by the individual states could such homogeneity be found. Given the variety of climates, productions, laws, and customs among the United States, a legislature formed of representatives from all parts of the country "would be composed of such heterogeneous and discordant principles, as would constantly be contending with each other."[29] The preservation of homogeneity required, for many of the Anti-Federalists, protection against foreign contamination. "To what purpose have you expended so freely the blood and treasures of this country? To have a government with unlimited powers administered by foreigners?"[30] Arguing that the general government should not be given the power to naturalize aliens, Agrippa pointed to the contrasting results of Pennsylvania's policy of open immigration and the eastern states' freedom from foreign mixture. Whereas Pennsylvania purchased her size and population at the expense of religion and good morals, "the eastern states have, by keeping separate from the foreign mixtures, acquired their present greatness in the course of a century and a half, and have preserved their religion and morals." At the same time they have preserved "that manly virtue which is equally fitted for rendering them respectable in war, and industrious in peace."[31]

Homogeneity implied, for the Anti-Federalists, not only likeness but likeness of a certain kind: a society in which there are no extremes of wealth, influence, education, or anything else—the homogeneity of a moderate, simple, sturdy, and virtuous people.[32] Republican government depends on civic virtue, on a devotion to fellow citizens and to country so deeply instilled as to be almost as automatic and powerful as the natural devotion to self-interest. Many Anti-Federalists joined Patrick Henry in praise of the Swiss, who "have retained their independence, republican simplicity and valour."[33]

---

29. Brutus I, 2.9.16.
30. Republican Federalist 4.13.26.
31. Agrippa IX, 4.6.34.
32. See Impartial Examiner 5.14.6; [Pennsylvania] Farmer 3.14.7.
33. Henry 5.16.8; cf. *Federalist* 19, pp. 122–23.

These qualities are encouraged in the restricted sphere of the small republic, which offers little inducement or opportunity for the exercise of divisive and corrupting talents and which daily reminds each man of the benefits derived from and the duties owed to his little community.

Wherever they looked in the new Constitution the Anti-Federalists saw threats to civic virtue. The federal city provided for would breed monarchical institutions and courtly habits, with their oppressive tendencies and with the effect "above all [of] the perpetual ridicule of virtue."[34] The standing army would be not only a potential instrument of oppression but a source of moral corruption. With interests and habits different from the rest of the community, a standing army "will inevitably sow the seeds of corruption and depravity of manners. Indolence will increase, and with it crimes cannot but increase. The springs of honesty will gradually grow lax, and chaste and severe manners be succeeded by those that are dissolute and vicious. When a standing army is kept up, virtue never thrives."[35] Commerce itself, the benefits of which were one of the major reasons for the American Union, seemed to threaten republican simplicity and virtue.[36] Commerce is the vehicle of distinctions in wealth, of foreign influence, and of the decline of morals. "As people become more luxurious, they become more incapacitated of governing themselves."[37] Anti-Federalists constantly complained of America's hankering after European luxury. They agreed generally with John Adams that "frugality is a great revenue, besides curing us of vanities, levities, and fopperies, which are real antidotes to all great, manly, and warlike virtues."[38]

---

34. Cato IV, 2.6.27. See Friend to the Rights of the People 4.23.3; [Maryland] Farmer VII, 5.1.111; Turner 4.18.2; Columbian Patriot 4.28.1.

35. Federal Republican 3.6.21. See "The Congress under the New Constitution," *New York Journal* 28 January 1788; [New Hampshire] Farmer 4.17.4; Impartial Examiner, 5.14.8.

36. See discussion of Agrippa, *What the Anti-Federalists Were* For, pp. 24–25.

37. Turner 4.18.1. See Cato V, 2.6.34; Alfred 3.10.5; Lansing (New York), Elliot II, 218; Williams, Elliot II, 240; Warren 6.14 *passim*; Delegate Who Has Catched Cold 5.19.9. See Andrew Carnegie, *The Gospel of Wealth and Other Timely Essays* (1933), Edward C. Kirkland, ed. (Cambridge, Mass., 1962) p. 3; Montesquieu, *The Spirit of Laws* XX, ch. 1.

38. *Thoughts on Government*, John Adams, *Works* IV, 109. See Livingston, Elliot II, 341. Some of the Anti-Federalists for this reason favored sumptuary laws. See [Maryland] Farmer V, 5.1.82; George Mason, Farrand II, 344 (20 August), 606 (13 September). See below, pp. 73–75

Implicit in all of these opinions relating to republican citizenship is a concern with civic education, broadly conceived. Mercy Warren, who saw as deeply into this question as any of her contemporaries, flirted with the isolationism that tempted many of the Anti-Federalists. Could the pure republican spirit of the Americans be preserved, she reflected, by walling the country off from European luxury, on the one hand, and western empire on the other? It could not. However high the walls of separation, the fingers of avarice and ambition would find their ways through or around them. The danger to the republican spirit of America was illustrated by American attraction to European luxury and skepticism; but the source of the danger was not external. It lay, as it always lies, in the restless ambition and avarice in the heart of every man and every people; and that is where it must be met, principally by education. "[I]f the education of youth, both public and private, is attended to, their industrious and economical habits maintained, their moral character and that assemblage of virtues supported, which is necessary for the happiness of individuals and of nations, there is not much danger that they will for a long time be subjugated by the arms of foreigners, or that their republican system will be subverted by the arts of domestic œconomies."[39] A few Anti-Federalists made specific proposals. Thus A [Maryland] Farmer proposed the establishment of local "seminaries of useful learning, with professorships of political and domestic economy." The citizens should be instructed not in "the philosophy of the moon and skies," but in "what is useful in this world—the principles of free government, illustrated by the history of mankind—the sciences of morality, agriculture, commerce, the management of farms and household affairs." If this were done, in a short time "the people instead of abusing, would wade up to their knees in blood, to defend their governments."[40] More often the Anti-Federalist thought of the whole organization of the polity as having an educative function. The small republic was seen as a school of citizenship as much as a scheme for government. An important part—much more important than we are today likely to remember—of their argument for a federal bill of rights was the educative function of such a document in reminding the citizen of the ends of civil government and in strengthening his attachment to it. The provisions of a bill of rights "can inspire and conserve the affection for the native country, they will be the first lesson of the young citizens becoming men, to sustain the dignity of their being. . . ."[41]

39. Warren 6.14.157.

40. [Maryland] Farmer VI, 5.1.82; see Warren 6.14.132–33.

41. Delegate Who Has Catched Cold 5.19.16. See Federal Farmer XVI, 2.8.190; Henry 5.16.37; *What the Anti-Federalists Were For*, ch. 8.

Finally, many Anti-Federalists were concerned with the maintenance of religious conviction as a support of republican government. "Refiners may weave as fine a web of reason as they please, but the experience of all times," Richard Henry Lee wrote to James Madison in 1784, "shews Religion to be the guardian of morals."[42] The opinions of men need to be formed "in favour of virtue and religion. . . ."[43] Religious support of political institutions is an old idea, and here again the Anti-Federalists tended to be the conservatives. The view was well expressed by an anonymous Massachusetts writer in 1787.[44] He explained that there are but three ways of controlling the "turbulent passions of mankind": by punishment; by reward; and "by prepossessing the people in favour of virtue by affording publick protection to religion." All are necessary, but especially the last. "[I]t is not more difficult to build an elegant house without tools to work with, than it is to establish a durable government without the public protection of religion." By 1787, however, the opinion seemed to be growing that organized religion could be dispensed with or taken for granted. This was, at any rate, the Anti-Federal reading of the situation. The indifference of the constitution and its main defenders to organized religion was striking. In the words of Federalist writer Elihu, "the light of philosophy has arisen," and "mankind are no longer to be deluded with fable." "Making the glory of God subservient to the temporal interest of men, is a worn-out trick. . . ."[45]

Anti-Federalists saw quite clearly the implications of such arguments and challenged them. They would have agreed with an anonymous Virginian who urged that steps be taken to revitalize religion: "Whatever influence speculative vanity may ascribe to the indefinite principle termed honor, or political refinement, to an artful collusion of interest, sound reason as well as experience proves that a due sense of responsibility to the Deity, as the author of those moral laws, an observance of which constitutes the happiness and welfare of societies as well as individuals, is the mean most likely to give a right

---

42. R. H. Lee, letter to James Madison, 26 November 1784, Lee, *Letters* II, 304.

43. David 4.24.2.

44. See Clinton Rossiter, *Political Thought of the American Revolution* (New York 1963) 204–6. See Alexis de Tocqueville, *Democracy in America* I, part 1, ch. 9; II, part 2, chs. 15–19. Alan Aichinger, "Civic Education in the New Republic" (University of Chicago Ph.D. diss. 1970).

45. David 4.24 n.1. See the satire of Aristocrotis (3.16.3) describing the free-thinking origin of the Constitution as an attempt to deny any divine limits on civil rulers.

direction to the conduct of mankind."[46] The Anti-Federalists feared that the Americans would follow the example of the Europeans as described by Mercy Warren: "Bent on gratification, at the expense of every moral tie, they have broken down the barriers of religion, and the spirit of infidelity is nourished at the fount; thence the poisonous streams run through every grade that constitutes the mass of nations." Warren insisted that skepticism is not, as some hold, necessarily fostered by republican liberty. Indeed, the history of republics is the history of strict regard to religion.[47]

It is less easy to say what concrete form the Anti-Federalists thought this concern with religion ought to take. They favored religious toleration and sometimes criticized the Constitution for the absence of protection of liberty of conscience; but this was assumed to mean, in practice, toleration of Christian (or only Protestant) sects and was rarely extended even in principle to the protection of professed atheists. They saw no inconsistency between liberty of conscience and the public support of the religious, and generally Protestant, community as the basis of public and private morality.

Many Anti-Federalists supported and would even have strengthened the mild religious establishments that existed in some states. Richard Henry Lee wrote in 1784 that "he must be a very inattentive observer in our Country, who does not see that avarice is accomplishing the destruction of religion, for want of a legal obligation to contribute something to its support. The [Virginia] declaration of Rights, it seems to me, rather contends against forcing modes of faith and forms of worship, than against compelling contribution for the support of religion in general."[48] More generally, the Anti-Federalist position was not so much that government ought to foster religion as that the consolidating Constitution threatened the healthy religious situation as it then existed. The religious diversity of the whole United States seemed so great as to strain to breaking point any publicly useful religious foundation for the nation as a whole. Consolidation would require, then, substituting for religion some other

---

46. *Virginia Independent Chronicle* 31 October 1787. See Federal Republican 3.6.21.

47. Warren 6.14.148, 135–37. See Agrippa IX, 4.6.34; XII, 4.6.48. Also Federal Farmer IV, 2.8.53. American fears about American corruption are considered at length by Gordon Wood in *Creation* chs. 3 and 10.

48. R. H. Lee, letter to James Madison, 26 November 1784, Lee, *Letters* II, 304. "William Penn" (Penn 3.12.18) found a contradiction in state constitutional provisions for liberty of conscience alongside provisions for religious oaths for officeholders; but he made no attempt to resolve it.

foundation of political morality—which the Anti-Federalists foresaw would be an aggregate of selfish interests held together by force. This tendency would be strengthened by the absence from the Constitution of any religious test for officeholding, which seemed intended to further undermine the public significance of religious conviction.[49]

The Constitution and its defenders deliberately turned away from religion as the foundation of civil institutions. Among the Anti-Federalists, on the other hand, there was a great deal of sympathy with views like those of Charles Turner: "without the prevalance of *Christian piety and morals*, the best republican Constitution can never save us from slavery and ruin." Turner hoped that the first Congress under the Constitution would recommend to the states the institution of such means of education "as shall be *adequate* to the *divine, patriotick purpose* of training up the children and youth at large, in that solid learning, and in those pious and moral principles, which are the *support*, the *life* and SOUL of republican government and liberty, of which a free Constitution is the body. . . ." He expressed a central Anti-Federal thought when he urged that the new rulers should turn their attention to the task, which surpasses the framing of constitutions, of fostering religion and morals, thereby making government less necessary by rendering "the people more capable of being *a Law to themselves*."[50] Such self-government was possible, however, only if the center of gravity of American government remained in the states.

The Federalist Reply

Most of the major Federalists spoke the language of the new federalism, and some were content to rest their defense of the Constitution on this ground. The general and the particular governments have their different spheres and objects: the Constitution has defined these spheres reasonably well; and there is reason to hope that future adjustments will preserve a healthy balance.

---

49. See, for example, the remarks of Amos Singletary, Elliot II, 44. For a good statement of the Federalist case against test oaths (and civil religion in general), see A Landholder (Oliver Ellsworth) in *Essays on the Constitution of the United States*, Paul Leicester Ford (Brooklyn, N.Y.: 1892), pp. 168–71, who, however, approved of "our laws against drunkenness, profane swearing, blasphemy, and professed atheism." See letter of William Williams, Ford, *Essays* 207–9.

50. Turner 4.18.2; see David Caldwell, Elliot IV, 199; Friend to the Rights of the People 4.23.3(9).

The most able Federalists, however, had reservations not merely about the feasibility of the new federalism but about its underlying premises. Men like James Madison thought that the solution of the internal as well as the external problems of American government was to be found not fundamentally in an equilibrium between states and Union, even if that could be achieved, but in a properly organized and empowered American republic. This view was prominent in the Philadelphia debates. Explaining the Virginia Plan, Edmund Randolph "observed that the general object was to provide a cure for the evils under which the U.S. labored; that in tracing these evils to their origin every man had found it in the turbulence and follies of democracy. . . ."[51] Later James Madison explicitly challenged the narrow view expressed by Roger Sherman that the objects of Union were confined to dealing with foreign powers and preventing disputes among the states. To these should be added, Madison said, "the necessity of providing more effectually for the security of private rights, and the steady dispensation of Justice. Interferences with these were evils which had more perhaps than anything else, produced this convention. Was it to be supposed that republican liberty could long exist under the abuses of it practiced in [some of] the states?"[52] This argument denies the basic premise of the Anti-Federal position and of the new federalism, the presumed superiority of the small republic in securing individual liberty and domestic tranquillity. On the contrary, the trouble with small republics is not mainly that they are weak and need to confederate for external purposes; it is that they cannot perform adequately the very tasks they are supposed to be best at.[53] The extended American republic organized under the Constitution, while surely necessary for defense and commercial prosperity, will also be able to do the internal work of free republican government better than the states or any ideal small republic could do it. There are two parts of this crucial Federalist argument, the first having to do with the characteristic problem of republican government and the second with its solution.

The characteristic problem of republican government is, in the words of Publius, majority faction, which is the majority "united and actuated by some common impulse of passion, or of interest, adverse

---

51. Farrand I, 51 (31 May).

52. Ibid. 134 (6 June). Brackets indicate James Madison's revision; see Chief Justice Taney in *Ableman v. Booth*, 21 How. 506, 516 (1859).

53. This leaves aside the additional and practically very powerful argument that the states were mostly larger than the traditional small republics anyway. See *Federalist 9*, pp. 52–53.

to the rights of other citizens, or to the permanent and aggregate interests of the community."[54] This is not the traditional problem of popular licentiousness leading to resistance of authority and anarchy. Majority faction is the particular danger of popular government precisely because under popular government majorities can tyrannize under the cover of law.[55] This does not mean that Publius and the Federalists opposed majorities—Publius makes clear that not all majorities are factious—or that they were, as is sometimes inferred, enemies of popular government.[56] They did often declare against democracy (or against "pure democracy"), but democracy was understood in such contexts as a corrupt or extreme form of popular government.[57] The Federalists were preoccupied with majority faction (or democracy, in some formulations) precisely because of their commitment to the kind of government of which majority faction is the characteristic evil. The point is, as Madison explained in a letter to Jefferson, that "wherever the real power in a Government lies, there is the danger of oppression. In our Governments the real power lies in the majority of the community, and the invasion of private rights is *chiefly* to be apprehended, not from acts of Government contrary to the sense of its constituents, but from acts in which the Government is the mere instrument of the major number of the Constituents."[58]

Among the opponents of the Constitution there was some equivocation over majority faction. A few argued for pure democracy: "America under [a government] purely democratical, would be rendered the happiest and most powerful nation in the universe. . . ."[59] A very few seemed to deny that there can be such a thing as majority tyranny. When Brutus defined tyrannical government as that which, instead of serving the public good, promotes "the happiness and aggrandisement of one, or a few," he seemed to suggest, by omission, that there can be no tyrannical government of the many, though

---

54. *Federalist* 10, p. 57.

55. See Gordon Wood's excellent discussion of this point, *Creation* 409–13.

56. See Parrington, *Main Currents in American Political Thought*, 3 vols. (New York: Harcourt, 1927–1930), I, chs. 1, 2; III, pp. 401–3; Jensen, *New Nation* (New York: Knopf, 1950), pp. 424–27; Jensen, *The Articles of Confederation* (Madison: University of Wisconsin, 1940, 1970) *passim*; Wood, *Creation* 513.

57. See for example Farrand I, 51 (31 May), 288 (18 June); Elliot II, 10.

58. Letter from James Madison to Thomas Jefferson, 17 October 1788. Madison, *Writings*, 9 vols. (New York: Putnam, 1900–1910), V, 272.

59. Philadephiensis X, 3.9.76.

on the whole it is more accurate to say that, while not denying the possibility of majority tyranny, he did not see any need to discuss it.[60] Governor Clinton perhaps came closest to a denial in principle of the very possibility of majority tyranny when he insisted that the only true definition of free government is that "the will of the people . . . is law."[61]

In general, however, the Anti-Federalists acknowledged the possibility of majority faction and the need to guard against it, even though this danger typically occupied a less conspicuous place in their catalog of dangers than in that of the Federalists.[62] Impressed as they were by the English "Real Whigs," or Commonwealthmen, as Caroline Robbins has called them, the Anti-Federalists had been taught by their own experience that there were other dangers than kings, lords, and magistrates. Few of them would have agreed with Burgh that to argue that "the representatives of the people be checked and clogged in promoting the interest of their constituents" is like arguing that "there ought to be a check to prevent individuals from being too healthy, or too virtuous. . . ."[63] Government by the people or, in practice, majority rule was accepted by the Anti-Federalists as the foundation of free government in America;[64] but (Cato to the contrary notwithstanding) majority rule was not generally thought to be the very definition of free government, because it can lead to unjust deprivations of individual liberty. This was, indeed, one of the reasons some of the Anti-Federalists wanted a bill of rights. Thus Agrippa met the Federalist denial that a bill of rights is necessary in a representative government by insisting that it would serve "to secure

---

60. Brutus IV, 2.9.45 and passim.

61. Clinton 6.13.2.

62. "He had," Elbridge Gerry told his fellow delegates at Philadelphia, "been too republican heretofore: he was still however republican, but had been taught by experience the danger of the levilling spirit." Farrand I, 48 (31 May); see Mason, Farrand I, 101 (4 June).

63. James Burgh, *Political Disquisitions*, 3 vols. (London: Dilly, 1774) I, 117. See Caroline Robbins, *The Eighteenth-Century Commonwealthman* (Cambridge, Mass.: Harvard University Press, 1959).

64. The difficult question of the franchise played little part in the ratification debate, since the Constitution left this matter to the states. While James Madison initially favored some form of freehold suffrage requirements as a way of checking the excesses of popular government, he later concluded that such a restriction on the franchise was dubious both in practice and in principle. See Farrand II, 203–4 (7 August) and Madison's very interesting fuller and more mature views in Farrand III, 450–55. See Wood, *Creation* 167–70.

the minority against the usurpation and tyranny of the majority."[65] A [Maryland] Farmer made the point even more emphatically:

> The truth is, that the rights of individuals are frequently opposed to the apparent interests of the majority—For this reason the greater the portion of political freedom in a form of government the greater the necessity of a bill of rights—Often the natural rights of an individual are opposed to the presumed interests or heated passions of a large majority of democratic government; if these rights are not clearly and expressly ascertained, the individual must be lost; and for the truth of this I appeal to every man who has borne a part in the legislative councils of America. In such government the tyranny of the legislative is most to be dreaded.[66]

Jackson Turner Main's disappointed estimate is "that less than half of the Anti-Federalist leaders had democratic inclinations, and that these were muted."[67] But the terms of this estimate are vague in the extreme. It would be difficult to find a single articulate American of this period who did not have very significant democratic "inclinations"; yet there were very few whose democratic inclinations were not, in some significant sense, "muted."

Gordon Wood, on the other hand, characterizes the Anti-Federalists as genuine populists, as "majoritarians with respect to the state legislatures," as "true champions of the most extreme kind of democratic and egalitarian politics expressed in the Revolutionary era."[68] But what precisely does this mean? There were very few "democrats" among the Anti-Federalist writers (or probably among Americans of any kind) if by that is meant those who believe simply that the will of the majority of the people is law and that that will ought to be exercised as directly and with as little restraint as possible.[69] How-

---

65. Agrippa XVI, 4.6.73.

66. [Maryland] Farmer I, 5.1.15.

67. Jackson Turner Main, *The Antifederalists: Critics of the Constitution* (Chapel Hill, N.C., 1960), p. 173. Whether unmuted democratic views were as common as Main assumes even among the obscure people may well be questioned on the basis of the available evidence.

68. Wood, *Creation* 516.

69. On the other hand, there were very few nondemocrats among the Federalists if by that is meant those who deny (1) that all powers derive from the consent of the governed and (2) that in general the will of the majority should prevail. Indeed, in his very important restoration of the thought of *The Federalist*, Martin Diamond insists on the founders' "democratic" intentions. Martin Diamond, "Democracy and *The Federalist*: A Reconstruction of the Framers' Intent," *American Political Science Review* March 1959 (reprinted in Richard Stevens and Morton Frisch, *American Political Thought* [New York:

ever, the Anti-Federalists *were* typically more democratic than the Federalists in the specific sense that they were less likely to see majority faction as the most dangerous and likely evil of popular government. They were inclined to think, with Patrick Henry, that harm is more often done by the tyranny of the rulers than by the licentiousness of the people.[70] Moreover, so far as there may be a threat of licentiousness, it is to be met in the same way, fundamentally, as the threat to tyranny: by the alert public-spiritedness of the small, homogeneous, self-governing community.

To the Federalists, Henry's and the other Anti-Federalists' view

---

Charles Scribner's Sons, 1971]); "The Federalist," in *History of Political Philosophy*, Leo Strauss and Joseph Cropsey, eds., 2d ed. (Chicago: Rand MacNally, 1972), pp. 636–41. There is usage to support this view. Madison spoke in the Constitutional Convention of the need to remedy "the inconveniences of democracy" in ways "consistent with the democratic form of Govt." Farrand I, 135 (6 June). John Marshall said that the Federalists (in contrast to their opponents who had praised monarchy) "idolize democracy" and consider the Constitution to provide for "a well-regulated democracy." Elliot III, 222. Nathaniel Gorham asserted that the preponderance of the landed interest will enable it to prevent the introduction "of any other than a perfectly democratical form of government." Elliot II, 69. A Federalist essayist, A Patriotic Citizen, in New Hampshire stressed that "the people are the sole, the great source from which all powers delegated to the federal government, by this truly democratic constitution, are to flow. . . ." See also [Pennsylvania] Farmer 3.14.2–3; Monroe 5.21 *passim*; Cato II, 2.6.8; Elliot II, 242; Penn 3.12.12. Nevertheless, while it is not inaccurate to say that the Founders favored a "well regulated democracy," to say that they favored "democracy" does not reflect dominant contemporary usage nor, I think, does it foster analytical clarity. The term "democracy" is ambiguous, containing a range of ideas from simple, direct popular rule to a regulated, checked, mitigated rule of the people. Generally, especially when aiming at precision of expression, both the Federalists and the Anti-Federalists used the term "popular government" to contain this whole range of ideas, reserving "democracy" for the former end of the scale and "republic" for the latter. See Elliot III, 394, and the very clear distinction drawn in *The Federalist* nos. 14 and 10. John Adams provides a good explanation in his *Defence of the Constitutions of Government of the United States of America*, in *The Works of John Adams*, Charles Francis Adams, ed., 10 vols. (Boston: Little and Brown, 1851), vol. I, pp. 308–9.

70. Henry 5.16.2. Cf. Federal Farmer V, 2.8.59; VII, 2.8.100. Cf. Madison, Elliot III, 87. On their side, the Federalists did not deny that rulers might be tyrannical, but they saw it as the secondary danger. But see the comment by Fabius (John Dickinson) that history "holds up the *licentiousness* of the people, and *turbulent temper* of some of the states, as *the only causes* to be dreaded, not the conspiracies of federal officers." Ford, *Pamphlets* 200. See *What the Anti-Federalists Were For*, pp. 50, 51.

of both the problem and the solution missed the main points. Having established the centrality to republican government of the problem of majority tyranny, the Federalists went on to challenge the Anti-Federalist preference for the small republic in all of the three essential aspects that we have considered.[71] Rather than attempting to secure the patriotic attachment and law-abidingness of the citizens through a small republic, the Federalists would bind the citizens to their polity by effective government and good administration. Rather than trying to secure responsibility through a numerous representation, the Federalists would stress the filtering effect of representation; they would accept the natural leadership of the influential few, attaching it to the government and directing it toward the public good. And finally, rather than trying to foster republican simplicity, virtue, and self-restraint, the Federalists would rely on the many diverse private gratifications available in the extended republic, with its spaciousness and opportunity, to make it unlikely that any faction (and particularly a majority faction) would have the inclination or opportunity to tyrannize over others. Let us consider each of these challenges to the Anti-Federalist position in turn.

The Anti-Federalists thought, as we have seen, that a large republic cannot attract the voluntary obedience of the people and is therefore driven to execute its resolutions by military force. In the words of the Federal Farmer, "The general government, far removed from the people, and none of its members elected oftener than once in two years, will be forgot or neglected, and its laws in many cases disregarded, unless a multitude of officers and military force be continually kept in view, and employed to enforce the execution of the laws, and to make the government feared and respected."[72] If a government of force is to be avoided, the bonds of political union must be woven from the strands of the natural human association.

> The strongest principle of union resides within our domestic walls. The ties of the parent exceed that of any other; as we depart from home, the next general principle of union is amongst citizens of the same state, where acquaintance, habits, and fortunes, nourish affection, and attachment; enlarge the circle still further, and, as citizens of different states, though we acknowledge the same national denomination, we lose the ties of acquaintance, habits, and fortunes, and thus, by degrees, we lessen in our attachments,

---

71. See above, pp. 37–51.
72. Federal Farmer II, 2.8.23; see Brutus I, 2.9.18.

till, at length, we no more than acknowledge a sameness of species.[73]

Significantly, Alexander Hamilton used exactly this thought in the New York ratifying convention and in *The Federalist* to show that the states need not fear being undermined by the new general government because they will always enjoy the attachment of the people. Followed with some care, however, Hamilton's discussion points to the Federalist alternative to the small natural community.

> It is a known fact in human nature that its affections are commonly weak in proportion to the distance or diffusiveness of the object. Upon the same principle that a man is more attached to his family than to his neighborhood, to his neighborhood than to the community at large, the people of each State would be apt to feel a stronger bias towards their local governments than towards the government of the Union; *unless the force of that principle should be destroyed by a much better administration of the latter.*[74]

What is presented here as the incidental and apparently unlikely possibility of a better federal administration turns out to be crucial. Hamilton later makes it clear that there is "a probability that the general government *will* be better administered than the particular governments," being composed of a more select group of men, with more information and free of the taint of faction.[75] Thus the

---

73. Cato III, 2.6.20.

74. *Federalist* 17, p. 107; italics added. See Elliot II, 354–55. Publius goes on to argue that this consideration is strengthened by the state's administration of ordinary criminal and civil justice, thus involving itself in the daily lives of the people.

75. *Federalist* 27, p. 172; italics added. Added to this consideration is the increased mingling of federal authority in the ordinary life of the people. Ibid. 173–74; no. 16, 102–3; cf. Plebeian 6.11.2.

Some of the Anti-Federalists saw the implication for the states of this line of argument. John Smilie thought that, for just such reasons as Publius gave, the people would become unwilling to support the state governments at all. "For, Sir, the attachment of citizens to their government and its laws is founded upon the benefits which they derive from them, and it will last no longer than the duration of the power to confer those benefits. When, therefore, the people of the respective States shall find their governments grown torpid, and divested of the means to promote their welfare and interests, they will not, Sir, vainly idolize a shadow, nor disburse their hard earned wealth without the prospect of a compensation. The constitution of the States having become weak and useless to every beneficial purpose, will be suffered to dwindle and decay, and thus if the governors of the Union are not too impatient for the accomplishment of unrivalled and absolute domin-

advantages of the close-knit natural community in inspiring the trust and confidence of the people can be replaced by the attractive benefits of the more effective government of the large republic.

Indeed, the Federalists claimed that their opponents mistook the political ground of trust, confidence, and even public morality, which is not intimate government but effective government. It is "not generally true," Hamilton told the New York convention, "that a numerous representation [is] necessary to obtain the confidence of the people. The confidence of the people will easily be gained by a good administration. This is the true touchstone." Public attachment to government "is more strongly secured by a train of prosperous events, which are the result of wise deliberation and vigorous execution," to which large bodies are less competent than small ones.[76]

Governments attract the confidence of the people in the long run by deserving it. This includes, among other things, giving effective support to the virtues that all admit are desirable. The qualities of industry, economy, honesty, and civic virtue, about which the Anti-Federalists preach so much, are in fact undermined by the kind of governments the Anti-Federalists defend. Tender laws and paper money, the products of weak government, had led in America to well-known (and, by most Anti-Federalists, admitted) evils. "If virtue is the foundation of republican government, has it not been fatally sapped by these means? The morals of the people have been almost sunk into depravity; and the government of laws has been almost superseded by a licentious anarchy."[77] The crucial need, even for those who are the immediate losers, is wise and effective government and the confidence that only such a government can inspire. This is the source of civic prosperity. "The circulation of confidence is better than the circulation of money," and the pump of confidence is sound government, not government close to the people.

An aspect of any good government is a capacity to coerce obedience when necessary. To that extent the Anti-Federalists were right in saying that the new government would rest ultimately on force; they were wrong, in the Federalists' opinion, in thinking that

---

ion, the destruction of State jurisdiction will be produced by its own insignificance." *Pennsylvania and the Federal Constitution*, pp. 270–71.

76. Elliot II, 254. See Wilson, ibid. 474; Philadelphiensis X, 3.9.80: "The allegiance of freemen to government will ever be a consequence of protection."

77. Jasper Yeates, *Pennsylvania and the Federal Constitution*, p. 298; cf. Charles Cotesworth Pinckney, John Marshall, Elliot III, 231; Tench Coxe, Ford, *Pamphlets* 147; John Dickinson, ibid. 174.

there is any other kind. "[A]ll government is a kind of restraint" and "founded in force," Charles Pinckney told the South Carolina House of Representatives; "he could not conceive that either the dignity of a government could be maintained, its safety ensured, or its laws administered, without a body of regular forces to aid the magistrate in the execution of his duty."[78] Coercion also has a broader moral and political effect: "While it compels the obedience of the refractory, it redoubles the alertness of the virtuous by inspiring a confidence in the impartiality of its burthens."[79]

The Federalist view, then, was that an effective government, in addition to being intrinsically desirable, is also the key to the attachment of the people and to civic virtue itself. A government that can actually accomplish its resolves, that can keep the peace, protect property, and promote the prosperity of the country will be a government respected and obeyed by its citizens. It will, moreover, promote private and public morality by providing them with effective protection.

The second element of the Federalist solution of the problem of popular government is a proper system of representation. In the main, the Anti-Federalists accepted representation reluctantly, as a necessary device in a community where the people cannot assemble to do their common business. The representative body is seen in consequence as a substitute for an assembly of all the citizens, which ought to be as like the whole body as possible. The Federalists, on the other hand, saw representation not as an unfortunate necessity but as an opportunity. It permits, in the first place, an extension of popular government. Through representation, especially in a federal system, "the people of a large country may be represented as truly as those of a small one."[80] Representation is the device that makes the large republic possible. But it is more. Arguing that representation was not new, but was put to a new use in the American governments, Publius made the striking observation that the difference between ancient governments and the American governments lay *"in the total exclusion of the people in their collective capacity from any share in the latter,* and not in the *total exclusion of representatives of the people,* from the administration of the former." To secure the full effect of this benefit, however, it must be connected to an extensive territory. "For it cannot be believed that any form of representative government,

---

78. Elliot IV, 261, 260–61.

79. Edward Carrington to Thomas Jefferson, 9 June 1787, *Proceedings of the Massachusetts Historical Society* 2d series, XVII, 463.

80. Hamilton, Elliot II, 353; see Randolph, Elliot III, 84–85.

could have succeeded within the narrow limits occupied by the democracies of Greece."[81]

Thus representation is necessary to secure the benefits of the large republic; but the large republic is also necessary to secure the benefits of representation. These benefits are to be found, negatively expressed, in the capacity of a representative system to provide for a popular government in which the people collectively play no part and in which the danger of popular excesses is thereby reduced. As a Virginia Federalist argued, "the more independent a government is . . . of the people, under proper restraints," the more likely it is to produce the security of persons and property which is the end of government.[82]

As we have seen, the Anti-Federalists complained that in a large republic the people will not in practice be able to choose men like themselves, and the representative body will inevitably be composed of the natural aristocracy. In large districts, "a common man must ask a man of influence how he is to proceed, and for whom he must vote," and the only men with a chance of being elected are those of "conspicuous military, popular, civil or legal talents."[83]

The Federalists replied that it is inevitable and natural that the people should choose such men to represent them; they cannot and should not be prevented from doing so. The small manufacturer sees that the merchant can represent him in public councils better than he could represent himself. The small landholder sees that his basic interests are shared with and protected by the great landholder. And what is wrong with electing men of conspicuous talents? Who composes this "natural aristocracy" before which the opponents of the Constitution tremble? They are the most distinguished, the most trusted, the most able men (and that is, on the whole, how the Anti-Federalists themselves identified them). But are not these precisely the kinds of men who ought to be the people's representatives? Even the radical constitution of Pennsylvania, James Wilson pointed out, declared that "representatives should consist of those most noted for

---

81. *Federalist* 63; cf. Montesquieu, *The Spirit of Laws* XI, ch. 6. Some Federalists did describe representation as a new idea. Thus Noah Webster asserted that "the moderns have invented the doctrine of *representation*, which seems to be the perfection of human government." Ford, *Pamphlets* 30, 42–43. See also Gorham, Elliot II, 68–69; Wilson, ibid. 423ff and *Pennsylvania and the Federal Constitution*, pp. 221ff.

82. State Soldier, *Virginia Independent Chronicle* 19 March 1788; cf. Ames, Elliot II, 8; *Federalist* 10.

83. Henry 5.16.27; Smith 6.12.17.

wisdom and virtue." "If this is [what is] meant by a natural aristocracy, and I know no other, can it be objectionable that men should be employed that are most noted for their virtue and talents?"[84]

In New York, Chancellor Livingston argued against rotation on the same grounds. It is "an absurd species of ostracism—a mode of proscribing eminent merit, and banishing from stations of trust those who have filled them with the greatest faithfulness." Moreover, should not virtue and talents be encouraged by honors and rewards? "The acquisition of abilities is hardly worth the trouble, unless one is to enjoy the satisfaction of employing them for the good of one's country."[85]

Thus the positive side of the Federalist case for representation is the likelihood that it will produce a government with a capacity to govern well. The probability is increased in an extensive republic, which is more likely to put forward "proper guardians of the public weal" and less susceptible to electoral corruption than a small one. Corruption is difficult where there are many to bribe, and the large district is protection against other forms of "bribery" such as demagoguery and appeals to narrow interests.[86] Petty republics and small districts are the natural homes of petty men. "It is only in remote corners of a government," James Wilson thought, "that little demagogues arise. Nothing but real weight of character, can give a man real influence over a large district."[87] In a large district an aspiring politician has to seek a wide base of support, and this increases the likelihood of his taking a broad view or at least decreases the chances of narrow partiality. "The little demagogue of a petty parish or county will find his importance annihilated, and his intrigues useless, when several counties join in an election; he probably would not be known, certainly not regarded, out of his own circle; while the man whose abilities and virtue had extended a fair reputation beyond the limits of his county, would, nine times out of ten, be the person who

---

84. *Pennsylvania and the Federal Constitution,* p. 335. The Pennsylvania Constitution of 1776 provided (II, sec. 7): "the house of representatives of the freemen of this commonwealth shall consist of persons most noted for wisdom and virtue, to be chosen by the freemen of every city and county of this commonwealth respectively." John Adams in his influential *Thoughts on Government* wrote of deputing power "from the many to a few of the most wise and good." *Works* IV, 194.

85. Livingston, Elliot II, 293; replied to by Smith, ibid. 310–11.

86. *Federalist* 10, p. 62. Cassius (a Federalist reply to R. H. Lee), *Virginia Independent Chronicle* 2 April 1788; see Gouverneur Morris, Farrand II, 30–31 (17 July).

87. *Pennsylvania and the Federal Constitution,* p. 336.

would be the choice of the people."[88] For the Federalists, then, representation is a mode of selecting for rulers the best men, or at least men better than average; and the large districts of the large republic increase the chance of securing such men.

Consistent with this view that, as Publius said, the first aim of every constitution should be "to obtain for rulers men who possess most wisdom to discern, and most virtue to pursue, the common good of the society," the Federalists saw the duty of representatives as extending beyond the particular interests of their constituents to the common good.[89] Noah Webster said, for example, that while a delegate is bound to represent "the true local interest" of those who elect him, "when each provincial interest is thus stated, every member should act for the *aggregate interest* of the whole confederacy. The design of representation is to bring the collective interest into view."[90] The Federalists were not naive about the tendencies of representatives to act for narrow and selfish views; but the aim was a system in which the collective interest will emerge. Representation is not sufficient, but it is the basic device through which the people not merely represents but transcends itself. As Fisher Ames put it, "The representation of the people is something more than the people."[91]

Against the third part of the Anti-Federalist defense of the small republic, the need for republican simplicity and public-spiritedness, the Federalists put forward the diversity of the extended commercial republic. Most of the Anti-Federalists thought, with Brutus, that "in

---

88. Charles Cotesworth Pinckney, Elliot IV, 302. Consider, however, Hamilton's reflection that demagogues are not always petty men. Farrand I, 147 (6 June). Publius concedes that the case is equivocal. If the large republic has a larger proportion of fit characters, it also has a larger proportion of bad ones; if corruption is more difficult, so is popular supervision of representatives. *Federalist* 10, p. 63.

89. *Federalist* 57, p. 384. Nevertheless, it goes too far to say, as Gordon Wood does, that putting "good men into the administration" is "the crux of the Federalist argument," as indeed Wood's summary chapter sufficiently shows. *Creation* 508, 602–6. See *What the Anti-Federalists Were* For, pp. 53, 54, on limited government.

90. Ford, *Pamphlets* 40.

91. Elliot II, 8. Wood sees behind such views the old notion of virtual representation based on an "organic" and homogeneous society, together with the clever rhetoric of a social elite seeking to maintain its position. The more plausible foundation is the ostensible one, the belief that even in a civil society devoted to the preservation of individual liberty, there is an objective collective interest which does not necessarily coincide with popular inclinations. Cf. Wood, *Creation* chs. 5, 12; *The Federalist* no. 71, 482–83.

a republic, the manners, sentiments, and interests of the people should be similar. If this is not the case, there will be a constant clashing of opinions; and the representatives of one part will be continually striving against those of the other."[92] The Federalists contended that such a homogeneous republic was possible only under the primitive, harsh conditions of a precommercial society, which no man—certainly no American—would choose to endure. John Adams had made the point well in his discussion of the little republic of San Marino:

> A handful of poor people, living in the simplest manner, by hard labor, upon the produce of a few cows, sheep, goats, swine, poultry and pigeons, on a piece of rocky, snowy ground, protected from every enemy by their situation, their superstition, and even by their poverty, having no commerce nor luxury, can be no example for the commonwealth of Pennsylvania, Georgia, or Vermont, in one of which there are possibly half a million of people, and in each of the others at least thirty thousand, scattered over a large territory.[93]

A safe mediocrity can be maintained in conditions like those of San Marino; but "in every community where industry is encouraged, there will be a division of it into the few and the many."[94] And when this occurs, the innocence of the primitive community is lost. The Anti-Federalists could not deny this; yet they did not really desire the simple, precommercial society, even if they could have had it. It is true that they criticized the man of commerce, "immersed in schemes of wealth" and thus "the last to take the alarm when public

---

92. Brutus I, 2.9.16; cf. Impartial Examiner 5.14.6.

93. *A Defence of the Constitutions of Government of the United States of America* (Adams, *Works* IV, 309–10). On citations to the *Defence*, see Martin 2.4.38 n. 9.

94. Hamilton, Farrand II, 288 (18 June). See the very interesting discussion in [Carter Braxton] *An Address to the Convention of . . . Virginia . . . By a Native of that Colony* (Philadelphia 1776). Braxton describes the severe limits that a democratic regime based on public virtue requires. "Schemes like these may be practicable in countries so sterile by nature as to afford a scanty supply of the necessaries and none of the conveniences of life," but in a more bountiful country men "will always claim a right of using and enjoying the fruits of their honest industry, unrestrained by any ideal principles of government. . . . These are rights which freemen will never consent to relinquish, and after fighting for deliverance from one species of tyranny, it would be unreasonable to expect they should tamely acquiesce under another" (p. 17).

liberty is threatened."[95] He has no permanent attachments and can pack up and move, leaving the farmer to suffer the consequences of a bad constitution. But this was the half-hearted criticism of children of the modern commercial world who worried about its implications. There was no attempt to articulate an alternative, no account of the virtue of the agrarian way of life. There was some hankering after a simple, subsistence agricultural life, but the Anti-Federalists were irrevocably committed to a commercial order, as indeed American agriculture had always been.[96] The Federalists drew out the implications of the commitment. While they were about as likely as their opponents to write as "Farmer" or "Countryman," they denied that there was any real conflict between the landed and the commercial interests, because (as they suggested more or less explicitly) the American landed interest is fundamentally part of and dependent upon the commercial order. The Federalist Landholder argued, for example,

> It may be assumed as a fixed truth that the prosperity and riches of the farmer must depend on the prosperity, and good national regulation of trade. Artful men may insinuate the contrary—tell you let trade take care of itself, and excite your jealousy against the merchant because his business leads him to wear a gayer coat, than your economy directs. But let your own experience refute such insinuations.[97]

The American world is the world of commerce.

The basic problem of the Anti-Federalists was that they accepted the need and desirability of the modern commercial world while attempting to resist certain of its tendencies with rather half-hearted appeals to civic virtue. But such restraints, the Federalists replied, have never worked and will never work; the solution is to be found in another direction entirely:

> *Virtue,* patriotism, or love of country, never was and never will be, till mens' natures are changed, a fixed, permanent principle and support of government. But in an agricultural country, a general possession of land in fee simple, may be rendered perpetual, and the inequalities introduced by

---

95. Centinel VIII, 2.7.126; see also [New Hampshire] Farmer 4.17.8.

96. See Harry V. Jaffa, "Agrarian Virtue and Republican Freedom: An Historical Perspective," *Equality and Liberty: Theory and Practice in American Politics* (New York: Oxford University Press, 1965).

97. Ford, *Essays* 140. A Landholder explains to his readers that he is a merchant, now retired to the country—the best of both worlds, as it were. See also *Federalist* 12, and cf. Charles Pinckney's different view, Elliot IV, 321–22.

commerce, are too fluctuating to endanger government. An equality of property, with a necessity of alienation, constantly operating to destroy combinations of powerful families, is the very *soul of a republic*.[98]

To this James Madison added the extended republic.[99] For even in the absence of primogeniture and under the constant churning of commerce, distinct interests will eventually form and find their way into the political realm. Despite unparalleled opportunity for individual enterprise, the time will come even under American conditions where the many will resent the greater goods enjoyed by the few. And in a popular government where the majority are united by a common interest or passion, the rights of the minority are in danger.

> The only remedy is to enlarge the sphere, & thereby divide the community into so great a number of interests & parties, that in the 1st place a majority will not be likely at the same moment to have a common interest separate from that of the whole or of the minority; and in the 2d place, that in case they shd. have such an interest, they may not be apt to unite in the pursuit of it. It was incumbent on us then to try this remedy, and with that view to frame a republican system on such a scale and in such a form as will controul all the evils wch. have been experienced.[100]

What Brutus saw as a great defect of the Constitution—that the legislature "would be composed of such heterogeneous and discor-

---

98. Noah Webster, Ford, *Pamphlets* 59.

99. See "Vices of the Political System of the U. States," April 1787, Madison, *Writings* II, 366–69; Farrand I, 134–36 (6 June); *Federalist* 10; letter to Thomas Jefferson, 24 October 1787, Madison, *Writings* V, 17–41, esp. 32. Douglass Adair has shown that Charles Beard was largely responsible for initiating the present-day prominence of *Federalist* 10 and for giving it a peculiar interpretation. Adair shows without difficulty that Beard's description of Madison's theory as a form of economic determinism is wrong. He also shows that Madison had carefully worked out his defense of the extended republic and that it had played a prominent role in Madison's argument in the Constitutional Convention. The influence of Madison's arguments or the role played, more broadly, by various versions of the notion of the extended republic are questions that have yet to receive satisfactory examination. Adair, "The Tenth Federalist Revisited," *William and Mary Quarterly* January 1951; " 'That Politics May Be Reduced to a Science': David Hume, James Madison and the Tenth Federalist," *Huntington Library Quarterly* August 1957; both articles reprinted in Adair, *Fame and the Founding Fathers* (New York: Norton, 1974), chs. 3, 4.

100. Farrand I, 136 (6 June).

dant principles, as would constantly be contending with each other"[101]—James Madison and others saw as its greatest virtue. In a large, diverse, wealthy country, men can find ample opportunity to gratify their private wants; they will be less likely to resent the success and to encroach on the rights of others, and such resentment as they do feel will be less likely to take dangerous political form. "Divide et impera," the reprobated axiom of tyranny, is, under certain qualifications, the only policy by which a republic can be administered on just principles.[102]

The trouble with the Anti-Federalists, in this view, was that they saw civil society as a teacher, as a molder of character, rather than as a regulator of conduct. Their mentality was like that expressed in a 1776 proclamation of the Massachusetts General Court:

> That piety and virtue, which alone can secure the freedom of any people, be encouraged, and vice and immorality suppressed, the Great and General Court have thought fit to issue this Proclamation, commanding and enjoining it upon the good people of this colony that they lead sober, religious, and peaceable lives, avoiding all blasphemies, contempt of the Holy Scriptures and of the *Lord's* Day, and all other crimes and misdemeanors, all debauchery, profaneness, corruption, venality, all riotous and tumultuous proceedings and all immoralities whatsoever, and that they decently and reverently attend the publick worship of God.[103]

Preaching like this, whether in the form of a direct injunction or the supposed functioning of the small republic, seemed to the Federalists ineffective, or at least grossly insufficient. No matter how strong the preaching or the community surveillance, men's interests will not be subdued or governed by considerations of public good, moral duty, or religious salvation.[104] To warnings like that of Anti-Federalist Thomas Wait that to try to subject the vast continent of America to a

---

101. Brutus I, 2.9.16; see Federal Farmer VIII, 2.8.110.

102. See Charles Pinckney, Elliot IV, 326–27; G. Morris, Farrand II, 54 (19 July).

103. Elisha Douglass, *Rebels and Democrats* (Chapel Hill: University of North Carolina Press, 1955) 148, quoting *American Archives* 4th series, III, 1514.

104. See A Citizen of America [Noah Webster], Ford, *Pamphlets* 55–56. Nevertheless, the Federalists preached, too, though relying on it less. See, for example, James Wilson's Fourth of July Address, *Boston Gazette and Country Journal* 28 July 1788; Ralph Lerner, "The Supreme Court as Republican Schoolmaster," *Supreme Court Review* 1967.

democracy would be as futile as trying "to rule Hell by Prayer,"[105] the Federalist reply was, in effect, that little democracies can no more be ruled by prayer than large ones. Men act mainly from passion and interest. The Constitution was deliberately and properly designed not to try to stifle or transform those motives—to try to rule them by prayer—but to channel them in the direction of the public good.

Conclusion

The Anti-Federalists lost the debate over the Constitution not merely because they were less clever arguers or less skillful politicians but because they had the weaker argument. They were, as Publius said, trying to reconcile contradictions. There was no possibility of instituting the small republic in the United States, and the Anti-Federalists themselves were not willing to pay the price that such an attempt would have required. A basis for republican government and the solution of the problems of republican government had somehow to be found in the great and complex republic. To this task the framers directed their attention, and the Constitution was their magnificent response. The Federalists, moreover, reminded Americans that the true principle of the Revolution was not hostility to government but hostility to tyrannical government. They sought to recover the balance that Americans had lost in the zeal of revolution: "There is no quarrel between government and liberty; the former is the shield and protector of the latter. The war is between government and licentiousness, faction, turbulence, and other violations of the rules of society, to preserve liberty."[106]

> In the commencement of a revolution which received its birth from the usurpations of tyranny, nothing was more natural than that the public mind should be influenced by an extreme spirit of jealousy. To resist these encroachments, and to nourish this spirit, was the great object of all our public and private institutions. The zeal for liberty became predominant and excessive. In forming our Confederation, this passion alone seemed to actuate us, and we appear to have had no other view than to secure ourselves from despotism. The object certainly was a valuable one, and deserved our utmost attention; but, sir, there is another object, equally important, and which our enthusiasm ren-

---

105. Letter from Thomas B. Wait to George Thatcher, 22 November 1787, "Thatcher Papers," *Historical Magazine* November 1869, 258.

106. Pendleton, Elliot III, 37; cf. Nicholas, ibid. 98; State Soldier, *Virginia Independent Chronicle* 12 March 1788.

dered us little capable of regarding: I mean a principle of *strength* and *stability* in the organization of our government, and *vigor* in its operations.[107]

The framers of the Articles of Confederation, misled by the vigor and good sense displayed by the people during the war, made the "amiable mistake" of thinking that the Americans needed no government, "that the people of America only required to know what ought to be done to do it."[108] The Americans are, however, like other men, which is to say that they cannot be relied on to govern themselves voluntarily. The Anti-Federalists' fondness for the small republic and their concern with the inculcation of civic virtue amounted to an attempt to push aside this harsh truth.[109] Thus they refused to accept, or they accepted only halfheartedly, that the prime need was a government with a capacity to govern and not dependent for its goodness and trustworthiness on the everyday goodness and trustworthiness of the people or their representatives. The Constitution was designed so that, as far as possible, the ordinary operations of government would call for little more than the reliable inclination of men to follow their own interests, fairly narrowly understood. This system has been remarkably, if not gloriously, successful.

If, however, the foundation of the American polity was laid by the Federalists, the Anti-Federalist reservations echo through American history; and it is in the dialogue, not merely in the Federalist victory, that the country's principles are to be discovered. The Anti-Federalists were easily able to show that the Constitution did not escape reliance on republican virtue. One of the chief replies to the critics' descriptions of dangers of the new and powerful general government was that the American people could be trusted to elect good men to office and to keep them under scrutiny while there.

---

107. Hamilton, Elliot II, 301. Similarly, cheap government is not necessarily good government. See Noah Webster, Ford, *Pamphlets* 47; also Oliver Ellsworth's formulation: "The cheapest form of government is not always the best, for parsimony, though it spends little, generally gains nothing. Neither is that the best government which imposes the least restraint on its subjects; for the benefit of having others restrained may be greater than the disadvantage of being restrained ourselves. That is the best form of government which returns the greatest number of advantages in proportion to the disadvantages with which it is attended." The Landholder, Ford, *Essays* 192. See A Native of Virginia, in *The Writings of James Monroe*, Stanislaus Murray Hamilton, ed., 7 vols. (New York: G. P. Putnam's Sons, 1898–1903), vol. I, p. 352; Impartial Examiner 5.14.2.

108. John Jay, Ford, *Pamphlets* 71.

109. *Federalist* 51, p. 349.

There were frequent remarks like that of James Wilson that the framers must have assumed that the people and the states would give proper attention to the men elected to the legislature: "If they should now do otherwise, the fault will not be in Congress, but in the people . . . themselves. I have mentioned oftener than once, that for a people wanting to themselves, there is no remedy."[110] "Let the Americans be virtuous," an anonymous Federalist wrote, "let them be firm supporters of Republicanism—let them have confidence in their representatives—then their Liberties will be secured to them, and peace and prosperity will ensue."[111]

Nor were these only the arguments of lesser Federalist thinkers or the ones least free of the old reliance on civic virtue. Madison himself defended the provisions for representation on the ground that "the people will have virtue and intelligence to select men of virtue and wisdom." He went on to ask:

> Is there no virtue among us? If there be not, we are in a wretched situation. No theoretical checks, no form of government, can render us secure. To suppose that any form of government will secure liberty or happiness without any virtue in the people is a chimerical idea. If there be sufficient virtue and intelligence in the community, it will be exercised in the selection of these men; so that we do not depend on their virtue, or put confidence in our rulers, but in the people who are to choose them.[112]

Publius, too, perhaps the least equivocal advocate of the constitutional system of channeled self-interest, remarked that the genius of the American people is such as to make it unlikely that they will put up with the loss of their liberty, or will take no interest in the activities of the government, or will choose ignorant or bad men as representatives. The crucial point is conceded in *Federalist 55*, where Publius argues that "as there is a degree of depravity in mankind which requires a certain degree of circumspection and distrust, so there are other qualities in human nature, which justify a certain

---

110. *Pennsylvania and the Federal Constitution*, p. 351.

111. Maecenas, *State Gazette of South Carolina* 6 December 1787. "What the government may terminate in depends on the people. . . ." Civis Rusticus, *Virginia Independent Chronicle* 30 January 1788, reply to Mason: ". . . the liberties of the people never can be lost, until they are lost to themselves, in a vicious disregard of their dearest interests, a sottish indolence, a wild licentiousness, a dissoluteness of morals, and a contempt of all virtue." Ibid. See Governor Huntington, Elliot II, 199–200.

112. Elliot III, 536–37.

portion of esteem and confidence. Republican government presupposes the existence of these qualities in a higher degree than any other form."[113] Publius did not here name the "other qualities"—itself a point of some interest—but they must include an enlightened understanding of the objects of government, a degree of public-spiritedness, a participation in citizenship as distinct from a merely private life.

Given this kind of argument, the Anti-Federalists could rightly contend that the new Constitution does, after all, depend on something like republican virtue. It is distinguished not by emancipation from this old dependence but by a lack of much attention to the question of how that necessary republican virtue can be maintained. As they took for granted a certain kind of public-spirited leadership,[114] so they took for granted the republican genius of the people; but that cannot prudently be taken for granted.

The Federalist solution not only failed to provide for the moral qualities that are necessary to the maintenance of republican government; it tended to undermine them. Will not the constitutional regime, the Anti-Federalists asked, with its emphasis on private, self-seeking, commercial activities, release and foster a certain type of human being who will be likely to destroy that very regime?

> It is alledged that the opinions and manners of the people of America, are capable to resist and prevent an extension of prerogative or oppression; but you must recollect that opinion and manners are mutable, and may not always be a permanent obstruction against the encroachments of government; that the progress of a commercial society begets luxury, the parent of inequality, the foe to virtue, and the enemy to restraint; and that ambition and voluptuousness aided by flattery, will teach magistrates, where limits are not explicitly fixed to have separate and distinct interests from the people, besides it will not be denied that government assimilates the manners and opinions of the community to it. Therefore, a general presumption that rulers will govern well is not a sufficient security.[115]

113. *Federalist* 55, p. 378; cf. no. 76, pp. 513–14.

114. For a revealing picture of Federalist government to contrast with Federalist principles of government, see Leonard D. White, *The Federalists* (New York: Macmillan, 1948) chs. 2, 3, 8, 9, and 40, and *The Jeffersonians* (New York: Macmillan, 1951) chs. 3–5 and 35.

115. Cato V, 2.6.34. "Where then is our republicanism to be found? Not in our constitution but merely in the spirit of our people. That would oblige even a despot to govern us republicanly." *Memoirs, Correspondence and Miscellanies from the Papers of Thomas Jefferson*, Thomas Jefferson Randolph, ed., 2d ed. (Boston 1830) IV, 287.

Can a legal system for the regulation of private passions to the end that those passions may be more fully gratified serve as the foundation of civic virtue? Montesquieu argued that the virtue required in a republican government is "the love of laws and of our country," that such love "requires a constant preference of public to private interest," that "every thing . . . depends on establishing this love in a republic; and to inspire it ought to be the principal business of education. . . ."[116] The question is whether the Constitution, as the Federalists understood it, succeeded in laying that argument to rest. The Anti-Federalists contended that it did not: "Whatever the refinement of modern politics may inculcate, it still is certain that some degree of virtue must exist, or freedom cannot live." They rejected "Mandervill's [sic] position . . . 'that private vices are public benefits.'"[117]

The Federalists did not, it should be emphasized, rely on some unseen hand to produce public good out of individual selfishness. The foundation was the Constitution, and the working of the system depended upon an attachment of the people to the Constitution. It was admitted that that attachment was not sufficiently assured by narrow self-interest. Whereas the Federalists regarded this as a somewhat peripheral problem, however, to be dealt with by avoiding certain kinds of mistakes and providing auxiliary institutions, such as judicial review, the Anti-Federalists saw it as a permanent and central concern of the republic.

The matter was canvassed most profoundly on the Federalist side by Publius in *Federalist* 49 and by Chief Justice John Marshall in his opinion in *Marbury v. Madison*.[118] A brief consideration of the former will suffice for the present purpose. The specific question was how to settle disputes between the different departments of government and whether provision should be made, as Jefferson had suggested, for appeals in such cases to the people. Publius treated this proposal with great respect, due not only to its author but also to its theoretical cogency, given the principles of popular government; but he rejected it.

Two arguments are of special importance here. First, he suggested that every appeal to the people "would carry an implication of some defect in the government," and "frequent appeals would in great measure deprive the government of that veneration, which time bestows on every thing, and without which perhaps the wisest and

---

116. *The Spirit of Laws* IV, ch. 5.
117. Federal Republican 3.6.21.
118. 1 Cranch 137, 176–78 (1803).

freest governments would not possess the requisite stability." While a nation of philosophers would be led to revere the laws by an enlightened reason, "in every other nation, the most rational government will not find it a superfluous advantage, to have the prejudices of the community on its side." Second, Publius pointed to the danger of "disturbing the public tranquillity by interesting too strongly the public passions. . . . Notwithstanding the success which has attended the revisions of our established forms of government and which does so much honor to the virtue and intelligence of the people of America, it must be confessed that the experiments are of too ticklish a nature to be unnecessarily multiplied."[119]

The basis of this argument is a radical disjunction between the founding of the government and its operation. The circumstances conducive to the good operation of a government under a properly constructed constitution (for example, a wide variety of interests) are extremely pernicious in the making or altering of the Constitution.[120] American constitutional reform occurred during a time when sharp diversities of opinion were muted and patriotic sentiments relatively great, when confidence in leaders was high, and when excesses of liberty had made the people willing to accept a sound constitution. It was the Americans' good fortune that the need for constitutional reform coincided with circumstances conducive to it, but these circumstances are rare and the coincidence unlikely. As a general rule, "a people does not reform with moderation."[121]

It is necessary that every precaution be taken not to upset that original patriotic act and to preserve and foster reverence for the laws, and particularly for the highest law. The Federalist authors did not argue, as Lincoln later did, that reverence for the laws ought to become the political religion of the nation. They took a narrower view of the problem and proposed more modest means. The task of basic lawmaking having been done, in the main successfully, the aim must be to avoid reopening the fundamental political questions, which were hardly likely to be so well answered another time, and to let

---

119. *Federalist* 49, pp. 340–41. Cf. Madison to Jefferson, 4 February 1798, Madison, *Writings* V, 438–39. John Marshall described the adoption of the Constitution as "a very great exertion." *Marbury v. Madison*, 1 Cranch 137, 176 (1803).

120. *Federalist* 37, p. 238.

121. [John Dickinson] "Letter from a Farmer in Pennsylvania to the Inhabitants of the British Colonies" (1767), in *Empire and Nation*, Forrest McDonald, ed. (Englewood Cliffs, N.J., 1962) 69. See *Federalist* 37; A Citizen of New York [John Jay], "An Address to the People of the State of New York," Ford, *Pamphlets* 69–86.

time do its work of fostering veneration. Publius's argument was a negative one: do nothing to disturb "that veneration, which time bestows on everything."

But will the mere passage of time be enough? Many of the Anti-Federalists thought that it would not, that the passage of time would magnify the difficulty of preserving the American republic, rather than overcoming it. The revolutionary preoccupation with liberty, which may have made men forget the need for government, nevertheless had a profound effect in holding the American governments true to their ends. And the spirit of the Revolution was a spirit of dedication to the common good:

> It is next to impossible to enslave a people immediately after a firm struggle against oppression, while the sense of past injury is recent and strong. But after some time this impression naturally wears off;—the ardent glow of freedom gradually evaporates;—the charms of popular equality, which arose from the *republican plan*, insensibly decline;—the pleasures, the advantages derived from the new kind of government grow stale through use. Such declension in all those vigorous springs of action necessarily produces a supineness. The altar of liberty is no longer watched with such attentive assiduity;—a new train of passions succeeds to the empire of the mind;—different objects of desire take place;—and, if the nation happens to enjoy a series of prosperity, voluptuousness, excessive fondness for riches, and luxury gain admission and establish themselves—these produce venality and corruption of every kind, which open a fatal avenue to bribery. Hence it follows, that in the midst of this general contageon a few men—or one—more powerful than all the others, industriously endeavor to obtain all authority; and by means of great wealth—or embezzling the public money,—perhaps totally subvert the government, and erect a system of aristocratical or monarchic tyranny in its room. . . . It is this depravation of manners, this wicked propensity, my dear countrymen, against which you ought to provide with the utmost degree of prudence and circumspection. All nations pass this *parokism* of vice at some period or other;—and if at that dangerous juncture your government is not secure upon a solid foundation, and well guarded against the machinations of evil men, the liberties of this country will be lost—perhaps forever![122]

---

122. Impartial Examiner 5.14.15. See Mercy Warren, this volume 76. After the Revolution, Federalist John Jay wrote, "the spirit of private gain expelled the spirit of public good, and men became more intent on the means of enriching and aggrandizing themselves than of enriching and aggrandizing their country." Ford, *Pamphlets* 70–71; see Jay in New York convention, Elliot

This view is strikingly like that of Abraham Lincoln in his speech in 1838 on "The Perpetuation of Our Political Institutions."[123] And some of the Anti-Federalists also saw the need, if the country was to survive its great moral crises, of leaders "who have genius and capacity sufficient to form the manners and correct the morals of the people, and virtue enough to lead their country to freedom."[124]

Indeed, the crisis might not be so far off. The postrevolutionary period was a time, Federalists and Anti-Federalists seem to have agreed, when men's lives, thoughts, and guiding principles were increasingly detached from the community. The Anti-Federalists thought that the Constitution would strengthen this tendency, and they feared for the Republic. It is a simplification, but not a misleading simplification, to say that the crisis faced by Abraham Lincoln seventy years later required a synthesis of the Federalist solution and the Anti-Federalist reservation. And if the major element in the synthesis was still the federal one, yet it is due the Anti-Federalists to say that it was they, more than the defenders of the Constitution, who anticipated the need. The Anti-Federalists saw, although sometimes only dimly, the insufficiency of a community of mere interest.[125] They saw that the American polity had to be a moral community if it was to be anything, and they saw that the seat of that community must be the hearts of the people.

Mercy Warren's reflections a decade after the adoption of the Constitution—not bitter or partisan reflections, but somewhat melan-

---

II, 284. Columbian Patriot 4.28.3: "But there are certain seasons in the course of human affairs, when Genius, Virtue, and Patriotism, seems to nod over the vices of the times, and perhaps never more remarkably, than at the present period."

123. Lincoln, *Collected Works*, Roy P. Basler, ed., 9 vols. (New Brunswick, N.J.: Rutgers University Press, 1953), vol. I, pp. 108–115. See Harry V. Jaffa, *Crisis of the House Divided* (Garden City, N.Y., 1959) ch.9.

124. Columbian Patriot 4.28.12; see Mercy Warren on Washington, 6.14.54–77.

125. The Federalists were not, generally speaking, less antislavery than the Anti-Federalists (indeed, one of the very few attempts to provide any kind of moral justification of slavery was made by Anti-Federalist Rawlins Lowndes); but their commitment to a policy of interest made it relatively easy to say, as did Oliver Ellsworth of the participation by the Southern states in the slave trade, that "their consciences are their own, tho' their wealth and strength are blended with ours." The Landholder, Ford, *Essays* 164; see also William Heath, Elliot II, 115. See Ford, *Pamphlets* 146; Martin 2.4.45, 68–70. The Anti-Federalists were less easily persuaded that questions of politics can be freed from questions of conscience.

4
The "Other" Federalist Papers:
A Preliminary Sketch

The wise CONSTITUTION let's truly revere,
It points out the course for our EMPIRE to steer,
For oceans of bliss do they hoist the broad sail,
And peace *is the current, and* plenty *the gale.*
  Our Freedom we've won, and the prize let's maintain,
    Our *hearts* are all right—
      Unite, Boys, Unite,
  And our *EMPIRE* in glory shall ever remain.

The Grand Constitution: Or,
The Palladium of Columbia. A New Federal Song
  —New Hampshire Recorder, *October 23, 1787*

To an even greater extent than the Anti-Federalists, the "other" Federalist writings stand in the shadow cast by the towering *Federalist* papers. The neglect they have suffered is not altogether undeserved. Taken as a whole, they tend to be rather shallow and routine. That can of course be said of most wide samples of political writing, but it is striking how much of the Federalist effort was directed to mere explication of the Constitution or to criticizing the opposition. Neither of these will concern us much here; but it is worth reporting that nearly half of the one hundred or so essays and pamphlets that form the basis of the present review are mainly criticisms of specific Anti-Federalist writings. It is hardly too much to say that among the "front line" debaters, the Anti-Federalists criticized the Constitution and the Federalists criticized the Anti-Federalists.

There is nothing in the Federalist writings comparable to the range and depth of *The Federalist;* nor are there the intriguing glimpses of an alternative American polity that emerge from the writings of

---

This chapter originally appeared in the *Political Science Reviewer*, vol. 6, Fall 1976. It is reprinted with permission.

the Anti-Federalists.[1] Yet these "other" Federalist writings carried the main burden of the public defense of the proposed Constitution in 1787 and 1788; many of them are quite substantial; several of them were vastly more influential than *The Federalist*. Considering the writings of men such as James Wilson, John Dickinson, Tench Coxe, Roger Sherman, Oliver Ellsworth, Noah and Pelatiah Webster, Alexander Hanson, John Jay, James Iredell, and the many still-anonymous Federalist writers enables us to fill in our picture of the debate over the Constitution, to see more fully the diversity of Federalist views, and to identify some major themes or issues. What follows is based on a wide though not exhaustive survey of Federalist essays, pamphlets, and published speeches appearing in 1787 and 1788, with the main emphasis on the more penetrating writers and the more fundamental issues.[2] It is meant to be suggestive rather than definitive.

It may be helpful to begin with a sketch of a typical Federalist essay, assuming that it was not merely attacking one of the Anti-Federalists. Our author would be likely to begin with an account of the precarious state of the American Union, emphasizing the economic stagnation, loss of credit, and dangers to commerce and safety caused by American weakness. Looking inward, he would probably refer to Shays' Rebellion and warn of the likelihood of increased domestic turmoil unless the governing capacity of the Union is strengthened. He would show the defects of the government under the Articles of Confederation, a government incapable of enforcing its resolves. He would describe in fulsome terms the Constitutional Convention under the leadership of the venerable Franklin and the virtuous Washington. All America agrees that the government of the Union requires additional powers; and the new general government

---

1. See Herbert J. Storing, ed., *The Complete Anti-Federalist*, 7 volumes (Chicago: University of Chicago Press 1981), the introduction to which should be read together with the present essay.

2. A list of the main Federalist writings on which this account is based is provided at the end of this essay. Footnote references will be to author (or pseudonym) and number in that list. Where appropriate, page references will be given to reprints in Paul Leicester Ford, *Pamphlets on the Constitution of the United States* (Brooklyn, 1888); Paul Leicester Ford, *Essays on the Constitution of the United States* (Brooklyn, 1892); or John Bach McMaster and Frederick Stone, *Pennsylvania and the Federal Constitution* (Philadelphia, 1888). These will be cited *FP, FE*, and *M/S* respectively. The state ratifying conventions are not considered here except for one or two speeches that were widely circulated in the press.

will possess only the powers specifically granted to it, which are no more than are required to deal with national concerns.

The much criticized powers of sword and purse, to which our author would give considerable attention, are indispensable to any government worthy of the name and are as well guarded as possible. All power can of course be abused, but the solution is to be found not in withholding necessary power but in a well-constructed government. Contrary to a common Anti-Federal claim, the states will not be destroyed by the new Constitution; they remain the organs of government for most domestic matters and they are vital to the operation of the general government itself. The new government, deriving from the pure source of all political authority, the people, will secure all of the advantages of monarchy, aristocracy, and democracy, while avoiding their disadvantages.

Our author would show at length why the representatives of the people will continue true to their trust; and he would explain the rational apportionment of power among the parts of the general government, together with the carefully devised scheme of checks and balances, all designed to reinforce governmental responsibility and secure wise government. He would deny, again probably at some length, that a bill of rights is necessary, contending that a good Constitution, such as the one proposed, is the proper "bill of rights" for a free people.

In conclusion he would return to the theme of Union and strongly urge that the alternative facing Americans is either acceptance of the new Constitution or the destruction of the Union. To insist on amendments prior to ratification or to call for a second convention is equivalent to rejecting the Constitution altogether. There is no likelihood that future deliberation would display anything like the spirit of patriotism and mutual concession achieved in Philadelphia in the summer of 1787. Having successfully defended their liberties against one of the foremost powers of the world, having freely established governments designed to secure those liberties, having through a convention of their wisest leaders devised and improved their Union, the American people now have it in their power to conclude a political founding unique in the annals of human history. They can give an example to mankind of an excellent constitution adopted by open deliberation and free choice.

Union

The precarious state of the American Union is the first article in the Federalist defense of the Constitution. Relaxing after their great public act of independence, Americans allowed selfish, partial interests to emerge, threatening the objects for which the Revolution had been fought. During the war, John Jay wrote, Americans worshipped their Union as the pagans worshipped their tutelar deities. "That union was the child of wisdom—heaven blessed it, and it wrought out our political salvation."[3] During those times, "a sense of the common danger united every heroic, every patriotic soul in the great cause of liberty." Selfishness itself was stilled.[4] So prevalent was this view that Americans made the "amiable mistake" of thinking that they were unlike other men and could do without coercive government. The ineffective Articles of Confederation were the result. "It was an honest and solemn covenant among our infant States, and virtue and common danger supplied its defects."[5] When the danger disappeared, however, "a sense of security loosened the bands of union." "The spirit of private gain expelled the spirit of public good, and men became more intent on the means of enriching and aggrandizing themselves, than of enriching and aggrandizing their country."[6] Americans need to resolve anew to "cling to Union as the political Rock of our Salvation,"[7] and they need to face the fact that their Union requires a real government.

The Anti-Federalists admitted the inadequacy of the Articles of Confederation, but they thought that the new Constitution would sacrifice the states to a great national government. Responding to this claim that the Constitution was a "consolidation" rather than a strengthened federal government, the Federalists made two main arguments. First, they showed that the states were indispensable participants in the new general government itself. State qualifications for electors were to be the qualifications for the electors of the House of Representatives; states were to choose the members of the Senate and were to be parties in the choosing of the president. In these and other ways, the Federalists repeatedly contended, the states would be so involved in the actual constitution of the general government that it could not exist without them.

The second and more fundamental defense, however, was that, despite the increase in the powers of the general government, the new Constitution leaves with the states the whole responsibility of internal government except for those few areas that concern the

---

3. John Jay (#97), *FP*, p. 70.
4. A Federalist (#40), *M/S*, p. 165.
5. A Citizen of Pennsylvania (#27), *M/S*, p. 106.
6. Jay (#97), *FP*, pp. 70–71.
7. John Dickinson (#92), *FP*, p. 167.

Union as a whole. The standard argument here is one that is very familiar to Americans today. It describes the American system as dividing the powers of government between the general government, which concerns itself with matters that affect the Union as a whole, and the state governments, which concern themselves with those matters purely domestic. According to Pelatiah Webster, "the Constitution does not suffer the federal powers to controul in the least, or so much as to interfere in the internal policy, jurisdiction, or municipal rights of any particular State: except where great and manifest national purposes and interests make that controul necessary."[8] Nor did the problem of drawing a line between state and federal jurisdictions seem so difficult: "the objects of federal government will be so obvious that there will be no great danger of any interference."[9]

These arguments did not satisfy the Anti-Federalists, and with good reason. State participation in filling the offices of the general government would mean little if the state were not secured an independent and significant sphere of power. And even granting the (doubtful) proposition that a clear line could now be drawn between the general concerns of the Union and the particular concerns of the states, the principle of distinction clearly implies a radical and, over time, almost complete subordination of the states. Some Federalists were happy to draw precisely that conclusion and only feared that federal supremacy would not occur soon or decisively enough. But most were at least equivocal, and it is that equivocation that we must examine.

One side of the Federalist view had been displayed by James Wilson in his speech of June 8, 1787, in the Constitutional Convention, when he said, "Among the first sentiments expressed in the first Congress, one was that Virginia is no more. That Massachusetts is no [more], that Pennsylvania is no more, etc. We are now one nation of brethren. We must bury all local interests and distinctions." This language continued for some time, Wilson said; but "no sooner were the States Governments formed than their jealousy and ambition began to display themselves. Each endeavored to cut a slice from the common loaf, to add to its own morsel, till at length the confederation became frittered down to the impotent condition in which it now stands."[10] Wilson here suggests that the Union is prior

---

8. P. Webster (#104), *FP,* p. 128; see P. Webster (#103), *M/S,* p. 99; N. Webster (#102), *FP* 46.

9. A Citizen of New Haven (#26), *FE,* p. 239; for detailed discussion see A Freeman (#43) and A Native of Virginia (#99).

10. Max Farrand, *Records of the Federal Convention,* 4 vols. (New Haven: Yale University Press, 1966), vol. I, p. 166 (June 8).

to the states in principle and even historically; the state governments, he says, were formed after the first Congress. "Indulge no narrow prejudices to the disadvantage of your brethren of the other states," another Federalist wrote, following this same line of thought; "consider the people of all the thirteen states, as a band of brethren, speaking the same language, professing the same religion, inhabiting one undivided country, and designed by heaven to be one people."[11]

In an interesting Federalist speech from Maryland, intended to be delivered to the ratifying convention but only published in July 1788, the historical and legal priority of the Union is asserted quite explicitly. Responding to the tyrannical impositions of the king and Parliament, this Federalist explained, the colonists united and appointed the first of the continental congresses which resisted British encroachments, determined upon separation, and prosecuted the war of independence. The state governments were instituted only later. "It is to be remembered, that congress existed before the [state] legislatures, and that it exercised all the powers, which are conferred by these articles [of confederation], and perhaps greater."[12]

The priority of the Union to the states, which was later to be so eloquently and profoundly argued by Lincoln, may, I think, be said to be the "true" or "best" Federalist position. Yet what is surprising is that the Federalists did not make the Marylander's argument more often; usually they conceded the historical and legal priority of the states. Indeed in the same speech of June 8 in which he urged the primacy of Union James Wilson made another argument which denied it. "Federal liberty," he said, "is to States, what civil liberty, is to private individuals. And States are not more unwilling to purchase it, by the necessary concession of their political sovereignty, than the savage is to purchase Civil liberty by the surrender of the personal sovereignty, which he enjoys in a State of nature."[13] This "federal liberty" view was prominent in Wilson's defense of the Constitution in Pennsylvania, and it was very widespread among

---

11. Ramsay (#101), *FP,* p. 379; see *Federalist* 2.

12. Anonymous Speech to Have Been Delivered . . . (#14). "Upon what basis does our Independence rest, so far as respects the recognition of Foreign Powers? Upon the basis of the UNION. In what capacity did France first acknowledge our Independence? In the capacity of UNITED STATES. In what capacity did Britain accede to it, and relinquish her pretensions? In the capacity of UNITED STATES.—In what character have we formed Treaties with other Nations? In the character of UNITED STATES.—Are we, in short, known in any other Independent character to any Nation on the face of the Globe?" Philo-Publius (#73).

13. Farrand, *Records,* vol. I, p. 166 (June 8).

Federalist writers. Wilson explained to his fellow Pennsylvanians that as civil liberty is that portion of natural liberty resigned by men to government, so federal liberty consists in the aggregate of the civil liberty which is surrendered by each state to the national government; "and the same principles that operate in the establishment of a single society, with respect to the rights reserved or resigned by the individuals that compose it, will justly apply in the case of a confederation of distinct and independent States."[14] The federal and the state governments are not (as was often said) coordinate sovereignties, another Federalist insisted: "The general government is *foederal*, or an union of *sovereignties*, for *special* purposes. The state governments are *social*, or an association of *individuals*, for all the purposes of society and government."[15] Many Federalists claimed that a bill of rights was unnecessary under the new Constitution because the federal government was an association of states, not of individuals.

There are two implications of the federal liberty/civil liberty analogy that are problematical from the Federalist viewpoint. First, it seems to demand that the states in a federal system have equal votes, as individuals do in civil society, regardless of their different strength and wealth. William Paterson had made this point in the Constitutional Convention: "there was no more reason that a great individual State contributing much, should have more votes than a small one contributing little, than that a rich individual citizen should have more votes than an indigent one."[16] In the convention Wilson had opposed an equal representation of the states and insisted rather on representation according to population, but he never gave Paterson a satisfactory reply. Some Federalists were more consistent and defended the equal representation of the states in the Senate as not merely a compromise (as Wilson regarded it) but a principled recognition of the "federal" character of the American Union.

A second and more fundamental implication of the "federal liberty" view is that the states are the crucial parties to, and presumably therefore ultimately the judges of, the general government. With independence from the crown, most of the Federalists seemed to think, the colonies also became independent of one another (as Luther Martin, later a prominent Anti-Federalist, had urged so forcefully in the Philadelphia convention). The states then determined on and were of course the parties of a new union.

---

14. Wilson, Speech of November 24, 1787 (#105), *M/S*, p. 227; see also Ramsay (#101), *FP*, p. 373.

15. A Pennsylvanian (#68), February 27, 1788.

16. Farrand, *Records*, vol. I, p. 178 (June 9).

As one thoughtful Pennsylvanian put it, since the center of the Union had been the crown, "the act of independence dissolved the political ties that had formerly existed among the states. . . ." However, the former colonies did not wish to continue "distinct bodies of people." "The remains of our ancient governments kept us in the form of thirteen political bodies, and from a variety of just and prudent considerations, we determined to enter into an indissoluble and perpetual *union*." The expression "We the people of the United States" means "We the People of the *Several* States," to whom reference was necessary because the new Constitution implied changes in the various state constitutions. Had the framers meant to refer to the American people at large, they would have said, "We the People *of America*," which is the term "constantly used in speaking of us *as a nation*." "Had the foederal convention meant to exclude the idea of *'union,'* that is, of *several and separate* sovereignties joining in a confederacy, they would have said, we, *the people of America*; the union necessarily involves the idea of component states, which complete consolidations exclude. But the severality of the states is frequently recognized in the most distinct manner in the course of the constitution."[17] "The Constitution now before the public," a Federalist from New Hampshire wrote, "is not a compact between individuals, but between several sovereign and independent political societies already formed and organized."[18] A view of this kind is the basis for the rather typical description of the Constitution by Roger Sherman: "The Powers vested in the federal government are clearly defined, so that each state still retain its sovereignty in what concerns its own internal government, and a right to exercise every power of a sovereign state not particularly delegated to the government of the United States."[19] But does not this view of the Constitution as a compact among states lead straight to the Virginia and Kentucky Resolutions and beyond? Is the authentic legacy of the Federalists expressed not by Abraham Lincoln but by John C. Calhoun?

It must be acknowledged of course that no view of the American Union that is true to history and the play of principle in the American founding can avoid ambiguity. Moreover, the Federalists had the usual motive of the political debater to take as much as he can of his opponent's ground. Nevertheless, it is striking how widely the

---

17. A Freeman (#43), January 23, 1788.

18. Alfredus (#1), January 18, 1788; compare with the discussion of ratification in *The Federalist* #39 and John Marshall's Opinion in McCulloch v. Maryland, vol. 4, Wheat, p. 316 (1819).

19. A Citizen of New Haven (#26), *FE*, p. 238.

Federalists adopted the view of the Union as a coming together of sovereign states. Yet that is not the end of the matter, for it still somehow misses the way most of the Federalists really understood the American Union. Can their widespread acknowledgment of the origin of the Union in state sovereignty be reconciled with their deeper view of the Union as the basic, defining political association of this American nation?

At least a hint of such a reconciliation may be found in the Federalist essays of John Dickinson, writing as *Fabius*. One of the Old Republicans, Dickinson pressed the need for "humility and benevolence" to take the place of "pride and overweening selfishness" if successful free government was to be established. He presents a standard account of the origins of civil society, in which each individual gives up some share of his rights in order to secure the rest. In a confederation a similar principle operates; but Dickinson emphasizes that men are the materials of confederation as well as of simple government; the purpose of a confederation is to promote the happiness of individuals. "Herein there is a progression, not a contradiction. As *man*, he becomes a citizen; as a citizen, he becomes a federalist. The generation of one, is not the destruction of the other. He carries into society his naked rights: These thereby improved, he carries still forward into confederation."[20]

Dickinson's argument was not widely imitated, the way Wilson's "federal liberty" idea was, but it nevertheless conveys, I think, a good deal of the spirit of the Federalist view of Union. The movement from man to citizen to federalist is a moral progression. Civil society is entered into to secure private rights; this requires a moderation of the pride and overweening selfishness of man in his natural state, which Dickinson sees as not only a means to but as a benefit of civil society. The same kind of observation applies to the next stage. "Federalist" here means a member of a wider association concerned with a wider and thereby somehow higher public good. Thus a Boston Federalist complained that the American people had become "destitute of FEDERAL FEATURES and HABITS—the several *State Constitutions* are *local, partial,* and *selfish. . . .*" The new Constitution, on the other hand, is well designed "to form us to a *national spirit,*

---

20. Dickinson (#92), *FP,* p. 177. The ordinary use of the word "federalist" had at this time an ambiguity that should be noted. It referred to the principle of "federalism" (or "confederalism"), but it also referred to the *agencies* of the federation. When a man said he was "federal" in disposition, he meant he was inclined to strengthen and support the general government. This was the usage that entitled the Federalists to their name.

and to diffuse those generous *federal* sentiments, without which we never can be a happy and flourishing people."[21]

There are repeated references by the Federalists to American nationality as something intrinsically worth preserving and superior to the claims of statehood. The line of thought here is that as civil society not only secures the rights of the natural man but improves him, so the government of the Union does not merely secure the states (admitting them to be the parties) but improves or perfects them. And Dickinson makes clear, what many Federalists do not, that even in a confederation the true parties are men. States may be the formal parties—and in this sense the narrower view of American Union may be correct—but an association of states is justified ultimately not in terms of "state" interest but as a broader or higher association of human beings. The new Constitution will "diffuse a *national spirit,* and inspire every man with sentiments of dignity, when he reflects that he is not merely the individual of a State, but a CITIZEN OF AMERICA."[22] This view of the American Union explains both the Federalists' claim that the significance of the states will be increased, not destroyed, by a stronger Union and their very widespread association of the states with narrow selfishness and the Union with a morally more elevated benevolence and public spirit. Thus in appealing to the "mothers, wives, daughters and sisters of America" to use their influence in behalf of the Constitution, a Boston Federalist said *"your hearts are naturally federal,* prone to friendship, pity, love and generosity."[23]

It is not inconsistent with this view that most of the Federalists described the specific objects of Union in terms of fairly narrow calculations of self interest. There are a few exceptions, as when the writer just quoted defends the Constitution as providing the civil order that is necessary "for the promotion of piety and every moral virtue."[24] In the main, however, the objects of Union are described in terms like those of Roger Sherman: "The great end of the federal government is to protect the several states in their enjoyment of those rights ["the civil and domestic rights of the people"], against foreign invasion, and to preserve peace and a beneficial intercourse among themselves, and to regulate and protect our commerce with foreign

---

21. A Federalist (#39).
22. Convention (#30); see Philodemos (#72).
23. Anonymous. "It is devoutly . . ." (#9).
24. Ibid.; see Wilson (#105).

nations."[25] In a word, a perfected Union will make us "respectable as a nation abroad, and rich as individuals at home."[26]

Wealth and national security are good in themselves—they are the primary goods of Union—but they are also means to moral improvement. The aim of securing national prosperity, reluctantly accepted by the Anti-Federalists, was much more enthusiastically embraced by the Federalists, partly because of what they took to be its beneficial moral consequences. The love of wealth, properly regulated, fosters industry. "Industry is most favourable to the moral virtue of the world; it is therefore wisely ordered by the Author of Nature, that the blessings of this world should be acquired by our own application in some business useful to society. . . ."[27] Similarly with "national respectability," Federalist writers saw advantages going beyond mere national security. They often displayed a rather aggressive pride in the greater significance to be enjoyed by Americans under the new Constitution. Under it Americans can achieve "a distinguished rank among the nations of the earth."[28] Indeed, "a mighty empire may be formed upon this basis, which shall make its enemies tremble."[29] Anti-Federalists were not mistaken in seeing among the defenders of the Constitution a desire that Americans should play a vigorous part on the world stage. Some, at least, of the moral ascent the Federalists saw in the movement from citizen to federalist depended on looking beyond the petty business of the states to greater scenes of national significance, empire, and glory.

The Federalist writings abound with elements of this line of reasoning, from man to citizen to federalist; and it does help to reconcile their view of the historical and even legal primacy of the states on the one hand, and the ultimate primacy of the Union on the other hand. The reasoning is, however, mostly implicit—even Dickinson is cryptic. Perhaps what is involved is less a matter of reasoning than the expression of a strong moral sentiment. What is very clear, however, is the conclusion: "Hear then ye people of the United States! reason dictates, every feeling of the heart entreats, and Heaven commands, *be federal and happy forever*."[30]

---

25. A Citizen of New Haven (#26), *FE*, p. 238; see A Landholder (#57), *FE*, pp. 146–47.
26. State Soldier (#81), February 6, 1788.
27. A Landholder (#57), *FE*, p. 200.
28. Pennsylvania Farmer (#67), *M/S*, p. 129.
29. Anonymous, "Observe . . ." (#11).
30. Anonymous, "It is devoutly . . ." (#9).

Government

If Union is the frame of the Federalist argument, energetic government is the heart. The Federalists' crucial task, as they saw it, was
not to show the desirability of Union, or the ends of Union, or even
the need for a Union-wide government. That was common ground.
The real task was to make Americans understand what their commitment to Union and to freedom itself implies in the way of government. "If you would be free and happy a power must be created to
protect your persons and property; otherwise you are slaves to all
mankind."[31] Government is "the foundation of all human happiness"; "there is no way more likely to lose one's liberty in the end
than being too niggardly of it in the beginning."[32] To acknowledge
the need for a *government* is to acknowledge the need for power and
compulsion. "A government capable of controling the whole, and
bringing its force to a point, is one of the prerequisites for national
liberty."[33] Such a government inevitably displays a somewhat harsh
aspect. "Were we to view only the gaols and dungeons, the gallows
and pillories, the chains and wheel-barrows, of any state, we might
be induced to think the government severe; but when we turn
our attention to the murderers and parricides, and robberies and
burglaries, the piracies and thefts, which merit these punishments,
our idea of cruelty vanishes at once, and we admire the justice, and
perhaps clemency, of that government which before shocked us as
too severe."[34]

Of course power can be abused, but would anyone choose a
lame horse, lest a sound one should run away with him? The tiresome
Anti-Federal complaints about possible abuses of the powers under
the Constitution and the absence of a bill of rights overlook that this
government will be in the hands of representatives chosen by the
people. Defense of the Constitution as providing a responsible government through the instrument of representation is a prominent,
though as we shall see somewhat superficial, aspect of Federalist
writing. James Wilson, for example, contended that the ancients had
no proper idea of representation; and even in Great Britain the
principle of representation was confined to a narrow corner. To
America has been left "the glory and happiness of forming a government where representation shall at once supply the basis and the

---

31. A Landholder (#57), *FE*, p. 191.
32. State Soldier (#81), February 6, 1788.
33. A Landholder (#57), *FE*, p. 147.
34. P. Webster (#103), *M/S*, p. 103.

cement of the superstructure. For representation, Sir, is the true chain between the people and those to whom they entrust the administration of the government; and though it may consist of many links, its strength and brightness should never be impaired."[35]

This view pervades Wilson's thinking and that of many other Federalists. Echoing the Revolutionary slogan of "no taxation without representation," representation here is seen as the necessary and almost the sufficient condition of good government. In a properly arranged system, the representatives *are* the people. "The distinction between the powers of the *people* and of their *Representatives* in the Legislature, is as absurd in *theory*, as it proves pernicious in *practice*."[36] The question, then, is not the power of the legislature but "how are Congress formed? how far have you a control over them? Decide this, and then all the questions about their power may be dismissed for the amusement of those politicians whose business it is to catch flies. . . ."[37] The representatives under the proposed Constitution will be chosen by the people and will be bound to them by considerations of honor and gratitude as well as self-interest. Every member of Congress is liable to all the operations of the laws he himself passes and "this circumstance alone, is a sufficient security."[38] Roger Sherman sums up this traditional view: "The greatest security that a people can have for the enjoyment of their rights and liberties, is that no laws can be made to bind them nor any taxes imposed upon them, without their consent by representatives of their own chusing, who will participate with them in the public burthens and benefits; this was the great point contended for in our controversy with Great Britain, and this will be fully secured to us by the new constitution."[39]

To the extent that they relied upon representation, these Federalist writers joined most of their Anti-Federalist opponents in defending what is basically a *simple* form of government, a government in which the representatives are elected by the people, responsible to the people, and presumed to be fundamentally identical to the people with regard to their interests and opinions. At this level the dispute is between the Federalists' heavy reliance on the mechanism of representation and the Anti-Federalists' insistence that genuine re-

---

35. Wilson, Speech of November 24, 1787 (#105), *M/S*, pp. 222–23; compare with *Federalist* 63.

36. America (#3).

37. A Countryman (#31), *FE*, p. 220.

38. America (#3).

39. A Citizen of New Haven (#26), *FE*, p. 237; see A Countryman (#31), *FE*, p. 220.

sponsibility can be found only in the smaller, more homogeneous states. So long as the issue is phrased in this way, the Anti-Federalists seem to have the better of it. But the deeper Federalist argument sees representation as something much more than a device for mirroring popular opinions and interests.

The notion of simple representative government has several clear difficulties, a consideration of which shows the weakness of the Federalists' argument at one level and its power at a deeper one. First is the issue of the fidelity of representatives. The Federalists rely heavily on two arguments, both of which are open to question. It is said that since under the new Constitution the representatives will be chosen by the people in open and free elections, they can also be displaced by the people if they should violate their trust. The Federalists do not in fact spend very much time considering the practical effectiveness of this electoral check, but their opponents point out with a great deal of plausibility that the actual capacity of the people to supervise and control their representatives through the electoral machinery, especially in the very large-scale American republic, will be very limited. Representatives will inevitably be chosen from among a relatively small group of widely known men, and their activities as rulers will be largely obscure to the mass of the electors. Moreover, the argument that the representatives are subject to the laws along with their constituents and therefore have identical interests is clearly an oversimplification. Even granting (what the Anti-Federalists did not grant) that there will not grow up a separate class of rulers, it is still clear that any group of representatives will have certain interests distinct from those of their constituents, another tendency certain to be magnified in the new, large federal government. To take the simplest case, the representatives will indeed have to share the cost of the government, but obviously they benefit from those expenditures in a way that the ordinary citizen does not. If a relationship of responsibility or identity of interests between representative and constituent is the central principle of the new government, as some of the Federalists did in fact contend, then it was not difficult for the Anti-Federalists to show the tenuousness of the connection.

This argument was met by other Federalists who, tacitly conceding that the chain of representation is not enough, showed that the Constitution provides additional and very effective safeguards, based solidly on interest, to secure the fidelity of representatives. These are the familiar checks and balances. "The perfection of political science consists chiefly in providing mutual checks amongst the several departments of power, preserving at the same time, the dependance of the greatest on the people."[40] In fact a very considerable part of the Federalist writings was addressed to this issue. The structure and working of the proposed Constitution were explained in detail in order to show how well devised were the internal arrangements and how difficult and unlikely would be major breaches of trust by the representatives.[41]

There is still a deeper problem with simple representative government seen as a mirror of society. Granting that such a government is responsive and safe, is it likely to be stable and competent? Many Federalists thought not and tried to show that the Constitution provides for "responsible" government in the broader (and now common) as well as in the narrower sense. Noah Webster elaborates well this line of reasoning.[42] He describes a chain of ideas about government followed by sober second thoughts, leading to the principle of a bicameral legislature (his immediate concern, writing as he was in Pennsylvania with its unicameral state legislature). Unanimous consent is the basis of all law, Webster begins; but experience shows that civil society is impossible unless the opinions of a majority are allowed to give law to the whole.

Similarly, at first sight it seems reasonable for all members of a society to meet together to decide on legislation; but it soon becomes evident that this is neither practical nor desirable, and a scheme of representation is substituted. Again, in the government thus established it seems very natural at first that all the representatives should be collected into one body; but on reflection the benefits of a more complex legislative arrangement are perceived. A second body can protect against sudden and violent passions and against being led astray by one extraordinary man; it can also instill qualities of wisdom and experience into governmental deliberations. The mutual checks of a complex government can provide, then, not only fidelity but also stability, prudence, and wisdom. Federalist descriptions of the Constitution to this effect abound. One further example will suffice here. The president, through the use of his veto and his veto messages, it was explained, will provide a useful channel of communication between those who make and those who execute the law. "Many things look fair in theory which in practice are impossible. If lawmakers, in every instance, before their final decree, had the opinion of those who are to execute them, it would prevent a

---

40. Hanson (#93), *FP*, p. 222 (italics omitted); see Anonymous, Speech to Have Been Delivered . . . (#14).

41. See Dickinson (#92), *FP*, p. 182; Hanson (#93), *FP*, p. 272.

42. N. Webster (#103), *FP*, pp. 30ff.

thousand absurd ordinances, which are solemnly made, only to be repealed, and lessen the dignity of legislation in the eyes of mankind."[43]

In arrangements like these lies the great strength of the new Constitution. Carefully framed in the light of experience in the states, it provides all of the qualities desirable in government: "fidelity, or firm attachments to the good of the people—wisdom to discern what is for the public good—and dispatch in business, or speedy execution of the measures determined upon."[44]

The basis of these arrangements is of course a written constitution. The document framed in 1787 was the completion—and was seen, more or less clearly, by Federalists to be the completion—of the development of constitutional government in the United States since the Revolution. Constitutional government embraces and transcends the principle of representation. Establishing a constitution as supreme law is the act (the only act) of the sovereign people. The Constitution may be amended, a wise feature pointed out by many Federalists, but even amendment does not involve recourse to the original popular source but is an exercise of constitutional authority. Election, the essence of "representative" government as traditionally understood, becomes merely a method of choosing, not a method of authorizing. The legislature is a body of constitutional officers, not a microcosm of the sovereign people. The legislators, like other officers of government, derive their authority from the Constitution, not from their election. There is, thus, contrary to the view expressed by Noah Webster, a crucial distinction between the power of the people (as an original matter) and the power of their representatives.[45] This is the basis of the whole system of checks and balances as well as of the doctrine, accepted by most Federalists, that acts of the legislature contrary to the Constitution are void. "When the powers to be exercised, under a certain system, are in themselves consistent with the people's liberties, are legally defined, guarded, and ascertained, and ample provision made for bringing to condign punishment all such as shall overstep the limitations of law,—it is hard to conceive of a greater security for the rights of the people."[46]

---

43. A Landholder (#57), *FE*, p. 158.

44. A Citizen (#25).

45. See the discussion of representation above.

46. *Atticus* (#17), November 22, 1787. Most but not all of the Federalists seem to have assumed that the courts would regard such acts as void. See Hanson (#93), *FP*, p. 234; Dickinson (#92), *FP*, pp. 181–83; Iredell (#95), *FP*, p. 357. See also James Wilson's extremely influential explanation of the limited powers delegated to the general government in contrast to the broad

Not all Federalists grasped the significance of constitutional government. As we have seen, there is still in many cases a heavy reliance on traditional notions of representation. There are occasional statements like that of Noah Webster, who disputed the claim for a bill of rights by contending that "the very attempt to establish a permanent, unalterable Constitution, is an act of consummate arrogance." He argued that susceptibility of the representatives to their acts as legislators is alone "a sufficient security."[47] Most Federalists saw the proposed Constitution, however, not merely as a set of agencies of popular consent, but also as the legal foundation for a government limited in its powers and in its interior arrangements. If all of these arrangements "can not keep the public decision within the bounds of wisdom, natural fitness, right and convenience, it will be hard to find any efforts of human wisdom that can do it."[48]

Popular Government

We must now look deeper into the Federalist understanding of popular government. While most Federalists saw that the Constitution was meant to provide a complex and not a simple representative government, they insisted on its fundamentally popular character. Whatever their other disagreements, most Federalists would have accepted this striking description by James Wilson:

> of what description is the constitution before us? In its principles, Sir, it is purely democratical; varying indeed, in its form, in order to admit all the advantages, and to exclude all the disadvantages which are incidental to the known and established constitutions of government. But when we take an extensive and accurate view of the streams of power that appear through this great and comprehensive plan, when we contemplate the variety of their directions, the force and dignity of their currents, when we behold them intersecting, embracing, and surrounding the vast possessions and interests of the continent, and when we see them distributing on all hands beauty, energy and riches, still, however numerous and wise their courses, however diversified and remote the blessings they diffuse, we shall be able to trace them to one great and noble source, THE PEOPLE.[49]

---

powers enjoyed by the state governments in his early and widely distributed "State House" speech of October 6, 1787 (#68).

47. America (#3).

48. P. Webster (#103), *M/S*, p. 96.

49. Wilson, Speech of November 24, 1787 (#105), *M/S*, pp. 230–31; see Coxe (#90), *FP*, p. 147.

It is doubtless true that the emphasis placed by the Federalists on the popular character of the new Constitution was in part a response to Anti-Federalist criticism. Yet I think it is a distortion to picture them as an elite cleverly scrambling to retain control in a new democratic age. Their sincerity is manifest. Again and again they contend that this new government derives, as all legitimate government must, from the great source of political authority, the people. There must be, Wilson said, in every government one supreme sovereign power from which there is no appeal. "That the supreme power . . . should be vested in the people, is in my judgment the great panacea of human politics. It is a power paramount to every constitution, inalienable in its nature, and indefinite in its extent."[50] Madison himself, the great teacher of the danger of majority faction, had urged in Philadelphia that "the people were in fact, the fountain of all power, and by resorting to them, all difficulties were got over."[51] Even *Caesar*, usually cited as strongly critical of the people, while doubting their majesty and political wisdom, never denied their right to accept or reject a proffered government.[52] Under the Constitution the power of the people is not only the ultimate authority but it pervades the whole system. This government will secure the freedom and promote the happiness of America, Dickinson said, "by giving *the will of the people* a decisive influence over the whole, and over all the parts."[53]

The disagreement among the Federalists concerned not the truth but the sufficiency of the principle of popular sovereignty. In the days of struggle against the King, it had seemed to many that if only the people could grasp the government, the political problem would be solved; the means, as we have seen, is an adequate system of representation. But as popular rule is achieved, it becomes clear to everyone (what was always clear to some) that popular government is problematic because, among other reasons, "the people" is not homogeneous. Old problems of injustice, oppression, and tyranny emerge out of conflicts within "the people."

A traditional way of viewing this problem is that even a "democratic" society tends to divide into the natural elements of one/few/many, which are more or less in conflict with one another. This view was perhaps expressed most fully among the Americans by John Adams in his *Defence of the Constitutions of Government of the United*

---

50. Wilson, Speech of November 24, 1787 (#105), *M/S*, p. 230.
51. Farrand, *Records*, vol. II, p. 476 (August 31).
52. Caesar (#20), *FE*, p. 288.
53. Dickinson (#92), *FP*, pp. 173–74.

States. In the Constitutional Convention it found expression in statements by men like Gouverneur Morris and Alexander Hamilton. It is frequently expressed by the Anti-Federalists and helps to explain their admiration for the British government, despite their preference for the simple, small republic. Among Federalist writers this view is rather rare. They generally saw the Constitution as providing a new kind of complex government, an arrangement of constitutional powers rather than of social orders.

The different branches in the new government were not intended to "balance" one class against another, the way British branches are. "The sole intention of it is to produce wise and mature deliberation."[54] Our senate, Noah Webster explained, is not a different order of men; "but the same reasons, the same necessity for distinct branches of the legislature exists in all governments." In the United States "we have all the advantages of checks and balance, without the danger which may arise from a superior and independent order of men."[55] This is a constant Federalist theme. The Constitution "unites in its different parts all the advantages, without any of the disadvantages, of the three well-known forms of government, and yet it preserves the attributes of a republic."[56] Thus the Anti-Federalist, *Centinel,* was several times attacked for his claim that the Constitution was designed to secure something like the mixed regime described by Adams; on the contrary, it was said, the new government is in every sense a popular government, one that secures the advantages without the disadvantages of the traditional mixed regimes.[57]

There are, however, significant traces of this older view in some Federalist writing, which should be noted before we return to the main line of argument. Especially interesting are the essays of a Boston writer, *Atticus,* whose topic is party and republican governments.[58] *Atticus* presents a version of the traditional view of government as representing and mediating between the basic elements of society. He begins by criticizing monarchy (it is not necessary for effective government) and parties (no violent party man can be a good citizen); but it turns out that parties are inevitable and useful and that their management does require a strong monarchical ele-

---

54. A Citizen (#24).

55. N. Webster (#102), *FP,* pp. 34–35; see the good discussion of the difference between the American "second house" and the British House of Lords by a *Democratic Federalist* (#33).

56. One of the Four Thousand (#62), *M/S,* p. 116.

57. See A Citizen (#24); P. Webster (#103), *M/S,* p. 95.

58. Atticus (#17).

ment. Two parties tend to emerge in all nondespotic governments. A democratic party, consisting of small property owners and debtors, tends towards levellism and democratic turbulence; an aristocratic party, consisting of large property owners, especially moneyed men, tends toward rigid aristocracy. Properly blended, *Atticus* argues in somewhat deceptively modern-sounding terms, parties give life to politics; they keep alive attention to public measures; they produce attendance and care in elections; and they keep any one interest from swallowing the rest. However, a third party is necessary to balance the democratic and aristocratic elements; and that must be found, after all, in the monarchical principle. This principle is represented in the American governments in the executive and judicial departments, supported by that class of the population dependent upon salaries, the natural supporters of monarchy. *Atticus* here is describing the American governments in general, and it is not always clear how he connects these principles to the new Constitution; but we have seen enough for our purpose.

Most of the Federalists, to repeat once more, did not see the Constitution as a mixing of social orders. The only American "order" is the people. That is decisive. Yet the "people" is not homogeneous and, according to the Anti-Federalists, will become less so if the relatively small republics of the states are submerged into a huge national aggregation. In the large commercial republic to be formed under the Constitution, the population will shatter into contending groups, with the inevitable emergence of a *de facto* aristocracy which will eventually control the government and the whole society. Thoughtful Federalists acknowledged the problem. The singularity of the order of "the people" in principle must rest on fact.

But what is wanted is not the petty, static homogeneity of the small, self-sufficient, and presumably public-spirited republic but what might be called the dynamic homogenizing tendency of the great commercial republic. The problem is not to prevent division or inequality but to prevent permanent division and inequality. The old defenders of popular government have looked to the wrong principle. "*Virtue*, patriotism, or love of country, never was and never will be, till men's natures are changed, a fixed, permanent, principle and support of government," Noah Webster insisted. Rather, "an equality of property, with a necessity of alienation, constantly operating to destroy combinations of powerful families, is the very *soul of a republic*—While this continues, the people will inevitably possess both *power* and *freedom;* when this is lost, power departs, liberty expires, and a commonwealth will inevitably assume some other form."[59]

---

59. N. Webster (#102), *FP,* p. 59.

Differences in wealth can be great, so long as they cannot become permanent. Fortunately the circumstances of America foster such fluidity. Opportunities are great, commerce is vigorous. There is no need to squabble over a limited pie and little likelihood that a small class can permanently control the wealth and therefore the government of the country. Besides the abundant wealth of America, the system depends on an unqualified acceptance of a modern commercial society. The old vestiges of feudal tenure and the old idea of the landed interest as somehow unique and superior must be firmly abandoned. Eliminate primogeniture, destroy entailment, "leave real estates to revolve from hand to hand, as time and accident may direct; and no family influence can be acquired and established for a series of generations—no man can obtain dominion over a large territory—the laborious and saving, who are generally the best citizens, will possess each his share of property and power, and thus the balance of wealth and power will continue where it is, in the *body of the people*."[60] One Federalist went so far as to argue that the states should provide for equality in descent without will of females as well as males and in the most remote collateral branches. "By these means, poverty and extreme riches would be avoided, and a republican spirit would be given to our laws, not only without a violation of private rights but consistently with the principle of justice and sound policy."[61]

The elimination of primogeniture and entail and the consequent tendency for large estates to be broken up was not a uniquely Federalist policy and is indeed most often associated with Jefferson and the small agrarian republic. The Federalists, however, were pressing in a different and on the whole more consistent direction. There was among Federalists little of that holding back from the modern commercial world that provides one strand of Jefferson's and the Anti-Federalists' thought. There were about as many "Farmers" and "Countrymen" among the Federalists as among the Anti-Federalists; and the defenders of the Constitution typically deny that there is any antagonism between the landed and the commercial interest, often contending that commerce is but the handmaiden of agriculture. At bottom, however, the Federalists affirm the fundamentally commercial character of agriculture itself. Thus Oliver Ellsworth, writing as *A Landholder*, described himself as a former merchant, now retired (thanks to industry and economy) to a farming life.

Throughout his essays, Ellsworth quietly but persistently presses

---

60. Ibid.
61. A Freeman (#43), January 30, 1788.

the claim of commerce, on which the prosperity of agriculture itself depends. "It may be assumed as a fixed truth that the prosperity and riches of the farmer must depend on the prosperity, and good national regulation of trade." He warns against the "artful men" who "tell you let trade take care of itself, and excite your jealousy against the merchant because his business leads him to wear a gayer coat, than your economy directs."[62] The United States will continue to be a country where the vast bulk of the people labor on the land; yet it will be a country in which the basic interest is commerce. The country will contain substantial differences of wealth, but old combinations will tend always to be broken up and new ones built.

Webster lays down two other conditions of free republican government, which are discussed at length by the Federalists but which can be passed over here, as well known and clear-cut views: the possession of information by the people and free and popular elections. "In a country like ours, abounding in free men all of one rank, where property is equally diffused, where estates are held in fee simple, the press free, and the means of information common, tyranny cannot reasonably find admission under any form of government; but its admission is next to impossible under one where the people are the source of all power, and elect either mediately by their representatives, or immediately by themselves the whole of their rulers."[63] These three conditions, then, are the essential bulwarks of republican freedom: a diffusion or fluidity of property, free press, and free and popular elections.[64]

The main concern of the arguments examined thus far is still the traditional (in the American context) fear that an aristocracy will tend to control the government and the society to the disadvantage of the mass of the people. The Anti-Federalists remained unpersuaded that the people would remain their own masters in the vast commercial empire to be established under the Constitution. Many of the Federalists, on the other hand, doubted that this was the main problem

---

62. A Landholder (#57), *FE*, pp. 139–40.

63. Ramsay (#101), *FP*, p. 379. Ellsworth wrote that the American governments are safe from monarchy or aristocracy "so long as the present descent of landed estates last and the mass of the people have, as at present, a tolerable education. . . ." A Landholder (#57), *FE*, p. 166; see America (#3).

64. A good deal of Federalist energy was devoted to showing that the press and elections would be free. This involved defending the Constitution against two major anti-Federalist criticisms: that there was no guarantee of freedom of the press and that the provision of Art. I, Sec. 4(1) permitting Congress to regulate the times, places, and manner of federal elections was a source of danger to free elections.

(though because of the reflexive character of Federalist writing, it is the one they spend most of their time dealing with). On the whole the Federalists inclined to the view that more was to be feared in American government from licentious democracy than from aristocratic oppression.[65] This view had been expressed by Edmund Randolph when he initiated the deliberations of the Constitutional Convention; and it is a persistent Federalist theme, though perhaps not so prominent as the Federalists' antidemocratic reputation might suggest.

"Many plausible things may be said in favor of pure democracy—many in favor of uniting the representatives of the people in one single house—but uniform experience proves both to be inconsistent with the peace of society, and the rights of freemen."[66] Dickinson himself, for all of his emphasis on the will of the people, describes the two main problems of American government as the turbulence of the states and the licentiousness of the people.[67] It is perhaps not accidental, however, that Dickinson, like most of the Federalist writers, discusses the problem of the turbulence of the states at considerable length, while only glancingly considering the problem of the licentiousness of the people or its solution.[68]

One answer to popular excess is that the government itself should be strong and independent enough to resist foolish or unjust popular impulses. The American governments have been "too feeble and too popular," *A State Soldier* said forthrightly. "The more independent a government is therefore of the people, under proper restraints, the more likely it is to produce . . . justice; and the more substantial and efficient under such restraints, the better calculated to protect both the persons and property of mankind."[69] One of the characteristics of constitutional government is that it restrains the people as well as the government. If a constitutional government is strong it is, in principle and practice, independent of immediate popular impulses. This describes precisely the government under the new Constitution. We have come almost full circle back to the need for effective government. The Constitution provides a government with the vigor, competence, and independence that can resist popular licentiousness and secure individual liberty.

This is, however, not sufficient. The Federalists emphatically

---

65. Cato (#12); see Caesar (#20).
66. N. Webster (#102), *FP*, p. 34.
67. Dickinson (#92), *FP*, p. 200; see State Soldier (#81), February 6, 1788.
68. Dickinson (#92), *FP*, p. 120.
69. State Soldier (#81), February 6, 1788, March 19, 1788.

concede that the government under the Constitution is and must be firmly (if not simply or directly) tied to and dependent on the popular will. The government under the Constitution, Dickinson explained, is *balanced* by the power from which it proceeds.[70] *Publius* would insist on a different formulation that would stress the absence of any direct agency by the people in the government. Nevertheless all Federalists must concede that in a popular government security from popular excess cannot finally be found in a strong, independent governmental force, or even in a supreme constitution. The soundness and health of the popular regime must depend finally on the health of its primary element.

Here the Anti-Federalists bring to bear their powerful argument that the civic virtue of the populace can be fostered only in a small republic.[71] The aggregate selfishness encouraged by the great commercial republic will destroy those qualities of moderation and public-spiritedness on which republican government depends. Many of the Federalists simply did not meet this objection. Wilson, for example, seems willing simply to trust in the vigor, good sense, and patriotism of the American people, without troubling himself very much about the extent to which the trust is justified. "[T]he citizens of the United States can never be wretched beyond retrieve, unless they are wanting to themselves."[72] More thoughtful Federalists, James Madison among them, saw that the problem was the likelihood that the people very frequently *would* be "wanting to themselves."[73]

Madison rejects the traditional solution, that the people must be formed by the small republic into citizens. He opposes this with his now well known defense of the large republic: "Extend the sphere, and you take in greater variety of parties and interests; you make it less probable that a majority of the whole will have a common motive to invade the rights of other citizens; or if such a common motive exists, it will be more difficult for all who feel it to discover their own strength, and to act in unison with each other." There are bits and pieces of this view of the extended republic in other Federalist writings; but it is nowhere referred to specifically by other Federalist writers, so far as I can discover, and there is little evidence that it was

---

70. Dickinson (#92), *FP*, p. 183.

71. This is fully elaborated in Storing's introduction to *The Complete Anti-Federalist*.

72. Wilson, Speech of November 24, 1787 (#88), *M/S*, p. 230. But see below, p. 240.

73. See *Federalist* 49.

influential or even widely understood.[74] This is not the place to try to solve the still perplexing problem of the influence and the authority (which are not the same) of Madison's famous account of the large republic. It is perhaps not surprising that the great body of Federalists stayed closer to the surface and to traditional views.

On the whole the Federalist view of both the problem and the solution was more conventional than Madison's. "Popular licentiousness" was likely to be the way a typical Federalist described the problem. In this he would betray a less penetrating understanding than Madison, who saw that the fundamental problem of popular government is not popular uprisings or disturbances along the lines of Shays' "rebellion" but the unjust use that can be made by the majority of its lawful authority.

In seeking a solution, too, the typical Federalist was likely to look to the traditional principles of civic education and character-molding, precisely the principles that Madison found so unreliable, although there is more question here whether the usual view was quite so superficial as it might appear within the Madisonian perspective (or indeed whether Madison himself escaped the traditional reliance). The typical Federalist was likely, in a word, to preach. "Let the Americans be virtuous—let them be firm supporters of Republicanism—let them have confidence in their representatives— then their liberties will be secured to them, and peace and prosperity will ensue."[75] The point could be put rather more favorably by saying that many of the Federalists saw the continuing need for political leadership to form the manners and character of the people. Thus James Wilson, on the occasion of a Fourth of July speech in 1788, instructed the American people in the duties as well as the benefits of American citizenship. Frugality and temperance, industry, a warm and uniform attachment to liberty and the Constitution—these are the duties of citizenship. All the activities of government "spring from the *original* movement of the *people at large.*" The people must provide "a sufficient force and a just direction" to all parts of the government. Especially, the people must choose good representatives, for on that all else depends. "It is the first *connection* in politics: if an *error* is made *here*, it can never be *corrected* in any subsequent

---

74. *Federalist* 10. See A State Soldier (#81), *passim;* Plain Truth (#74), *M/S,* p. 193; A Countryman (#31), *FE,* p. 215; Wilson, Speech of November 24, 1788 (#105), *M/S,* p. 220; Hanson (#93), *FP,* p. 247; Cato (#23); Cassius (#22), April 2, 1788; Dickinson (#92), *FP,* pp. 203–6; Anonymous, Speech to Have Been Delivered . . . (#14), July 25, 1788.

75. Maecenas (#58).

process." Each citizen should vote as if his were the vote that would decide the election.[76]

Teaching, and even preaching, are important for the Federalists, more important than a reading of *The Federalist* would suggest.[77] But that teaching of the duties of citizenship rests on the solid ground of the effective government provided by the Constitution. This is, again, the bedrock of the Federalist position. Civic morality is fostered where civic morality is effectively protected. Want of energetic government is followed by disobedience among the governed; that is followed in turn by general licentiousness, typically giving rise to a harsh antirepublican response that is likely to destroy liberty for the sake of order.[78] "Nothing tends more to the honour, establishment, and peace of society, than public decisions, grounded on principles of right, natural fitness and prudence; but when the powers of government are *too limited,* such decisions can't be made and enforced; so the mischief goes without a remedy. . . ." When the powers of government are in dispute, "the administration dare not make decisions on the footing of impartial justice and right" but must temporize, with the result that "the *righteous* go off injured and disgusted." Controversy must have "a just, *speedy,* and effectual decision that right may be done before the contention has *time* to grow up into habits of malignity, resentment, ill nature, and ill offices."[79] A good government on an enlarged scale is a far better teacher of justice and patriotism than is the petty republic, with its inherent weakness and turbulence. The excellent government provided by the Constitution will enforce, habituate to, and teach civic virtue while going about its business of providing security, order, and justice between man and man.

"Virtue or good habits are the result of good laws—and from the excellent American Constitution those *habits* will be induced, that shall lead to those *exertions, manufactures,* and *enterprises,* which will give a scope to the American genius, and 'find employment for their activity.' "[80] Reject the Constitution, went a typical warning, and "you will possess popular liberty with a vengeance," with the result that "no man's property will be secure, but each one defrauding his neighbour under the sanction of law,—thus subverting every princi-

---

76. Wilson, Speech of July 4, 1788 (#89).

77. See Ralph Lerner, "The Supreme Court as Republican Schoolmaster," *The Supreme Court Review,* 1967.

78. Pennsylvania Farmer (#67), *M/S,* pp. 127–28.

79. P. Webster (#104), *FP,* pp. 119–20.

80. Convention (#30).

ple of morality and religion." Accept it, and "you will enjoy the blessing of a well balanced government, capable of inspiring credit and respectability abroad, and virtue, confidence, good order and harmony at home."[81]

A Selected List of Federalist Writings

By Pseudonym

1. Alfredus (Samuel Tenny or Tenney), New Hampshire *Freeman's Oracle*, 18 January, 8 February, 13 June, 11 July, 23 August, 13 September 1788.
2. Amen., *Massachusetts Centinel*, 13 October 1787.
3. America (Noah Webster), New York *Daily Advertiser*, 31 December 1787.
4. An American Citizen (Tench Coxe), Philadelphia *Independent Gazetteer*, 26 September, 28 September, 29 September, 24 October 1787 (also published as a pamphlet); in *Ford Pamphlets*.
5. Americanus, *Virginia Independent Chronicle*, 5 December, 19 December 1787.
6. An Annapolitan, Baltimore *Maryland Gazette*, 31 January 1788.
7. Anon., "A correspondent observes . . . ," *Boston Gazette*, 29 October 1787.
8. Anon., "The following dialogue . . . ," *Boston Gazette*, 29 October 1787.
9. Anon., "It is devoutly to be wished . . . ," *Boston Gazette*, 26 November 1787.
10. Anon., (Francis Hopkinson), The New Roof, *Pennsylvania Packet*, 29 December 1787, in *McMaster and Stone*.
11. Anon., "Observe . . . ," Northampton, Massachusetts, *Hampshire Gazette*, 17 October 1788.
12. Anon., On the National Constitution, New Hampshire *Freeman's Oracle*, 13 June 1788.
13. Anon., "Should the wisdom . . . ," *Connecticut Journal*, 17 October 1787.
14. Anon., Speech to Have Been Delivered in Maryland Convention, Baltimore *Maryland Journal*, 25 July, 29 July, 1 August, 8 August 1788.
15. Anon., The Triumph of Reason, Poughkeepsie *Country Journal*, 11 March 1788.

---

81. Cato (#23).

16. Aristides (Alexander Hanson), Baltimore, *Maryland Gazette*, 4 March, 1 April, 22 April 1788 (see #93).
17. Atticus, Boston *Independent Chronicle*, 9 August, 18 October, 22 November, 27 December 1787.
18. Avenging Justice, *Massachusetts Gazette*, 23 November 1787.
19. Brutus, Alexandria *Virginia Journal*, 22 November, 6 December 1787.
20. Caesar, New York *Daily Advertiser*, 1 October, 17 October 1787, in *Ford Essays*.
21. Cassius (James Sullivan), *Massachusetts Gazette*, 18 September, 2 October, 16 November, 23 November, 27 November, 30 November (2 essays), 14 December, 18 December, 21 December, 25 December 1787, in *Ford Essays*.
22. Cassius, *Virginia Independent Chronicle*, 2 April, 9 April, 23 April 1788.
23. Cato, Poughkeepsie *Country Journal*, 12 December 1787.
24. A Citizen, Carlisle *Gazette*, 24 October 1787.
25. A Citizen, New York *Daily Advertiser*, 6 February 1788.
26. A Citizen of New Haven (Roger Sherman, *New Haven Gazette*, 4 December, 25 December 1787, in *Ford Essays*.
27. A Citizen of Pennsylvania, *Pennsylvania Packet*, 12 October 1787, in *MacMaster and Stone*.
28. Common Sense, *Massachusetts Gazette*, 11 January 1788.
29. Conciliator (Benjamin Rush?), Philadelphia *Independent Gazetteer*, 9 January, 15 January, 21 January, 12 February, 20 February 1788.
30. Convention, *Massachusetts Centinel*, 13 October 1787.
31. A Countryman, *New Haven Gazette*, 14 November, 22 November, 29 November, 6 December, 20 December 1787, in *Ford Essays*.
32. Curtiopolis, New York *Daily Advertiser*, 8 January 1788.
33. Democratic Federalist, Philadelphia *Independent Gazetteer*, 26 November 1787.
34. A Dutchess County Farmer, Poughkeepsie *Country Journal*, 26 February 1788.
35. Elihu, Hartford, Connecticut *American Mercury*, 18 February 1788.
36. Examiner, *New York Journal*, 14 December, 19 December, 24 December 1787; 4 January 1788.
37. Ezekiel, *Connecticut Journal*, 31 October 1787.
38. A Farmer, *Massachusetts Centinel*, 9 January 1788.
39. A Federalist, *Boston Gazette*, 3 December 1787.
40. A Federalist, Philadelphia *Independent Gazetteer*, 25 October 1787, in *McMaster and Stone*.

41. Foreigner, Boston *American Herald*, 26 November 1787.
42. A Freeholder, *Virginia Independent Chronicle*, 9 April (extraordinary), 23 April 1788.
43. A Freeman (Tench Coxe), *Pennsylvania Gazette*, 23 January, 30 January, 6 February 1788.
44. A Friend, Poughkeepsie *Country Journal*, 18 March 1788.
45. A Friend to the Constitution, Baltimore *Maryland Journal*, 16 October 1787.
46. A Friend to Good Government, Poughkeepsie *Country Journal*, 8 April, 15 April 1788.
47. A Friend to Honesty, Boston *Independent Chronicle*, 10 January 1788.
48. A Friend to Society and Liberty, Pennsylvania Gazette, 23 July 1788.
49. A Gentleman, *Connecticut Journal*, 24 October 1787.
50. Hambden, Baltimore *Maryland Journal*, 14 March, 25 April 1788.
51. Harrington, Boston *American Herald*, 15 October 1787.
52. Hermenius, *Carlisle Gazette*, 16 January 1788.
53. Honestus (Benjamin Austin, Jr.), *Massachusetts Centinel*, 9 January 1788.
54. Honorius, Boston *Independent Chronicle*, 3 January 1788.
55. Junias, *Massachusetts Gazette*, 22 January, 29 January, 5 February 1788.
56. Juvenis, *New Hampshire Recorder*, 5 August 1788.
57. A Landholder (Oliver Ellsworth), *Connecticut Courant*, 5 November, 12 November, 19 November, 26 November, 3 December, 10 December, 17 December, 24 December, 31 December 1787; 3 March, 10 March, 17 March, 24 March 1788; Baltimore *Maryland Journal*, 29 February 1788; in *Ford Essays*.
58. Maecenas, *State Gazette of Georgia*, 6 December 1787.
59. Monitor, *Massachusetts Gazette*, 30 October 1787.
60. New England, *Connecticut Courant*, 24 December 1787.
61. An Old Planter, *Virginia Independent Chronicle*, 27 February 1788.
62. One of the Four Thousand, Philadelphia *Independent Gazetteer*, 15 October 1787, in *McMaster and Stone*.
63. One of the Middle Interest, *Massachusetts Centinel*, 28 November 1787.
64. One of the People, *Massachusetts Centinel*, 17 October, 17 November 1787.
65. P. Valerius Agricola, *Albany Gazette*, 8 November, 6 December 1787.
66. A Patriotic Citizen, *Carlisle Gazette*, 21 May 1788.

67. Pennsylvania Farmer, Philadelphia *Independent Gazetteer*, 27 September 1787, in *McMaster and Stone*.
68. A Pennsylvanian, *Pennsylvania Gazette*, 6 February, 13 February, 20 February, 27 February 1788.
69. A Pennsylvanian, *Pennsylvania Gazette*, 11 June 1788.
70. Philanthrop, Northampton, Massachusetts *Hampshire Gazette*, 23 April 1788.
71. Philanthropos, *Pennsylvania Gazette*, 16 January 1788.
72. Philodemos, Boston *American Herald*, 12 May 1788.
73. Philo-Publius, New York *Daily Advertiser*, 1 December 1787.
74. Plain Truth, Philadelphia *Independent Gazetteer*, 10 November, 28 November 1787, in *McMaster and Stone*.
75. A Plebeian, *Maryland Journal*, 14 March 1788.
76. Poplicola, *Massachusetts Centinel*, 31 October 1787.
77. Remarker, Boston *Independent Chronicle*, 27 December 1787, 17 January 1788.
78. Remarker ad corrigendum, Boston *Independent Chronicle*, 3 January 1788.
79. A Republican, Boston *Independent Chronicle*, 28 February 1788.
80. Socius, *Carlisle Gazette*, 14 November 1787.
81. State Soldier, *Virginia Independent Chronicle*, 16 January, 6 February, 12 March, 19 March, 2 April 1788.
82. A Steady and Open Republican (Charles Pinckney), *State Gazette of South Carolina*, 5 May 1788, in *Ford Essays*.
83. Truth, *Massachusetts Centinel*, 24 November 1787.
84. Uncus, Baltimore *Maryland Journal*, 30 November 1787.
85. Union, *Boston Gazette*, 12 November 1787.
86. Valerius, *Massachusetts Centinel*, 28 November 1787.
87. Hugh Williamson, Remarks, *State Gazette of North Carolina*, in *Ford Essays*.
88. James Wilson, "State House Speech, 6 October 1787," *Pennsylvania Packet*, 10 October 1787, in *McMaster and Stone* and *Ford Pamphlets*.
89. James Wilson, Speech of 4 July 1788. *Pennsylvania Gazette Supplement*, 9 July 1788.

By Author's Name, Where Known

90. Tench Coxe (American Citizen), An Examination of the Constitution of the United States, Philadelphia, 1788, in *Ford Pamphlets* (also published as newspaper essays).
91. William Davie (Publicola), Address to the Freeman of North Carolina, Newbern, 1788, in *Ford Pamphlets*.

92. John Dickinson (Fabius), Letters of Fabius, Wilmington, Delaware, 1787, in *Ford Pamphlets.*
93. Alexander Hanson (Aristides), Remarks on the Proposed Plan of a Federal Government, Annapolis, in *Ford Pamphlets* (See #16).
94. Federal Party, An Impartial Address to the Citizens of Albany, Albany, 1788.
95. James Iredell (Marcus), Answer to Mr. Mason's Objections to the New Constitution, Newbern, 1788, in *Ford Pamphlets.*
96. Jonathan Jackson (A Native of Boston), Thoughts Upon the Political Situation, Worcester, 1788.
97. John Jay (A Citizen of New York), An Address to the People of the State of New York, New York, 1788, in *Ford Pamphlets.*
98. Dr. James Montgomery (Decius), Decius's Letters on the Opposition, Richmond, 1789 (originally published in Virginia Independent Chronicle).
99. A Native of Virginia, Observations Upon the Proposed Plan of Federal Government, Petersburg, 1788, in M. Hamilton, *The Writings of James Monroe,* Vol. I.
100. Charles Pinckney, Observations On the Plan of Government, New York, 1787, in Farrand, *Records of the Federal Convention,* Vol. III.
101. David Ramsay (Civis), An Address to the Freeman of South Carolina on the Federal Constitution, Charleston, 1788, in *Ford Pamphlets.*
102. Noah Webster (A Citizen of America), An Examination into the Leading Principles of the Federal Constitution, Philadelphia, 1787, in *Ford Pamphlets.*
103. Pelatiah Webster, Remarks on the Address of Sixteen Members of the Assembly of Pennsylvania, Philadelphia 1787, in McMaster and Stone, *Pennsylvania and the Federal Constitution.*
104. Pelatiah Webster (A Citizen of Philadelphia), The Weakness of Brutus Exposed, Philadelphia, 1787, in *Ford Pamphlets.*
105. James Wilson, The Substance of a Speech Delivered by James Wilson . . . on 24 November 1787, Philadelphia, 1787, in McMaster and Stone, *Pennsylvania and the Federal Constitution* (also widely printed in newspapers).

5
The Constitution and the Bill of Rights

The foundation of the American constitutional system was not completed, it is widely agreed, until the adoption of the first ten amendments in 1791. The absence of a bill of rights from the original Constitution had, of course, been a major item in the Anti-Federalist position. "No sooner had the Continental Congress laid the proposed Constitution before the people for ratification," Irving Brant writes, "than a great cry went up: it contained no Bill of Rights."[1] According to Robert Rutland, whose book *The Birth of the Bill of Rights, 1776–1791* is the major history of these events, "The Federalists, failing to realize the importance of a bill of rights, miscalculated public opinion and found themselves on the defensive almost from the outset of the ratification struggle."[2] Another scholar, Bernard Schwartz, says: "Here, the Anti-Federalists had the stronger case and their opponents were on the defensive from the beginning. It was, indeed, not until the Federalists yielded in their rigid opposition on Bill of Rights Amendments that ratification of the Constitution was assured. On the Bill of Rights issue, it is the Anti-Federalist writings which are the more interesting and even the more influential."[3]

So, as the story is generally told, the Federalists gave us the Constitution, but the Anti-Federalists gave us the Bill of Rights. Moreover, it seems quite plausible today, when so much of constitutional law is connected with the Bill of Rights, to conclude that the Anti-Federalists, the apparent losers in the debate over the

This essay originally appeared in M. Judd Harmon, ed., *Essays on the Constitution of the United States* (Port Washington, N.Y.: Kennikat Press, 1978).

1. Irving Brant, *The Bill of Rights: Its Origin and Meaning* (Indianapolis: The Bobbs Merrill Co., 1965), p. 46.

2. Robert Rutland, *The Birth of the Bill of Rights* (Chapel Hill: University of North Carolina Press, 1955), p. 125.

3. Bernard Schwartz, *The Bill of Rights: A Documentary History* (New York: Chelsea House Publishers, 1971), p. 527.

Constitution, were ultimately the winners. Their contribution to the scheme of American constitutional liberty seems to be a more fundamental one. Rutland puts this point well: "The facts show that the Federal Bill of Rights and the antecedent state declarations of rights represented, more than anything else, the sum total of American experience and experimentation with civil liberty up to their adoption."[4]

We all have a tendency to look at the past through the glass of our present concerns and presuppositions. That is altogether understandable; it can be given a plausible justification; it is sometimes said to be the only thing we can do. The result, however, is that we tend to speak to the past rather than to let the past try to speak to us. I want to try to reconstruct some of the debate over the Bill of Rights in a way that will enable it to speak to us. I think the result will be to show that the common view that the heart of American liberty is to be found in the Bill of Rights is wrong. That view rests, I think, on a misreading of the events of the American founding and reflects and fosters a misunderstanding of the true basis of American constitutional liberty.

To begin, we need to remind ourselves of some of the central facts about the way the Constitution was ratified. On September 17, 1787, the convention sitting in Philadelphia finished its business and sent its proposed constitution to Congress for transmittal to the states, there to be considered in conventions specially elected for that purpose. The Federalists in several states moved quickly to secure ratification. The Pennsylvania legislature began discussing the calling of a convention, even before the Constitution had been acted upon by Congress, and provided for a convention to meet on November 21. Delaware was, however, the first to ratify, on December 7, followed by Pennsylvania on December 12. The Pennsylvania ratification was accompanied by charges of steamrolling and unfair tactics; the opposition remained unreconciled and demanded a second national convention. There followed ratification in rapid succession by New Jersey, Georgia, and Connecticut. By the middle of January 1788, however, no major state had ratified except Pennsylvania, where the opposition was still strong.

The Massachusetts convention met on January 14, and the evidence suggests that there was probably a majority against the Constitution or at least that the Anti-Federalists were very strong. The Massachusetts convention saw intensive debate, accompanied by equally intensive parliamentary and political maneuvering. Finally,

---

4. Rutland, *The Birth of the Bill of Rights*, p. v.

for reasons that will always be debated, John Hancock, the hitherto absent president of the convention, made an appearance and proposed that along with ratification the convention recommend a series of amendments to "remove the fears and quiet the apprehensions of many of the good people of the commonwealth, and more effectually guard against an undue administration of the federal government. . . ."[5] This proposal, supported by Samuel Adams, secured ratification in Massachusetts on February 6 by the still close vote of 187 to 168. Indeed, it is scarcely too much to say that this formula secured the ratification of the Constitution; for some version of it was used in every state that ratified after Massachusetts, with the exception of Maryland but including the crucial and doubtful states of Virginia and New York. The Constitution was ratified, then, on the understanding that an early item on the national agenda would be the consideration of widely desired amendments.

The story is completed in the First Congress. When the new government began functioning in 1789, James Madison introduced in the House of Representatives a series of amendments which, after consideration there and in the Senate, were framed as twelve proposed amendments and sent to the states for ratification. Two of these amendments (of minor importance) were not ratified by the states.[6] The others were ratified in 1791 and became the first ten amendments to the Constitution—our Bill of Rights.

The reader of the debates of the First Congress can hardly avoid being struck by the persistence with which Madison pressed his proposals and the coolness with which they were initially received. The House of Representatives was hard at work getting the government organized and under way. It was engaged in establishing the executive departments and providing for a national revenue system; the Senate was working on a bill to establish the federal judiciary (where several of the main questions raised in proposals for amendment would have to be faced). It seemed sensible to most of Madison's colleagues to concentrate on getting the government well launched, to acquire some experience in it, and to avoid a premature reopening of the divisive debate over ratification. It is true that Madison had explicitly committed himself to the position that the First Congress should propose amendments to be submitted to the states; "amendments, if pursued with a proper moderation and in a proper mode, will be not only safe, but may serve the double purpose

---

5. Jonathan Elliot, ed., *Debates in the Several State Conventions on the Adoption of the Federal Constitution*, vol. 2, pp. 122–23, 177.

6. See below, note 10.

of satisfying the minds of well meaning opponents, and of providing additional guards in favour of liberty."[7] Nevertheless, Madison could have explained, altogether plausibly, to his Virginia constituents that he had introduced amendments as promised, but that they had been postponed until the House could finish the obviously more pressing business of launching the new government. Yet in the face of resistance from political friends as well as foes, Madison pressed forward. Why?

Madison's insistent sponsorship of amendments has to be seen, I think, as the final step in the strikingly successful Federalist strategy to secure an effective national government. I do not claim that this strategy was conceived at the beginning of the ratification debate—it developed as events emerged—or that all Federalists were parties to it; if they had been, Madison would not have had the opposition he did at the outset of the debate on amendments. But I think it is fairly clear that Madison knew what he was doing: he meant to complete the Federalist ratification victory, and in fact he did so.

Madison's proposals were designed primarily to prevent two things from happening. The first aim was to thwart the move for a general convention to consider amendments under the authority of Article V of the Constitution. A second convention was a favorite plan of the Anti-Federalists; the Federalists feared that such a convention might be—was, indeed, intended to be—a time bomb that would destroy the essentials of the Constitution. The second and related aim was to snuff out the attempt to revise the basic structure and powers of the new federal government, which was the main thrust of Anti-Federal opposition. All the state ratifying conventions that proposed amendments included suggestions to strengthen the states and limit the powers of Congress relating to such crucial matters as federal elections, taxes, military affairs, and commercial regulation. Madison made clear that he had no intention of proposing, or accepting, any amendments along these lines. "I should be unwilling to see a door opened for a reconsideration of the whole structure of Government—for a reconsideration of the principles and the substance of the powers given; because I doubt, if such a door were opened, we should be very likely to stop at that point which would be safe to the Government itself."[8] Madison's strategy was to seize the initiative for amendments, to use the Federalist majority in the

---

7. Letter to George Eve, January 2, 1789, Gaillard Hunt, ed., *The Writings of James Madison* (New York: G. P. Putnam's Sons, 1904), vol. 5, p. 320.

8. *The Debates and Proceedings of the Congress of the United States* (Washington, 1834), vol. 1, p. 433.

First Congress to finish the unavoidable business of amendments in such a way as to remove from the national agenda the major Anti-Federalist objections—and incidentally to secure some limited but significant improvements in the Constitution, especially in securing individual rights.

Thus, on June 6 Madison offered his proposals, mustering all his remarkable influence to urge on the friends of the Constitution the prudence of showing their good faith and tranquilizing the public mind by putting forward amendments "of such a nature as will not injure the Constitution" and yet could "give satisfaction to the doubting part of our fellow-citizens." He urged also that "it is possible the abuse of the powers of the General Government may be guarded against in a more secure manner than is now done, while no one advantage arising from the exercise of that power shall be damaged or endangered by it." "We have," he said, "in this way something to gain, and, if we proceed with caution, nothing to lose."[9]

Secure in the knowledge of a large majority back of him (once he could get it to move), Madison proposed amendments designed to correct minor imperfections in the structure of government, which I pass over here,[10] to secure traditional individual rights, and to reserve to the states powers not granted to the federal government. These proposals were recast by the House, but little of substance was added or taken away. A comparison of Madison's original proposals and the first ten amendments of the Constitution shows both the value of a serious and thoughtful deliberative process in improving the original language and the dominance of Madison's impulse. The crucial fact is that none of the amendments regarded by the opponents to the Constitution as fundamental was included.

Indeed, in one of his proposals Madison tried to turn the table on the Anti-Federalists by using the Bill of Rights momentum to make what he regarded as a substantial improvement in the constitutional design. He proposed that "no state shall violate the equal right of conscience, or the freedom of the press or the trial by jury in criminal cases." Admitting that many state constitutions already had such

---

9. Ibid., p. 432.

10. Amendments were proposed (1) to ensure at least one representative for each 30,000 people until the size of the House should reach a certain limit, when the proportion would be reduced; and (2) to make increases in the salaries of congressmen apply only after the next election of representatives. Versions of these two amendments were included in the twelve amendments proposed by the Congress, but failed to be ratified by a sufficient number of states.

provisions, Madison saw no reason against double security. And he shrewdly observed that

> nothing can give a more sincere proof of the attachment of those who opposed this Constitution to these great and important rights, than to see them join in obtaining the security I have now proposed; because it must be admitted, on all hands, that the State Governments are as liable to attack these individual privileges as the General Government is, and therefore ought to be as cautiously guarded against.[11]

This amendment, which Madison thought "the most valuable amendment in the whole list,"[12] was eventually rejected by the Senate, as perhaps he expected it would be. It reflected, nonetheless, Madison's long-standing view that the chief danger to American liberty lay in the incapacity, instability, and injustice of state governments.

Madison's proposals were first referred to the committee of the whole house; later, after a good deal of controversy about how to proceed, they were referred to a select committee of eleven, on which Madison sat. To this select committee were also referred, pro forma, all the amendments proposed by the state ratifying conventions. But the committee reported out Madison's amendments only. The majority had now committed itself to action, and Madison's proposals were briskly moved through the House, over some objections of unseemly haste, echoing similar briskness and similar complaints in the early stages of the ratification of the Constitution itself. Attempts by Anti-Federalists such as Aedanus Burke and Elbridge Gerry to secure consideration of the more fundamental amendments proposed by the state ratifying conventions were courteously but firmly and quickly turned aside.

The objective of amendments, Madison had said, was to "give satisfaction to the doubting part of our fellow-citizens." But they did not give satisfaction. Burke spoke for most of his fellow Anti-Federalists when he contended that Madison's amendments were "very far from giving satisfaction to our constituents; they are not those solid and substantial amendments which the people expect. They are little better than whip-syllabub, frothy and full of wind, formed only to please the palate; or they are like a tub thrown out to a whale to secure the freight of the ship and its peaceable voyage." Samuel Livermore thought Madison's amendments were "no more

---

11. *Debates and Proceedings of the Congress,* p. 441.
12. Ibid., p. 755.

than a pinch of snuff; they went to secure rights never in danger."[13] And when later the amendments went to the states the main opposition to their ratification came not from the friends but from the former enemies of the Constitution, whose opinion the amendments were supposed to placate. Their view, generally speaking, was that expressed by Samuel Chase to John Lamb of New York. "A declaration of rights alone will be of no essential service. Some of the powers must be abridged, or public liberty will be endangered and, in time, destroyed."[14]

Of course, Madison knew that his amendments would not satisfy the hard-core Anti-Federalists. His strategy was rather to isolate them from the large group of common people whose opposition did rest, not on fundamental hostility to the basic design of the Constitution, but on a broad fear that individual liberties were not sufficiently protected. By conciliatory amendments, he told Jefferson, he hoped "to extinguish opposition to the system, or at least break the force of it, by detaching the deluded opponents from the designing leaders."[15] However little the Anti-Federalist leaders ultimately relied on the absence of a bill of rights, too many reams of paper and hours of speaking had been devoted to it to make it now very plausible for them to dismiss a Federalist-sponsored bill of rights as mere froth. Bristling (pleasurably, one supposes) at accusations from the Anti-Federalists of lack of candor, Madison could ask "whether the amendments now proposed are not those most strenuously required by the opponents of the Constitution?" Have not the people been "taught to believe" that the Constitution endangered their liberties and should not be adopted without a bill of rights?[16]

And by whom had they been taught? That liberty had never been in serious danger under the Constitution is what the Federalists had claimed; but under Madison's prodding they were now moderately yielding to their opponents' sensibilities. Those opponents could not expect to make much headway by admitting that the Federalists had been right on the bill of rights issue all along. "It is a fortunate thing," Madison solemnly declared in the House, "that the objection to the Government has been made on the ground I stated; because it will be practicable, on that ground, to obviate the objection,

---

13. Ibid., pp. 745, 775.

14. January 13, 1788, Isaac Leake, *Memoir of the Life and Times of General John Lamb* (Albany: J. Munsell, 1850), p. 310.

15. Letter to Thomas Jefferson, March 29, 1789, Hunt, ed., vol. 5, p. 335. See *Debates of the Congress of the United States*, vol. 1, pp. 432–33.

16. Ibid., p. 746.

so far as to satisfy the public mind that their liberties will be perpetual, and this without endangering any part of the Constitution, which is considered as essential to the existence of the Government by those who promoted its adoption."[17] The Anti-Federalist leaders objected to what Madison had *not* included in his amendment, but they had been neatly boxed in.

In September 1789 Edmund Pendleton wrote to Madison:

> I congratulate you upon having got through the Amendments to the Constitution, as I was very anxious that it should be done before your adjournment, since it will have a good effect in quieting the minds of many well meaning Citizens, tho' I am of opinion that nothing was further from the wish of some, who covered their Opposition to the Government under the masque of uncommon zeal for amendments and to whom a rejection or a delay as a new ground of clamour would have been more agreeable. I own also that I feel some degree of pleasure, in discovering obviously from the whole progress, that the public are indebted for the measure to the friends of Government, whose Elections were opposed under pretense of their being averse to amendments.[18]

My argument thus far is that the primary significance of the Bill of Rights is seen most clearly in what it does not include. Madison's successful strategy was to finish the debate over ratification by pushing forward a set of amendments that almost everyone could accept and that excluded all the Anti-Federalists' fundamental proposals. There is also a more positive and substantial significance. To consider this we need to understand first why there was no bill of rights in or attached to the Constitution as originally drafted. The most obvious answer is that it was only after the convention in Philadelphia had spent three months constructing a government that it occurred to anyone to attach a bill of rights to it. By the time Mason and Gerry did propose a bill of rights on September 12, it was clear to almost everyone that the convention needed to finish its business and put its proposal to the country. It seemed likely, moreover, despite Mason's contention to the contrary, that the drafting of a bill of rights would turn out to be a long and difficult business.

But why was a bill of rights not considered earlier? And why,

---

17. Ibid., p. 433.

18. September 2, 1789, *The Letters and Papers of Edmund Pendleton, 1734–1803*, ed. David John Mays (Charlottesville: University Press of Virginia, 1967), vol. 2, p. 558.

even admitting that it might be difficult to draw up, could it be dispensed with? There is a bewildering diversity of arguments made by defenders of the Constitution to explain why a bill of rights was undesirable or unnecessary. These are not always consistent or very plausible; but at bottom there are a couple of powerful and, I think, deeply compelling arguments.[19] The most widely discussed argument against a federal bill of rights was made by James Wilson in his influential "State House" speech on October 6, 1787. Wilson pointed to the fact that the general government would possess only specifically enumerated powers, unlike the state governments, which possessed broad, general grants of authority. Thus, in the case of the states, "everything which is not reserved is given," but in the case of the general government "everything which is not given is reserved." Once this distinction is understood, the pointlessness of a federal bill of rights emerges:

> for it would have been superfluous and absurd to have stipulated with a federal body of our own creation, that we should enjoy those privileges of which we are not divested, either by the intention or the act that has brought the body into existence. For instance, the liberty of the press, which has been a copious source of declamation and opposition— what control can proceed from the Federal government to shackle or destroy that sacred palladium of national freedom?[20]

Wilson articulated here a fundamental principle of the American Constitution, that the general government possesses only enumerated powers. It is, however, open to the objection that enumerated powers must imply other powers (an implication strengthened by the necessary and proper clause) and that a train of implied powers may lead to encroachments on state prerogatives. Madison made a kind of concession to this argument by proposing in one of his amendments that "the powers not delegated by this Constitution, nor prohibited by it to the States, are reserved to the States respectively." Attempts to insert "expressly" before "delegated," thus restoring the language of the Articles of Confederation and more tightly restraining

---

19. One of the arguments made by the Federalists was that specific restrictions might imply powers not intended to be granted and that a listing of powers might endanger rights not listed. There was enough plausibility in this argument to lead the First Congress to add and the states to ratify what is now the Ninth Amendment.

20. John B. McMaster and Frederick Stone, *Pennsylvania and the Federal Constitution* (Lancaster: Historical Society, Pennsylvania, 1888), pp. 143–44.

federal authority, failed (though the ubiquitous "expressly" proved extremely difficult to eliminate from American political debate). Indeed, the House accepted Charles Carroll's motion to add "or to the people," which was presumably meant to narrow the states' claim to reserved powers.[21] Thus emerged what is now the Tenth Amendment. But this amendment was quite rightly seen by the Anti-Federalists as no substantial concession at all. It merely stated the obvious in a coldly neutral way: that what was not granted was reserved.

Losing the battle of "expressly delegated" was merely the sign of the Anti-Federalists' loss of the battle over the basic character of the Constitution. They threw up, however, a second, less than best, defense against the possibility of unjust enlargement of federal powers, and that was the campaign to give specific protection to especially important or exposed individual rights. This was part of the serious argument for a bill of rights; and Madison's response here was more substantial, as we have seen. The result is the prudent and successful scheme of limited government that we now enjoy in the United States, with both its Constitution and its Bill of Rights. Security is provided at both ends: limited grants of power; protection of individual rights. This scheme is well known enough to require from me little in the way of either explanation or praise. Perhaps a view from the founding might caution us, however, not to exaggerate its benefits. Justice Black to the contrary notwithstanding, it is impossible in any interesting case to define the rights protected in the amendments with sufficient exactness to permit their automatic application. A bill of rights cannot eliminate the need for political judgment, and therewith the risk of abuse. James Iredell, in his reply to George Mason's "Objections" to the Constitution, displayed the ambiguity, for example, of "cruel and unusual punishments" and at the same time the impossibility of exhaustive particularization.[22] Alexander Hamilton defied anyone to give a definition to "liberty of the press" "which should not leave the utmost latitude for evasion." "I hold it to be impracticable; and from this, I infer that its security, whatever fine declarations may be inserted in any constitution respecting it, must altogether depend on public opinion, and on the general spirit of the people and of the government. And here, after all . . . must we seek for the only solid basis of all our rights."[23]

---

21. *Debates of the Congress of the United States*, vol. 1, pp. 436, 761, 767–68.

22. Paul Leicester Ford, *Pamphlets on the Constitution* (Brooklyn, N.Y., 1888), p. 360.

23. *Federalist* 84. "It would be quite as significant to declare that government ought to be free, that taxes ought not to be excessive, etc., as that the liberty of the press ought not to be restrained." The state bills of rights did

It is interesting to consider what our constitutional law would be like today if there had been no Bill of Rights. Its focus would presumably be to a far greater extent than it is today on the powers of the government. We might expect a more searching examination by the Supreme Court of whether federal legislation that seems to conflict with cherished individual liberties is indeed "necessary and proper" to the exercise of granted powers. We might expect a fuller articulation than we usually receive of whether, in Marshall's terms, "the end" aimed at by given legislation "is legitimate." Might this not foster a healthy concern with the problems of *governing*, a healthy sense of responsible self-government?

Doubtless a jurisprudence without a Bill of Rights would also have to find ways of scrutinizing the impact of legislation on the individual. How could that be done? Could the individual "take advantage of a natural right founded in reason," one Anti-Federalist asked; "could he plead it and produce Locke, Sydney, or Montesquieu as authority?"[24] Perhaps he could. One Federalist said that while there was no way to predict in advance what laws may be "necessary and proper," "this we may say—that, in exercising those powers, the Congress cannot legally violate the natural rights of an individual."[25] Another insisted that "no power was given to Congress to infringe on any one of the natural rights of the people by this Constitution; and, should they attempt it without constitutional authority, the act would be a nullity, and could not be enforced."[26] Such views have found expression in the Supreme Court by men who would rest their findings of governmental usurpation squarely on the inherent purposes and limitations of all legitimate, free government. "I do not hesitate to declare," Justice Johnson said in *Fletcher v. Peck*, "that a state does not possess the power of revoking its own grants. But I do it on a general principle, on the reason and nature of things: a principle which will impose laws even on the Deity."[27] And Justice Chase, in *Calder v. Bull,* insisted that

> There are certain vital principles in our free Republican governments, which will determine and overrule an appar-

---

in fact contain many such "ought" statements, which were intended to foster that "spirit of the people" on which Hamilton depends.

24. "Essay by a Farmer," *Maryland Gazette*, February 15, 1788.

25. Essay by "Aristides," *Maryland Journal and Baltimore Advertiser*, March 4, 1788.

26. Theophilus Parsons in the Massachusetts ratifying convention, Elliot, ed., vol. 2, p. 162.

27. 6 Cranch 87, 143 (1810).

ent and flagrant abuse of legislative power; as to authorize manifest injustice by positive law; or to take away that security for personal liberty, or private property, for the protection whereof the government was established. An act of the Legislature (for I cannot call it law) contrary to the great first principles of the social compact, cannot be considered a rightful exercise of legislative authority.[28]

Of course, government *does* "violate" the natural rights of the individual, at least in the sense that it legitimately prevents him from enjoying the fullness of his rights. The question that always has to be asked is whether individual rights have been unnecessarily or unreasonably abridged. Such questions are not easy to answer, with or without a bill of rights. Any formulation of the standard of natural rights is problematical and obscure. But is it much more cloudy or contingent than "cruel and unusual punishment," "excessive bail," or "freedom of the press?" Would the nationalization of civil rights have been less well guided by something like Cardozo's standard of "implicit in the concept of ordered liberty"[29] than it has been by the tortuous reasoning induced by preoccupation with the issue of "incorporation"? Without a bill of rights our courts would probably have developed a kind of common law of individual rights to help to test and limit governmental power. Might the courts thus have been compelled to confront the basic questions that "substantive due process," "substantive equal protection," "clear and present danger," etc. have permitted them to conceal, even from themselves? Is it possible that without a bill of rights we might suffer less of that ignoble battering between absolutistic positivism and flaccid historicism that characterizes our constitutional law today?

I stray from my principal concern, though not, I think, from the spirit of the argument I am examining. The basis of the Federalist argument was that the whole notion of a bill of rights as generally understood is alien to American government. It was derived from Britain, where there was no written constitution and where individual liberties were secured by marking out limits on royal prerogative. Here the Constitution itself is a bill of rights, the Federalists often argued, meaning that it was derived from the people themselves, that it provided for a sound system of representation, and that it granted limited powers to a balanced government. Quoting from the opening of the preamble, *Publius* said, "Here is a better recognition of popular rights than volumes of aphorisms which make the princi-

---

28. 3 Dallas 386, 387 (1798).
29. Palko v. Connecticut, 302 U.S. 319 (1937).

pal figure in several of our State bills of rights and which would sound much better in a treatise of ethics than in a constitution of government."[30] This argument shows the redundancy of any declaration of the right of people to establish their own government, but it does not reach the chief problem of popular government, which is majority tyranny. Protecting individuals and minorities against unjust action by the majority, or the government reflecting the wishes of the majority, is a major benefit of a bill of rights in the Anti-Federalist view. Like most Federalists, Madison never denied this, but he did not think it very reliable. The solution has to be found at a deeper level, in the functioning of a large, differentiated commercial society. And so far as the possible dangers from government are concerned, protection must be found in the very constitution of that government. Thus, Thomas McKean told his Pennsylvania colleagues that although a bill of rights "can do no harm, I believe, yet it is an unnecessary instrument, for in fact the whole plan of government is nothing more than a bill of rights—a declaration of the people in what manner they choose to be governed."[31] In the words of another Federalist:

> Where the powers to be exercised, under a certain system, are in themselves consistent with the people's liberties, are legally defined, guarded and ascertained, and ample provision made for bringing condign punishment to all such as shall overstep the limitations of the law—it is hard to conceive of a greater security for the rights of the people.[32]

But admitting that a bill of rights was not necessary, what harm could it do? "A bill of rights may be summed up in a few words," Patrick Henry told his fellow Virginians. "What do they tell us?—That our rights are reserved. Why not say so? Is it because it will consume too much paper?"[33] By 1789 Madison conceded this; he told Congress that we have nothing to lose and something to gain by amendments to secure individual rights. Why not concede the point earlier? Madison admitted that "some policy had been made use of, perhaps, by gentlemen on both sides of the question."[34] On the Federalist side, an unyielding resistance to a bill of rights is to be explained by a fear that it would divert the campaign for ratification of the Constitution into what surely would have been a long and circuitous

---

30. *Federalist* 84.
31. McMaster and Stone, *Pennsylvania and the Federal Constitution*, p. 252.
32. Essay by "Atticus," *Boston Independent Chronicle*, November 28, 1787.
33. Elliot, *Debates in the State Conventions*, p. 448.
34. *Debates of the Congress of the United States*, vol. 1, p. 436.

route to amendments, a route along which the essentials of the Constitution would have been extremely difficult to protect. As long as the Constitution remained unratified, Madison wrote to George Eve in 1783, "I opposed all previous alterations as calculated to throw the States into dangerous conventions, and to furnish the secret enemies of the Union with an opportunity of promoting its dissolution."[35]

There was also, I think, a deeper and more positive reason for what appears to many scholars a rigid and defensive opposition to a bill of rights. The Federalists were determined that Americans not be diverted, in a more fundamental sense, from the main task of providing themselves with effective government. Jefferson, writing from France, admitted to Madison that bills of rights have an occasional tendency to cramp government in its useful exertions; but he thought that such inconvenience was short-lived, moderate, and reparable.[36] The friends of the Constitution, on the other hand, feared that an undue concern with rights might be fatal to American liberty. "Liberty may be endangered by the abuses of liberty," *Publius* warned, "as well as by the abuses of power, and the former rather than the latter is apparently most to be apprehended by the United States."[37] James Iredell saw in the old state bills of rights evidence that "the minds of men then [were] so warmed with their exertions in the cause of liberty as to lean too much perhaps toward a jealousy of power to repose a proper confidence in their own government."[38] The Federalists feared that Americans were all too wont to fall into easy and excessive criticism of all proposals for effective government. They saw in the arguments against the Constitution a tendency to drift into the shallow view that Americans could somehow get along without government—without the tough decisions, the compulsion, the risk that government must always involve. The main political business of the American people, they thought, was and would continue to be not to protect themselves against political power but to accept the responsibility of governing themselves. The Federalists did not deny that government, once established, may need protecting against, but they tried to make sure that that would always be seen

---

35. Letter to George Eve, January 2, 1789, Hunt, *Writings of James Madison*, p. 318.

36. Letter to James Madison, March 15, 1789, Julian Boyd, ed., *The Papers of Thomas Jefferson* (Princeton: Princeton University Press, 1958), vol. 14, p. 660.

37. *Federalist* 63.

38. Ford, *Pamphlets on the Constitution*, pp. 359–60.

for the secondary consideration it is. The lesson that the furor over a bill of rights threatened to obscure was, in Edmund Pendleton's words, that "there is no quarrel between government and liberty. The war is between government and licentiousness, faction, turbulence, and other violations of the rules of society, to preserve liberty."[39]

It was altogether appropriate, from this Federalist point of view, that the Bill of Rights should have emerged from a separate set of deliberations, occurring after the Constitution had been framed and accepted and its government set in motion. Even at this point, however, the Federalist concession was less than might at first appear. We have seen that by taking the initiative for amendments Madison confined discussion to a bill of rights (plus a few, noncontroversial changes) and excluded that whole set of major Anti-Federalist proposals that would limit the powers of the general government or otherwise change the basic design of the Constitution. We must now see that Madison also took a narrow view of the meaning of a bill of rights as such, with the aim of preserving not only the constitutional scheme but also the vigor and capacity of government.

In their extraordinary exchange of views between 1787 and 1789, Thomas Jefferson pressed on Madison his opinion in favor of a bill of rights.[40] But the significant fact is not that Madison came to favor a bill of rights—he said truthfully that he had always favored it under the right circumstances. What is significant is the time he chose to move for a bill of rights, the kinds of rights protected, and the form the Bill of Rights took.

> I will own that I never considered this provision [of a bill of rights] so essential to the Federal Constitution as to make it improper to ratify it, until such an amendment was added; at the same time, I always conceived, that in a certain form, and to a certain extent, such a provision was neither improper nor altogether useless.[41]

Jefferson repeatedly described the kinds of protection he wanted in terms like the following: "a bill of rights providing clearly and without the aid of sophisms for freedom of religion, freedom of press, protection against standing armies, restriction against monop-

---

39. Elliot, *Debates in the State Conventions*, p. 37.

40. The main letters in this exchange are Madison to Jefferson, October 24, 1787, October 17, 1788, December 8, 1788; and Jefferson to Madison, December 20, 1787, July 31, 1788, March 15, 1789. These are conveniently available in Boyd, *Papers of Thomas Jefferson*, and in Schwartz, *A Documentary History*.

41. *Debates of the Congress of the United States*, vol. 1, p. 436.

olies, the eternal and unremitting force of the habeas corpus laws, and trials by jury in all matters of fact triable by the law of the land and not by the law of Nations."[42] Three of these amounted to substantial restrictions on the power of government to act—the restrictions on monopolies, standing armies, and the suspension of habeas corpus; Jefferson clearly thought that they were vital barriers against governmental tyranny. It is equally clear that Madison consistently opposed all such amendments as obstacles to effective government. He did not include them in his original proposals (though there had been such proposals from the state ratifying conventions), and he and the Federalist majority beat down all attempts to secure such amendments.

There is, moreover, a deeper stratum in Madison's concern to prevent bills of rights from inhibiting government. The Anti-Federalists' advocacy of a bill of rights was concerned with more than specific protections; their overriding concern here was to make sure that government was rooted firmly in natural rights and justice. One of the confusions to the modern ear in the debate over the Bill of Rights and in the language of the old state bills of rights is the jumbling together of natural rights, civil rights, basic principles of justice, maxims of government, and specific legal protections. The state bills of rights were full of "oughts" and general principles. The Virginia Declaration of Rights of 1776 provides, for example: "That all men are by nature equally free and independent, and have certain inherent rights, of which, when they enter into a state of society, they cannot, by any compact deprive or divest their posterity; namely, the enjoyment of life and liberty, with the means of acquiring and possessing property, and pursuing and obtaining happiness and safety." Again, "Government is, or ought to be, instituted for the common benefit, protection, and security of the people, nation or community." The legislative and executive powers "should be separate and distinct from the judiciary"; "elections . . . ought to be free"; jury trial in civil cases "is preferable to any other, and ought to be held sacred."

Bills of rights were often described by their advocates as having as their purpose "to secure to every member of society those unalienable rights which ought not to be given up to any government."[43] Yet bills of rights, as we know them today, do not protect natural rights. And there seems to be something empty in the declarations of natural

---

42. Jefferson to Madison, December 20, 1787, Boyd, *Papers of Thomas Jefferson*, p. 440.

43. Elliot, *Debates in the State Conventions*, p. 137.

rights in a Constitution. That was the Federalist view. Thus, the acerbic Dr. Rush praised the framers for not disgracing the Constitution with a bill of rights: "As we enjoy all our natural rights from a pre-occupancy, antecedent to the social state," it would be "absurd to frame a formal declaration that our natural rights are acquired from ourselves."[44] The Anti-Federalists insisted, on the contrary, that the main purpose of a bill of rights is to provide an explicit set of standards in terms of which a government can be judged and, when necessary, resisted. A good bill of rights is a book in which a people can read the fundamental principles of their political being. "Those rights characterize the man, essentially the true republican, the citizen of this continent; their enumeration, in head of the new constitution, can inspire and conserve the affection for the native country, they will be the first lesson of the young citizens becoming men, to sustain the dignity of their being. . . ."[45] This is what explains the affirmation of natural rights, the "oughts," the unenforceable generality of the state bills of rights and of many of the Anti-Federalists' proposals. In Patrick Henry's words:

> There are certain maxims by which every wise and enlightened people will regulate their conduct. There are certain political maxims which no free people ought ever to abandon—maxims of which the observance is essential to the security of happiness. . . . We have one, sir, *that all men are by nature free and independent, and have certain inherent rights, of which, when they enter into society, they cannot by any compact deprive or divest their posterity.* We have a set of maxims of the same spirit, which must be beloved by every friend to liberty, to virtue, to mankind: our bill of rights contains those admirable maxims.[46]

This was the reason that the state bills of rights preceded their constitutions and could be described as the foundation of government. Edmund Randolph put it as well as anyone in his comment on the Virginia bill of rights:

> In the formation of this bill of rights two objectives were contemplated: one, that the legislature should not in their acts violate any of those cannons [sic]; the other, that in all the revolutions of time, of human opinion, and of govern-

---

44. McMaster and Stone, *Pennsylvania and the Federal Constitution*, p. 295.

45. *Virginia Independent Chronicle*, June 25, 1788. See *An Additional Number of Letters from the Federal Farmer to the Republican* (New York, 1788), p. 144.

46. Elliot, *Debates in the State Conventions*, p. 137; see essay by "A Delegate" in *Virginia Independent Chronicle*, June 18, June 25, 1787.

ment, a perpetual standard should be erected around which the people might rally, and by a notorious record be forever admonished to be watchful, firm and virtuous. The corner stone being thus laid, a constitution, delegating portions of power to different organs under certain modifications, was of course to be raised upon it.[47]

The problem with a bill of rights as a "perpetual standard" or a set of maxims to which people might rally is that it may tend to undermine stable and effective government. The Virginia Declaration of Rights asserted that free government depends on "a frequent recurrence to fundamental principles." The Federalists doubted that. Recurrence to first principles does not substitute for well-constituted and effective government. In some cases, it may interfere. Does a constant emphasis on unalienable natural rights foster good citizenship or a sense of community? Does a constant emphasis on popular sovereignty foster responsible government? Does a constant emphasis on a right to abolish government foster the kind of popular support that any government needs? The Federalists did not doubt that these first principles are true, that they may be resorted to, that they provide the ultimate source and justification of government. The problem is that these principles, while true, can also endanger government. Even rational and well-constituted governments need and deserve a presumption of legitimacy and permanence.[48] A bill of rights that presses these first principles to the fore tends to deprive government of that presumption.

For this reason, I think, Madison drastically limited the kind of standard-setting, maxim-describing, teaching function of bills of rights that the Anti-Federalists thought so important. In the hands of Madison and the majority of the First Congress, the Bill of Rights became what it is today: not the broad principles establishing the ends and limits of government, not "maxims" to be learned and looked up to by generations of Americans, not statements of those first principles to which a healthy people should, according to the Virginia Declaration of Rights, frequently resort; but specific protections of traditional civil rights.

With two exceptions, all the "oughts," all the statements of general principle, were excluded from Madison's original proposals—and these two were themselves eliminated before the House of Representatives finished its work. One of Madison's amendments would have declared that the powers delegated by the Constitution

---

47. Schwartz, A Documentary History, p. 249.
48. See Federalist 49.

"are appropriated to the departments to which they are respectively distributed" so that no department shall exercise powers vested in another.[49] This was rather weakly defended by Madison in the House, where it was accepted; but it was rejected by the Senate, and no one seems to have regretted its loss. The second and most important residue of the old maxims was Madison's first proposal, which was a statement that all power derives from the people, that government ought to be instituted for the benefit of the people, and that the people have a right to change the government when they find it adverse or inadequate to its purposes.[50] This proposal was later reduced by a committee (on which Madison sat) to a brief and ill-fitting preface to the preamble ("Government being intended for the benefit of the people, and the rightful establishment thereof being derived from their authority alone. We the People of the United States. . . ."). It was finally dropped altogether as a result of the acceptance of Roger Sherman's proposal to have the amendments added at the end of the Constitution. The separation of powers amendment was to be given a separate article of its own, a clear breach of the economy of the Constitution; yet there was no other place for it. Even more striking is the awkward placing of Madison's first proposal prior to the preamble and the intolerable grammatical cumbersomeness of the Committee of Eleven version. Both these drafting inelegancies derived from Madison's determination to fit all of the amendments into the existing text of the Constitution.

Virtually all the advocates of a bill of rights assumed that it should come at the head of the Constitution; Madison wanted it in the body; it came finally at the tail.[51] Madison's argument was that "there is a neatness and propriety in incorporating the amendments

---

49. *Debates of the Congress of the United States*, vol. 1, pp. 435–36.

50. Ibid., pp. 433–34. Already this proposal significantly modified the language of the Virginia Declaration of Rights and the proposal of the Virginia convention, from which it was drawn, in the direction of supporting government. It does not begin, as the earlier versions do, with any declarations of natural rights of individuals; Madison's beginning point is already a society. The "inherent rights of which man cannot be divested," of the Virginia Declaration of Rights, are here converted into "benefits of the people" for the sake of which government is instituted. The right "to reform, alter or abolish government" (in the Virginia Declaration of Rights) or the rejection of the "slavish doctrine of non-resistance" (in the proposals of the Virginia ratifying convention) is moderated to a right to "reform or change government."

51. This debate appears in *Debates of the Congress of the United States*, vol. 1, pp. 707–17.

into the Constitution itself; in that case the system will remain uniform and entire. . . ." He wanted to avoid a form that would emphasize the *distinction,* common in the states, between the Constitution and the Bill of Rights. On the other hand, Roger Sherman, who was far from keen on having amendments at all, argued that to try to interweave the amendments with the Constitution was to mix brass, iron, and clay; "The Constitution is the act of the people and ought to remain entire." George Clymer supported Sherman; the amendments should be kept separate so that the Constitution "would remain a monument to justify those who made it; by a comparison the world would discover the perfection of the original and the superfluity of the amendments."

Madison sought to secure his amendments against the possibility of their being held merely redundant and ineffective; he wanted them to "stand upon as good a foundation as the original work." When he said that a separate set of amendments would "create unfavourable comparisons," he was concerned to avoid a denigration of the amendments. But neither did he wish to elevate them to a distinct, primary position. His proposed form was designed to secure protection for the most widely agreed rights that would be both authoritative and inconspicuous. Sherman had his way, for reasons that do not fully emerge from the report of the debate. Ironically, the result seems to have been exactly the opposite of what Sherman intended, and yet to have gone beyond what Madison wanted. Separate listing of the first ten amendments has elevated rather than weakened their status. The overall result is a Bill of Rights that is much less than the broad, preambular statement of basic principles that the enthusiastic proponents of bills of rights had in mind. At the same time it is—or has in this century become—rather more significant (not less, as Sherman and his friends wanted) than scattered protections of individual rights inserted into the Constitution would have been.

What can we say in conclusion in answer to our original questions? What is the significance of the absence of a bill of rights from the original Constitution and of its subsequent addition?

First, the basic justification for the absence of a bill of rights was that the main business of a free people is to establish and conduct good government; that is where the security of freedom must be sought. For the Americans in the 1780s, still warm with the ultimate truths of natural rights and revolution, the rhetoric of bills of rights might serve as a delusive substitute for the hard tasks of self-government.

Yet, second, bills of rights are an appropriate second step. Governments do tend to abuse their powers; and while the main protections are to be found in representation and social and political checks, a bill of rights can provide useful supplemental security.

Third, the initiative seized by Madison in the First Congress enabled the Federalists to complete their ratification victory by using amendments to better secure individual rights as the vehicle for decisively (if not finally) laying to rest the major Anti-Federal objections to the powers of the general government.

Fourth, the traditional notion of a bill of rights was drastically narrowed by largely eliminating the usual declarations of first principles, frequent resort to which Madison thought caused serious harm to government by disturbing that healthy crust of prejudice needed to support even the most rational government.

At the same time, however, and finally, the civil rights that were secured by the new Bill of Rights were limited and defined enough to be capable of effective (though not unproblematical) enforcement. The oft-described transformation of the moralistic "ought nots" of the old bills of rights into the legal "shall nots" of the United States Bill of Rights *is* a true and important part of the story. But I hope it is now clear that that transformation was possible only as a result of a drastic narrowing and lowering deliberately intended to secure the central place for the establishment and conduct of free government as the main business of a free people.

Yet there is still in our Bill of Rights an echo of the earlier declarations of natural rights and maxims of well-constituted free governments. This is especially true of the First Amendment, which might be described as a statement in matter-of-fact legal form of the great end of free government, to secure the private sphere, and the great means for preserving such a government, to foster an alert and enlightened citizenry. In the form of a protection of civil liberties, then, the First Amendment echoes the great principles of natural liberty and free government that played so large a role in the state bills of rights.[52] The preamble contains a similar echo of the basic principle of human equality and popular sovereignty. The Bill of Rights provides a fitting close to the parentheses around the Constitution that the preamble opens. But the substance is a design of government with powers to act and a structure arranged to make it act wisely and responsibly. It is in that design, not in its preamble or its epilogue, that the security of American civil and political liberty lies.

---

52. It is of course significant in this connection that the First Amendment is addressed to Congress (the structure of the Bill of Rights is provided by the traditional legislative, executive, judicial sequence) and that for that reason, and because of the breadth of its terms, its interpretation and enforcement are unusually problematical.

PART TWO

Slavery and Race in American Politics

6
Slavery and the Moral Foundations of the American Republic

"It is refreshing," said one of the dissenters in the case of *Dred Scott v. Sandford*, "to turn to the early incidents of our history and learn wisdom from the acts of the great men who have gone to their account."[1] It is a common opinion today, however, that, admirable as the American founders may be in other respects, in their response to the institution of Negro slavery their example is one to be lived down rather than lived up to. A good expression of this opinion has recently come from the distinguished American historian John Hope Franklin. We need to face the fact, Franklin contends, that the founders "betray[ed] the ideals to which they gave lip service." They failed to take an unequivocal stand against slavery. They regarded "human bondage and human dignity" as less important than "their own political and economic independence." They spoke "eloquently at one moment for the brotherhood of man and in the next moment den[ied] it to their black brothers." They "degrad[ed] the human spirit by equating five black men with three white men." The moral legacy of the founders is shameful and harmful. "Having created a tragically flawed revolutionary doctrine and a Constitution that did *not* bestow the blessings of liberty on its posterity, the Founding Fathers set the stage for every succeeding generation of Americans to apologize, compromise, and temporize on those principles of liberty that were supposed to be the very foundation of our system of government and way of life."[2]

This view of the American founding—that the founders excluded

This essay appeared in Robert H. Horwitz, ed., *The Moral Foundations of the American Republic*, 3rd ed. (Charlottesville, Va.: University Press of Virginia, 1986). It is reprinted with permission from the University Press of Virginia.

1. Scott v. Sandford 19 How 393, 545 (1857) (Justice McLean).
2. "The Moral Legacy of the Founding Fathers," *University of Chicago Magazine*, Summer 1975, pp. 10–13.

the Negroes from the "rights of man" expressed in the Declaration of Independence and sanctioned slavery and Negro inferiority in the Constitution—is a view that the radical abolitionists, from whom John Hope Franklin descends, share with their proslavery antagonists. Indeed, one of the best, and surely most authoritative, expressions of this view came in the opinion of Chief Justice Roger B. Taney in the famous Supreme Court case of *Dred Scott v. Sandford* in 1857, in which the Supreme Court, for the second time in its history, held an act of Congress unconstitutional, and in which Taney tried to secure once and for all the place of slavery under the Constitution. I want to examine Taney's carefully worked out reasoning, for there one can confront most clearly what is today the dominant opinion about the founders and slavery.

Dred Scott was a slave owned by a Doctor Emerson, a surgeon in the United States Army. In 1834 Scott was taken by his master from Missouri to Rock Island, Illinois, where they lived for about two years, and from there to Fort Snelling in the federal "Louisiana territory," where they lived for another couple of years before returning to Missouri. On Emerson's death Scott tried to purchase his freedom from Mrs. Emerson. Failing in that, he sued in the Missouri courts for his freedom, on the ground that he had become free by virtue of his residence in a free state and a free territory. He won in the lower court, but the decision was reversed on appeal. The Supreme Court of Missouri, abandoning eight Missouri precedents and departing from the then almost universal adherence of Southern courts to the principle "once free, always free," held that, whatever his condition in Illinois and in federal territory, Scott was a slave upon his return to Missouri.

On Mrs. Emerson's remarriage, Scott became the property of her brother, John Sandford, a citizen of New York; and this enabled Scott to sue for his freedom in federal court under the provision of the Constitution that gives federal courts jurisdiction in cases between citizens of different states. He lost in the lower court and appealed to the Supreme Court, which in 1857 finally handed down its opinion— or rather its opinions, for all nine justices expressed their opinions, most at considerable length. I will be concerned here only with the opinion "of the court" given by Chief Justice Taney.

Taney held, in the first place, that because he was a Negro, Scott was not and could not be a citizen of the United States (whether he was free or not) and could therefore not sue in the federal courts on the grounds he had chosen. (I pass over Taney's dubious assumption that for a citizen of a state to be entitled to sue under the diversity clause he must establish citizenship of the United States.) Taney held, in the second place, that the federal act under which Scott claimed freedom, the Missouri Compromise Act of 1820 outlawing slavery in the northern part of the Louisiana Purchase, was unconstitutional: for Congress to prohibit slavery in federal territory was to deprive slave-owning citizens who might move into that territory of their property without due process of law.

These two holdings are the conclusions of two lines of argument, one concerning the status of Negroes and the other concerning the status of slavery, that provide my two themes. Taney emphasized throughout his opinion that he was merely giving effect to the Constitution. It was not his business to read into the Constitution the more favorable views toward the Negro that had emerged since the time of the founding. Actually, as Lincoln correctly argued, opinion about Negroes had hardened rather than softened in the seventy years since the adoption of the Constitution.[3] But more important is the fact that Taney's reading of the Constitution and the views of the founders was wrong, except perhaps in one very important respect.

Taney takes up first the question of Negro citizenship, then the question of Negro slavery; but it will be clearer if I reverse the order and look first at slavery. According to Taney, the founders assumed the legitimacy of slavery; and back of that was a universal opinion of the inferiority of the Negro race.[4] Negroes "had for more than a century before been regarded as beings of an inferior order; and altogether unfit to associate with the white race, either in social or political relations; and so far inferior, that they had no rights which the white man was bound to respect; and that the negro might justly and lawfully be reduced to slavery for his benefit." "No one thought," Taney said, "of disputing" such opinions. Negroes "were never thought of or spoken of except as property."

Only on such a basis, it seemed to Taney, could the framers of the Declaration of Independence be absolved from utter hyprocrisy. They *said* that "all men are created equal and are endowed by their Creator with certain unalienable rights." Yet they were, many of them, slaveholders; and they certainly did not destroy slavery. But there was no hypocrisy, because the writers of the Declaration "perfectly understood the meaning of the language they used, and how it would be understood by others; and they knew it would not, in any part of the civilized world, be supposed to embrace the negro

---

3. "The Dred Scott Decision," Speech at Springfield, June 26, 1857, in Roy P. Basler, ed., *Abraham Lincoln: His Speeches and Writings* (New York: World Publishing Co., 1946), p. 359.

4. Scott v. Sandford 19 How 407–10 (1857).

race, which, by common consent, had been excluded from civilized governments and the family of nations, and doomed to slavery." The men of that age (that is, the white men) simply did not regard Negroes as included among the "all men" who are, according to the Declaration of Independence, "created equal"; and, Taney concluded, "no one misunderstood them."

This whole argument—and I repeat, it is identical to the common view today—is a gross calumny on the founders. The truth is almost the exact opposite of Taney's account. The founders understood quite clearly that Negroes, like men everywhere, were created equal and were endowed with unalienable rights. They did not say that all men were actually secured in the *exercise* of their rights or that they had the power to provide such security; but there was no doubt about the *rights*. Far from it being true that "negroes were never thought of except as property," not only Negroes but slaves were very frequently spoken of and treated as persons. All of the constitutional provisions relating to slaves, for example, refer to them as persons. And while slaves were typically deprived of *civil* rights, they were regarded as persons under criminal law. As rational and, to some degree, morally responsible human beings, they were held capable of committing crimes, and they were protected by the law—in principle and surprisingly often in practice—against crimes committed against them. In the first three or four decades of our history, the injustice of slavery was very generally acknowledged, not merely in the North but in the South and particularly in Southern courts.

Since this is likely to be unfamiliar territory to most readers, let me give a couple of examples.

In 1820 the superior court in Mississippi was confronted with the question, there being no positive legislation covering the matter, whether the killing of a slave was murder under the common law.[5] The court held that it was; and this was the usual view of Southern courts that considered this question. The Mississippi judge began by emphasizing that "because individuals may have been deprived of many of their rights by society, it does not follow that they have been deprived of all their rights." The slave "is still a human being, and possesses all those rights, of which he is not deprived by the positive provisions of the law. . . ." Since the common law definition of murder is the taking away of the life of a reasonable creature with malice aforethought and since a slave is a reasonable being, such a killing of a slave is murder.

Slavery is the creature, Southern as well as Northern judges said

---

5. State v. Jones 1 Miss 83 (1820).

again and again, of positive law only; it has no support in natural law or in transcendent principles of justice. Yet slavery existed; it was lawful in the Southern states. Even when the judges were giving effect to the positive law of slavery (which they had a clear duty to do), they typically acknowledged the injustice of the institution.

In a Supreme Court case fifteen years before *Dred Scott*, *Prigg v. Pennsylvania* (1842), the Supreme Court upheld the constitutionality of the Fugitive Slave Act of 1793, which implemented the fugitive slave clause of the Constitution; the Court held that this federal power was exclusive, thereby invalidating state "personal liberty laws," which had been passed in a number of Northern states to try to give greater protection than the federal law provided to Negroes claimed as fugitive slaves.[6] The opinion was written by a strong antislavery man, Joseph Story, and many of Story's friends wondered how he could make such a decision. Story replied that his first obligation was to the law but that, in any case, he thought his opinion a great "triumph of freedom."[7] It was a triumph of freedom mainly because, while upholding the Fugitive Slave law, Story took the opportunity to stress that slavery is a mere creature of positive law and has no support in natural law. "The state of slavery is deemed to be," in Story's words, "a mere municipal regulation, founded upon and limited to the range of the territorial laws." That means that the presumption is always against slavery, even while provisions of the positive law protecting slavery are being enforced.

The same view was common in the South. Indeed, contrary to Taney's claim that no one questioned the legitimacy of slavery, nothing was more common than Southern judges giving public utterance to the excruciating agony of trying to reconcile the law that protected slavery with the principle of justice that condemns it. One of the most interesting of these cases is an 1829 North Carolina case, *State v. Mann*, where the court held that a master cannot commit a legal battery upon his slave.[8] The court had held earlier that a white person could be punished for assault and battery against someone else's slave.[9] But the law cannot protect the slave, Judge Ruffin held, against his master, even in case of a wanton, cruel, senseless beating. Ruffin was offered by counsel the analogy of parent and child or

---

6. Prigg v. Pennsylvania 16 Pet 539, 611 (1842); compare Taney's different view, 628.

7. William W. Story, ed., *Life and Letters of Joseph Story* (Boston: Charles C. Little and James Brown, 1851), vol. 2, pp. 390 ff.

8. State v. Mann 13 N.C. 263 (1829).

9. State v. Hale 9 N.C. 582 (1823).

master and apprentice, where the authority of the superior is limited and supervised by law. He reluctantly, but surely correctly, rejected the analogy on the ground that the end of these relations is the good and happiness of the child or the apprentice, whereas in U.S. slavery the end is nothing but the profit of the master. It is the wrongness of slavery that makes it impossible to limit it. "We cannot allow the right of the master to be brought into discussion in the courts of justice." To question that right is to deny it, and that cannot be the business of a judge in a slave state.

> The slave, to remain a slave, must be made sensible that there is no appeal from his master. . . . I most freely confess sense of the harshness of this proposition; I feel it as deeply as any man can; and as a principle of moral right every person in his retirement must repudiate it. But in the actual condition of things it must be so. There is no remedy. . . . It constitutes the curse of slavery to both the bond and free portion of our population. But it is inherent in the relation of master and slave.

I should add that ten years later, nevertheless, Ruffin upheld a conviction of murder in the case of an especially brutal, but probably not premeditated, killing by a master of his own slave.[10]

Another kind of case that was common in the Southern courts was like *Dred Scott;* it arose where a person who had been a slave but who had been taken to reside in a free state and then returned to a slave state sued in the courts of the latter for his freedom. As I have said, in such a case the Southern courts held (at least until the 1840s or 1850s) that such a person was free. Once the chains of slavery enforced by positive law are broken, they can never be restored.

A slave, Lydia, was taken in 1807 by her master from Missouri to free Indiana, where he registered her as his servant under Indiana's gradual emancipation law. He sold his right to her but when her new master brought her back to Missouri, the court there upheld her claim to freedom.[11] The rights of her master had been destroyed in Indiana, "and we are not aware of any law of this state which can or does bring into operation the right of slavery when once destroyed." Can it be thought, the judge asked, that "the noxious atmosphere of this state, without any express law for the purpose, clamped down her newly forged chains of slavery, after the old ones were destroyed? For the honor of our country, we cannot for a moment admit,

---

10. State v. Hoover 4 Dev & Bat (N.C.) 365 (1839).
11. Rankin v. Lydia 2 AK Marshall (Ky.) 470 (1820).

that the bare treading of its soil, is thus dangerous, even to the degraded African."

The American founders and their immediate descendants, North and South, not only believed in but emphasized the wrongness of slavery, at the same time that they wrestled with the fact of slavery and the enormous difficulty of getting rid of it. It was a fact; it seemed for the time being a necessity; but it was a curse—the curse of an unavoidable injustice.

It is true, as Taney said, that Negroes were thought to be inferior to whites; but it is not true that this was thought to justify slavery. In a famous section of his *Notes on the State of Virginia*, published in 1784, Thomas Jefferson reflected on Negroes and Negro slavery in terms which are today generally found offensive and which are in consequence usually distorted and misunderstood.[12] Proceeding in the spirit of the eighteenth-century student of natural history, and emphasizing the shameful lack of systematic study of this subject, Jefferson examined the differences between the races. He thought that the blacks "participate more of sensation than reflection." He judged them inferior to whites in physical beauty, in reason, and in imagination, though in many physical attributes and in what he called "endowments of the heart," or the "moral sense," they are equal. Jefferson did conclude that this inferiority was an obstacle to Negro emancipation; but the reason was not that it makes Negroes less entitled to liberty than whites or that their enslavement is in some way just—Jefferson emphatically and consistently held the contrary. He would have agreed fully with Lincoln's view that "in some respects [a Negro woman] certainly is not my equal, but in her natural right to eat the bread she earns with her own hands without asking leave of anyone else, she is my equal, and the equal of all others."[13] Negro inferiority hindered emancipation in Jefferson's view, not because it justified slavery, but because it increased the difficulty of knowing how to deal with Negroes, once freed. Before pursuing this, however, we need to return to Taney's defense of slavery in the Constitution.

Taney held that Congress cannot prohibit slavery in federal territory: "an Act of Congress which deprives a citizen of the United States of his liberty or property, merely because he came himself or brought his property into a particular Territory of the United States,

---

12. *Notes on the State of Virginia*, Query 14, in Adrienne Koch and William Peden, eds., *The Life and Selected Writings of Thomas Jefferson* (New York: Modern Library, 1944).

13. Lincoln, "The Dred Scott Decision," p. 360.

and who had committed no offense against the laws, could hardly be dignified with the name of due process of law." Nor, Taney contended (and this is crucial and the point on which Taney abandoned both federal and state precedents), is there any difference between property in slaves and other property. In fact, he said, "the right of property in a slave is distinctly and expressly affirmed in the Constitution."[14] These words are striking: if one had to think of two adverbs that do *not* describe the way the Constitution acknowledged slavery, he could not do better than "distinctly and expressly."

No form of the word *slave* appears in the Constitution, and one would not know from the text alone that it was concerned with slavery at all. Today's beginning law students, I am told, are generally not aware that there are three provisions of the Constitution relating to slavery. This is testimony to the skill with which the framers wrote. Some concessions to slavery were thought to be necessary in order to secure the Union, with its promise of a broad and long-lasting foundation for freedom; the problem was to make the minimum concessions consistent with that end, to express them in language that would not sanction slavery, and so far as possible to avoid blotting a free Constitution with the stain of slavery. Frederick Douglass described it this way:

> I hold that the Federal Government was never, in its essence, anything but an anti-slavery government. Abolish slavery tomorrow, and not a sentence or syllable of the Constitution need be altered. It was purposely so framed as to give no claim, no sanction to the claim, of property in man. If in its origin slavery had any relation to the government, it was only as the scaffolding to the magnificent structure, to be removed as soon as the building was completed.[15]

"Scaffolding" catches the intention exactly: support of slavery strong enough to allow the structure to be built, but unobtrusive enough to fade from view when the job was done.

Let us look at the provisions. Article I, sec. 2(3) provides, in a masterpiece of circumlocution: "Representatives and direct Taxes shall be apportioned among the several States which may be included within this Union, according to their respective Numbers, which shall be determined by adding to the whole Number of free Persons, including those bound to Service for a Term of Years, and excluding

---

14. 19 How 450–51 (1857).

15. "Address for the Promotion of Colored Enlistments," July 6, 1863, in Philip S. Foner, ed., *The Life and Writings of Frederick Douglass* (New York: International Publishers, 1950), vol. 3, p. 365.

Indians not taxed, three fifths of all other Persons." "All other Persons" are slaves. Thus in counting population for purposes of determining the number of representatives and also apportioning land and poll taxes, five slaves count as three free persons. What this provision signifies in principle is extremely complex, and I will not exhaust the matter here.[16] The question came up in the Constitutional Convention in the course of a debate over whether numbers or wealth is the proper basis of representation. That issue was resolved, or avoided, by use of Madison's suggestion that numbers are in fact a good index to wealth. In the case of slaves, however, that is not so clear, partly because the productivity of slaves is thought to be lower than that of free men, so some kind of discount seemed appropriate.

This line of reasoning is supported by recalling that the three-fifths rule originated under the Articles of Confederation as a way of apportioning population for purposes of laying requisitions on the states. Suggestions that the three-fifths rule implies a lack of full humanity in the slave, while not without some basis, are wide of the main point. The three-fifths clause is more a way of measuring wealth than of counting human beings represented in government; wealth can claim to be the basis for apportioning representation and is of course the basis for apportioning direct taxes. Given the limited importance of direct taxation, the provision was understood to be a bonus for the Southern slave states. That gives the common argument against the three-fifths clause an unusual twist. While it may be that the provision "degrades the human spirit by equating five black men [more correctly, five slaves] with three white men," it has to be noted that the Southerners would have been glad to count slaves on a one-for-one basis. The concession to slavery here was not in somehow paring the slave down to three-fifths but in counting him for as much as three-fifths of a free person.

Regarding the second constitutional provision relating to slavery, Justice Taney said, "the right to trade in [slave property], like an ordinary article of merchandise and property, was guaranteed to the citizens of the United States, in every State that might desire it, for twenty years."[17] Clearly this is a major concession to slavery. It protects not merely an exiting slave population but the creation of new slaves. Practically, it allowed a substantial augmentation of the slave population and thus, of course, of the slave problem.

Yet the concession is less than Taney suggests. Even on the

---

16. See Donald L. Robinson, *Slavery in the Structure of American Politics, 1765–1820* (New York: Harcourt Brace Jovanovich, 1971), chaps. 4, 5.

17. 19 How 451 (1857).

basis of Taney's account, one might wonder why the slave trade is guaranteed only to those citizens "in every State that might desire it" rather than to all citizens; and one would surely ask why this guarantee was limited to twenty years. These qualifications suggest that there is something that is *not* ordinary about this particular article of merchandise and property.

When we look at the clause itself, this suggestion is reenforced. The clause reads: "The Migration or Importation of such Persons as any of the States now existing shall think proper to admit, shall not be prohibited by the Congress prior to the year one thousand eight hundred and eight, but a tax or duty may be imposed on such Importation, not exceeding ten dollars for each Person" (Art. I, sec. 9[1]). We note that the form is not a guarantee of a right but a postponement of a power to prohibit. Moreover we see, what Taney neglects to point out, that the postponement of federal power to prohibit applies only to the states "now existing." We have here, apparently, a traditional or vested right or interest which is to be preserved for a time but which Congress need not allow to spread to new states. The clause, fairly interpreted, gives a temporary respite to an illicit trade; the presumption was that Congress would, after twenty years, forbid this trade (as it would not and perhaps could not prohibit trade in ordinary articles of merchandise), and in fact Congress did so.

Finally, to quote Taney again, "the government in express terms is pledged to protect [slave property] in all future times, if the slave escapes from his owner."[18] Here is another major concession. It is a clear case of a new legal right of slavery—there was nothing like it under the Articles of Confederation. It amounts, moreover, to a kind of nationalization of slave property, in the sense that everyone in a free state has an obligation to assist in the enforcement, so far as fugitive slaves are concerned, of the institution of slavery. It is not surprising that this clause turned out to be the most intensely controversial of the three provisions dealing with slavery. Yet it was hardly noticed in the Northern ratification conventions. The fugitive slave clause in the Constitution, like its model in the Northwest Ordinance which outlawed slavery in the Northwest Territory, was the price of a broader freedom. And the price was grudgingly, at least narrowly, defined.

Here are what Taney called "plain words—too plain to be misunderstood": "No Person held to Service or Labour in one State, under the Laws thereof, escaping into another, shall, in Consequence of

---

18. 19 How 451–54 (1857).

any Law or Regulation therein, be discharged from such Service or Labour, but shall be delivered up on Claim of the Party to whom such Service or Labour may be due" (Art. IV, sec. 2[3]). Whether or not these words are plain, they were carefully chosen.[19] The suggestion for such a provision was first made in the Constitutional Convention on August 28 by Pierce Butler and Charles Pinckney of South Carolina, who moved "to require fugitive slaves and servants to be delivered up like criminals." Following some discussion (in which, incidentally, Roger Sherman equated "a slave or servant" and "a horse" for the purpose of limiting the slaveowner's claim), the motion was withdrawn, to be replaced the next day by the following version: "If any person *bound to service or labor* in any of the U——States shall escape into another State, he or she shall not be discharged from such service or labor, in consequence of any regulations subsisting in the State to which they escape, but shall be delivered up to the person *justly claiming* their service or labor," which was agreed to.[20]

This was later revised by the Committee on Style to something close to the final version: "No person *legally held to service or labour* in one state, escaping into another, shall in consequence of regulations subsisting therein be discharged from such service or labour, but shall be delivered up on claim of the party to whom such service or labour *may be due*." Thus the Committee on Style withdrew from the master the claim that he "justly claimed" the services of his slave, acknowledging only that the slave's labor "may be due." On September 15, the Committee on Style's description of a slave as a "person legally held to service or labour" (already probably a narrowing of the previous and morally more comprehensive description, "bound to service or labour") was objected to by some who, in Madison's words, "thought the term (legal) equivocal, and favoring the idea that slavery was legal in a moral view." Thus "legally" was struck out and "under the laws thereof" inserted. Supposing that a concession to return fugitive slaves had to be made, it is hard to see how it could have been made in any way that would have given less sanction to the idea that property in slaves has the same moral status as other kinds of property.

The founders did acknowledge slavery, they compromised with it. The effect was in the short run probably to strengthen it. Perhaps

---

19. The following deliberations are reported in Max Farrand, ed., *The Records of the Federal Convention of 1787*, four vols. (New Haven: Yale University Press, 1911–37), vol. 2, pp. 443, 453–54, 601–2, 628.

20. The emphases here and throughout this and the next paragraph are mine.

they could have done more to restrict it, though the words of a Missouri judge express what the founders thought they were doing and, I think, probably the truth. "When the States assumed the rights of self-government, they found their citizens claiming a right of property in a miserable portion of the human race. Sound national policy required that the evil should be restricted as much as possible. What they could, they did."[21] "As those fathers marked it," Lincoln urged on the eve of the Civil War, "so let it be again marked, as an evil not to be extended, but to be tolerated and protected only because of and so far as its actual presence among us makes that toleration and protection a necessity."[22] Slavery was an evil to be tolerated, allowed to enter the Constitution only by the back door, grudgingly, unacknowledged, on the presumption that the house would be truly fit to live in only when it was gone, and that it would ultimately be gone.

In their accommodation to slavery, the founders limited and confined it and carefully withheld any indication of moral approval, while they built a union that they thought was the greatest instrument of human liberty ever made, that they thought would lead and that did in fact lead to the extinction of Negro slavery. It is common today to make harsh reference to the irony of ringing declarations of human rights coming from the pens of men who owned slaves. But I think that Professor Franklin is wrong when he says that "they simply would not or could not see how ridiculous their position was." They saw it all right, and they saw better than their critics how difficult it was to extricate themselves from that position in a reasonably equitable way. But they saw, too, a deeper irony: these masters knew that they were writing the texts in which their slaves would learn their rights.

Having, I hope, rescued the founders from the common charge that they shamefully excluded Negroes from the principles of the Declaration of Independence, that they regarded their enslavement as just, and that in their Constitution they protected property in man like any other property, I must at least touch on a deeper question, where they do not come off so well. But at this deeper level the problem is not that they betrayed their principles, the common charge; the problem lies rather in the principles themselves. That very principle of individual liberty for which the founders worked so brilliantly and successfully contains within itself an uncomfortably

---

21. Winny v. Whitesides 1 Mo Rep 472 (1824).

22. "Address at Cooper Institute," New York, February 27, 1860, in Basler, *Lincoln*, p. 526.

large opening toward slavery. The principle is the right of each individual to his life, his liberty, his pursuit of happiness as he sees fit. He is, to be sure, subject to constraints in the pursuit of his own interests because of the fact of other human beings with similar rights. But are these moral constraints or merely prudential ones? Locke says that under the law of nature each individual ought, as much as he can, "to preserve the rest of mankind" "when his own preservation comes not in competition."[23] Each individual is of course the judge of what his own preservation does require, and it would be a foolish man, an unnatural man, who would not, under conditions of extreme uncertainty, give himself every generous benefit of the doubt. Does this not tend to mean in practice that each individual has a right to pursue his own interests, as he sees fit and as he can? And is there not a strong tendency for that "as he can" to become conclusive? In civil society, indeed, each of us gives up the claim of sovereign judgment for the sake of the milder, surer benefits of a supreme judge. Even in that case there is a question whether the first principle does not remain that one may do what one can do. The founders often described the problem of civil society as resulting from that tendency. In any case, regarding persons outside civil society, there is a strong implication that any duty I have to respect their rights is whatever residue is left after I have amply secured my own.

Now, in the case of American slavery, especially in the South at the time of the writing of the Constitution, there clearly was a conflict between the rights of the slaves and the self-preservation of the masters. "[W]e have a wolf by the ears," Jefferson said, "and we can neither hold him, nor safely let him go. Justice is in one scale, and self preservation in the other."[24] Only an invincible naiveté can deny that Jefferson spoke truly. But the deeper issue, as I think Jefferson knew, is the tendency, under the principles of the Declaration of Independence itself, for justice to be reduced to self-preservation, for self-preservation to be defined as self-interest, and for self-interest to be defined as what is convenient and achievable. Thus the slave owner may resolve that it is necessary to keep his slaves in bondage for the compelling reason that if they were free they would kill him; but he may also decide, on the same basic principle, that he must keep them enslaved in order to protect his plantation, his children's patrimony, his flexibility of action, on which his preservation ulti-

---

23. John Locke, *Two Treatises of Government*, Book 2, chap. 2, section 6.

24. Thomas Jefferson to John Holmes, April 22, 1820, Jefferson, *Selected Writings*, Koch and Peden, eds., p. 698.

mately depends; and from that he may conclude that he is entitled to keep his slaves in bondage if he finds it convenient to do so. All of this presumes of course that he *can* keep his slaves in bondage. Nor does it in any way deny the right of the slave to resist his enslavement and to act the part of the master if he can. This whole chain of reasoning is a chilling clarification of the essential war that seems always to exist, at bottom, between man and man.

American Negro slavery, in this ironic and terrible sense, can be seen as a radicalization of the principle of individual liberty on which the American polity was founded. Jefferson wrote in his *Notes on the State of Virginia* of the demoralization of the masters caused by slavery and its threat to the whole institution of free government. Masters become tyrants and teach tyranny to their children (and, incidentally, to their slaves). Even more important, slavery, through its visible injustice, tends to destroy the moral foundation of civil society. "And can the liberties of a nation be thought secure when we have removed their only firm basis, a conviction in the minds of the people that these liberties are of the gift of God? That they are not to be violated but with His wrath? Indeed I tremble for my country when I reflect that God is just; that his justice cannot sleep forever; that . . . an exchange of situation [between whites and blacks] is among possible events; that it may become probably [*sic*] by supernatural interference! The Almighty has no attribute which can take side with us in such a contest."[25] I do not think that Jefferson was literally concerned with divine vengeance, but he was concerned with the underlying tension—so ruthlessly exposed in the institution of Negro slavery—between the doctrine of individual rights and the necessary moral ground of any government instituted to secure those rights.

Let me proceed, more briefly, to my second theme, Negro citizenship. Justice Taney was wrong in his claim that the founding generation excluded Negroes from the principles of the Declaration of Independence. But he was not wrong in his claim that the founders excluded Negroes from that "We the People" for whom and whose posterity the Constitution was made. Or rather, he was wrong in detail but right fundamentally.

Taney's reasonable contention was that citizens of the United States in 1787—the "People" by and for whom the Constitution was made—were all those people who were then citizens of the states. He went on to claim that Negroes were not then citizens of any states and are therefore forever excluded from United States citizenship. But it was easy to show, as Justice Benjamin R. Curtis did, that free

---

25. *Notes on the State of Virginia*, Query 18, ibid., pp. 278–79.

Negroes were citizens in many of the states; and Taney's argument excluding Negroes from United States citizenship collapses.

In this matter Taney is simply wrong; but he had a better case at a deeper level. The way to this level is through the privileges and immunities clause, which was Taney's real concern here, even though it was not involved in the legal dispute. This clause provides that "the Citizens of each State shall be entitled to all Privileges and Immunities of Citizens in the several States." Taney said that the Southern states cannot be presumed to have agreed to a Constitution that would give any Northern state the power to make citizens of free blacks, who could then go to Southern states, claim there all of the privileges and immunities of citizens, and by their agitation and example disrupt the whole police system on which the maintenance of slavery, and the preservation of the white South, depended. The privileges and immunities clause was the knife by which Northern freedom cut into the South, as the fugitive slave clause was the knife by which Southern slavery cut into the North. And it could be said of the privileges and immunities clause that the South did agree, as the North agreed to the fugitive slave clause, even if it did not anticipate all the consequences; and that the bargain should be kept. But the deeper question is whether the Constitution was really meant to provide for a large-scale racially mixed polity. Here I think Taney was right, for although the answer is less clear than he says, it is nevertheless a fairly resounding no.

The position of most American statesmen from the time of the Declaration of Independence through the Civil War was well expressed by Jefferson in his autobiography: "Nothing is more certainly written in the book of fate, than that these two people are to be free; nor is it less certain that the two races, equally free, cannot live in the same government."[26] And in his *Notes on the State of Virginia* Jefferson gave perhaps the best explanation of this widely held view.[27] He gives an account of a scheme he had helped draft for reforming the laws of Virginia. Included in that plan was a provision for the emancipation of slaves, to be followed by their colonization to some suitable place, "sending them out with arms, implements of household and of the handicraft arts, seeds, pairs of the useful domestic animals etc., to declare them a free and independent people, and extend to them our alliance and protection, till they have acquired strength." At the same time, it was proposed that vessels be sent to other parts of the world for an equal number of white emigrants.

26. "Autobiography," ibid., p. 51.
27. Query 14, ibid., pp. 255–62.

145

Jefferson naturally anticipated the question, Why not leave the free blacks where they were and save the expense of resettling them and securing replacements? His answer can be collected under three heads. The first obstacle was the race prejudice of the whites—deep, aggressive, and invincible. Second was the blacks' sense of the injustice done to them, a sense sure to be kept alive by new injuries. Third were the natural differences between the races and particularly the actual and probably inherent inferiority of the blacks in certain respects that affect crucially the quality of civil society.

The first and second causes seemed to Jefferson and his generation to ensure that there would never be that sense of fellow feeling and mutual trust between the races that forms the indispensable social basis of civil society. The third (supposed Negro inferiority) expressed a concern not with the bare possibility but with the quality of civil life. Many of the advocates of Negro rights, Jefferson said, "while they wish to vindicate the liberty of human nature, are anxious also to preserve its dignity and beauty. Some of these, embarrassed by the question, 'What further is to be done with them?' join themselves in opposition with those who are actuated by sordid avarice only." Race prejudice, a tangled history of injustice, natural differences suggesting Negro inferiority—these are not promising materials for civil society.

These early American statesmen (including, by the way, many blacks) may have been wrong, as most of us would think today, in believing that a long-term biracial society was unfeasible and undesirable. They surely did not in fact provide any real alternative in their American Colonization Society and its minute settlement in Liberia. But we are likely to be too quick to assume that in trying to get rid of both slavery and Negroes they were being simply hypocritical or unprincipled. We have lost sight of the crucial difference between the two questions I am discussing: the question of freedom and the question of citizenship. To concede the Negro's right to freedom is not to concede his right to United States citizenship. And, on the other hand, to deny his right to United States citizenship is not to affirm that he is justly enslaved. There is nothing contradictory in arguing that while the Negroes have a human right to be free, they do not have a human right to be citizens of the United States. This distinction, which is today muddled inadvertently, was deliberately muddled by Stephen Douglas, and probably by Taney also. The former, Lincoln said in his magnificent speech on the *Dred Scott* decision, "finds the Republicans insisting that the Declaration of Independence includes ALL men, black as well as white; and forthwith he boldly denies that it includes negroes at all, and proceeds to argue gravely that all who contend it does, do so only because they want to vote, and eat, and sleep, and marry with negroes. He will have it that they cannot be consistent else. Now I protest against that counterfeit logic which concludes that, because I do not want a black woman for a *slave* I must necessarily want her for a *wife*. I need not have her for either, I can just leave her alone."[28]

Of course the problem was that while an individual could "leave the Negro alone," the American polity could not. Unless there was to be a permanent class of underlings, Negro emancipation had to imply either political and social equality of the races in the United States or separation of the races into distinct polities. For Lincoln, as for nearly all American statesmen up to his time, only the latter seemed to hold any promise for the long-term viability and quality of the American polity. In advocating a policy of emancipation and colonization, the founders may have been cold or unwise or inequitable, but they were not acting contrary to the principles of the Declaration of Independence. To put the point differently, American Negroes may have had a valid claim to United States citizenship (I think they did); but it was a claim depending on particular circumstances and history (and thus discussable on such grounds) quite distinct from their claim to freedom, which depended upon nothing but their humanity.

The American founders would have done their work better, it is now generally thought, if they had seen the need for, and responded to, the challenge of a multiracial, heterogeneous, open society. Instead, they toyed with unrealistic schemes of colonization, temporized with racism and racial segregation, delayed justice for blacks unconscionably long, sanctioned second-class citizenship. They "set the stage," in John Hope Franklin's terms, "for every succeeding generation of Americans to apologize, compromise, and temporize on those principles of liberty that were supposed to be the very foundation of our system of government and way of life."[29]

What might one of the thoughtful founders say in response to these charges and in the light of present-day circumstances in the United States?

First, I think he would be amazed at the degree to which blacks and whites have progressed in making a civil society together. I think he would frankly admit that he would never have expected anything like the degree of harmony, mutual trust and toleration, and opportunity for blacks that have been achieved in the United States at the

---

28. Lincoln, "The Dred Scott Decision," p. 360.
29. *University of Chicago Magazine*, Summer 1975, p. 13.

bicentennial of our beginning. At the same time, on closer inspection, he might wonder whether even the elementary question of whether the races can live together in peace has yet been settled beyond doubt. Are the races so well bonded that long-term economic depression or large-scale war (fought perhaps mainly by black American soldiers against black or yellow enemies) could not still tear them apart?

Moreover, in defense of his "temporizing" with racism and segregation and injustice, our founder might ask what else he could have done? What, he might slyly ask our generation, has been your most successful (perhaps your only successful) large-scale integration program? Surely the desegregation in the United States military forces. That example is interesting in two respects. First the success seems increasingly problematical, as festering racial antagonism and the worrisome prospect of an all-black army, or infantry, suggest. Second, to the extent that it is a success, why was that possible? Because an army is an army. But a political democracy is not an army. It rests on and is severely limited by opinion, which cannot be commanded. Prejudice—arbitrary liking and trust and, of course, also disliking and mistrust—is inherent in political life, and its role is greater as the polity is more democratic. To criticize a Jefferson or a Lincoln for yielding to, even sharing in, white prejudice is equivalent to demanding either that he get out of politics altogether—and leave it to the *merely* prejudiced—or that he become a despot.

Regarding the quality of civil life, as distinct from its bare possibility, our founder might say much. He might point to the extraordinary vulgarity and triviality of American popular culture, to the difficulty that America has in generating any high culture of its own, to the superficiality of social bonds and community values. And he might ask whether these oft-observed and deplored characteristics of American civil life are not connected with its attempt to be all things to all men, with its attempt to embrace the most extreme heterogeneity, so that it can be nothing much to any of them.

Finally, however, I think our founder might be intrigued, if not altogether persuaded, by the prospect of a free society consisting not merely of a huge aggregation of individuals but of diverse ethnic and religious and other groups. He would be interested in the possibility of a civil society, viable yet capable of exploring and exemplifying diverse significant human possibilities. He would see the point, I think (especially if he had read his Tocqueville), of criticisms by Negroes like W. E. B. Du Bois of the Declaration of Independence itself for a radical individualism that cuts each man off from his fellows and from God. While he would be skeptical, I think he would be interested in exploring the world into which Du Bois offers a window, a world that is built (perhaps more than Du Bois realized) on our founders' principles and institutions, but that is nevertheless quite different from anything they imagined.

> [I]f . . . there is substantial agreement in laws, language and religion; if there is a satisfactory adjustment of economic life, then there is no reason why, in the same country and on the same street, two or three great national ideals might not thrive and develop, that men of different races might not strive together for their race ideals as well, perhaps even better, than in isolation. Here, it seems to me, is the reading of the riddle that puzzles so many of us. We are Americans, not only by birth and by citizenship, but by our political ideals, our language, our religion. Farther than that, our Americanism does not go. At that point, we are Negroes, members of a vast historic race that from the very dawn of creation has slept, but half awakening in the dark forests of its African fatherland. We are the first fruits of this new nation, the harbinger of that black to-morrow which is yet destined to soften the whiteness of the Teutonic to-day. We are that people whose subtle sense of song has given America its only American music, its only American fairy tales, its only touch of pathos and humor amid its mad money-getting plutocracy. As such, it is our duty to conserve our physical powers, our intellectual endowments, our spiritual ideals; as a race we must strive by race organization, by race solidarity, by race unity to the realization of that broader humanity which freely recognizes differences in men, but sternly deprecates inequality in their opportunities of development.[30]

Reflecting on thoughts like these and on present circumstances in the United States, our founder might concede that the huge problem of racial heterogeneity, which his generation saw but could not master, may show the way to deal with another problem, which they did not see so clearly, the political and moral defects of mere individualism. He would surely point out that the foundation of this new polity is the old one; and he might wryly observe that his own principle of racial separation is, after all, an essential element in the

---

30. W. E. B. Du Bois, "The Conservation of the Races," Washington, 1897, in Herbert J. Storing, ed., *What Country Have I? Political Writings by Black Americans* (New York: St. Martin's Press, 1970), pp. 82–83.

new polity of racial and ethnic diversity. But I think he would concede, finally, that while in his heart of hearts he had thought that he and his generation had finished in its essentials the task of making the American polity, there is after all work still to be done.

7
Frederick Douglass

One of the major themes of American statesmanship and political thought is the indelible impression made upon the American polity by the institution of slavery. Few men understood that institution so well as Frederick Douglass. Few men labored so wisely and effectively to destroy it. Few men saw so deeply into its implications. Douglass never abandoned the perspective of the black American. He was always and deliberately a partisan, in the sense that he adopted the stance and the duties of one who speaks for only a part (though in this case a uniquely important part) of the political whole. Yet few men deserve so fully the rank of American statesman.

Douglass began his public career when, not three years after his escape from slavery and while leading the hard life of a common laborer in New Bedford, Massachusetts, he accepted an invitation to speak a few words at an 1841 antislavery convention on his experiences as a slave. He spoke so well that he was invited by the Massachusetts Anti-Slavery Society to become one of its agents, telling of his experiences throughout the Eastern states. But it was not enough for him to follow the advice of his white abolitionist friends: "Give us the facts," they said, "we will take care of the philosophy." Douglass's mind was always working; he could not talk about slavery without thinking about it. "It did not entirely satisfy me to *narrate* wrongs—I felt like *denouncing* them."[1]

Inevitably doubts were expressed whether a man who reasoned so well and in such fine and eloquent language could ever have been a slave. Partly in response to these doubts Douglass wrote the first of his several autobiographical works, *A Narrative of the Life of Frederick*

This essay is from Morton J. Frisch and Richard G. Stevens, eds., *American Political Thought: The Philosophical Dimension of American Statesmanship*, 2d ed. (Itasca, Ill.: Peacock Publishers, 1983). It is reprinted with permission from Peacock Publishers.

1. Frederick Douglass, *Life and Times of Frederick Douglass, the Complete Autobiography* (New York, 1962), p. 217. Hereafter cited as *Life and Times*.

Douglass, An American Slave, published in 1845.[2] The facts were established—at considerable risk to Douglass, for his whereabouts thereby became known in Maryland—but the small volume is a good deal more than a narrative. It is, in fact, an excellent treatise, in narrative form, on the inner workings and principles of the institution of American slavery. Like Harriet Beecher Stowe, who drew on his volume, Douglass showed how the best in slavery is implicated in the worst and pulled down to it. He described how his kind and tenderhearted Baltimore mistress, who first taught him to read, painfully learned "that I sustained to her the relation of a mere chattel, and that for her to treat me as a human being was not only wrong, but dangerously so"; and he described the evil effects upon her of the lesson. He described the slave-breaker, Covey, who could rent slaves cheaply because of his reputation for restoring them to their masters chastened and despirited. But at what a cost! Covey lurked around his own plantation, spying on the slaves, sometimes crawling on his hands and knees to surprise them—utterly degrading himself in the exercise of his miserable mastership. Though Douglass spent his rare moments of rest with Covey "in a sort of beast-like stupor," the natural human desire for liberty continued to burn fitfully. It burst into flame when, unjustly attacked by Covey, Douglass successfully defended himself in a two-hour struggle. From that time on he ceased being a slave in fact, though he might remain a slave in form; for he determined that in the future no one should succeed in beating him without succeeding in killing him.

Covey represented the depths of slavery; and Douglass's condition improved thereafter, but the improvements only made the slave less contented with his bonds. Hired by his master to a fair and kind man who treated him well, Douglass responded by making an unsuccessful attempt to escape. Instead of selling him south, his master permitted him to return to Baltimore, where he was hired out and later permitted to hire his own time. Yet the experience only flaunted the robbery of slavery before Douglass's eyes and made him more anxious to escape. The more slavery adopted the characteristics of freedom, the more intolerable it became. Douglass experienced the contradiction of the house divided against itself, and he understood it fully:

> I have observed this in my experience of slavery,—that whenever my condition was improved, instead of its increasing my contentment, it only increased my desire to be free,

2. Frederick Douglass, *A Narrative of the Life of Frederick Douglass, An American Slave* (Garden City, N.Y., 1963).

and set me to thinking of plans to gain my freedom. I have found that to make a contented slave, it is necessary to make a thoughtless one. It is necessary to darken his moral and mental vision, and, as far as possible, to annihilate the power of reason. He must be able to detect no inconsistencies in slavery; he must be made to feel that slavery is right; and he can be brought to that only when he ceases to be a man.[3]

Moral Reform and Political Action

During his first years as a public man Douglass was a devoted disciple of William Lloyd Garrison, fully accepting his argument that the Constitution was a proslavery document and his doctrine of nonvoting. "With him, I held it to be the first duty of the non-slaveholding states to dissolve the union with the slaveholding states, and hence my cry, like his, was 'No union with slaveholders.' "[4] Douglass liked "radical measures," whether by the abolitionists or the slaveholders. "I like to gaze upon these two contending armies, for I believe it will hasten the dissolution of the present unholy Union, which has been justly stigmatized as 'a covenant with death, an agreement with hell.' "[5] He held the Constitution to be "radically and essentially slave-holding." "For my part I had rather that my right hand should wither by my side than cast a ballot under the Constitution of the United States."[6]

Douglass carried these views with him when he moved to Rochester, New York, and established his own abolitionist newspaper. "Slavery will be attacked in its stronghold—the compromises of the Constitution, and the cry of disunion shall be more fearlessly proclaimed, till slavery be abolished, the Union dissolved, or the sun of this guilty nation must go down in blood."[7] The Constitution and government of the United States are "a most foul and bloody conspiracy" against the rights of the slaves. "Down with both, for it is not fit that either should exist!"[8] The oath to support the Constitution "requires that which is morally impossible."[9] As for the Free Soilers,

---

3. Douglass, *A Narrative*, p. 98. See *Life and Times*, p. 150.

4. Douglass, *Life and Times*, p. 260.

5. Philip S. Foner, ed., *The Life and Writings of Frederick Douglass* (New York, 1950), vol. 1, pp. 269–70. Hereafter cited as *Life and Writings*.

6. Ibid., vol. 1, pp. 274–75.

7. Ibid., p. 347.

8. Ibid., p. 379.

9. Ibid., vol. 2, p. 117.

who attempted to justify their support of the Constitution as a way of promoting beneficial measures, "they have our sympathies, but not our judgment." Douglass rejected their "theory of human government, which makes it necessary to do evil, that good may come." A Constitution at war with itself cannot be lived up to, and therefore "the platform for us to occupy, is outside that piece of parchment."[10]

As he exercised his always strong and independent judgment, Douglass became increasingly doubtful of the Garrisonian position, and in 1851 he announced his break with it.[11] He adhered to the opinion that the basic problem was a moral one and that the abolition of slavery depended upon a moral regeneration. But he concluded that the Garrisonians had no adequate answer to the question of how this was to be done. Moreover, he came to see that the Garrisonian position was not only politically but morally defective. For all their righteousness, the Garrisonians needed to learn morality in the politics of a free (though imperfect) republic. "As a mere expression of abhorrence of slavery," the Garrisonian sentiment of no union with slaveholders was a good one; "but it expresses no intelligible principle of action, and throws no light on the pathway of duty. Defined, as its authors define it, it leads to false doctrines, and mischievous results."[12] It amounted, in fact, to an abandonment of the great idea with which the antislavery movement began: "It started to free the slave. It ends by leaving the slave to free himself."[13]

Douglass adopted the position of the political abolitionists that slavery was "a system of lawless violence; that it *never was lawful, and never can be made so. . . .*"[14] He was "sick and tired of arguing on the slaveholders' side of this question,"[15] and he came to the conclusion that the slaveholders were not only wrong about slavery but were also wrong about the Constitution. He adopted the view "that the Constitution, construed in the light of well established rules of legal interpretation, might be made consistent in its details with the noble purposes avowed in its preamble; and that hereafter we should insist upon the application of such rules to that instrument, and demand that it be wielded in behalf of emancipation."[16] Douglass came to understand the design of the framers of the Constitution who tried,

---

10. Ibid., p. 119.
11. Douglass, *Life and Times*, pp. 260–61.
12. Douglass, *Life and Writings*, vol. 2, p. 351.
13. Ibid., p. 350.
14. Ibid., p. 156.
15. Ibid., p. 149.
16. Ibid., p. 155.

while making necessary provision for the existing institution of slavery, to leave no principle in the Constitution that would sanction slavery and no word that would defile the constitution of a free people. Once he penetrated this design, Douglass seized the opportunity it provided. The black could now speak fully the language of the law, the language of defense of the Constitution. He could now call upon the country to return, not only to the fundamental political principles of the republic as expressed in the Declaration of Independence, but to its fundamental legal principles as expressed in the Constitution.

Under his new persuasion Douglass held that "it is the first duty of every American citizen, whose conscience permits him so to do, to use his *political* as well as his *moral* power for its overthrow."[17] "Men should not, under the guidance of a false philosophy, be led to fling from them such powerful instrumentalities against Slavery as the Constitution and the ballot."[18] Thus Douglass embarked upon a course of political activity that sought to maintain the moral purity and therefore the moral power of abolition, while at the same time finding ways of making it politically effective. Defending his support of the Free Soil candidate in 1852, Douglass stated the following rule of political action:

> It is evident that all reforms have their beginning with ideas, and that for a time they have to rely solely on the tongue and pen for progress, until they gain a sufficient number of adherents to make themselves felt at the ballot-box. . . . We ask no man to lose sight of any of his aims and objects. We only ask that they may be allowed to serve out their natural probation. Our rule of political action is this: the voter ought to see to it that his vote shall secure the highest good possible, at the same time that it does no harm.[19]

With his tongue and pen Douglass continued to fight for uncompromising abolition: but when the time came to go to the polls he focused on the good that he could do in the immediate future rather than on the good he was aiming for in the long run.

> The mission of the political abolitionists of this country is to abolish slavery. The means to accomplish this great end is, first, to disseminate anti-slavery sentiment; and, secondly, to combine that sentiment and render it a political force which shall, for a time, operate as a check on violent mea-

17. Ibid., p. 156.
18. Ibid., p. 177.
19. Ibid., pp. 213–14.

sures for supporting slavery; and, finally, overthrow the great evil of slavery itself.[20]

Douglass's problems well illustrate the apparent dilemma of the reformer in politics. In 1856, for example, writing on "What is My Duty as an Anti-Slavery Voter?" Douglass argued that "the purity of the cause is the success of the cause." While he might participate in politics, "the first duty of the Reformer is to be right. If right, he may go forward; but if wrong, or partly wrong, he is as an house divided against itself, and will fall." Since the Republican party did "not occupy this high Anti-Slavery ground, (and what is worse, does not mean to occupy it)," Douglass urged his readers to vote for the presidential candidate of the Radical Abolitionists, even at the risk of throwing the election to the Democrats and losing Kansas to slavery. "We deliberately prefer the loss of Kansas to the loss of our Anti-Slavery integrity."[21] Yet four months later, in August 1856, Douglass abandoned the Abolitionist candidate, Gerrit Smith, and announced his support of Republicans John Fremont and William Dayton. The purity of the cause was subordinate, even for the partisan reformer, to a higher morality.

> The time has passed for an honest man to attempt any defence of a right to change his opinion as to political methods of opposing Slavery. Anti-Slavery consistency itself, in our view, requires of the Anti-Slavery voter that disposition of his vote and his influence, which in all the circumstances and likelihoods of the case tend most to the triumph of Free Principles in the Councils and Government of the nation. It is not to be consistent to pursue a course politically this year, merely because that course seemed the best last year, or at any previous time. Right Anti-Slavery action is that which deals the severest deadliest blow upon Slavery that can be given at that particular time. Such action is always consistent, however different may be the forms through which it expresses itself.[22]

On this basis, Douglass later supported Abraham Lincoln, although often with grave doubts and usually with impatience and exasperation. His criticisms of Lincoln, especially during the years prior to the Emancipation Proclamation, were often cutting and even harsh. He found Lincoln's first Inaugural Address a "double-tongued document"; he accused him of being destitute of antislavery principle;

---

20. Ibid., p. 220.
21. Ibid., pp. 391–94.
22. Ibid., p. 397.

he contended that he was "active, decided, and brave" for the support of slavery, "and passive, cowardly, and treacherous to the very cause of liberty to which he owes his election"; he questioned his honesty.[23] He found the Emancipation Proclamation itself disappointing, making a burden of what should have been a joy, touching neither justice nor mercy.[24] "Abraham Lincoln, President of the United States, Commander-in-Chief of the army and navy, in his own peculiar, cautious, forbearing and hesitating way, slow, but we hope sure, has, while the loyal heart was near breaking with despair, proclaimed and declared" the Emancipation Proclamation.[25]

As circumstances drew the black leader and the white statesman closer together, Douglass grew in his understanding of Lincoln. This is not to say that their relations were ever smooth or that Douglass saw matters as Lincoln saw them. Regarding the use by the Union of black troops, for example, they were constantly at odds. After months of urging that black troops should be used and long negotiations about how they would be used, Douglass reluctantly agreed to support a system that was in some respects unfair to black troops, because he thought that the cause of black freedom was served by cooperation even on such terms.

Douglass met in Lincoln true statesmanship and came to understand his own and his people's place in relation to it. While Charles Sumner was "to me and to my oppressed race . . . higher than the highest, better than the best of all our statesmen," Lincoln was simply "the greatest statesman that ever presided over the destinies of this Republic."[26] Douglass gave expression to this understanding in 1876 on the occasion of the unveiling of the Freedmen's Monument in Washington, D.C.[27] Lincoln was not, he said, "in the fullest sense of the word, either our man or our model. In his interests, in his associations, in his habits of thought, and in his prejudices, he was a white man." He came to office on the principle of opposition to the extension of slavery, but he was prepared to defend and perpetuate slavery where it existed, and his whole policy was motivated by "his patriotic devotion to the interests of his own race." Yet, "while Abraham Lincoln saved for you a country, he delivered us from a bondage, according to Jefferson, one hour of which was worse than ages of the oppression your fathers rose in rebellion to oppose."

23. Ibid., vol. 3, pp. 72, 186, 268, 127, 267.
24. Ibid., p. 309.
25. Ibid., p. 273.
26. Ibid., vol. 4, pp. 239, 368.
27. Ibid., pp. 309ff.

Lincoln's very prejudices were an element of his success in preparing the American people for the great conflict and bringing them safely through it. "Viewed from the genuine abolition ground, Mr. Lincoln seemed tardy, cold, dull, and indifferent; but measuring him by the sentiment of his country, a sentiment he was bound as a statesman to consult, he was swift, zealous, radical, and determined."

The blacks believed in Lincoln, despite acts and words that tried the faith and taxed the understanding.

> When he tarried long in the mountain; when he strangely told us that we were the cause of the war; when he still more strangely told us that we were to leave the land in which we were born; when he refused to employ our arms in defence of the Union; when, after accepting our service as colored soldiers, he refused to retaliate our murder and torture as colored prisoners; when he told us he would save the Union if he could with slavery; when he revoked the Proclamation of Emancipation of General Freemont; when he refused to remove the popular commander of the Army of the Potomac, in the days of its inaction and defeat, who was more zealous in his efforts to protect slavery than to suppress rebellion; when we saw all this, and more, we were at times grieved, stunned, and greatly bewildered; but our hearts believed while they ached and bled.

Nor was this merely a blind, unreasoning faith. "Despite the mist and haze that surrounded him; despite the tumult, the hurry, and confusion of the hour, we were able to take a comprehensive view of Abraham Lincoln. . . ." Douglass never abandoned his point of view as a black spokesman and leader, but he did come to understand the deeper harmony of black and white of which Lincoln was the guardian.

> It mattered little to us what language he might employ on special occasions; it mattered little to us, when we fully knew him, whether he was swift or slow in his movements; it was enough for us that Abraham Lincoln was at the head of a great movement, and was in living and earnest sympathy with that movement, which, in the nature of things, must go on until slavery should be utterly and forever abolished in the United States.[28]

"What Country Have I?"

In England between 1845 and 1847, where he had fled to prevent recapture and to preach abolitionism, Douglass often explained that

---

28. Ibid., p. 314.

he was "an outcast from the society of my childhood, and an outlaw in the land of my birth." "That men should be patriotic is to me perfectly natural; and as a philosophical fact, I am able to give it an *intellectual* recognition. But no further can I go."[29]

> I have no love for America, as such; I have no patriotism. I have no country. What country have I? The institutions of this country do not know me, do not recognize me as a man. . . . I have not, I cannot have, any love for this country, as such, or for its Constitution. I desire to see its overthrow as speedily as possible, and its Constitution shivered in a thousand fragments, rather than this foul curse should continue to remain as now.[30]

When Douglass abandoned Garrisonianism he no longer saw the black as, strictly speaking, an "outlaw," because he now held that slavery was not lawful under the Constitution. The black was still an "outcast," because he was in fact held a slave; but he had a moral and a legal claim to the protection of "his" country. This is the theme of one of Douglass's major prewar statements, an oration given in Rochester, New York, in 1852, on "The Meaning of July Fourth for the Negro."

> Fellow-citizens, pardon me, allow me to ask, why am I called upon to speak here to-day? What have I, or those I represent, to do with your national independence? Are the great principles of political freedom and of natural justice, embodied in that Declaration of Independence extended to us? . . .
> Would to God, both for your sakes and ours, that an affirmative answer could be truthfully returned to these questions. . . .
> This Fourth July is *yours* not *mine*. You may rejoice, I must mourn. To drag a man in fetters into the grand illuminated temple of liberty, and call upon him to join you in joyous anthems, were inhuman mockery and sacrilegious irony. Do you mean, citizens, to mock me, by asking me to speak to-day?[31]

In return for mockery, Douglass gave his audience the whip of America's self-betrayal. Looking at the day from the slave's point of view, he declared that the character and conduct of the nation had never looked blacker. "America is false to the past, false to the

---

29. Ibid., vol. 1, p. 126.
30. Ibid., p. 236.
31. Ibid., vol. 2, pp. 188–89.

present, and solemnly binds herself to be false to the future." To those who said that the abolitionists denounce when they ought to persuade, Douglass asked, what is it that needs argument? That the slave is a man? That a man is entitled to liberty? That slavery is wrong? That slavery is not divine? Words are valuable now only as they move to action.

> At a time like this, scorching irony, not convincing argument, is needed. O! had I the ability, and could reach the nation's ear, I would to-day pour out a fiery stream of biting ridicule, blasting reproach, withering sarcasm, and stern rebuke. For it is not light that is needed, but fire; it is not the gentle shower, but thunder. We need the storm, the whirlwind, and the earthquake. The feeling of the nation must be quickened; the conscience of the nation must be roused; the propriety of the nation must be startled; the hypocrisy of the nation must be exposed; and its crimes against God and man must be proclaimed and denounced.[32]

And so Douglass flayed his fellow-citizens:

> Fellow-citizens, I will not enlarge further on your national inconsistencies. The existence of slavery in this country brands your republicanism as a sham, your humanity as a base pretense, and your Christianity as a lie. It destroys your moral power abroad: it corrupts your politicians at home. It saps the foundation of religion; it makes your name a hissing and a bye-word to a mocking earth. It is the antagonistic force in your government, the only thing that seriously disturbs and endangers your *Union*. It fetters your progress; it is the enemy of improvement; the deadly foe of education; it fosters pride; it breeds insolence; it promotes vice; it shelters crime; it is a curse to the earth that supports it; and yet you cling to it as if it were the sheet anchor of all your hopes.[33]

Strong words; yet words directed to "fellow citizens," as Douglass repeatedly addressed his audience. Five years later, however, the Supreme Court in the *Dred Scott* decision denied Douglass's interpretation of the Constitution, holding that blacks could claim none of the rights and privileges secured by the Constitution to citizens of the United States. In his speech on this decision Douglass was not scorching fellow citizens (a term he used here only once, and that in the formal salutation) but defending himself against an en-

32. Ibid., p. 192.
33. Ibid., p. 201.

emy. The decision was "infamous," "devilish," "the judicial incarnation of wolfishness," "an open, glaring, and scandalous tissue of lies." Douglass appealed against "this hell-black judgment of the Supreme Court, to the court of common sense and common humanity." He declared that "all that is merciful and just, on earth and in Heaven, will execrate and despise this edict of Taney."[34]

On most occasions, as Douglass gave ample evidence of understanding, such an unqualified partisan attack on the supreme instrument of lawfulness would be utterly irresponsible and self-defeating. But the Court's decision in *Dred Scott* amounted to an act of outright war against the black, excluding him from participation in the American political community; and the black had to defend himself in like manner, even at the risk of seriously damaging that very political community in which he sought to secure his rightful place. Thus Douglass confessed in his autobiography to a feeling allied to satisfaction at the prospect of a war between North and South. "Standing outside the pale of American humanity, denied citizenship, unable to call the land of my birth my country, and adjudged by the Supreme Court of the United States to have no rights which white men were bound to respect, and longing for the end of the bondage of my people, I was ready for any political upheaval which should bring about a change in the existing condition of things."[35]

It is instructive in this connection to compare Douglass's speech on the *Dred Scott* decision with his speech in 1883 on the *Civil Rights* case, striking down federal legislation prohibiting discrimination against blacks. The war was over, for the country and for the black, and the character of the speech was determined by that great fact. This is not to suggest that the *Civil Rights* case was not a serious blow. Douglass saw it as standing in a line that included the forcing of slavery into Kansas, the enactment of the Fugitive Slave Act, the repeal of the Missouri Compromise, and the *Dred Scott* decision. "We have been, as a class, grievously wounded, wounded in the house of our friends," he said at the mass meeting called to protest the *Civil Rights* decision.[36]

But although wounded, the blacks were not turned out of their political house, as they had been in *Dred Scott*; and Douglass's rhetoric was governed by that difference. Here there was none of the violence of his attack on the Taney decision. He began by noting that he had taken the trouble to write out his remarks, that they might

---

34. Ibid., pp. 410–12.
35. Douglass, *Life and Times*, p. 329.
36. Douglass, *Life and Writings*, vol. 4, pp. 392ff.

be "well-chosen, and not liable to be misunderstood, distorted, or misrepresented." He suggested that it may be that "the hour calls more loudly for silence than for speech," and he exhibited an unusual reluctance to enter into the criticism he had to utter. He aimed to achieve a certain kind of silence, while speaking. He contended that the most serious evil in the land, "which threatens to undermine and destroy the foundations of our free institutions," is—not race prejudice or injustice to blacks, as one might have expected, but—"the great and apparently increasing want of respect entertained for those to whom are committed the responsibility and the duty of administering our government."

Douglass urged his partisan audience never to forget that "whatever may be the incidental mistakes or misconduct of rulers, government is better than anarchy, and patient reform is better than violent revolution." While not interfering with fair criticism, he would give "the emphasis of a voice from heaven" to the repugnance felt by all good citizens to any disrespect for governors.[37] Coming "a little nearer to the case now before us," he began his criticism, but again interrupted himself to caution that "if any man has come here tonight with his breast heaving with passion, his heart flooded with acrimony, wishing and expecting to hear violent denunciation of the Supreme Court, on account of this decision, he has mistaken the object of this meeting and the character of the men by whom it is called."[38] Douglass then entered into a vigorous criticism, but he did so only after having introduced the subject with the greatest circumspection and concern for maintaining the dignity and authority of the Court and the law for which it spoke. This was now the blacks' Court as well as the whites'. Better to have a Court that does serious harm to blacks than to have none at all.

Indeed, the privilege of having a part in the American political institutions was a precious victory that Douglass had helped to win. This privilege did not, as Douglass clearly understood, necessarily accompany emancipation. Emancipation could justly be claimed on the basis of the fundamental principles of the American Declaration of Independence and Constitution, and it could therefore be justly argued that in this respect the black's interest was fundamentally identical with the interest of the rest of the nation. Even in his speech on *Dred Scott*, Douglass concluded, "all I ask of the American people is, that they live up to the Constitution, adopt its principles, imbibe

37. Ibid., p. 394.
38. Ibid., pp. 395–96.

its spirit, and enforce its provisions."[39] But while the black fought to be a free man, he also fought to be a free *American*. And while the best American statesmen had always agreed that American principles demanded freedom for the black, there was much less agreement about whether they demanded freedom for the black *in the United States*. With respect to this question—whether the blacks, once freed, should stay in the United States or go elsewhere—it was not so clear that the good of the black and the good of the country were identical. It is of some interest to note that the first official reception by any president of a group of blacks came in 1862 when Abraham Lincoln invited a committee of blacks to lend their support to a plan for colonizing blacks in Central America.[40]

The colonization issue was, of course, an old one. The first printed notice of Frederick Douglass, indeed, was a report in the Garrisonian *Liberator* of March 29, 1839, that the young ex-slave had addressed an anticolonization meeting, arguing "that the inordinate and intolerable scheme of the American Colonization Society shall never entice or drive *us* from our native soil."[41] From this time until the very end of his long career Douglass fought the numerous schemes of colonization put forward as solutions to the "Negro problem."[42]

Douglass argued the civilizing effect of a permanent location, which the American blacks were just beginning to experience. "We say to every colored man, *be a man where you are*. . . . You must be a man here, and force your way to intelligence, wealth and respectability. If you can't do that here, you can't do it there. By changing your place, you don't change your character." The argument was not simply directed against restless nomadism, although that is part of it. "We believe that contact with the white race, even under the many unjust and painful restrictions to which we are subjected, does more toward our elevation and improvement, than the mere circumstance of being separated from them could do."[43] Although he despised many who made the argument, Douglass nevertheless saw "that the

---

39. Ibid., vol. 2, p. 424.

40. Abraham Lincoln, in Roy P. Basler, ed., *The Collected Works of Abraham Lincoln* (New Brunswick, N.J., 1953), vol. 5, pp. 370–75.

41. Douglass, *Life and Writings*, vol. 1, p. 25.

42. The last two substantive pieces in Foner's *Life and Writings* are a "Lecture on Haiti" (1895, vol. 4, p. 478) and a long essay on "Why the Negro is Lynched" (1894, vol. 4, p. 491), both of which contain substantial discussions of the colonization issue.

43. Douglass, *Life and Writings*, vol. 2., p. 173.

condition of our race has been improved by their situation as slaves, since it has brought them into contact with a superior people, and afforded them facilities for acquiring knowledge,"[44] and he fought to keep the blacks in contact with that superior people—superior, it is hardly necessary to add, not in nature but in fact. Douglass saw that the contact was not of equal advantage to the two sides. Speaking of the profit to himself of association with the son of his former master, he said "the law of compensation holds here as well as elsewhere. While this lad could not associate with ignorance without sharing its shade, he could not give his black playmates his company without giving them his superior intelligence as well."[45]

Whatever the whites might think was best for America, the blacks knew what was best for them; and, according to Douglass, they would fight to stay. "Our minds are made up to live here if we can, or die here if we must; so every attempt to remove us, will be, as it ought to be, labor lost. Here we are, and here we shall remain."[46] The black has stayed despite his great differences from the European, despite "greater hardships, injuries and insults than those to which the Indians have been subjected," and despite cunning schemes to teach his children that this is not his home.

> It is idle—worse than idle, ever to think of our expatriation, or removal. . . . *We are here,* and here we are likely to be. To imagine that we shall ever be eradicated is absurd and ridiculous. We can be remodified, changed, and assimilated, but never extinguished. We repeat, therefore, that *we are here*; and that this is *our* country; and the question for the philosophers and statesmen of the land ought to be, what principles should dictate the policy of the action toward us?[47]

Douglass did argue that there was no ineradicable prejudice against blacks and that the proper response to prejudice is to root it out rather than to pander to it. He argued that the South had a positive need for the blacks' labor. He argued on the basis of human brotherhood, and he sometimes suggested that greater intercommunication of the races was historically necessary and morally desirable. But he never formed these various suggestions into a comprehensive argument that colonization would be, like slavery, as bad for the country as for the black. Douglass's argument here might be paraphrased as follows. "I think that the United States has a duty to keep

---

44. Ibid.
45. Douglass, *Life and Times,* p. 44.
46. Douglass, *Life and Writings,* vol. 1, p. 351.
47. Ibid., p. 417.

her black stepchildren; I think that she will be enriched by so doing, and that the problems involved in it can be solved. However, the cost to the country of retaining the freedman and its possible damage to the fabric of American political life are not questions that it is my duty to ponder deeply. The black is willing—must be willing—to see the American polity pay almost any price, run almost any risk, to admit him. For him it is a matter, not, it is true, of life or death or freedom or slavery, but of that for the sake of which life and freedom are sought; and he will resist any attempt, however reasonable to others, to loosen his grip on the white man's civilization."

The colonization issue was the last great battle in the black's paradoxical war with America to become part of America, and it was in principle his most difficult battle, more difficult than emancipation, on the one side, or the securing of civil and political rights, on the other. The black's victory in this struggle was commemorated in Douglass's oration at the unveiling of the Freedmen's Monument in 1876, from which we have already quoted.[48] This speech contains one of the most profound statements ever made of the relations between the American blacks and the American polity. Douglass described, in stately terms, the setting in the capital of the nation and the audience drawn from all the segments of the government, present to give witness to the blacks' entry into the American community through their praise of America's greatest statesman. He did not succumb to the temptation of shallow praise: he did not claim Lincoln for the blacks; he felt no need to blur the truth. "We fully comprehend the relation of Abraham Lincoln both to ourselves and to the whole people of the United States." Lincoln was a white man, an American of the Americans.

> He was preeminently the white man's President, entirely devoted to the welfare of white men. He was ready and willing at any time during the first years of his administration to deny, postpone, and sacrifice the rights of humanity in the colored people to promote the welfare of the white people of this country. In all his education and feeling he was an American of the Americans. . . . The race to which we belong were not the special objects of his consideration. . . . We are at best only his step-children; children by adoption, children by forces of circumstances and necessity.

But the circumstances were such that Lincoln could not promote the welfare of whites without promoting the welfare of blacks, for both rested on the same principle, individual freedom; and their destinies

---

48. Ibid., vol. 4, pp. 309ff.

were too entwined ever to be separated. The Freedmen's Monument stood for the blacks' praise of Lincoln but also for their *title* to praise him—stepchildren, indeed, but, for better or worse, his and the country's children. "Fellow-citizens, I end, as I began, with congratulations. We have done a good work for our race today. In doing honor to the memory of our friend and liberator, we have been doing highest honors to ourselves and those who come after us; we have been fastening ourselves to a name and fame imperishable and immortal. . . ."

What Shall We Do with the Black?

If, then, the blacks were to stay in the United States, the question was asked, what shall we do with them? Douglass answered, "Do nothing with them; mind your business, and let them mind theirs. Your *doing* with them is their greatest misfortune." The question implies "that slavery is the natural order of human relations, and that liberty is an experiment." But the reverse is true, and consequently human duties are mostly negative. "If men were born in need of crutches, instead of having legs, the fact would be otherwise. We should then be in need of help, and would require outside aid; but according to the wiser and better arrangement of nature, our duty is done better by not hindering than by helping our fellow-men; or, in other words, the best way to help them is just to let them help themselves."[49] While not wishing to check any benevolent concern, Douglass suggested pointedly, "Let the American people, who have thus far only kept the colored race staggering between partial philanthropy and cruel force, be induced to try what virtue there is in justice." The black's misfortune is precisely that "he is everywhere treated as an exception to all the general rules which should operate in the relations of other men."[50] "[I]f the Negro cannot stand on his own legs, let him fall. . . . All I ask is, give him a chance to stand on his own legs! Let him alone!"[51]

Let the Negro alone. This was the touchstone; obviously it was not exhaustive. Douglass was well aware that the black did need crutches, for his limbs were stiff from the shackles of slavery. "Time, education, and training will restore him to natural proportions, for, though bruised and blasted, he is yet a man."[52] Douglass knew the

---

49. Ibid., vol. 3, pp. 188–90.
50. Ibid., p. 190.
51. Ibid., vol. 4, p. 164.
52. Ibid., p. 435.

debt owed the black, but he did not harp on it. He knew, and in various ways presented, the black's need for generous help as well as his demand for justice; but there was never any question about the priority of the black's demand to be allowed to stand or fall as he is capable of standing or falling.

The demand to be let alone is, however, not so negative as it might sound, due to the scope and character of the whites' "doing" for the blacks in the past. Douglass demanded "the most perfect civil and political equality, and . . . all the rights, privileges and immunities enjoyed by any other members of the body politic." "Save the Negro and you save the nation, destroy the Negro and you destroy the nation, and to save both you must have but one great law of Liberty, Equality and Fraternity for all Americans without respect to color."[53]

The two main objectives of Douglass's campaign to have the blacks "left alone," in this fundamental sense of being subject only to the one great law for all Americans, were the right to vote and freedom from color prejudice. The former need not detain us here. Blacks wanted the vote, as Douglass repeatedly explained, because it was their right, because it was a means of education, because its denial was "to brand us with the stigma of inferiority," because it was a means of self-defense in a hostile South, and because it was an instrument for maintaining federal authority in the South.[54]

Douglass's concern with prejudice against the black requires more attention. From the beginning he saw this prejudice as arising from and contributing to the black's enslavement, his proposed expatriation, and his actual degradation. "This prejudice must be removed; and the way for abolitionists and colored persons to remove it, is to act as though it did not exist, and to associate with their fellow creatures irrespective of all complexional differences." Douglass marked out this path for himself and pursued it "at all hazards."[55] He spoke and acted against any form of public discrimination whatsoever against blacks. On trains and ships, in hotels and restaurants, in meetings and other public places, he resisted the conventional expressions of race prejudice. He described what might in modern parlance be called a "stroll-in," when he passed the time waiting for a steamer in New York City walking with two white ladies and had to beat off the attentions of several ruffians as a result. He engaged in such behavior, he said, "with no purpose to inflame the

---

53. Ibid., vol. 3, pp. 348–49.
54. Ibid., vol. 4, pp. 159–60.
55. Ibid., vol. 1, p. 387.

public mind; not to provoke the popular violence; not to make a display of my contempt for public opinion; but simply as a matter of course, and because it was right to do so."[56] Douglass certainly had that love of sheer combat that is necessary to the good politician—"I glory in the fight as well as in the victory"[57]—but he rarely did something that was right unless he thought it was also politic. This was certainly true of his persistent testing and challenging of conventions of race discrimination.

"The question is not can there be social equality?" for that does not exist anywhere. The question is rather, "Can the white and colored people of this country be blended into a common nationality, and enjoy together, in the same country, under the same flag, the inestimable blessings of life, liberty and the pursuit of happiness, as neighborly citizens of a common country?" This is not simply a matter of public behavior. It is true that Douglass argued that "men who travel should leave their prejudices at home,"[58] but fundamentally Douglass believed that men should not *have* any color prejudice that needs to be left at home. For blacks and whites to live together as fellow-citizens, color prejudice must be eradicated. In an essay in 1866 on "The Future of the Colored Race" Douglass stated as his "strongest conviction" that the black would neither be expatriated nor exterminated, nor forever remain a separate and distinct race, "but that he will be absorbed, assimilated, and will only appear finally . . . in the features of a blended race."[59] He emphasized that this would not happen quickly or by any forced process or "out of any theory of the wisdom of such blending of the two races." He did not, he said, advocate intermarriage between the two races; neither did he deprecate it. But seeing this as the only condition finally in which the Negro could survive and flourish in the United States, he naturally advocated a course of action that would prepare for it.

Douglass often displayed the concern with the psychological effects of segregation with which we are today so familiar. Thus an aspect of his campaign to get blacks into the army during the Civil War was the effect that this would have on the blacks' own self-regard, both directly and indirectly through an enhanced regard in the eyes of others. He had a similar concern in other areas, such as voting, but the psychological consideration was never the only reason for Douglass's policy and seldom a major one.

---

56. Ibid., vol. 2, p. 126.
57. Ibid., vol. 1, p. 137.
58. Ibid., vol. 2, p. 450.
59. Ibid., vol. 4, p. 195.

Such considerations were of more than usual importance in the education of the young. Douglass indignantly described how he withdrew his nine-year-old daughter from a private school when it was proposed to teach her separately, "as allowing her to remain there in such circumstances, could only serve to degrade her in her own eyes, and those of the other scholars attending the school."[60] More than twenty years later he urged passage of a bill providing for mixed schools in the District of Columbia "in order that the mad current of prejudice against the Negro may be checked; and also that the baleful influence upon the children of the colored race of being taught by separation from the whites that the whites are superior to them may be destroyed." "Educate the poor white children and the colored children together; let them grow up to know that color makes no difference as to the rights of a man; that both the black man and the white man are at home; that the country is as much the country of one as of the other, and that both together must make it a valuable country." "We want mixed schools not because our colored schools are inferior to white schools—not because colored instructors are inferior to white instructors, but because we want to do away with a system that exalts one class and debases another."[61]

There is, then, a connection between the views of Douglass and those of today's integrationists with regard to race prejudice and segregation. But the main lesson lies in the differences. First, although all such segregation carries an implication of black inferiority in the opinion of the white segregators, not all segregation is equally harmful merely on that account. The harm is great in the case of black children, Douglass thought, but it is small as more mature blacks are the objects of segregation. Unlike Martin Luther King, Jr., Douglass did not see segregation as doing any harm *to himself*.[62] Describing harassment by a Syracuse mob in 1861, Douglass said that the aim was to humble and mortify him. "Just as if a man could feel himself insulted by the kick of a jackass, or the barking of a bull-dog. It is, to be sure, neither pleasant to be kicked nor to be barked at, but no man need to think less of himself on account of either."[63] At the same time that he fought to prevent the damage that segregation can do the self-respect of black children and to childlike adults, Douglass held himself forward as an example of the man who has risen above that kind of harm.

---

60. Ibid., vol. 1, p. 372.

61. Ibid., vol. 4, pp. 288–89.

62. Martin Luther King, Jr., *Stride toward Freedom* (New York, 1958), pp. 20–21.

63. Douglass, *Life and Writings*, vol. 3, p. 182.

Douglass fought prejudice and all its manifestations fundamentally not because of its psychological effect, but because of the objective harm to which prejudice leads. He did express the belief that "the tendency of the age is unification, not isolation; not to clans and classes, but to human brotherhood"; but he did not rest his political case on it. Indeed he expressed this belief in the context of the deep and firm moral and political hold the black has upon *this* country.[64] Douglass's political concern was to free the black from very clear and objective oppression, provide him with the platform of equal opportunity, and show him how to use his opportunity to live a decent, independent, civilized life.

> Having despised us, it is not strange that Americans should seek to render us despicable; . . . having denounced us as indolent, it is not strange that they should cripple our enterprise; having assumed our inferiority, it would be extraordinary if they sought to surround us with circumstances which would serve to make us direct contradictions to their assumption.[65]

What concerned Douglass was not fundamentally the whites' despising, denouncing, or assuming, but their rendering despicable, their crippling of enterprise, their imposition of degrading circumstances. The black's fight against prejudice was not, in Douglass's view, fundamentally a fight for "integration"; it was a fight to establish the outworks of his claim to be left alone. "The spirit which would deny a man shelter in a public house, needs but little change to deny him shelter, even in his own house."[66] Douglass was concerned mainly with the shelter, not the spirit.

Consistently with this view, Douglass linked almost every one of his criticisms of social and other forms of segregation with observations on the black's duty to exert himself. "It is too true, that as a People, our aspirations have not been sufficiently elevated; and it is also equally true, that we have been and still are the victims of an ostracism as relentless as the grave. . . ." Yet, "our elevation as a race, is almost wholly dependent upon our own exertions."[67] "He who would be free must strike the first blow," Douglass repeated again and again. But this is not enough—at least in Douglass's opinion. Not all restrictions on freedom are imposed by others. Not all prejudice has its source simply in the mind of the bigot. While striking off

64. Ibid., vol. 4, p. 412.
65. Ibid., vol. 2, p. 268.
66. Ibid., vol. 4, p. 295.
67. Ibid., vol. 2, pp. 373, 360.

his shackles, the black also had to take a responsibility for the good use of his freed limbs and mind.

What Shall the Black Man Do with Himself?

Douglass was acutely aware of the extremely limited means for self-improvement available to the blacks. Speaking of Southern blacks in 1886, he said, "They are asked to make bricks without straw. Their hands are tied, and they are asked to work. They are forced to be poor, and laughed at for their destitution."[68] Nevertheless every major part of Douglass's argument—whether dealing with abolition, black troops, the vote, color prejudice, or anything else—was accompanied by stern calls to the black man to exert himself.

> We have but to toil and trust, throw away whiskey and tobacco, improve the opportunities that we have, put away all extravagance, learn to live within our means, lay up our earnings, educate our children, live industrious and virtuous lives, establish a character for sobriety, punctuality, and general uprightness, and we shall raise up powerful friends who shall stand by us in our struggle for an equal chance in the race of life. The white people of this country are asleep, but not dead.[69]

Again and again, Douglass asked, as he did, for example, in his newspaper in 1848, "What is the use of standing a man on his feet, if, when we let him go, his head is again brought to the pavement?" No matter how much we beg and pray our white friends for assistance, he said, and no matter how generously they provide it, "unless we, the colored people of America, shall set about the work of our own regeneration and improvement, we are doomed to drag on in our present miserable and degraded condition for ages."

> What we, the colored people, want is *character*, and this nobody can give us. It is a thing we must get for ourselves. We must labor for it. It is gained by toil—hard toil. Neither the sympathy nor the generosity of our friends can give it to us. . . . It is attainable; but we must attain it, and attain it each for himself. I cannot for you, and you cannot for me. . . . We must get character for ourselves, as a people. A change in our political condition would do very little for us without this. . . . Industry, sobriety, honesty, combined with intelligence and a due self-respect, find them where

---

68. Ibid., vol. 4, p. 436.
69. Ibid., p. 441.

you will, among black and white, must be *looked up to*—can never be *looked down upon*. In their presence, prejudice is abashed, confused and mortified.[70]

Here, as usual, Douglass speaks of what he clearly regards as good in itself, regeneration and character, as means to the end of removing prejudice. Douglass's argument is, "Be a man and you will, in time, be treated as a man." In a comprehensive view, as Douglass saw, the end is to be a man. While we urge that Congress and the country perform their duties toward the black,

> we must never forget that any race worth living will live, and whether Congress heeds our request in these and other particulars or not, we must demonstrate our capacity to live by living. We must acquire property and educate the hands and hearts and heads of our children whether we are helped or not. Races that fail to do these things die politically and socially, and are only fit to die.[71]

Nevertheless from the point of view of the black, hampered and oppressed by the effects of prejudice, the immediate end is to be treated like a man, to which being one is a means. Douglass's statements typically contain the more comprehensive view but focus on the more particular one. The following is one further example, taken from dozens, written in 1883.

> [A]fter all, our destiny is largely in our own hands. If we find, we shall have to seek. If we succeed in the race of life, it must be by our own energies, and our own exertions. Others may clear the road, but we must go forward, or be left behind in the race of life.
>
> If we remain poor and dependent, the riches of other men will not avail us. If we are ignorant, the intelligence of other men will do but little for us. If we are foolish, the wisdom of other men will not guide us. If we are wasteful of time and money, the economy of other men will make our destitution the more disgraceful and hurtful. If we are vicious and lawless, the virtues and good behavior of others will not save us from our vices and our crimes.
>
> We are now free, and though we have many of the consequences of our past condition to contend against, by union, effort, co-operation, and by a wise policy in the direction and the employment of our mental, moral, industrial and political powers, it is the faith of my soul, that we

---

70. Ibid., vol. 1, pp. 316–18.
71. Ibid., vol. 4, p. 388.

can blot out the handwriting of popular prejudice, remove the stumbling-blocks left in our way by slavery, rise to an honorable place in the estimation of our fellow-citizens of all classes, and make a comfortable way for ourselves in the world.[72]

Conclusion

In Frederick Douglass we find a deep understanding of the dependence of the partial good, the good of blacks, on the good of the whole American community. It is well that there are leaders who take upon themselves the duty of promoting the good of the part, but that duty includes a recognition of and participation in a higher statesmanship. A Douglass knows the horizons of a Lincoln, although he does not himself need often to climb so high and scan so widely. The partisan and the statesman have ultimately the same end, but they begin from different points. They meet, in our system of government, in the political arena, where the parts take (at least implicitly) some responsibility for the whole, while they make demands on the whole—as Douglass did when he supported John Fremont for the presidency in 1856 and when he criticized and defended the Supreme Court in 1883.

Douglass argued that the black's greatest struggle was the struggle to become a part of the American political community and that the reason for that struggle was his creditable desire to keep his grip on the civilization that the white man possessed. Douglass was not assailed by refined doubts about "identity" or about the meaning of "civilization." For the time being, at any rate, the matter seemed clear enough. Speaking in 1868 at the inauguration of the Douglass Institute in Baltimore, Douglass elaborated on the grounds and the structure of civilization:

> Now, what are those elemental and original powers of civilization about which men speak and write so earnestly, and which white men claim for themselves and deny to the Negro? I answer that they are simply consciousness of wants and ability to gratify them. Here the whole machinery of civilization, whether moral, intellectual or physical, is set in motion. . . .
>
> We who have been long debarred the privileges of culture may assemble and have our souls thrilled with heavenly music, lifted to the skies on the wings of poetry and song. Here we can assemble and have our minds enlightened upon

72. Ibid., pp. 366–67.

the whole circle of social, moral, political and educational duties. Here we can come and learn true politeness and refinements. Here the loftiest and best eloquence which the country has produced, whether of Anglo-Saxon or of African descent, shall flow as a river, enriching, ennobling, strengthening and purifying all who will lave in its waters. Here may come all who have a new and unpopular truth to unfold and enforce, against which old and respectable bars and bolts are iron gates.[73]

Douglass saw, moreover, that if the object is to share in this civilization the means of securing that share must be designed so as to do no damage, or as little as possible, to that civilization.

Above all Douglass taught that the black, like every man, must walk the road of opportunity himself. As the black makes good use of the opportunities he has, more opportunities will open up; as he gives less reason for prejudice, prejudice will decline.

Without pretending to have exerted ourselves as we ought, in view of an intelligent understanding of our interest, to avert from us the unfavorable opinions and unfriendly action of the American people, we feel that the imputations cast upon us, for our want of intelligence, morality and exalted character, may be mainly accounted for by the injustice we have received at your hands. What stone has been left unturned to degrade us? What hand has refused to fan the flame of popular prejudice against us? What American artist has not caricatured us? What wit has not laughed at us in our wretchedness? What songster has not made merry over our depressed spirits? What press has not ridiculed and condemned us? What pulpit has withheld from our devoted heads its angry lightning, or its sanctiminious hate? Few, few, very few: and that we have borne up with it all—that we have tried to be wise, though denounced by all to be fools—that we have tried to be upright, when all around us have esteemed us knaves—that we have striven to be gentlemen, although all around us have been teaching us its impossibility—that we have remained here, when all our neighbors have advised us to leave, proves that we possess qualities of head and heart, such as cannot but be commended by impartial men.[74]

It is said that in 1895 a young man asked Frederick Douglass's advice about what the young black just starting out should do. "The

---

73. Ibid., pp. 181–82.
74. Ibid., vol. 2, pp. 266–67.

patriarch lifted his head and replied, 'Agitate! Agitate! Agitate!' "
Four years later the same youth asked the same question of Booker
T. Washington, "who answered, 'Work! Work! Work! Be patient and
win by superior service.' "[75] The contrast is full of significance, but
for the present it is sufficient to reiterate that this agitator laid a
striking amount of emphasis upon work. Some tell you to go to
Africa or Canada or to go to school, Douglass told his readers in
1853. "We tell you to go to work; and to work you must go or die.
Men are not valued in this country, or in any country, for what they
are; they are valued for what they can *do*. It is vain that we talk about
being men, if we do not do the work of men."[76]

"Agitate!" but at the same time, "Work!" Work because that is a
good form of agitation, and work because the opportunity to work is
what you are agitating *for*. External obstacles are not, after all,
decisive. Obviously that is no reason placidly to accept them. Douglass in fact spent most of his energy and most of his words in trying
to remove them. But while he was concerned, partly by chance and
partly by deliberate choice, mainly with helping to provide the
conditions of the good life for the black, Douglass did not lose sight
of the fact that possession of the opportunity to live well is not living
well. Concluding his autobiography, Douglass described what he
had tried to teach:

> . . . that knowledge can be obtained under difficulties—that
> poverty may give place to competency—that obscurity is not
> an absolute bar to distinction, and that a way is open to
> welfare and happiness to all who will resolutely and wisely
> pursue that way—that neither slavery, stripes, imprison-
> ment, nor proscription need extinguish self-respect, crush
> manly ambition, or paralyze effort—that no power outside
> of himself can prevent a man from sustaining an honorable
> character and a useful relation to his day and generation—
> that neither institutions nor friends can make a race to stand
> unless it has strength in its own legs—that there is no power
> in the world which can be relied upon to help the weak
> against the strong or the simple against the wise—that races,
> like individuals, must stand or fall by their own merits. . . .[77]

---

75. *Life and Writings*, vol. 4, in Philip S. Foner, "Frederick Douglass,"
p. 149.

76. Douglass, *Life and Writings*, vol. 2, p. 224.

77. Douglass, *Life and Times*, p. 479.

8
The School of Slavery:
A Reconsideration of
Booker T. Washington

You ask that which he found a piece of property and turned into a free American citizen to speak to you tonight on Abraham Lincoln. I am not fitted by ancestry or training to be your teacher tonight for, as I have stated, I was born a slave.

> —Booker T. Washington,
> an address before the
> Republican Club of New
> York City, February 12,
> 1909

"One hesitates," wrote W. E. Burghardt Du Bois in 1903, "to criticise a life which, beginning with so little, has done so much. And yet the time is come when one may speak in all sincerity and utter courtesy of the mistakes and shortcomings of Mr. Washington's career, as well as of his triumphs, without being thought captious or envious, and without forgetting that it is easier to do ill than well in the world."[1] It is the premise of this essay that these words apply now to the very movement of which Du Bois's critical essay, "Of Mr. Booker T. Washington and Others," was one of the first major documents and of which the National Association for the Advancement of Colored People is the major instrument. Is it not time to "speak in all sincerity and utter courtesy of the mistakes and shortcomings," not of this man or this organization, but of the understanding they represent of the principles that govern or ought to govern the conduct of American citizens and free men, white and black, in their relations with one another?

This essay was originally published in Robert A. Goldwin, ed., *One Hundred Years of Emancipation* (Chicago: Rand McNally & Co., 1964).

1. W. E. Burghardt Du Bois, *The Souls of Black Folk* (Chicago: A. C. McClurg & Co., 1903), pp. 43–44.

Although the movement headed by the NAACP has never enjoyed the same degree of unity of purpose or widespread support that characterized the leadership of Booker T. Washington, it is scarcely less preeminent in its day and in its chosen field than Washington was in his. Here too is a life, albeit an institutional one, that began with little and has done much; and one hesitates to criticize it for fear, not so much of seeming captious and envious, as of seeming infected with one or another of the forms of bigotry through which the NAACP and its allied groups have had to steer and to which no respectable man would resort. Yet unwillingness to speak on these grounds can hardly be justified if there is reason to think, as Du Bois thought of Washington, that the standard to which men are invited to repair is false or in important respects defective.

Our concern is not, any more than Du Bois's was, with particular mistakes or superficial shortcomings. We are not concerned with tactics; we are somewhat more concerned with broad strategy, where means and ends mix; and we are above all concerned with the ends sought and the reasons for thinking them good. But why approach these questions through Booker T. Washington instead of looking at present-day leaders addressing themselves to present-day problems? A strong historical justification may be found in the fact that the Negro "protest" movement of the twentieth century, of which the NAACP is still the major exponent, took form very largely in response to and rejection of Washington's policy of "accommodation." It was not a thoughtless response; it was surely not merely captious and envious. But it was heavily dependent on its picture of what it was against; it was against Booker T. Washington. Not that Washington plays much part in the rhetoric of the "protest" movement today. Yet it may be suggested, without here trying to prove, that the movement, understandably preoccupied today with specific policies, relies heavily for its higher justification on its early leaders and they, in turn, defined their position against the background that Washington provided.

We have used the customary terms, "accommodation" and "protest," in referring to Washington's position and that of his opponents. But although the terms are now common in the histories, they are the product of the anti-Washington movement; they convey, without explaining or justifying, the anti-Washington argument. The terms imply that the difference was a difference in strategy, or approach, or style. The question was *how* to go about promoting the advancement of colored people, to adopt the terminology of the new organization. Washington's answer to that question was summed up by many, not without some justification, as "accommodation"; and the

177

"protest" movement was born out of and rests upon a rejection of that answer. Of course all questions of strategy point to the ends served, and the higher principles of strategy are determined by the order of the ends, in principle and in time. Problems of higher strategy and questions about ends become more pressing when tactics at the lower levels are successful. Such is the condition of the "protest" movement today, and in this condition lies the need to speak of Washington again. For Washington always kept in central position the question that his successors push to the periphery: what constitutes the "advancement" of colored people, or any people?

Since the ranks of the "protest" movement were so largely formed in opposition to Washington and since that movement, for all its variety of forms and objectives, still finds its definition in that original protest, it is well to begin with the bill of particulars drawn against Washington's leadership. This was a bill drawn by men who felt deeply and reasoned well, men who concluded, often slowly and reluctantly, that the future of the Negro in the United States lay in a rejection of the position of the most powerful, most loved, and most feared Negro leader the country has ever seen. Their passion, reason, and organizational and political skill have prevailed. What was the indictment?

> First, that Washington advocated, successfully, that the Negro should enter into a compromise with the dominant white community, North and South, in which the Negro would in effect give up his claims for equal political, civil, and social rights and accept a position of indefinite tenure at the bottom of the ladder, in return for the opportunity to be left to earn and consume his crust of bread and, if he should work very hard, to enjoy the modest material comforts of a dutiful dependent class.
>
> Second, that Washington acceded to the disfranchisement of the Negro and to the use by the Negro of his vote, in the rare cases where he was permitted to vote, under the tutelage of his former masters, thus accepting and accelerating the withdrawal of the only weapon with which the Negro could enforce his civil rights, his economic opportunity, and his dignity as a human being.
>
> Third, that Washington insisted on the fundamental need for the Negro to secure and retain the good will and cooperation of the Southern whites and strengthened white prejudice and gave countenance to indignities practiced against the freedman by his counsel of silent submission.
>
> Fourth, that Washington practiced and encouraged a form of education designed to keep the Negro in the South and

on the land, designed to fit the Negro for menial labor and to content him with a more or less permanent position as a hewer of wood and a drawer of water; that in consequence he neglected and even deliberately stifled the efforts of others to further higher educational opportunities for Negroes, thus further contributing to their permanent depression.

Fifth, that Washington taught a mean materialism, mitigated only by the delusive hope that as the Negro succeeded in his pursuit of material well-being he would lay the foundation for increased acceptance by his white neighbors and for his own higher aspirations; that he adopted in fact the prevailing business philosophy of Northern businessmen with whom he came into increasing contact, sacrificing the best interests of Negroes to Northern Avarice as he sacrificed them to Southern Prejudice.

Sixth, that Washington was perennially and unreasonably optimistic about the improvement of the condition of the Negro and his acceptance by the white community, and that he used his enormous influence, cultivated with so much care and at so great a cost, to frustrate or suppress a more vigorous and varied Negro leadership, precisely at the time when his own program, however understandable or even justifiable it may have been as the best bargain that a people just emerging from slavery could make, proved increasingly narrow and insufficient.[2]

The Tuskegee movement was not a separatist or nationalist movement. It rested emphatically on the fact of "integration," although

---

2. I have omitted one count from this list, the soft indictment much favored by historians, that Washington was, after all, merely a "man of his times," sharing the widespread opportunism, accepting current notions of Negro education (and even Negro inferiority), moved by the fashionable currents of Social Darwinism and the Gospel of Wealth. We need not pause here to inquire whether this does not attempt to explain what is reasonably clear—what Washington said and did—by viewing it as a reflection of what is cloudy and vague—the "times" in which he lived; or whether these "times" were not formed out of the ideas of men, men like Washington. Our concern is more down to earth. If we are to presume of Washington that he is merely a "man of his times" (and treat him with the patronizing tolerance he would then deserve) are we not to presume (and to treat) similarly Washington's opponents and their successors? And have we not therefore cut away any ground upon which we might stand in addressing ourselves, as all of these men thought to address themselves, to questions about the "times" in which we live? The hard indictment is much preferable, because on that basis we can confront Washington, and thus his successors.

not the kind of integration that first comes to mind today. In the same year that Justice John Marshall Harlan said, in his dissent in *Plessy v. Ferguson*, that "the destinies of the two races in this country are indissolubly linked together," Washington said: "We rise as you rise; when we fall you fall. When you are strong we are strong; when we are weak you are weak. There is no power than can separate our destiny."[3]

Washington sought to work out that destiny within the limits set by the primitive condition of the Negro and the prejudice of the white. But whereas Harlan stressed the need to protect the Negro against irrational prejudice, Washington argued—can it have been seriously, we ask today?—that "the Negro can afford to be wronged; the white man cannot afford to wrong him," and that unjust laws directed by whites against Negroes harm the former but only inconvenience the latter. Whereas Harlan's underlying theme is race hate, Washington's is "the question of the highest citizenship." The inconveniences suffered by the Negro would diminish and diminish in significance to the extent that he could measure up to this highest citizenship. "This country demands that every race measure itself by the American standard. By it a race must rise or fall, succeed or fail, and in the last analysis mere sentiment counts but little."

But is not the American standard the Declaration of Independence? And is it not the Negro's task to act as the thorny, relentless conscience of America by demanding the equality, the rights, the freedom that American whites, professing adherence to the national standard, refuse to grant to American Negroes? So indeed Du Bois and his colleagues and successors argued. Washington speaks of duty; yet surely, they insisted and continue to insist, the language of America is rights. This is both the strongest case against Washington and the way to an understanding of his deepest justification; for Washington found in the pages of slavery—full of injustice and degradation as they were—instruction in freedom and in the highest citizenship.

There is irony in the condition of the American Negro, a hard irony but, Washington thought, a noble one. The white slave-trader violated the fundamental principles of his own civilization and thereby degraded himself, even in comparison with the black slave-traders with whom he had commerce; yet he introduced those slaves and their descendants to the civilization that he served so badly. The

---

3. 163 U.S. 560 (1896); E. Davidson Washington, ed., *Selected Speeches of Booker T. Washington* (Garden City, N.Y.: Doubleday, Doran & Co., 1932), pp. 75–77.

fact provides him no defense, as it provides no defense of those who bought from him and used men as animals; but it is a fact that few American Negroes would wish to see undone.

> Think of it: we went into slavery pagans; we came out Christians. We went into slavery pieces of property; we came out American citizens. We went into slavery without a language; we came out speaking the proud Anglo-Saxon tongue. We went into slavery with slave chains clanking about our wrists; we came out with the American ballot in our hands.[4]

This is not an argument that "all's for the best," nor is it an apology for injustice past or present, but Washington constantly sought to draw American Negroes' attention to the fact that slavery was their road to freedom and civilization and to explain the past and present implications of that fact. The Africans' very struggle against slavery was their first lesson in freedom; "the fugitive slaves learned in the United States, in their very efforts to be free, something about the nature of freedom that they could not have learned in Africa."[5] Washington often argued that, notwithstanding all the cruelty and moral wrong of slavery, "the ten million Negroes inhabiting this country, who themselves or whose ancestors went through the school of American slavery, are in a stronger and more hopeful condition, materially, intellectually, morally, and religiously, than is true of an equal number of black people in any other portion of the globe."[6] This is not, to repeat, to justify slavery, the net result of which is bad—"bad for the enslaved, and perhaps worse for the enslaver."[7] But Washington thought that the American Negro could not understand or improve his present condition without remembering that as he suffers arbitrarily indignities and injustice, so he came arbitrarily into possession of "the American standard" by which he measures the behavior of others and himself.

Washington often spoke of the contrast between the history of the Negro and the American Indian in their relations with the white man. The Indian, proud, free, ungovernable, refused to wear the yoke of slavery and when he was forced to do so rarely made a good

---

4. Washington, *Selected Speeches*, p. 37.

5. Booker T. Washington, *The Story of the Negro: The Rise of the Race from Slavery* (London: T. Fisher Unwin, 1909), vol. 1, p. 231.

6. Booker T. Washington, *Up from Slavery: An Autobiography* (1st ed.; New York: Doubleday, Page & Co., 1901), p. 16.

7. Booker T. Washington and W. E. Burghardt Du Bois, *The Negro in the South* (Philadelphia: George W. Jacobs & Co., 1907), p. 16.

slave; he elected to remain the noble savage or to die. The Negro, on the other hand, uprooted to an alien land, submitted mildly to being tamed, trained, and worked; he survived and even prospered. Observe the result. The Indian became increasingly merely savage, a despicable cur surviving (when he did survive) on scraps from the white man's table. The Negro became increasingly civilized; so that in 1879 the young Negro students at Hampton, only a very few years removed from slavery, agreed only with some muttering to accept among themselves a group of uncouth, evil-smelling, tobacco-smoking Indians so that the blacks might help to civilize the reds.

There is a good deal to be said, Washington suggests, for the noble savage in preference to the submissive slave—the stigma of slavery cuts deep and stays long. But that was not really the choice. The Negro seems to have been the only race, he repeatedly points out, to look the white man in the face and live. The Indian chose the way of degradation and destruction, while the Negro chose, not merely survival, but "the only method that existed at that time for getting possession of the white man's learning and the white man's civilization."[8] The irony of the history of the American Negro— heightened by the fact that he was the only man who did not choose to come to the New World but was brought unwillingly because he was needed there—did not end with emancipation. As he suffered the degradation and violence of his slavery as the price of his entry into the land of freedom, so he suffered and continues to suffer the discrimination and injustice of his partial freedom as the price of freedom itself. No one has a "right" to exact this price of him, and he might at any time refuse to pay it, as the Indian did. The Negro bent his back and lowered his eyes, not out of dumb submission or for the sake of mere survival, but to learn to stand straight and hold his head high.

With this as background, let us turn to Washington's much criticized policy with respect to the civil and especially the political rights of Negroes. Washington did seek to promote the rights of Negroes. He spoke out against lynching; he emphasized that the Negro must be dangerously dissatisfied until he gets equal justice; he argued against segregation laws; he criticized the grossly unequal educational facilities for Negroes; he helped to finance the test case against the "grandfather clause"; he sought to secure adequate accommodations for Negroes on Southern railroads; and he used his influence, often quietly and even under cover, to combat specific cases of injustice and discrimination. He insisted that "no question is

---

8. Washington, *The Story of the Negro*, vol. 1, p. 136.

ever permanently settled until it is settled on the principles of highest justice";[9] and he left no fair doubt of his opinion that the highest justice so far as the Negro was concerned included (but was not exhausted by) full civil and political rights. Yet Washington never made the active pursuit of these rights a major part of his policy, and he sought deliberately to turn Negroes' minds in other directions. "Brains, property, and character for the Negro will settle the question of civil rights," he argued in his first address in 1884. "The best course to pursue in regard to the civil rights bill in the South is to let it alone; let it alone and it will settle itself." Thirty years later, when growing discrimination caused Washington to speak out more sharply on questions of civil and political rights, he nevertheless adhered to the view that "no law of Congress or of the State Legislature can help us as much, in the last analysis, as things that we can do. . . ."[10]

So far as political rights are concerned, we have Theodore Roosevelt's plain-spoken testimony that no one was more alive than Washington to the threat "contained in the mass of ignorant, propertyless, semi-vicious Black voters, wholly lacking in the character which alone fits a race for self-government, who nevertheless have been given the ballot in certain Southern States." Roosevelt estimated that half of the considerable time that he spent in consultation with Washington was spent "discussing methods for keeping out of office, and out of all political power, the ignorant, semi-criminal, shiftless Black Man who, when manipulated by the able and unscrupulous politician, Black or White, is so dreadful a menace to our political institutions."[11] It is the duty of the Negro, Washington taught, "to deport himself modestly in regard to political claims, depending upon the slow but sure influences that proceed from the possession of property, intelligence, and high character for the full recognition of his political rights."[12] A heavy burden of justification lies on a Negro leader who spent so considerable a portion of his energy discouraging the exercise by Negroes of political rights that were legally theirs.

Before considering that justification, however, it is necessary to engage in the somewhat academic exercise of recalling and attempting to take seriously some distinctions, once generally accepted in

9. Washington, *Selected Speeches*, pp. 82–83.

10. Ibid., pp. 3, 243.

11. Preface to Emmett J. Scott and Lyman Beecher Stowe, *Booker T. Washington, Builder of a Civilization* (Garden City, N.Y.: Doubleday, Page & Co., 1917), pp. xiii–xiv.

12. Washington, *Up from Slavery*, p. 235.

the United States and implicit in Washington's program, which successive waves of the "protest" movement have caused to be almost forgotten. The three post–Civil War amendments to the Constitution are concerned with three distinct stages in the emancipation of the Negro. The Thirteenth Amendment granted him legal freedom; the Fourteenth made him a citizen and provided a constitutional guarantee of basic civil rights; the Fifteenth gave him the vote. No later one of these guarantees is necessarily implied in any earlier one. According to the principles of American law and political theory, a man (or a woman) might be a citizen enjoying full civil rights, for example, and yet not be permitted to vote or to hold office or to sit on juries. Participation in the political life of the community has always been thought to depend on qualifications, however minimal, set by the present citizenry or their representatives, acting according to their best judgment.

As a man might enjoy full civil rights and even be a citizen without being permitted to vote, so a man might be legally free, not a slave, without enjoying full civil rights; he might, for example, be subject to special regulations so far as the ownership of property or the making and enforcing of contracts or his personal liberty of movement are concerned. Admittedly this is a harder case. But if, as many have thought, a native-born free American who is not a citizen in possession of full civil rights is an anomaly, it is an anomaly suffered in recognition of the impossibility of transforming a man, much more a large body of men, from slave to citizen overnight. Indeed, the Fourteenth Amendment, following hard upon emancipation, although it removed the anomaly in law, did not remove, and at that time could not have removed, the anomaly in fact. We need not engage in loose talk about the Negro's "virtual re-enslavement" after Reconstruction or ignore the degree of legal protection which even the notorious black codes provided, and which large numbers of Negroes actually enjoyed, to see that the freedman was just that—no longer slave, not yet truly free. Washington describes the conditions of the freedman as a kind of serfdom, a natural and even necessary serfdom, which was "merely one of the stages through which a society, in which slavery has existed, has usually worked its way to freedom."[13]

It must immediately be said that freedom in the fullest or highest sense depends, and has always been understood to depend, on the enjoyment of all three of these degrees of freedom—bare legal freedom, civil rights, and political responsibility. Moreover, it is obvious

---

13. Washington, *The Story of the Negro*, vol. 2, p. 50.

that the actual enjoyment of the status legally guaranteed at one of the lower stages may in practice be impossible without the protection of a higher stage; for example, legally guaranteed civil rights may in practice be withheld from a group without political power. (That this is not necessarily the case is testified by the experience of many groups, for example women and aliens at various times and places.) But before entering into these important considerations, let us proceed academically a bit further and engage in an exercise of the imagination about the introduction of the freedmen to the full privileges and responsibilities of American citizenship. Our purpose is not to sigh about what might have been or to attempt to lay the blame for what is—to put such questions in any prominent place would violate the whole spirit of Washington's enterprise—but to see if we can thus understand Washington's policy.

Let us suppose that the doubts of men like President Andrew Johnson about the wisdom of admitting the Negro quickly into full political participation had prevailed. Suppose that a constitutional amendment had been passed opening the franchise only to individual Negroes who could meet reasonable but rather strict property and literacy qualifications to be set by Congress and administered by the states under federal supervision. What would have been some of the consequences? First, there is some reason to expect that the provisions, even though administered largely by Southern whites, would have been administered fairly and that Negro political participation, just because it was to be slow and limited, would have come to be accepted. Second, it is reasonable to expect that the groundwork would have been laid for a gradual but steady extension of the franchise, both by giving the white Southerner time to make the drastic adjustment required of him and by removing the basis of his fear, or alleged fear, of the sudden rise to political power of an unprepared group with many reasons to use its power against white interests. Third, it might be expected that, introduced to politics in this way, the Negro would have learned to use political power more independently and wisely than in fact he did. Fourth, it seems possible that such a policy, based on genuine American principles and directed to conditions and interests as they actually existed, might have led to a more harmonious development of relations between the races in the South. Finally, however, this policy would certainly have done injustice to many individual Negroes and in a sense to the whole race, for whites were not held to such standards. The freedman would have been required, before entering fully into citizenship, to show himself better prepared than many, perhaps most, whites.

When Booker T. Washington imagined that such a policy, despite its essential element of injustice to Negroes, would have been the least unsatisfactory way of integrating Negroes into American political life, he was standing in an eminently respectable line of statesmen, at the head of which, had he lived, we might have found Abraham Lincoln. Du Bois himself entertained similar speculations; but he thought that once federal protection of the Negro was withdrawn and he was handed back to the guardianship of those who were determined to thwart his freedom, the Negro's only defense lay in the ballot.

Du Bois concedes "that it is possible, and sometimes best, that a partially undeveloped people should be ruled by the best of their stronger and better neighbors for their own good, until such time as they can start and fight the world's battles alone." These conditions would be fairly well fulfilled "if the representatives of the best white Southern public opinion were the ruling and guiding powers in the South to-day"; but "the best opinion of the South to-day is not the ruling opinion." Consequently, "to leave the Negro helpless and without a ballot today is to leave him, not to the guidance of the best, but rather to the exploitation and debauchment of the worst. . . ."[14] "This truth," Du Bois says elsewhere, "the great Thaddeus Stephens saw, and with a statesmanship far greater than Lincoln's he forced Negro suffrage on the South."[15] "No one thought, at the time, that the ex-slaves could use the ballot intelligently or very effectively; but they did think that the possession of so great power by a great class in the nation would compel their fellows to educate this class to its intelligent use."[16]

Behind Washington's desire to see the Negro take up only slowly the exercise of his political rights lay his view that the Negro had been pushed too fast through the several stages of emancipation. Washington was not blind to the force of arguments like Du Bois's; but he was neither so sure as Du Bois that the best opinion in the South was, or could be assumed to be, beyond restoration, nor so hopeful about the educational effects upon Negroes of the possession of the ballot. Washington thought that the Negro's premature assumption of political power and responsibility found him so ill-prepared that he aroused legitimate fears and measures of self-defense in the white community and that he was unable to use his political power intelligently even to protect his own interests, to say nothing of exercising well the responsibilities of full citizenship.

---

14. Du Bois, *The Souls of Black Folk*, pp. 172–77.
15. Washington and Du Bois, *The Negro in the South*, p. 89.
16. Du Bois, *The Souls of Black Folk*, pp. 173–74.

Regarding white fears of a black political assault, it might be said that the Negroes were not to blame for what they were and that no harm done by their political activity could exceed the measure of just retribution. Washington saw that this kind of reasoning, however true, is a poor basis for any positive policy. In the history of the relations between Negro and white in the South there is scarcely any wrong on one side that cannot be shown to proceed from some prior wrong on the other. Washington's aim was to break out of the chain of mutual fear and injustice and to make, to the extent conditions permitted, a new beginning.

To make a policy of protesting injustice, laying the blame for it at the white man's door, and forcing that growth of Negro political power which was the very thing most feared by the whites was, he thought, only to lengthen the chain of mutual harm. The new beginning required the Negro to concede that the Southern whites (despite all their past and present guilt) had some legitimate reason to fear large-scale political participation by the Negro. Conceding this, Washington also conceded the necessity of applying special qualifications to Negro voters. He adhered to the principle that "whatever tests are required, they should be made to apply with equal and exact justice to both races."[17] Yet he was sufficiently realistic to know that such tests would in fact be applied more strictly, to say the least, to Negroes than to whites; and he was sufficiently statesmanlike to recognize that justice may be poorly served by a blind determination to do justice in every individual case—to insist on no tests or on tests applied strictly to all, even to those parts of the population not previously thought to need them. There was some unfairness in this policy, as there would have been in the better policy we have imagined, since the Negro is held to stricter requirements than the white. But while an individual white may be just as poor and ignorant as an individual Negro, it is of the utmost political relevance if the ignorant white is the exception and the ignorant Negro the rule.

Washington was willing to make substantial concessions to prepare for a new beginning, but that did not imply any concession or compromise so far as the *end* was concerned. In the end, he insisted, the only safe course for the South was also the right one: to admit the Negro to full citizenship when he should have become fit for it.

> It ought to be clearly recognized that, in a republican form of government, if any group of people is left permanently without the franchise it is placed at a serious disadvantage.

17. Washington, *Up from Slavery*, p. 237.

> I do not object to restrictions being placed upon the use of
> the ballot, but if any portion of the population is prevented
> from taking part in the government by reason of these
> restrictions, they should have held out before them the
> incentive of securing the ballot in proportion as they grow
> in property-holding, intelligence, and character.[18]

This was the duty of the South, and it was the course of both justice
and policy.

The Negro's duty was to make himself fit, and that is the basis
of Washington's efforts to turn Negroes from political to economic
activity. His aim, he said, was not "to give the people the idea that
political rights were not valuable or necessary, but rather to impress
upon them that economic efficiency was the foundation for every
kind of success."[19] Washington saw more clearly than Du Bois ever
did the relation of politics and economics so far as the American
Negro was concerned. Economics is fundamental; it is not sufficient.
The most immediate lesson the Negro had to learn was the former,
because the intelligent use of the vote requires a foundation that he
did not have. "Show me a race that is living on the outer edges of the
industrial world, on the skimmed milk of business, and I will show
you a race that is the football for political parties, and a race that
cannot be what it should be in morals and religion."[20] Unquestionably a race, even though permitted a considerable degree of economic
opportunity, is at a disadvantage without the vote (although Washington pointed out that a prosperous man is seldom without political
influence, whether or not he can vote); but so is a race that is
ignorant, untrained, and poverty-ridden at a disadvantage even if it
has the vote. The questions are which of these disadvantages is the
more fundamental, which can be removed, and which is it the
business of Negroes to remove? Washington argued that, under
existing conditions, if the Negro placed major emphasis on political
activity he offered himself up as a pawn in the political struggles of
others. There is something to be got out of being a pawn, and there
is a kind of education in it; but it is not the kind of reward or the kind
of education that the Negro ought to strive for.

Washington's famous policy of "accommodation" was based on
the belief that political wisdom, and political courage too, consists in
removing the evils that can be removed and doing the good that can
be done rather than crying out against all the injustice there is. But

---

18. Washington, *The Story of the Negro*, vol. 2, p. 370.
19. Ibid., p. 192.
20. Washington, *Selected Speeches*, p. 44.

Washington did more than trim his sails to the wind. He recognized that the progress of the Negro depended on the receptivity and cooperation of the white, as well as on the efforts of the Negro. And while he was, in the nature of the case, in a better position to influence the latter, he also did what he could to influence the former. If the Southern white was so intransigent that he simply would not permit the Negro to lay the economic foundation for his higher aspirations—if Negroes could not get contracts enforced, if they were not permitted in any significant numbers to own property, if they were forced to live in constant terror of violence—then Washington's policy collapses. Under such circumstances a resort to political power in sheer self-defense—mean and doubtful as the outcome must have been—would have been the only course open to the Negro short of abject submission or violent rebellion. The exact degree to which opportunities were, or are, open must remain a matter of debate; but it will be generally agreed that the Negro did not and does not confront such desperate extremity.

Washington was, by deliberate choice, an "optimist." "There is no hope for any man or woman, whatever his color, who is pessimistic; who is continually whining and crying about his condition. There is hope for any race of people, however handicapped by difficulties, that makes up its mind that it will succeed, that it will make success the stepping stone to a life of success and usefulness."[21] Again and again Washington insists on "the great human law, which is universal and eternal, that merit, no matter under what skin found, is, in the long run, recognized and rewarded." "The individual who can do something that the world wants done will, in the end, make his way regardless of his race." "Say what we will, there is something in human nature which we cannot blot out, which makes one man, in the end, recognize and reward merit in another, regardless of colour or race."[22]

Washington was sufficiently in contact with the life of the Negro in the South to know that "the long run" might be very long indeed, that there is also something in human nature that refuses to recognize merit, and that Negro success in economic matters might result immediately in further repression rather than in acceptance. (But before quoting Southern history too quickly to prove this point it would be necessary to consider how that history might have been different if the fear of Negro political power had been removed by the Negro.) His optimism was genuine but it was not simple-minded.

---

21. Ibid., p. 207.
22. Washington, *Up from Slavery*, pp. 40–41, 155, 235, and *passim*.

It was meant, of course, to stimulate the Negro; but it was also an attempt, by stating as a fact what was, in part, only what ought to be the fact, to stimulate the Southern white, in the best way that a Negro could do it, to the exercise of his better nature. Washington sought to strengthen the "best opinion" among the Southern whites which Du Bois admitted, or almost admitted, ought to rule.

In his first speech in 1884 Washington observed that Southerners have "a good deal of human nature"; they like to receive praise for doing good deeds and they resist outsiders who tell them to abandon the customs of centuries. He advocated no unmanly stooping to satisfy unreasonable whims but thought it prudent as well as charitable to remember what the South had to overcome.[23] "I early learned that it is a hard matter to convert an individual by abusing him, and that this is more often accomplished by giving credit for all the praiseworthy actions performed than by calling attention alone to all the evil done."[24]

Washington kept in the forefront the consideration that reform, wherever it might begin and whatever means it might use, is the making of just men, and that is rarely done by bitterness and abuse. Whether treating history or current affairs, Washington chose to see and to tell the Southern white side of the story as sympathetically and hopefully as was consistent with historical truth and fundamental principles of right. He found and praised Southern abolitionists, he assigned ample credit to the numerous Southerners who freed or wished to free their slaves, and he gave a balanced explanation of the fears that many white Southerners had of a large class of freedmen. He found it significant, in one of his last speeches, that the opinion in the *Guinn* case (1915), which outlawed the "grandfather clause," was written by a native-born Southerner, a former Confederate soldier, and a former slaveholder. He emphasized the good relations of individual whites and individual Negroes. He stressed the openness of many Southerners to straightforward criticism. Part of this same policy was Washington's careful avoidance of giving cause for irritation or resentment among Southern or other white people in the matter of the law and custom of segregation. Though necessarily involved in white society in the North, and to a considerable extent even in the South, Washington sought to avoid giving the impression of seeking social intercourse with whites, typically refusing invitations to purely social functions or attending doubtful ones without his wife and, we may be sure, wrapped in an aloof, businesslike dignity.

---

23. Washington, *Selected Speeches*, pp. 6–7.
24. Washington, *Up from Slavery*, p. 201.

This policy was saved, not from bootlicking, for only bitter or ignorant opponents could see that in it, but from a mere calculation about how to retain the cooperation of the Southern whites, by the fact that it was a policy also meant to minister to the whites. Washington is usually represented as a bridge between the white and the Negro communities, a broker making forays into the North and returning laden with money, a few political offices, and good wishes, and making humble explanation to the white South in return for at least bare tolerance and some modest support. For instance, Gunnar Myrdal says: "Washington's main motive . . . was accommodation *for a price*. . . . [H]e promised Negro patience, boosted Negro efforts, begged for money for his school and indulgence generally for his poor people."[25]

He was a bridge, but he bargained with the whites not only for money and support for the Negro but also for the sake of the whites' own souls. One of the remarkable characteristics of Washington is the extent to which he succeeded in living as well as mouthing the rule "that I would permit no man, no matter what his color might be, to narrow and degrade my soul by making me hate him."[26] He knew the hates and hurts of racial difference and strife; but he succeeded where so many other Negro leaders and writers have tried but failed, in wiping away all traces of bitterness and its accompanying corruption. Perhaps this was easier for Washington, who had experienced, even though as a mere child, the emergence from slavery into freedom, than it was for a man like Du Bois, born and reared in New England and scarcely part of the people he sought to lead; or for Walter White, whose features and complexion permitted him to live in both worlds; or for the other members of the Negro elite, largely Northern-born and Northern-educated, far from slavery yet not free of it. One of Washington's aims, indeed, was to keep alive that recollection of slavery, the source of the American Negro's instruction in and contribution to American freedom.

It was the school of slavery that gave Washington his deep understanding of and sympathy for the burden of the whites—a burden of guilt for past wrongs; of fears for the future, reasonable and unreasonable; of hate and prejudice. He took care not to add to that burden unnecessarily and to lighten it when he could. Washington did not give major emphasis to the wrongs done to Negroes, not fundamentally out of prudent reticence, but because Negroes were

---

25. Gunnar Myrdal, *An American Dilemma: The Negro Problem and Modern Democracy* (New York: Harper & Brothers, 1944), p. 726.

26. Washington, *Up from Slavery*, p. 165.

not the sufferers of the deepest wrong. It is on the side of the masters that the net disadvantage of slavery is to be counted. Through slavery, the Negro found or had thrust upon him freedom and civilization; his master betrayed them.

And the price continues to be paid. The most harmful effect, Washington reiterated, of Southern efforts to deprive the Negro of the ballot is not the wrong done to the Negro, which is temporary (and which, like slavery itself, may prove a net advantage by forcing the Negro to give his attention to more lasting methods of betterment), but in the permanent injury to the morals of the white man. In possession of this understanding, Washington could urge the ignorant black, bruised and maimed by the white man's boot, to let his heart go out to his tormentor, who condemned himself to stay in the ditch in order to keep the black man there. If the white man's guilt is greater, so is his hurt, because his contact with the black tends to pull him down, whereas the black can scarcely do anything but rise. But in his rise, Washington thought, he can help the white man up.

Speaking in Chicago on the duty owed by "the great and prosperous North" to "your less fortunate brothers of the white race South who suffered and are still suffering the consequences of American slavery," Washington spoke of Our New Citizen.

> Surely, surely, if the Negro, with all that is behind him, can forget the past, you ought to rise above him in this regard. When the South is poor you are poor, when the South commits crime you commit crime, when the South prospers you prosper. There is no power that can separate our destiny. Let us ascend in this matter above color or race or party or sectionalism into the region of duty of man to man, American to American, Christian to Christian. If the Negro who has been oppressed, ostracized, denied rights in a Christian land, can help you, North and South, to rise, can be the medium of your rising to these sublime heights of unselfishness and self-forgetfulness, who may say that the Negro, this new citizen, will not see in it a recompense for all that he has suffered and will have performed a mission that will be placed beside that of the lowly Nazarene?
>
> Let the Negro, the North, and the South do their duty with a new spirit and a new determination during this, the dawning of a new century, and at the end of fifty years a picture will be painted—what is it? A race dragged from its native land in chains, three hundred years of slavery, years of fratricidal war, thousands of lives laid down, freedom for the slave, reconstruction, blunders, bitterness between

North and South. The South staggers under the burden; the North forgets the past and comes to the rescue; the Negro, in the midst, teaching North and South patience, forbearance, long-suffering, obedience to law, developing in intellect, character and property, skill and habits of industry. The North and South, joining hands with the Negro, take him whom they have wronged, help him, encourage him, stimulate him in self-help, give him the rights of man, and, in lifting up the Negro, lift themselves up into that atmosphere where there is a new North, a new South—a new citizen—a new republic.[27]

The most famous expression of Washington's accommodation to segregation is his speech at the Atlanta Exposition in 1895: "In all things that are purely social we can be as separate as the fingers, yet one as the hand in all things essential to mutual progress." "The wisest among my race understand that the agitation of questions of social equality is the extremest folly, and that progress in the enjoyment of all the privileges that will come to us must be the result of severe and constant struggle rather than of artificial forcing."[28] These statements, called by Myrdal "the makeshift compromise with white society in the South,"[29] have been often discussed and criticized as leading to the strengthening of segregation. Justice Brown's opinion in the notorious Supreme Court case of *Plessy v. Ferguson*, which came the next year, does represent the judicial stamp of approval on the Washington policy. To avoid misunderstanding, even at the cost of straying for a bit from the immediate question, let me state what I understand to be the rationale of the *Plessy* decision and of Washington's policy.

First, it is not a violation of the equal protection clause of the Fourteenth Amendment—or of any standard of good law—for the law to make discriminations, provided they are reasonable, provided, that is to say, they are reasonably related to some legitimate end of the law. One legitimate end of the law is to preserve the peace and order and to promote the general convenience of the community. Distinctions of race may be reasonably related to such ends, as for example where two races (or two generally discernible groups of people) possessing significantly different habits (however caused) with respect to, say, hygiene, social behavior, and criminality, come into contact. Given conditions in the South forty years after emanci-

---

27. Washington, *Selected Speeches*, pp. 47–50.

28. Ibid., pp. 34–36. This speech is also printed in Washington, *Up from Slavery*, pp. 218–25.

29. Myrdal, *An American Dilemma*, p. 641.

pation, it was not unreasonable to require segregation of the races in certain public places. It may not have been necessary or even wise, but it was not unreasonable; that is, an argument can be made for it that would have weight in the mind of an intelligent, informed, and unbiased man.[30]

Second—and now I enter into interpretation and attribute a silent argument or assumption to Justice Henry B. Brown which I concede is open to debate—it may be admitted that in practice the "separate" facilities are not likely to be "equal." Nor is that inequality without some reason, for the specific relations being regulated are those between a superior and an inferior race, not intrinsically but in fact. Nevertheless, the standard of the law must be equality (and the standard of equality was set, not by the Supreme Court, but by the Louisiana statute, which put "equal" before "separate"). Whenever the law touches the actual conditions, it moves them in the direction of equality, not the equality of men, because that the law cannot provide, but the equality of civil rights: that platform on which every man in the United States is entitled to a place in his stretching out for true freedom.

Third, when Justice Brown says that if enforced separation is regarded as stamping the colored race with a badge of inferiority, "it is not by reason of anything found in the act, but solely because the colored race chooses to put that construction upon it"[31]—a remark so often subject to derision today and (rightly) put in contrast with Chief Justice Earl Warren's reasoning in *Brown v. Board of Education* (1954)—he was, I believe, not purporting to state the literal fact of the case but the higher truth of it. The literal fact is, as argued above, that the law finds its reason in an actual (although not inherent) inferiority and in that sense is a stamp of inferiority.

---

30. The fact that Jim Crow legislation was fairly late in coming is certainly relevant but it does not prove its unreasonableness or even that it was not a response to a deeply felt and legitimate need. A regulation of the relations between the races (if that be granted to be a legitimate end) at one time by the force of economic and political and moral superiority of one race might not suffice at another time when the progress of the second race had been sufficient to threaten the old methods of regulation but not yet sufficient to abolish the need for regulation. I repeat: it is not necessary to this argument that these Jim Crow regulations should have been wise or necessary (Washington argued that they were neither); it is only necessary that such an argument might have been seriously made by a reasonable man. See Booker T. Washington, "My View of Segregation Laws," *The New Republic*, December 4, 1915, pp. 113–14.

31. 163 U.S. 551 (1896).

The higher truth may be seen by comparing the reactions to segregated travel of Martin Luther King and Frederick Douglass. King reports that the first time he was seated behind a curtain in a dining car, "I felt as if the curtain had been dropped on my selfhood." He could never "adjust" to separate accommodations, not only because the separation was always unequal, but "because the very idea of separation did something to my sense of dignity and self-respect."[32] Washington reports that Frederick Douglass told how he was traveling in Pennsylvania and was forced to ride in the baggage car, despite having paid the same fare as other passengers. Upon receiving apologies for being "degraded in this manner" from some of the white passengers, "Mr. Douglass straightened himself up on the box upon which he was sitting, and replied: 'They cannot degrade Frederick Douglass. The soul that is within me no man can degrade. I am not the one that is being degraded on account of this treatment, but those who are inflicting it upon me.' "[33] Such a man is not stamped with inferiority by separate (and manifestly unequal!) accommodations, because he does not choose to put that construction on it.

Finally, neither Justice Brown nor Washington looked upon social integration as an end or even as a necessary means to an end; they both reject the argument "that equal rights cannot be secured to the negro except by an enforced commingling of the two races."[34] It is for this reason that Washington is often criticized. Admittedly, it is said, Washington did well enough for his time, but he tended to ignore and to obstruct others who wanted to hold up before Negroes the great end or ideal, which is a world without race-consciousness and willing, even anxious, to accept each man as an individual. As Dr. King says, "our ultimate goal is integration which is genuine intergroup and interpersonal living."[35] Washington was indeed silent about this great ideal, or only spoke to deny that the Negro hankered to mingle socially with whites. "I have never at any time asked or expected that any one, in dealing with me, should overlook or forget that I am a Negro."[36] He took the sensible view that racial differences and racial feelings would continue for as long as men could foresee,

---

32. Martin Luther King, Jr., *Stride toward Freedom: The Montgomery Story* (New York: Harper & Row, 1958), pp. 20–21.

33. Washington, *Up from Slavery*, p. 100.

34. 163 U.S. 551 (1896).

35. King, *Stride toward Freedom*, p. 220.

36. Booker T. Washington, *My Larger Education* (Garden City, N.Y.: Doubleday, Page & Co., 1911), p. 49.

and perhaps did not even wholly deserve being wiped out. The problem was not to obliterate a sense of racial difference, surely not by forcing one race on another, but to enable the races to live side by side in peace and mutual assistance. That would require some separation, as it required some integration. Above all, Washington refused to accept social integration as an end or even as a major means, because he saw that it would be fatal to the dignity of the Negro if he were to measure—as the standard of social integration inevitably encouraged him to measure—his own manhood (or "self-hood") according to the degree of his acceptance into every phase of white society.

Two major obstacles stood and stand between the status actually held by the American Negro and the status that he ought to enjoy: his own deficiencies and the unwillingness of his white fellows to admit him to his rightful place. Washington argued that both of these handicaps harmed both groups, that both required sympathetic understanding to be overcome, that the Negro's opportunity and duty lay mainly in overcoming the former, and that in doing that he would go far to help to overcome the latter.

> There is but one salvation for our country, and that is obedience to law, whether this law relates to human life, to property, or to our rights as citizens. For us, however, in our present condition, I believe that our greatest hope for salvation and uplift is for us to turn our attention mainly in the direction of progressive, constructive work. Let construction be our motto in every department of our lives North and South. Pursuing this policy, we will convince the world that we are worthy of the best treatment.[37]

While often reminding his audiences, colored and white, that there was neither justice nor policy in depriving the Negro of basic civil rights and the qualified Negro of political rights, he consistently and more emphatically tried to turn the Negro's attention from rights withheld to rights unwisely exercised or poorly prepared for, from limited opportunities to neglected opportunities, from social discrimination to social misbehavior. The protesters argued that the whites did the Negro a double wrong, causing his present situation and then blaming him for it. The NAACP insisted, in an early declaration, that the responsibility for the conditions of the Negro "rests chiefly upon the white people of the United States [and] that it is their duty to change them. . . ."[38]

---

37. Washington, *Selected Speeches*, p. 207; compare Booker T. Washington, *Working with the Hands* (New York: Doubleday, Page & Co., 1904), pp. 245–46.
38. *The Crisis*, May 1911, p. 24.

"If they accuse," Du Bois argued bitterly, "Negro women of lewdness and Negro men of monstrous crime, what are they doing but advertising to the world the shameless lewdness of those Southern men who brought millions of mulattoes into the world? . . . Suppose today Negroes do steal; who was it that for centuries made stealing a virtue by stealing their labor?"[39] Washington did not deny these facts—they are undeniable—but he quietly insisted upon what is also a fact, that "in spite of all that may be said in palliation, there is too much crime committed by our people in all parts of the country. We should let the world understand that we are not going to hide crime simply because it is committed by black people."[40] The task of Negro leadership, in Washington's view, was to hold the Negro American rather than the white American to the American standard, or rather to hold the white American to the American standard by holding the Negro to it.

The chief instrument of this task of leadership was the program of "industrial education," which Washington himself had learned, broom in hand, at the Hampton Institute. During Reconstruction, Washington says, two ideas agitated the minds of colored people, a desire to hold public office and a craze to learn Latin and Greek (both of which passions also gripped Washington). The instincts of the colored people toward the higher regions of freedom could scarcely have been better; their preparation for reaching them could not easily have been worse.

One of the saddest things Washington saw traveling through Alabama when he first came to Tuskegee in 1881 was "a young man, who had attended some high school, sitting down in a one-room cabin, with grease on his clothing, filth all around him, and weeds in the yard and garden, engaged in studying a French grammar."[41] Du Bois, the defender of higher education and the higher life, insisted, in some of his most powerful early writing against the Tuskegee movement, on "the rule of inequality:—that of the million black youth, some were fitted to know and some to dig; that some had the talent and capacity of university men, and some the talent and capacity of blacksmiths. . . ."[42]

Washington and Du Bois agreed, of course, that both industrial education and higher education were needed, but Washington emphasized, with a wisdom Du Bois appreciated only later, the need

---

39. Washington and Du Bois, *The Negro in the South*, pp. 181–82.
40. Washington, *Selected Speeches*, p. 237.
41. Washington, *Up from Slavery*, p. 122.
42. Du Bois, *The Souls of Black Folk*, p. 84.

to put first things first. Here as elsewhere Washington took the responsibility, which the protesters shun, of stating priorities: "Where the want of time and money prevents this broader culture (and a choice must be made by most), let us choose to give the student that training in his own language, in the arts and sciences that will have special bearing on his life and will thus enable him to render the most acceptable worship to God and the best service to man."[43] There is no need to deny Du Bois's affirmation (Washington emphatically asserted it) that "life [is] more than meat, and the body more than raiment"[44] to come to the conclusion that the Negro would be predominantly concerned for many years with food and clothing.

Washington's argument, then, was that the Negro was at the bottom and that his education had to begin there. He had to prepare to meet conditions as they were, to make a living, to learn the dignity of labor. He was building the foundations of his civilization so that later he might erect noble arches and elegant spires or study those put up by others. While insisting that as the industrial condition of a race improved, in the same degree its intellectual, moral, and religious life would improve, Washington did not take this to be an automatic process. He was in fact constantly exhorting Negroes to remember that material improvement was only the first step, and no pupil at Tuskegee, no member of the National Negro Business League (which he organized), no Negro within the range of his influence was allowed to forget it. It can certainly be said of Washington's program that it ran the risk of having people fix their attention on material comforts at the expense of higher things—it is hard to see how that risk could have been avoided under the circumstances. But it is unmerited to imply that Washington was careless in guarding against such a result or that he ever tacitly encouraged it. Du Bois's allegation that Washington's program was "a gospel of Work and Money to such an extent as apparently almost completely to overshadow the higher aims of life"[45] will not stand up to a fair examination of what Washington said and what he did.

Those who criticize Washington's industrial education on the grounds that it was intended to make the Negro a permanent peasant preoccupied with material things or that it did not keep pace with the onrush of the industrial revolution too often forget that, despite its name, industrial education was not merely or even basically a

---

43. Washington, *Selected Speeches*, pp. 18–19.
44. Du Bois, *The Souls of Black Folk*, p. 94.
45. Ibid., p. 50.

system of technical training.[46] It was aimed at the intellectual and moral improvement of the Southern Negroes, beginning where they were; it was the vehicle for instruction in the rudiments of civilization and true freedom. The goal, Washington reiterated, was to educate the hand, the head, and the heart. Washington taught skills and the love of labor, not only because his pupils needed to earn a living, but "for the independence and self-reliance which the ability to do something which the world wants done brings."[47] He taught neatness and personal cleanliness, the latter carried to such lengths that he insisted on his daily bath even under the most awkward circumstances, thus teaching those around him the value of the bath, "not only in keeping the body healthy, but in inspiring self-respect and promoting virtue."[48] He taught and vigorously insisted on the use of the toothbrush in the belief that "there are few single agencies of civilization that are more far-reaching."[49] He taught system, order, and regularity, and Tuskegee was operated according to a strict discipline. "A race or an individual which has no fixed habits, no fixed place of abode, no time for going to bed, for getting up in the morning, for going to work; no arrangement, order, or system in all the ordinary business of life, such a race and such an individual are lacking in self-control, lacking in some of the fundamentals of civilization."[50]

Washington aimed to start "the Negro off in his new life in a natural, logical, sensible manner instead of allowing him to be led into temptation to begin life in an artificial atmosphere without any real foundation."[51] Civilization begins with the things of most immediate importance, food, clothing, and shelter; it extends to skills, trade, commerce; and it leads finally to the broadest and most complete knowledge of the arts and sciences. The oft-told story of the rise of Tuskegee was meant to illustrate this natural development. "All the industries at Tuskegee have been started in natural and logical order, growing out of the needs of a community settlement.

---

46. Washington did sometimes call his system "industrial training." On the relation between training and education and the liberating effects of good vocational training, see *Working with the Hands*, p. 82 and *passim*. This volume is a sequel to *Up from Slavery* and contains a more detailed description of Washington's educational program.

47. Washington, *Up from Slavery*, p. 74.

48. Ibid., p. 58.

49. Ibid., p. 75.

50. From a talk to the students of Tuskegee, quoted in Scott and Stowe, *Booker T. Washington*, p. 231.

51. Washington and Du Bois, *The Negro in the South*, p. 51.

We began with farming, because we wanted something to eat." With few exceptions the buildings were reared by the students themselves, and although they were often crude and defective, "I felt that it would be following out a more natural process of development to teach them how to construct their own buildings." "It means a great deal, I think, to start off on a foundation which one has made for one's self."[52]

This same idea of a natural development was involved in Washington's emphasis on the soil as the place for Negroes, or for most Negroes. It was not merely that most Negroes were in fact on the soil, for Washington might have urged them to get into the towns (and into the North), as Du Bois and others did. He thought that the Negro was better off on the land; and he said of the aimless, foolish, foppish Negroes that he had observed in Washington that he wished he could remove the bulk of them "into the country districts and plant them upon the soil, upon the solid and never deceptive foundation of Mother Nature, where all nations and races that have ever succeeded have gotten their start,—a start that at first may be slow and toilsome, but one that nevertheless is real."[53]

Washington thought that the Negro was at his best in the rural districts and at his worst in the cities, and the great migration from the former to the latter does not itself disprove this judgment. It is not correct, as John Hope Franklin claims, that Washington "failed to see . . . that the industrial urban community was infinitely more attractive to Negroes as well as to whites."[54] He saw that quite well, but he thought that it was a superficial and harmful attraction which it was the duty of a Negro leader to resist. Perhaps it is true, as Franklin suggests, "that nothing represented more vividly the Negro's reflection of a typical American reaction than his inclination to move from the country to the city in the late nineteenth and early twentieth centuries," but Washington's point was that the Negroes were not typical Americans but unusually primitive and inexperienced ones and unusually open to the harmful effects of the products of high industrial civilization.

It may be, of course, that the pull of economic forces was so strong that the Negro was inevitably drawn to the cities and to the North, quite apart from what men like Washington or Du Bois might do to discourage or encourage him. In any case it is clear that, in

---

52. Washington, *Up from Slavery*, pp. 138, 149, 162, and *passim*.

53. Ibid., p. 90.

54. John Hope Franklin, *From Slavery to Freedom: A History of American Negroes* (New York: Alfred A. Knopf, 1947), p. 390.

general, the Negro today cannot be remade into a simple country toiler, even if that were desirable. Yet insufficient as the old Tuskegee system is now in its details, the principles of that education are as relevant in, say, Chicago or Washington, D.C., today as they were in Alabama a half century and more ago. "There is no position, however high, in science, or letters, or politics, that I would withhold from any race, but I would have the foundation sure."[55]

"After Emancipation," Du Bois writes, "it was the plain duty of some one to assume [the] group leadership and training of the Negro laborer," and Du Bois means that it was the duty of someone *other* than the Negro, as unquestionably it was.[56] It is characteristic that Washington was less concerned to point to the unfulfilled duties of others in the past than to discover and to take up the present duties of himself and his race.

> We have a right in a conservative and sensible manner to enter our complaints, but we shall make a fatal error if we yield to the temptation of believing that mere opposition to our wrongs, and the simple utterance of complaint, will take the place of progressive, constructive action, which must constitute the bedrock of all true civilization. The weakest race or individual can condemn a policy; it is the work of a statesman to construct one.[57]

Did Washington ask the Negro to carry a burden that was too heavy for him? Perhaps he did. Was it any wonder that many Negroes, bewildered and sorely tried, screamed out their bitterness and demanded their legal rights, and even more than their legal rights, often regardless of the consequences? It was not. Yet when the harsh words have been said, when the blame is assigned, when many rights have been granted and are actually enjoyed, Washington's soft, tough words still speak. Opportunities are limited. How

---

55. Washington, *Selected Speeches*, p. 45. Discussing a student's commencement oration on cabbages, Washington says: "As a matter of fact, there is just as much that is interesting, strange, mysterious, and wonderful; just as much to be learned that is edifying, broadening, and refining in a cabbage as there is in a page of Latin. There is, however, this distinction: it will make very little difference to the world whether one Negro boy, more or less, learns to construe a page of Latin. On the other hand, as soon as one Negro boy has been taught to apply thought and study and ideas to the growing of cabbages, he has started a process which, if it goes on and continues, will eventually transform the whole face of things as they exist in the South today." Washington, *My Larger Education*, pp. 142–43.

56. Du Bois, *The Souls of Black Folk*, p. 168.

57. Washington, *Selected Speeches*, p. 98.

well have we used those that are open? Rights are still curtailed. Have we prepared to exercise those we have? The Negro is blamed for too much of American crime. Are we nevertheless responsible for too much of it? The Negro is less than completely free. Do we know what freedom is? The Negro is a second-class citizen. Are we fit for first-class citizenship? The Negro can find deficiencies, in these respects and countless others, in every phase of American life, but his own deficiencies are not one whit removed by pointing out those of others. The Negro can serve himself, as he can serve his country, only by learning and thereby teaching the lesson that Theodore Roosevelt said was "more essential than any other, for this country to learn, . . . that the enjoyment of rights should be made conditional upon the performance of duty."[58]

In a speech in 1903, on the occasion of the birthday of George Washington, Booker Washington drew, as he often did, upon the history of the United States and the Negro's servitude and freedom in it to teach the meaning of freedom. Raising the question, "What is liberty for a race, and how is it to be obtained?" he warned against superficial or apparent freedom, the play that the child thinks is freedom, the spending that one man, the debauchery that another, the loafing that still another, mistakes for freedom.

> And so, all through human experience, we find that the highest and most complete freedom comes slowly, and is purchased only at a tremendous cost. Freedom comes through seeming restriction. Those are most truly free today who have passed through great discipline. Those persons in the United States who are most truly free in body, mind, morals, are those who have passed through the most severe training—are those who have exercised the most patience and, at the same time, the most dogged persistence and determination.[59]

The Negro's problem is to transform the restrictions and the discipline that were and are imposed upon him into the inner restrictions and discipline of the truly free man—to learn to work, Washington often said, having in the past only been worked. "It is a mistake," Washington said elsewhere, "to assume that the Negro, who had been a slave for two hundred and fifty years, gained his freedom by the signing, on a certain date, of a certain paper by the President of the United States. It is a mistake to assume that one man can, in any true sense, give freedom to another. Freedom, in the larger and

---

58. Preface to Scott and Stowe, *Booker T. Washington*, p. x.
59. Washington, *Selected Speeches*, pp. 108–11.

higher sense, every man must gain for himself."[60] There is, as Washington said, "nothing new or startling in this. It is the old, old road that all races that have got upon their feet and have remained there have had to travel."[61]

It was more than a policy of making the best of a bad situation that led Washington to stress, again and again, the advantages of having difficult obstacles to overcome, for that was intrinsic to his basic teaching about the nature of freedom. Here again, Washington found an ironical but real advantage to the Negro in his very disadvantages. "With few exceptions, the Negro youth must work harder and must perform his tasks even better than a white youth in order to secure recognition." The protester sees the unfairness of such a situation; Washington saw its high opportunity. "But out of the hard and unusual struggle through which he is compelled to pass, he gets a strength, a confidence, that one misses whose pathway is comparatively smooth by reason of birth and race."[62]

No doubt it is true that the training in civilization offered the Negro by his hard and unfriendly environment is only to be won by extraordinary patience, persistence, and labor. Many individuals, and perhaps the whole race, will succumb—and no one can blame them. Nevertheless, Washington's conclusion is hardly avoidable: "Standing as I do today before this audience, when the very soul of my race is aching, is seeking for guidance as perhaps never before, I say deliberately that I know no other road. If I knew how to find more speedy and prompt relief, I should be a coward and a hypocrite if I did not point the way to it."[63]

But does not Washington simplify? Doubtless he does; he was speaking to and for a simple people. But his simplification, particularly when taken with his actual policy, points more surely to the truth than those of the protesters. Du Bois contends that "in a world where it means so much to take a man by the hand and sit beside him, to look frankly into his eyes and feel his heart beating with red blood; in a world where a social cigar or a cup of tea together means more than legislative halls and magazine articles and speeches,—one can imagine the consequences of the almost utter absence of such social amenities between estranged races, whose separation extends even to parks and streetcars."[64] Washington would argue that the

---

60. Washington, *The Story of the Negro*, vol. 2, pp. 47–48.
61. Washington, *Selected Speeches*, p. 111.
62. Washington, *Up from Slavery*, p. 40. See Washington, *My Larger Education*, pp. 1–7 and *passim*.
63. Washington, *Selected Speeches*, p. 111.
64. Du Bois, *The Souls of Black Folk*, p. 185.

importance that this world, to which Du Bois and his successors accommodate themselves, attaches to sentimental social good fellowship is an indication of the extent to which this world has lost its sense of priority. Martin Luther King, for example, says of the Negroes of Montgomery, Alabama:

> Their minds and souls were so conditioned to the system of segregation that they submissively adjusted themselves to things as they were. This is the ultimate tragedy of segregation. It not only harms one physically but injures one spiritually. It scars the soul and degrades the personality. It inflicts the segregated with a false sense of inferiority, while confirming the segregator in a false estimate of his own superiority.[65]

It was the allegedly lamblike and submissive Washington who, a half century ago, stated what is surely the only manly response to this complaint:

> Character, not circumstances, makes the man. It is more important that we be prepared for voting than that we vote, more important that we be prepared to hold office than that we hold office, more important that we be prepared for the highest recognition than that we be recognized.[66]

The hardships and injustice faced by the Negro in America are not tragic or even exceptional. "On the contrary, they are common, and every race that has struggled up from a lower to a higher civilization has had to face these things. They have been part of its education."[67] There was for Washington no tormented introspection; no fondling of his psychological hurts; no wallowing, now in pride, now in shame, in the mysteries within the "Veil" of color; no self-conscious, self-pitying search for "identification." Washington had no need to repudiate white civilization, because he saw that, with all its faults, it *is* civilization; he had no need to repudiate his Negro heritage, because he saw in it a source of strength with which he and other Negroes might enter into civilization, earn the higher freedom, and through their example even help their former masters to recover it. It is not Washington who is the accommodationist.

It is much, perhaps it is too much, to ask the Negro to set himself as an example of devotion to duty, when his fellow Americans clamor for rights. It is much to ask the Negro to affirm that dignity and self-

---

65. King, *Stride toward Freedom*, p. 37.
66. Washington, *Selected Speeches*, p. 76.
67. Washington, *The Story of the Negro*, vol. 1, p. 15.

respect are not within the gift of any man or any law and to deny that a man consists of his psychological reactions to the psychological prejudices of those around him, when more and more whites look for themselves in the opinions of others. It is much to ask the Negro leader to teach his own people that a man is, finally, responsible for himself, when the other members of his society hanker to place the responsibility elsewhere. That is what Washington asked and taught. Could any lesson more noble or more needed issue from the school of slavery?

9
What Country Have I? Political Writings by Black Americans

The need for black Americans to recover and study their history and traditions is today a commonplace. This book is intended, among other things, to facilitate that recovery through the exploration of black political writing. But that writing is not the exclusive possession or concern of blacks, and it would be less significant, for blacks and for whites, if it were. These writers ascend through distinctively black problems and aspirations to a level of universal human concern. They stand out in the black tradition precisely because, remaining black, they speak, in ways that count, to men.

W. E. B. Du Bois, in a well-known passage, described the Negro as "a sort of seventh son, born with a veil, and gifted with second-sight in this American world. . . ." "One ever feels his two-ness,—an American, a Negro; two souls, two thoughts, two unreconciled strivings; two warring ideals in one dark body, whose dogged strength alone keeps it from being torn asunder."[1] No one perhaps has surpassed Du Bois's sensitive portrait of life within the Veil, and no one has been more concerned with the integrity and dignity of black identity, tradition, and principles. But Du Bois knew that all men live within their veils of prejudice, convention, and particularity, just as, at the same time, all thoughtful men reach out for the world beyond.

> I sit with Shakespeare and he winces not. Across the color line I move arm in arm with Balzac and Dumas, where smiling men and welcoming women glide in gilded halls. From out the caves of evening that swing between the strong-limbed earth and the tracery of the stars, I summon Aristotle and Aurelius and what soul I will, and they come

---

This essay was originally published as the preface and introduction to Herbert J. Storing, ed., *What Country Have I? Political Writings by Black Americans* (New York: St. Martin's Press, 1970).

1. W. E. B. Du Bois, *The Souls of Black Folk* (Chicago: A. C. McClurg & Co., 1903).

all graciously with no scorn nor condescension. So, wed with Truth, I dwell above the Veil.[2]

The black political thinkers represented in this book belong, first, to black Americans who will cherish them as fathers, brothers, friends, and leaders. They belong, next, to all Americans, for they stand among the noteworthy makers and critics of the American regime. They belong, finally, to those who seek to understand men and their relations with one another. They are teachers of all who aspire to wed with Truth and dwell above the Veil.

Introduction

When young Frederick Douglass, speaking before the American Anti-Slavery Society in 1847, asked, "What Country Have I?",[3] he put a question that circumstances compel every black American to ask. And when Douglass affirmed that he had no love for America and that, indeed, he had no country, he gave an answer that every thoughtful black in America has had to consider. This was not Douglass's final answer, as it has not been the final answer of most blacks in America; but the *question* does not thereby lose its potency. This question is the glass through which the black American sees "his" country. It is a glass that can distort. Anger, frustration, hopelessness, confusion, excessive inwardness often result from the black's situation; and they can lead to blindness and an utter incapacity to see the country in anything like its true shape. But the glass of the black's peculiar situation can also provide a clean, sharp view of America, exposing its innermost and fundamental principles and tendencies, which are largely ignored or vaguely seen through half-closed eyes by the majority of white Americans, whose circumstances do not compel them really to look at their country and to wonder about it. This does not mean that the black is necessarily revolutionary—most blacks are not; but it does mean that he takes seriously the possibility of revolution, or rejection, or separation. He thus shares the perspective of the serious revolutionary. He appeals, at least in thought, from the imperfect world of convention and tradition (very imperfect, indeed, from his point of view) to the world of nature and truth. In important respects, then, black Americans are like a revolutionary or, more interestingly perhaps, a founding generation. That is, they are in the difficult but potentially glorious position of

2. "Of the Training of Black Men," in ibid., p. 109.

3. Philip Foner, ed., *The Life and Writings of Frederick Douglass* (New York: International Publishers, 1950), vol. 1, p. 236.

not being able to take for granted given political arrangements and values, of having seriously to canvass alternatives, to think through their implications, and to make a deliberate choice. To understand the American polity, one could hardly do better than to study, along with the work and thought of the founders, the best writings of the blacks who are at once its friends, enemies, citizens, and aliens.

Although never dominant, there have always been articulate blacks who deny that America is their country. They insist that there is a fundamental incompatibility between America and the blacks who find themselves physically within, but in all significant respects alien to, this polity. "No, I'm not an American," Malcolm X protested, "I'm one of the 22 million black people who are victims of Americanism."

This view takes a number of forms. Some men argue that American society (or, more generally, Western society) is fundamentally and intrinsically corrupt, quite apart from any race problems. This was the view, for example, of the later Du Bois. "We tax ourselves into poverty and crime so as to make the rich richer and the poor poorer and more evil. We know the cause of this: it is to permit our rich business interests to stop socialism and to prevent the ideals of communism from ever triumphing on earth. The aim is impossible. Socialism progresses and will progress."[4] The criticism, if not the conviction of historical inevitability, continues to find expression in some radical black thought. "Societies and countries based on the profit motive will never insure a new humanism or eliminate poverty and racism."[5] Because the black is excluded from the society, he remains relatively uncorrupted by it and thus better able to see its true character; but the corruption does not, fundamentally, have anything to do with him. Capitalistic exploitation—or any evil of similar kind—may be exacerbated or given its specific form by racial conditions; but it exists and has its cause independently of racial conditions.

A more common argument points to America's views of and actions toward the black man as the essential flaw in American society. A version of this argument, rather common among early black separatists, is that America is not bad intrinsically, but that it is

---

4. *The Autobiography of W. E. B. Du Bois* (New York: International Publishers, 1968), p. 421.

5. H. Rap Brown, *Die Nigger Die!* (New York: Dial Press, 1969), p. 128. A more clearheaded view is presented in Julius W. Hobson's essay, "Black Power: Right or Left?" in Floyd E. Barbour, *The Black Power Revolt* (Boston: Porter Sargent, 1968).

bad for blacks. Much more common today is the view that white racism has eaten into the soul and psyche of America, harming not only (indeed, not mainly) the black but also the white, and corrupting the country perhaps beyond any possibility of reform. "America is mad with white racism," Eldridge Cleaver contends. "Whom the gods would destroy, they first make mad. Perhaps America has been mad far too long to make any talk of sanity relevant now."[6]

A third view of the incompatibility between the black and America is concerned less with the deficiencies of America and more with the needs of blacks. The argument here is that the black man has certain needs, certain opportunities, certain duties to bring himself to full manhood, and that he cannot do this successfully, or he can do it only with great difficulty, in the United States. It requires independence from the advanced, powerful, overwhelming, unfriendly white community and the establishment of a black nation. The building and managing of political communities is the highest business of man; it is the activity in which the highest development of human potential takes place. And unless a people finds or makes for itself opportunities to engage in that high business, on its own account and not just as laborers in someone else's garden, that people will suffer in its very character and competence as men. "Nationalism is a prerequisite for statehood," Floyd McKissick has written, "and membership in a state is imperative if a man is to have self-respect, if he is to command the respect of other men."[7] LeRoi Jones [Imamu Baraka] also had something like this in mind when he wrote, "The Black Man will always be frustrated until he has a land (A Land!) of his own. All the thought processes and emotional orientation of 'national liberation movements'—from slave uprisings onward—have always given motion to a Black National (and Cultural) Consciousness."[8]

The bulk of recent discussion among those who reject America has turned on the more immediate question, What is to be done? The prescriptions range from advice to leave the country to programs to destroy it or to engineer some more or less radical revolution (which are also forms of "leaving"). If none of these is possible, some way may have to be found of living among enemies, or living in the midst

---

6. Robert Scheer, ed., *Eldridge Cleaver: Post-Prison Writings and Speeches* (New York: Random House, 1969), p. 39.

7. Floyd McKissick, *Three-Fifths of a Man* (New York: William Morrow & Co., 1969), p. 101.

8. LeRoi Jones, *Home: Social Essays* (New York: William Morrow & Co., 1966), p. 244.

of an evil society. It is not surprising, when one considers the implications of these suggestions, that discussions about means so often degenerate into blind striking out, with little or no attempt to show any relation between means adopted and ends desired. Yet there is some reason even here. Just as no thoughtful black, however cool his reason and moderate his conclusions, can entirely discard the possibility that his country is at war with him, so he cannot entirely discard the possibility that under some circumstances the most rational and noble course may be, after all, naked defiance of an inhuman, oppressive society, even at the price of certain annihilation.

Most black Americans have decided that, for all its defects and injustice, America is their country. The black abolitionists like Frederick Douglass fought the American Colonization Society and all efforts to rid the country of its black population hardly less vigorously than they fought slavery; and typically they regarded these as but two sides of the same coin. We are here, Douglass affirmed repeatedly, and here we intend to stay. With all her faults, America is a better home and school for her black stepchildren, as Douglass called them, than any African or South American wilderness. The American principles of equality and individual liberty are, indeed, often violated or ignored in their application to the black, who has been closed out from the rights and opportunities that he ought to enjoy. The problem basically is to hold America to her own principles, so that the black can share American liberty and civilization.

This has, of course, been the basis of the twentieth-century civil rights movement, which has attempted to protect individuals from racially inspired injustices, such as job discrimination, or legal inhibitions on voting, or inferior education. The civil rights movement has not, generally speaking, been very philosophical. Partly this is because the battles of political and constitutional principle seemed to have been fought and won in an earlier day. Partly it is because, in its individualistic ends and its legal, conventional means, the civil rights movement accepted without reservation basic American political principles. The job seemed to be to keep up the pressure and to secure implementation of the civil rights program. The civil rights movement also accepted the widespread indifference among contemporary American political leaders and thinkers about what individuals *do* with their rights and opportunities, standing in this respect in striking contrast to the older fighters for civil rights, such as Frederick Douglass.

The recent civil rights movement shares with the older one the ultimate aim of assimilation. The focus, politically, legally, socially, and in every other conceivable way, is on the individual human beings, the color of their skin being fundamentally irrelevant. These were the views of the old CORE, described so charmingly by James Farmer, where a young white female worker failed to identify an attacker as black, for fear of somehow betraying the principle that race differences should not be "noticed."[9] Assimilation or racial amalgamation seems to provide the final step that completes the whole civil rights program. Whether because amalgamation is seen as the only way, finally, to destroy race prejudice, or because it seems demanded in principle by the brotherhood of all men, or because it seems to follow from the radical individualism of civil rights, "integration" as a goal has meant men living together without consciousness of color differences, which leads to, if it does not require, the elimination of those differences by racial amalgamation.

In the last few years the movement for civil rights and integration has come under criticism with respect to its commitment to legal and nonviolent means, its assimilationist ends, and even its individualistic philosophy. Questions that were considered closed in the heyday of NAACP legal action for civil rights have been reopened. There is again a good deal of agitation of basic theoretical issues, and while the result is often merely confusing, it can be highly illuminating. Separatism and other radical positions are again being taken seriously by thoughtful and responsible blacks. More common, however, are renewals of the old quest of the black American for a position that is neither assimilationist nor separatist and neither individualistic nor racist, but that attempts to unite these elements in theory and in practical programs. Although quite different from what has recently been thought of as "integration," this new (or new-old) line of thinking is nevertheless integrationist in the proper sense of the word. While the civil rights movement often assumed or looked forward to racial *amalgamation* or homogenization, the more recent thinking is in the direction of integration in the more precise sense of making a whole out of parts that are and remain distinct.

The recent movement toward Black Power is, by and large, integrationist in this sense, although it begins with a kind of separation. It begins with calls to blacks to "collect ourselves," but to do so in preparation for entering the broader community. The principle of "collecting ourselves" concerns both means and ends. On the level of means, Stokely Carmichael and Charles Hamilton, for example, argue that those who say that blacks ought to engage in coalition politics are putting the cart before the horse—or trying to pull the

---

9. James Farmer, *Freedom—When?* (New York: Random House, 1965), p. 85.

cart without any horse. The first requirement of coalition politics is to collect oneself, to collect one's power. The rule of the game is that if you go in with nothing, you come out with nothing; and that is the way the blacks have played it in the past.[10]

The more fundamental, philosophical ground of Black Power is to be found in the same principle of "collecting ourselves," but here in the sense of black self-understanding. The argument is that blacks need to collect themselves psychologically, morally, and socially, as well as in power terms; only then will they have a real basis for conducting their own lives and participating in the broader American community. Thus there has been a resurgence among blacks of interest in and commitment to black institutions and standards and black ways of thinking and acting. In the opinion of the advocates of Black Power, the practical result of the amalgamationist view, for all its individualism, was to teach that the Negro future lies in being white, whereas the practical result of Black Power is to teach pride in being black. Thus Carmichael and Hamilton say,

> The racial and cultural personality of the black community must be preserved and that community must win its freedom while preserving its cultural integrity. Integrity includes a pride—in the sense of self-acceptance, not chauvinism—in being black, in the historical attainments and contributions of black people. No person can be healthy, complete, and mature if he must deny a part of himself; this is what "integration" has required thus far. This is the essential difference between integration as it is currently practiced and the concept of Black Power.[11]

As Carmichael and Hamilton make clear, black cultural integrity is to be the basis not for leaving the American community but for significant participation in it.

This concern for cultural integrity obviously points to the need to understand and to give expression to the identity, the worth, the way of life associated with being black. To the exploration of these questions much of the best thought of American blacks has been and will no doubt continue to be directed, for the subject is far from having been exhausted.

One possible source for an understanding of the significance of

---

10. Stokely Carmichael and Charles V. Hamilton, "The Myths of Coalition," in *Black Power: The Politics of Liberation in America* (New York: Random House, 1967).

11. Carmichael and Hamilton, "Black Power: Its Need and Substance," in ibid.

being black is Africa. But except for some separatists and missionaries (who saw the black American as the model for Africa, rather than the other way around), Africa has seldom been more than a peripheral concern of American blacks. Africa has seemed to be capable of enriching but not of defining the identity of black Americans. Similar considerations apply to attempts to ground black identity in Islam. As James Baldwin said, "the Negro has been formed by this nation, for better or for worse, and does not belong to any other—not to Africa, and certainly not to Islam."[12]

A second possible source of black self-understanding is "black culture," a distinctive and valuable style of life developed by blacks in America. While many of the writers included here are concerned with black culture, in one form or another, a full exploration of it would lead to other writings and other authors, especially in literature and the arts.[13] The problem is to articulate exactly what black culture is (and, more basically, what "culture" in general is) and to show that it has sufficient substance and viability to serve as the basis for a people's self-conscious development. A simple but difficult question is whether the distinctive values of an oppressed people will not inevitably die with the removal of the oppression. W. E. B. Du Bois, for example, described the black man as "the sole oasis of simple faith and reverence in a dusty desert of dollars and smartness."[14] Yet Du Bois fought to secure for the black man an opportunity to function on equal terms in American society. There is an obvious question whether the simple faith and reverence with which the black responded to exclusion will or can be retained when the justice he demands is done him. Will he too not chase the dollar when he has a full opportunity to do so?

Another less obviously political version of the same problem arises out of the growing tendency to describe "black culture" as a distinctive experience or behavior and to resist any demand to explain it or talk about it. It is what it is. "The uniqueness of black culture can be explained," Julius Lester says, "in that it is a culture whose emphasis is on the nonverbal, that is, the nonconceptual. The lives of

---

12. Ibid., "Black Power: Its Need and Substance."

13. See LeRoi Jones, "The Need for a Cultural Base to Civil Rites & Bpower Mooments," in Floyd E. Barbour, ed., *The Black Power Revolt*, and Harold Cruse, *The Crisis of the Negro Intellectual* (New York: William Morrow & Co., 1967). This was a major concern of the New Negro Movement or Harlem Renaissance of the 1920s. See Alain Locke, ed., *The New Negro* (New York: Albert & Charles Boni, Inc., 1928).

14. Du Bois, "Of Our Spiritual Strivings," in *The Souls of Black Folk.*

blacks are rooted in the concrete daily experience. . . . In black culture it is the experience that counts, not what is said. . . ."[15] Yet culture seems to require at least some agency of transmission and interpretation, if it is to be more than a series of random responses to chance stimuli. Some of those concerned with black culture look to the nonverbal or largely nonverbal arts to perform this function in a way that does not fall into the white trap of verbalizing and conceptualizing. This view would have to be seriously considered in any full exploration of black revival. Lester's own work strongly suggests, however, the principal difficulty, which is that some "verbalizing" seems to be necessary, both to transmit the culture or experience, from man to man and generation to generation, and to make sense of it, to understand it. Can we know the lash of slavery, for example, for what it is—not merely as one bit of unpleasant experience but as something unjust and inhuman—without fundamental reliance on words and concepts?

A third source of black identity (and the most fruitful one) is the political and moral history of the black in America. The search here is for a higher harmony arising out of the antagonism between being black and being American. The broad answer—given in a variety of ways by black writers of differing views—is that the black has been placed in the position of being uniquely fitted to call America to be her true or best self. Thus when W. E. B. Du Bois wrote in 1903 that "there are to-day no truer exponents of the pure human spirit of the Declaration of Independence than the American Negroes,"[16] he was suggesting that what distinguishes the black American from the rest of the country is also what ties him to the country: his unique appreciation of the principles on which the country is based.

There is today a renewed understanding that in the history of slavery, oppression, and degradation of the black American there is much for him to be proud of. The assimilationists regarded that history as something to be put aside or lived down, which is another way of saying that being a Negro is degrading and has to be sloughed off in order to move into the mainstream and find one's liberty as an individual. On the contrary, it is now again argued, there is something ennobling in this tradition, which contains the materials of the self-understanding and dignity of black Americans. This is a tradition of fortitude, patience, dignity, and independence under extreme adversity, a tradition of persistent striving for freedom and civiliza-

---

15. Julius Lester, *Look Out, Whitey! Black Power's Gon' Get Your Mama* (New York: Dial Press, 1968), p. 87.

16. Du Bois, "Of Our Spiritual Strivings."

tion. It does not need to be ignored or discarded; nor, it should be added, does it need to be inflated or fictionalized. There is merit enough in the truth. "To accept one's past—one's history— is not the same thing as drowning in it; it is learning how to use it. An invented past can never be used; it cracks and crumbles under the pressures of life like clay in a season of drought."[17]

Properly understood, this tradition reveals the basis of the black American's own integrity and self-understanding and also the basis of his relation to America. Almost all of the nonassimilationist, nonseparatist writers have pursued this line of thought, but none more profoundly than Booker T. Washington. (Remember that we are not here discussing Washington's program but his philosophy.) Washington thought that the American black had gone through a school that had, paradoxically, taught him about freedom and civilization while holding him in slavery and degradation. It had taught him, Washington thought, something about the meaning and value of freedom and independence and self-respect; and these lessons were to be not only the basis of the black's rise but his gift to America. The American black learned that the kind of respect that counts is self-respect, not the fickle opinions of others. He learned that real freedom rests on a foundation of reason and order. He learned that the useful arts are respectable in themselves and are the beginning of the liberal arts. In all these ways, Washington thought, the black was put in the way of acquiring an understanding of freedom and self-respect that his former white masters were themselves sadly in need of. Here is a basis of black pride that is distinct from, yet harmonious with, the American whole.

In one of the most profound passages in Washington's writings, he reflects on a white man whose proud boast of never doing menial labor amounted to a confession of utter poverty with respect to the real purpose of education, "the making of men useful, honest, and liberal."

> Here is a citizen in the midst of our republic, clothed in a white skin, with all the technical signs of education, but who is as little fitted for the highest purpose of life as any creature found in Central Africa. My friends, can we make our education reach down far enough to touch and help this man? Can we so control science, art, and literature as to make them to such an extent a means rather than an end; that the lowest and most unfortunate of God's creatures shall be lifted up, ennobled and glorified; shall be a freeman

---

17. Baldwin, *The Fire Next Time*, p. 95.

> instead of a slave of narrow sympathies and wrong customs?[18]

The problem, this representative of the recently freed blacks suggested, was to find a way of reaching down far enough to touch this white "slave of narrow sympathies and wrong customs." This is the source of Washington's gentle concern for whites, often mistaken for pandering or weakness. It was the concern of the strong for the weak, the superior for the inferior, the teacher for the pupil.

The characteristic and perhaps most noble posture of the black American has been that of the friendly, though badly mauled, critic, calling America to live up to her own principles. Several versions of this profound and ironical theme—the oppressed and degraded black as the conscience of America, the teacher of America, the source of needed values and principles—will be found in this volume. According to this view, the problems could not be solved by separation, even if that were feasible, because the blacks and whites are in a relation of mutual dependence. Each would be worse off without the other. Writing of "Our Spiritual Strivings," W. E. B. Du Bois held up "the ideal of fostering and developing the traits and talents of the Negro, not in opposition to or contempt for other races, but rather in large conformity to the greater ideals of the American Republic, in order that some day on American soil two world-races may give to each other those characteristics both so sadly lack."[19]

America is our country, blacks as diverse as Washington, Du Bois, King, Baldwin, and even Malcolm X and Cleaver have thought, not only because blacks value and demand the rights and opportunities of American liberty and civilization, not only because the history of black and white in America has bound them together inextricably, but above all because America has a void that none can fill so well as America's black victims, citizens, friends, teachers. This is one of the deepest themes of black American political thought, and no serious consideration of American government and political theory can fail to give it a prominent place.

Like most other American political thought, black American political thought is not "closet philosophy." The viewpoint is usually not that of the scholar or the philosopher but of the statesman or the adviser to statesmen. The statesman, however, is carried beyond immediate practical issues by a need to understand the deeper ground on which they rest. Thus the writers here deal not only with

---

18. E. Davidson Washington, ed., "Democracy and Education," in *Selected Speeches of Booker T. Washington* (New York: Doubleday, Doran & Co., 1932).

19. Du Bois, "Of Our Spiritual Strivings."

problems of black Americans and of the United States but with many of the perennial questions of political life. These broader themes are often lost sight of or distorted in the clamor of everyday political contention; and it will take a deliberate effort for most readers to suspend judgment on the immediate issues long enough to follow the reflections of these writers on the broader implications. Four themes are especially important and worth watching for and thinking about.

First, there is the question of the extent of an individual's responsibility for what he is. Although there is still a considerable tendency in some circles to dismiss any criticism of or prescription for the behavior of blacks with the claim that the "fault" lies elsewhere, one of the consequences of the upsurge of black militancy is a renewed unwillingness by blacks to accept the implication of this easy explanation: that blacks are the mere product of white action and have no genuine independence of action or thought and therefore no independent responsibility. "What others did was their responsibility," James Baldwin wrote, reflecting on his early years in the church, "for which they would answer when the judgment trumpet sounded. But what *I* did was *my* responsibility, and I would have to answer, too—unless, of course, there was also in Heaven a special dispensation for the benighted black, who was not to be judged in the same way as other human beings, or angels."[20]

This is a question of individual morality, but it is also a political question of the first order. One of the major concerns of the best black writers has been to explore the relation between the inner and external obstacles to black advancement and independence, and to human fulfillment in general. One of the great questions of emigration, for example, was whether separation or integration would be the better condition under which blacks could develop those inner resources of character and independence that had been weakened by slavery but that were necessary to any meaningful progress. How does a leader, any leader, teach his people the duty of independent, manly use of such opportunities as are available without encouraging them to be satisfied with narrow and demeaning circumstances? How does he move his people to fight to remove unjust external obstacles without teaching them to think of themselves as being merely the product of such external forces? How far is it true, or in what sense is it true, that each man is finally responsible for himself, and what are the political implications of an answer to this question?

Second, there is the question of prejudice. Situated as he is, the

---

20. Ibid., p. 54.

black writer can scarcely avoid some reflection on the nature of prejudice in general and on its political function—and malfunctioning. Is prejudice the basic problem, as is so often said? If so, is that because prejudice causes objective injustice and harm to blacks? Or because it stands in the way of seeing men as individuals? Or because it is psychologically harmful to the holder? Each of these answers has different implications. There is the further question of how far prejudice has some foundation in reason. James Baldwin somewhere confessed a prejudice against doormen, but the sound and rational basis of this prejudgment is easy to understand and accept, even though it no doubt led often to injustice to particular doormen. How far is something like this true of prejudice generally? Can the victim of prejudice destroy or weaken it, as Frederick Douglass suggested, by acting so as to remove the basis in truth, thus making slanderers of his vilifiers? Can racial prejudice be overcome through the neutrality of the market, as Washington thought? Can it be destroyed by law? Or is there some deeper cause of prejudice, unreachable by any rational appeal? Further, there is the crucial question whether race prejudice is one species among many or a unique kind of prejudice. Do the depth and virulence of race prejudice require, as a political matter, the elimination of the race difference, either by separation or by assimilation? Finally, there is the question whether all political organizations or human associations depend on prejudice. Does race or group pride imply, at least in practice, race or group prejudice? Perhaps it is necessary to refine the issue, regarding both race prejudice and prejudice in general, by distinguishing between prejudice that is more or less in touch with some rational foundation, more or less conducive to beneficial group cohesion, more or less harmful to outside persons and groups.

Third, there is the ancient question of the relation between the political whole and its parts. Is government the tool and protector of the individual, and society an aggregate of homogeneous or undifferentiated individuals? This has been the view of many black American thinkers, as it has generally been the view of white American political thinkers. There has, however, also been a different line of argument, perhaps most fully and thoughtfully presented in Du Bois's early essay on "The Conservation of the Races," but explored also by Washington, Baldwin, and Carmichael, and currently undergoing a marked revival. The "new integration," in contrast to the old or assimilationist integration, rests on or points to a theoretical view that a polity is a unity of distinct and purposive social parts—*e pluribus unum*—and that an individual is part of a series of increasingly larger groups, including family, community, race, and country. The utterly homogeneous nation, in this view, is weak and sterile. "What a tiresome place America would be if freedom meant we all had to think alike or be the same color or wear that same gray flannel suit!"[21] These various social groups extend, define, and give significance to the individual; and they are in turn bound together in a diverse, mutually supporting and enriching whole. Social and political thought ought to aim to help men find their way into broader and higher levels of significance. The aim should be, however, not to abandon the narrower, particular associations but rather, by sustaining their integrity and exploring their implications, to enrich and elevate the whole community. The immediate thrust of this line of argument is in the direction of restoring and strengthening black cultural integrity as part of a broader association. Carried to its fullest extent, the argument suggests some basic questions, as Du Bois saw, about the accepted foundations of American government and politics and even about the accepted foundations of politics in the modern world.

Finally, there is the question of the relation between law and right. The black American, more than most others, suffers from imperfect and unjust laws. He is less likely to adopt the simple view that the law is right because it is the law. His circumstances make law-abidingness a larger question for him than it usually is for most other people. He is more likely to admit the legitimacy, under some circumstances, of disobedience to law. At the same time, however, the black American, as one of a disadvantaged and even hated minority, has a disproportionately great dependence on the protection of law. "Even poor whites do not have to rely on the law for protection as do Black People."[22] A victim of imperfect law, the black is nevertheless a prime beneficiary of law. What should he do? The situation of the black is only an extreme version of the situation that confronts every man who benefits from the law while suffering from its imperfections. Some argue for blind obedience to preserve the benefits. Others, on principle or in despair, argue for utter rejection to eliminate the imperfections. But most have seen that any viable solution must somehow combine the claims both of a stable legal system and of transcendent justice. Martin Luther King, Jr. is, of course, well known for his treatment of this theme, and his "Letter from the Birmingham Jail" is a major political document of recent

---

21. John Oliver Killens, *Black Man's Burden* (New York: Trident Press, 1965), p. 20.

22. McKissick, *Three-Fifths of a Man*, p. 85.

PART THREE

Rights, the Rule of Law, and the Public Interest

10
William Blackstone

Sir William Blackstone (1723–1780) was not a political philosopher, but an English lawyer and judge. His major piece of writing is not a book on justice or even on law, but the set *Commentaries on the Laws of England*. He was not original or inventive, but deliberately the opposite; and he often treats important and difficult questions in what seems to be an obscure or superficial way. Indeed, Blackstone is fairly widely regarded as having been contradictory or confused on important points of political philosophy. He is thought to exhibit a character that is amiable if a bit pompous; a style that is crisp and sometimes elegant; an intellect not strong in theory but capable of sound practical judgment and intrinsically bent to compromise—in short, to present himself a thorough Englishman. There is considerable ground for this view, but it is insufficient, and the reasons for its insufficiency are the reasons for giving note to Blackstone in a history of political philosophy.

When Blackstone first offered a course of lectures on the laws of England at Oxford University in 1753, he set a precedent that was intended to have a major effect on English legal and, more broadly, civic education.[1] Although the *Commentaries* are addressed to officers of every description and subjects of every order, they are aimed particularly at the lawyer and the gentleman. The lawyer was to be

This essay is from Leo Strauss and Joseph Cropsey, eds., *History of Political Philosophy*, 3rd ed. (Chicago: University of Chicago Press, 1987). It is reprinted with permission from the University of Chicago Press.

1. The four volumes of the *Commentaries on the Laws of England* first appeared in 1765, 1766, 1768, and 1769. The edition used here is the eighth, published in 1778 and the last published during Blackstone's lifetime; except where otherwise indicated, citations are to volume and page. The authenticity of the changes made by the editor of the ninth edition, on which many modern editions are based, is somewhat doubtful; but the differences are minor, and numerous standard editions reproduce the entire text with original pagination. The useful edition of William G. Hammond (San Francisco: Bancroft-Whitney, 1890) contains a collation of all changes in the first eight editions.

lifted from the confines of mere practice and directed to the elements and first principles upon which his practice was based. The gentleman was to be rescued from his dishonorable ignorance of the laws that it was his duty to safeguard, improve, and administer. In both cases what was required was academical instruction in the laws of the land which would enable the student not only to learn the outlines of the positive law but also to comprehend, and even himself to form, arguments "drawn *a priori*, from the spirit of the laws and the natural foundations of justice."[2] Blackstone invites examination of the laws of the land, their natural foundations, and the intervening "spirit of the laws." It is true that he also discusses divine law, for example, in his introductory treatment of law in general, but divine law typically makes an early and brief appearance, soon collapsing into natural law; and Blackstone makes little or no use of it in explaining, as distinguished from supporting, the laws of England. Religion does indeed have an important place under the laws of England, and Blackstone is a warm friend of the established church; but what is relevant is the influence of the church in making men sober, industrious, and good citizens.[3]

Blackstone's highest theme, then, deals with the relation between natural law and conventional law, as this relation presents itself to one who is a lawyer in the best and highest sense. The plan or organization of the *Commentaries* is characterized by a symmetry which contains, as a whole and in each of the parts, a movement or progression from the natural to the conventional.[4] Following an introduction, the four volumes of the *Commentaries* are divided into two parts, each comprising two volumes or books. First are "Rights," divided into the Rights of Persons (book 1) and the Rights of Things (book 2); there follow "Wrongs," divided into Private Wrongs (book 3) and Public Wrongs (book 4). The argument as a whole moves from individual rights to public wrongs.

The first chapter of book 1 begins with what Blackstone calls the absolute rights of individuals, which are those that appertain and belong to particular men as individuals and "would belong to their

---

2. Ibid., bk. 1, p. 32.

3. See ibid., bk. 3, pp. 100–103; bk. 4, chaps. 6, 8, 28.

4. In an early sketch of the ground covered later in the *Commentaries*, Blackstone remarks that he follows in many respects the plan of Sir Matthew Hale (*The Analysis of the Law . . . of England*, 3d ed., 1739); but he emphasizes that he has chosen "to extract a new Method of his own, [rather] than implicitly to copy after any." *An Analysis of the Laws of England* (3d ed., 1758), p. vii.

persons merely in a state of nature. . . ." The "first and primary end" of human laws is to maintain and regulate these absolute rights.[5] Blackstone spends little time, however, with the natural liberty of mankind, even in this first chapter, but moves quickly to the subject of civil rights and specifically the absolute rights of Englishmen, which are treated under the familiar Lockean headings of personal security, personal liberty, and private property. The remainder and by far the bulk of book 1 deals with relative rights, that is, the secondary and more artificial rights of individuals as they stand in legally established relationships to other individuals, first the public relationships of governors and governed, then the private relationships of master and servant, husband and wife, parent and child, and the like, which are consequent on civil society. Although the right of property is discussed, as has been said, in the first chapter of book 1 as one of the absolute rights of individuals, Blackstone treats property in a separate and subsequent book, subsequent, it may be noted, even to the relations of government. The reason for this is that the natural origin of rights of things is, compared with rights of persons, both less clear and less relevant to civil society. It is less clear because Blackstone finds the natural origin in occupancy or possession, and he seems to leave open the difficult question of what kind of right mere possession can be or grant; it is less relevant because, whereas natural personal rights, such as self-defense, are more or less regulated by positive law, the natural right to acquire property is substantially replaced or superseded by conventional rights to hold and transfer property.[6]

"Wrongs," the subject of the second part of the *Commentaries*, are said "for the most part [to] convey to us an idea merely negative, as being nothing else but a privation of right."[7] The second part contains no chapters comparable in philosophical intention to the first chapters of books 1 and 2, because wrongs are defined by and derivative from rights. The last pair of books is not, however, merely a mirror image of the first pair. Book 3 describes how the law provides for the redress of private wrongs relating to both persons and property (civil injuries), reflecting therefore the discussion in both book 1

---

5. *Commentaries*, bk. 1, pp. 123–24.

6. Ibid., bk. 2, pp. 3, 8–9, and *passim*. In Blackstone's significantly loose formulation, "The original of private property is probably founded in nature . . . : but certainly the modifications under which we at present find it, the method of conserving it in the present owner, and of translating it from man to man, are entirely derived from society." Bk. 1, p. 138.

7. Ibid., bk. 3, p. 2.

and book 2 and bringing to a conclusion, as it were, the whole subject of individual rights.

Public wrongs (crimes and misdemeanors), the subject of book 4, constitute that part of the law that is most artificial. Rights are the basis of Blackstone's jurisprudence, and there are, strictly speaking, no rights of the public but only rights of individuals. In book 4, however, political society, which is a means to the end of protecting individual rights, is treated—as it can and must be treated for many practical purposes—as if it were an end. That end is "the government and tranquillity of the whole," or more simply, peace; "for peace is the very end and foundation of civil society."[8] Without entering into detail, we may say that Blackstone's description of the several species of crimes and misdemeanors, for example crimes against God and religion and against the king and government, contains his negative or indirect discussion of the kind of artificial public or common good that must be constructed for the sake of the peaceful enjoyment of individual rights.

"The only true and natural foundations of society," Blackstone asserts, "are the wants and fears of individuals";[9] but it is not Blackstone's procedure to enter into any detailed or exhaustive examination of these wants and fears or of the natural liberty of mankind from which he begins. Rather he hastens on (not, we may imagine, to the displeasure of his English gentlemen and lawyers) to a discussion of civil rights, as if to define the rights of man in terms of the rights of Englishmen. The rights of Englishmen, however, are all rights *under law*. Personal liberty, to give but one example, "consists in the power of loco-motion, of changing situation, or removing one's person to whatsoever place one's own inclination may direct; without imprisonment or restraint, *unless by due course of law*."[10] But if the law were amended to permit arrest and imprisonment for indefinite periods on suspicion of executive officials, would that not constitute an abridgment of the Englishman's right of personal liberty? Putting the point more generally, Blackstone says, following Montesquieu, that in England as perhaps nowhere else, "political or civil liberty is the very end and scope of the constitution"; but he goes on to say that "this liberty, rightly understood, consists in the power of doing whatever the laws permit. . . ."[11] Blackstone seems to present a

---

8. Ibid., bk. 4, p. 7; bk. 1, p. 349.

9. Ibid., bk. 1, p. 47.

10. Ibid., p. 134; italics supplied. For the definitions of the rights of personal security and property, see bk. 1, pp. 129, 138.

11. Ibid., p. 6.

circular argument: defining good law as that which best maintains individual liberty and defining individual liberty as that which is permitted by law. This circularity or ambiguity is present throughout the *Commentaries*, not because of a defect in Blackstone's powers of reasoning or some irrational commitment to the English legal system, but because the theoretically sound argument, the argument taken from nature, tends to be practically self-defeating.

Even self-defense, "justly called the primary law of nature," is strictly confined, although "it is not, neither can it be in fact, taken away by the law of society."[12] The principle of law is "that where a crime, in itself capital, is endeavoured to be committed by force, it is lawful to repel that force by the death of the party attempting." Blackstone immediately goes on to warn that "we must not carry this doctrine to the same visionary length that Mr. Locke does; who holds, 'that all manner of force without right upon a man's person, puts him in a state of war with the aggressor; and, of consequence, that . . . he may lawfully kill him that puts him under this unnatural restraint.' " This principle may be just "in a state of uncivilized nature," but "the law of England, like that of every other well-regulated community, is too tender of the public peace, too careful of the lives of the subjects, to adopt so contentious a system; nor will suffer with impunity any crime to be *prevented* by death, unless the same, if committed, would also be *punished* by death."[13]

The law of England does, however, provide an exception to this rule of justifiable homicide, and that is, in the terminology of the law, excusable homicide. Where, for example, a man protects himself from assault and in the course of the quarrel kills his assailant, he is excused from legal penalty, provided that "certain and immediate suffering would [have been] the consequence of waiting for the assistance of the law" and that "the slayer had no other possible (or, at least, probable) means of escaping from his assailant."[14] A man attacked must turn his back and flee, if he can, and later bring his assailant to court. The presumption is always in favor of the law of civil society, not the law of nature.

The maintenance of government and therefore law itself is an even more delicate case. Blackstone is often pointed to as an exponent of parliamentary sovereignty, in contrast, for example, to American

---

12. Ibid., bk. 3, p. 4.

13. Ibid., bk. 4, pp. 181–82; cf. bk. 3, pp. 168–69. Italics original. The passage here from Locke is not a direct quotation but a paraphrase. See *Second Treatise*, secs. 18–19.

14. Ibid., bk. 4, p. 184.

ideas of limited government. In Parliament, consisting of king, lords, and commons, lies "that absolute despotic power, which must in all governments reside somewhere. . . ." Parliament can deal with matters outside the ordinary scope of law, it can remodel the succession to the crown, it can alter the established religion, it can change the constitution of the kingdom and Parliament itself. "It can, in short, do every thing that is not naturally impossible. . . ."[15] It is true that Blackstone frequently seems to assume that Parliament cannot do what it ought not to do (for example, substitute an elective for a hereditary monarchy); and he emphasizes "the true excellence of the English government, that all the parts of it form a mutual check upon each other."[16] But however great the safeguard provided in practice by the English system of mutual social and political checks, in the end Blackstone must return to the first principle of civil society, which is that Parliament, or the legislature, can do what it likes.

Is there not, however, a still more fundamental principle? "It must be owned that Mr. Locke, and other theoretical writers, have held, that 'there remains still inherent in the people a supreme power to remove or alter the legislative, when they find the legislative act contrary to the trust reposed in them. . . .' " Blackstone insists that, "however just this conclusion may be in theory"—and it *is* just in Blackstone's theory for precisely the same reasons that it is just in Locke's—"we cannot practically adopt it, nor take any *legal* steps for carrying it into execution, under any dispensation of government at present actually existing."

Such a devolution of power to the people at large presumes a dissolution of government, a reduction of the people to their "original state of equality," and the repeal of all positive laws. "No human laws will therefore suppose a case, which at once must destroy all

---

15. Ibid., bk. 1, pp. 160–61.
16. Ibid., bk. 1, pp. 154–55. See bk. 1, pp. 50–51:

> . . . as the legislature of the kingdom is entrusted to three distinct powers, entirely independent of each other; first, the king; secondly, the lords spiritual and temporal, which is an aristocratical assembly of persons selected for their piety, their birth, their wisdom, their valour, or their property; and, thirdly, the house of commons, freely chosen by the people from among themselves, which makes it a kind of democracy; as this aggregate body, actuated by different springs, and attentive to different interests, composes the British parliament, and has the supreme disposal of every thing; there can no inconvenience be attempted by either of the three branches, but will be withstood by one of the other two; each branch being armed with a negative power, sufficient to repel any innovation which it shall think inexpedient or dangerous.

law, and compel men to build afresh upon a new foundation; nor will they make provision for so desperate an event, as must render all legal provisions ineffectual."[17] The ultimate resort to first principle, to what Blackstone calls elsewhere the "law of nature" or "the God of battles,"[18] is at the foundation of law because it enforces, as no law and no internal checks can do, the limits on political authority. Yet the law cannot provide for or even suppose this ultimate resort and is, in fact, in tension with it: the maintenance of law and therefore the effective maintenance of individual rights depends upon a putting aside, as if for once and all, of the original state of lawless equality out of which civil society arose and into which it may, in desperate event, relapse. Mr. Locke and his theoretical friends are not wrong, but they may endanger the polity precisely because of their clear expression of its true foundation. "For civil liberty rightly understood, consists in protecting the rights of individuals by the united force of society: society cannot be maintained, and of course can exert no protection, without obedience to some sovereign power: and obedience is an empty name, if every individual has a right to decide how far he himself shall obey."[19] Blackstone is not fearful that his constant emphasis on law and law-abidingness will incapacitate the people for the resumption of their original right should that be necessary. Where the sovereign power becomes tyrannical and threatens desolation to the state, "mankind will not be reasoned out of the feelings of humanity; nor will sacrifice their liberty by a scrupulous adherence to those political maxims, which were originally established to preserve it."[20]

The origin of civil society, Blackstone suggests, is anarchy; its tendency, tyranny. There have been times when the rights of Englishmen were "depressed by overbearing and tyrannical princes; at others, so luxuriant as even to tend to anarchy, a worse state than tyranny itself," says Blackstone, as befits a lawyer, "as any government is better than none at all."[21] But the objective is to avoid both, as the British constitution has generally done. In support of this objective, Blackstone's jurisprudence acknowledges the extremes, while resisting their pull, for either is fatal to liberty. Stated positively, Blackstone seeks to maintain between the ground and the tendency of civil society the central position of law, particularly the law as it is understood by judges and administered in their courts.

---

17. Ibid., pp. 161–62. Italics original.
18. Ibid., p. 193.
19. Ibid., p. 251.
20. Ibid., p. 245.
21. Ibid., p. 127.

In a list of five "auxiliary subordinate rights," which serve principally as "barriers" to protect the three great primary rights, Blackstone gives central place to the right of every Englishman to apply to the courts for redress of injuries. The law (not Parliament or the people at large), Blackstone says here, is in England "the supreme arbiter of every man's life, liberty, and property. . . ." In this "distinct and separate existence" of the judiciary lies "one main preservative of the public liberty; which cannot subsist long in any state, unless the administration of common justice be in some degree separated both from the legislative and also from the executive power." In particular, "were it joined with the legislative, the life, liberty, and property, of the subject would be in the hands of arbitrary judges, whose decisions would be then regulated only by their own opinions, and not by any fundamental principles of law; which, though legislators may depart from, yet judges are bound to observe."[22]

Blackstone here expresses again the principle of mutual checks, but our present concern is with his comment that there are "fundamental principles of law; which, though legislators may depart from, yet judges are bound to observe." This seems curious when we consider what may be called Blackstone's basic (though not exhaustive) definition of law: "the will of one man, or of one or more assemblies of men, to whom the supreme authority is entrusted . . . is in different states, according to their different constitutions, understood to be *law*."[23] Law is the will of the sovereign; but good law, and therefore law properly speaking, requires something more. Not only consent, for "even laws themselves, whether made with or without our consent, if they regulate and constrain our conduct in matters of mere indifference, without any good end in view, are regulations destructive of liberty. . . ." The good end in view is genuine civil liberty, which is "no other than natural liberty so far restrained by human laws (and no farther) as is necessary and expedient for the general advantage of the publick."[24]

How far and in what respects the general advantage requires restraint of natural liberty is not a question that can be answered, except in a way that reformulates the question, by some general principle or rule. It is a matter of judgment. And free government depends on the maintenance within it of a central place for the judiciary, that peculiar body of men who are capable, by tradition,

---

22. Ibid., pp. 141, 269.

23. Ibid., p. 52. Italics original. An obvious misprint in the text of this passage has been corrected.

24. Ibid., pp. 125–26.

political position, and training, of judging well. While providing disinterested protection of the lives, liberties, and properties of the subjects, the judiciary also serves as a brake on the unwise use of parliamentary and popular authority and as a source (or at least a mouthpiece) of instruction in the true principles of civil liberty.

The fundamental principles of law to which judges must adhere, and which mitigate the view of law as the will of the sovereign, consist of or are drawn in the first place from custom. In English law, "The goodness of a custom depends upon it's [sic] having been used time out of mind; or, in the solemnity of our legal phrase, time whereof the memory of man runneth not to the contrary. This it is that gives it it's [sic] weight and authority: and of this nature are the maxims and customs which compose the common law, or *lex non scripta*, of this kingdom." When in his introduction Blackstone turns from a discussion of the nature of law to the laws of England, he does not begin with a contracting people or a sovereign legislature but with these common laws, of which judges are the "depositaries" and "living oracles." Written laws or statutes are merely declaratory or remedial of some defect in the common laws, which are "the first ground and chief corner stone of the laws of England. . . ."[25]

In innumerable ways throughout the *Commentaries* Blackstone recognizes, strengthens, and uses the authority of the old. He is often taken for a mere patriot or conservative, even though he gives ample indication that neither his praise of what is English nor his devotion to what is old is to be taken simply at face value.[26] Certainly Blackstone does emphasize the bindingness of precedent and the deference owed by the present generation to former times. He chooses, for example, to defend on the ground of authority rather than reason and justice the decision of the lords and commons to regard James II as having merely abdicated the throne, rather than as having subverted the government and broken the original contract. While making clear his own opinion that the decision was reasonable and just, in avoiding "the wild extremes into which the visionary theories of some zealous republicans would have led them," he fears that such speculation, if carried too far, "might imply a right of dissenting or revolting from [the decision], in case we should think it to have been unjust, oppressive, or inexpedient."[27]

Blackstone was as perceptive as those commentators who have pointed out that there is a defect in this argument because on

25. Ibid., pp. 67, 69, 73.
26. See ibid., pp. 172, 190–91; bk. 4, pp. 3–5.
27. Ibid., bk. 1, pp. 212–13.

Blackstone's own principles the present generation does have a right at any time to be judge of whether the contract has been broken. Blackstone's implicit argument is that if desperate circumstances arise, as they did in 1688, it must be hoped that the original right will be exercised as wisely and moderately as it was then, when the fabric of government and law was maintained while a revolution was made. But the exercise of this basic right is to be discouraged. The stability of any polity, not least a polity whose fundamental principles contain an intrinsic tendency toward instability, depends upon a widespread opinion of the bindingness of the old.

It is the duty of the judge, and the concern of Blackstone as his teacher, to articulate and maintain the integrity of the system of positive law as it stands. The reader of the *Commentaries* is frequently told of the nicety with which the old rules of law were framed, "and how closely they are connected and interwoven together, supporting, illustrating, and demonstrating one another."[28] He is cautioned that the very number and complexity of English municipal laws which vex him, whether as student or litigant, testify to the extent of the country, its commercial prosperity, and above all the liberty and property of the subjects.[29] He is reminded that every science has its terms and rules of art, the reason of which may not be immediately visible. Many of these artificial rules reflect the lawyer's preoccupation with forms and procedures, arising out of his trained understanding that if laws are cast in a certain form, promulgated in a certain way, and enforced according to certain processes, the likelihood of doing substantive justice is increased. The legal art provides the framework within which judgment is exercised and justice done. Thus, lawyer-like, Blackstone says that municipal law is "something permanent, uniform, and universal" and describes the procedure of trial by jury as "the most transcendent privilege which any subject can enjoy, or wish for. . . ."[30] But his concern with the integrity, or rationale, of the English legal system goes deeper than forms and procedures, important as they are and large a place as they inevitably occupy in an analysis of English law.

The *Commentaries* are full of intricate and seemingly endless "explanations" of the old rules of law, many of them apparently irrelevant or even in opposition to present needs and modern principles. Dizzy with the effort to comprehend the reason of a system

---

28. Ibid., bk. 2, p. 128; compare bk. 2, p. 376.

29. Ibid., bk. 3, pp. 325–27.

30. Ibid., bk. 1, p. 44; bk. 3, p. 379; compare Blackstone's discussion of equity in bk. 1, pp. 62, 91–92; bk. 3, pp. 429–41.

where, for example, a brother of the half blood may never succeed as heir to the estate of his elder brother even if they have the same father,[31] the reader is likely to conclude that the old maxim of the common lawyer that "what is not reason is not law"[32] is maintained only by an unshakable determination to assert, however artificially and at whatever cost in Latin maxims and patchwork fictions, that what is English law is reason.

If there is any consistent underlying principle it seems to lie in Blackstone's emphatic intention to draw his students away from "the rage of modern improvement." Yet "modern improvement" is the very foundation of the *Commentaries;* but it is essential to the modern enterprise itself that reform should wear a conservative cloak.[33] The weight and influence of the old are to be preserved and used to support the new:

> We inherit an old Gothic castle, erected in the days of chivalry, but fitted up for a modern inhabitant. The moated ramparts, the embattled towers, and the trophied halls, are magnificent and venerable, but useless. The inferior apartments, now converted into rooms of convenience, are chearful and commodious, though their approaches are winding and difficult.[34]

Blackstone helps to remodel the old castle, by means of which its comfort is improved, for example by relaxing some of the old legal restrictions on commerce; but he is careful to warn against reform that might loosen some apparently useless stone or weaken some inconvenient timber and cause the whole edifice, the pleasant apartments as well as the noble shell, vital damage.

Blackstone is therefore an extremely cautious reformer, but his metaphor also has a deeper significance. Civil society consists of a set of conventional, and in a sense arbitrary, rules and regulations whose purpose is the regularization and thereby the protection of natural rights. But the effectiveness of that conventional system depends upon its becoming confounded, for many practical purposes, with nature. Too persistent inquiry into the grounds of the conventional system may reveal too clearly and widely that it *is* a conventional system and not a set of natural rules, thereby encouraging self-

31. Ibid., bk. 2, pp. 227–33.

32. Ibid., bk. 1, p. 70.

33. Ibid., p. 10. For some of Blackstone's suggestions for reform, see bk. 3, pp. 381–85 (trial by jury); bk. 4, pp. 235–39 (capital punishment); bk. 4, pp. 388–89 (corruption of blood).

34. Ibid., bk. 3, p. 268.

destructive appeals from the artificial system to its natural foundation. "It is well if the mass of mankind will obey the laws when made, without scrutinizing too nicely into the reasons of making them."[35] And of course the older and better established the laws, the less likely that their reasons will be questioned. The general tendency to "mistake for nature what we find established by long and inveterate custom"[36] can be a trap for the academic student of law, but it is absolutely indispensable to the maintenance of law.

The classic case, because the most modified or artificial of individual rights, is the right of property, and Blackstone provides two versions of its origin. In his introductory discussion of property in general, he finds the origin in sheer possession or occupancy. He then shows how men's desire to hold their property in greater security drives them by stages from a "savage state of vagrant liberty" to civil society, and to civilization, with its increasingly complex and artificial system of law establishing property rights.[37]

The second version of the origin of property begins at the peak of the hierarchy rather than its base and describes a conquering general seizing lands, partitioning them among his followers, and eventually establishing a hierarchical military system.[38] English law, and English history as well, is presented here as a combination of these two developments. Thus the basic pattern of land law is feudal tenure, of which "the grand and fundamental maxim" is "that all lands were originally granted out by the sovereign, and are therefore holden, either mediately or immediately, of the crown."[39] But this fundamental maxim is a fiction; a fiction to which our ancestors consented under William only in order to establish a then generally useful military system; a fiction that later Norman lawyers made the engine of ecclesiastical tyranny; a fiction, now much modified and adapted to a commercial society, that signals the recognition that a man can most effectively preserve what is his own by consenting to regard it as the king's.

Indeed, the hereditary monarch is himself a kind of fiction, or he is an altogether artificial entity, the prime sign and example of the replacement of men's natural equality by that "due subordination of rank" that government requires.[40] While Blackstone praises the mod-

---

35. Ibid., bk. 2, p. 2.
36. Ibid., p. 11.
37. Ibid., pp. 6–8.
38. Ibid., pp. 45ff.
39. Ibid., p. 53.
40. Ibid., bk. 1, p. 271; compare bk. 1, pp. 208–9; bk. 4, p. 105; and Blackstone's discussion of allegiance, bk. 1, pp. 366–70.

ern freedom to discuss the limits of the king's prerogative, "a topic, that in some former ages was thought too delicate and sacred to be profaned by the pen of a subject," he discusses it nevertheless with "decency and respect." "For, though a philosophical mind will consider the royal person merely as one man appointed by mutual consent to preside over many others, and will pay him that reverence and duty which the principles of society demand, yet the mass of mankind will be apt to grow insolent and refractory, if taught to consider their prince as a man of no greater perfection than themselves. The law therefore ascribes to the king . . . certain attributes of a great and transcendant [sic] nature; by which the people are led to consider him in the light of a superior being, and to pay him that awful respect, which may enable him with greater ease to carry on the business of government."[41]

Thus the merely conventional superiority of the king is widely regarded, thanks partly to certain laws and writings about law, as a natural superiority; his conventional title to the throne a natural title; his contractual right to the loyalty of his subjects a natural right. As subjects we stand in awe of the king, without considering that he is our servant; we accept our subordinate rank in society, without considering our original equality; we accept the property that the laws assign us, without considering our original right to seize what we can. In sum, we obey, without considering our right to rid ourselves of the sovereign who commands and the law he administers; for to exercise this right would be the destruction of the security of our persons, our liberty, and our property. "The moated ramparts, the embattled towers, and the trophied halls," Blackstone says, "are magnificent and venerable, but useless." It is true that the noble and chivalrous purposes that they once supported and displayed are now displaced; newer and better ends are expressed in the comfortable apartments. But these apartments cannot provide for themselves that magnificence and venerability with which their own outer walls must be reinforced if the modern edifice is to stand. The Gothic labyrinth of hierarchy and duty, to which Blackstone provides the key, is the indispensable means to the regulation and thus the preservation of human equality and individual rights.

---

41. Ibid., bk. 1, pp. 237, 241.

11

The Case against Civil Disobedience

Author's note: In this essay, which was completed a few days before the assassination of Martin Luther King, I examine and criticize, among other matters, King's philosophy of nonviolent resistance. There is a bitter sorrow in seeing part of my argument underlined with the blood of this American leader and the consequent civil disorder. While I find some personal satisfaction in what I believe was King's growing understanding of the limits of civil disobedience, this only increases my sense of the loss to the nation. We have lost not only an eloquent advocate of civil disobedience but a leader who was in the course of transcending civil disobedience in the direction of statesmanship. We may pay heavily for the loss.

As a teacher, however, Martin Luther King is not lost to us. He still speaks; we may listen and think. I have no better way of paying him honor and respect than to seek instruction in a critical examination of his principles, and that is what I have tried to do here.

The most striking characteristic of civil disobedience is its irrelevance to the problems of today. The fashion in civil disobedience seems likely to die out as quickly as it burst into flame with the actions of the Montgomery bus boycotters and the words of Martin Luther King. Moreover, today's rejection of civil disobedience comes not mainly from right-wing defenders of law, order, and the *status quo,* but from the very sources of radical reform and protest from which the advocates of civil disobedience have drawn their principles and programs. Disobedience abounds, but it has thrust civility aside. We take up the question of civil disobedience, then, at a time when there is a good deal of agreement from all sides of the political compass that civil disobedience is obsolete or irrelevant. Nor should this be surprising. Civil disobedience, however important it seemed a short time ago, is an altogether secondary and derivative matter, scarcely

---

This essay was originally published in Robert A. Goldwin, ed., *On Civil Disobedience* (Chicago: Rand McNally & Co., 1969).

capable of being put in a form that is not contradictory, shallow, and a feeble guide to action. It deserves, nevertheless, serious consideration, for it is remarkable in its capacity to point to far more fundamental, timely, and relevant political questions.

Civil disobedience, I shall argue, is an unsuccessful attempt to combine, on the level of principle, revolution and conventional political action. The fundamental choice lies, as Malcolm X often said, between bullets and ballots. In both revolution and conventional political action something that could be called civil disobedience may play a part, but that part is altogether contingent, subject to prudential considerations, and subordinate to the greater principles of political action. Civil disobedience is the resort—always a theoretically and practically weak resort—of the *subject* of law, exercised because the subject cannot or will not take up the rights and duties of the citizen.

I will consider civil disobedience in the context of the Negro movement. This has, in recent years, been the main locus of civil disobedience and the area in which it has received its most thorough articulation. I will rely primarily, although not entirely, on the principles enunciated by Martin Luther King, who has stood since the Montgomery bus boycott of 1955–1956 as the most authoritative and best spokesman of civil disobedience in the Negro movement. According to King, civil disobedience is the open, nonviolent, even loving breaking of law with a willingness to accept the punishment.

It will be helpful to bear in mind two closely related distinctions. First, nonviolent resistance, as King taught and practiced it, does not always involve civil disobedience. The Montgomery bus boycott, at least in its early stages, was not illegal, but it was a form of nonviolent resistance. Nonviolent resistance may take the form of massive but legal protest. However, as King clearly saw, the heart of nonviolent resistance is disobeying a law or lawful authority in protest against injustice. Second, civil disobedience is to be distinguished from testing the constitutionality of law. This distinction is often obscured because what starts out as the former may end as the latter, and very often in practice the two kinds of activities are pressed forward at the same time. But the distinction in principle is clear. If a Negro makes use of facilities reserved by local law for whites and if upon being arrested and fined he appeals and secures a decision from the Supreme Court that the local law is unconstitutional, he has not committed an illegal act. (If, on the other hand, he loses his appeal but by his action persuades the federal or state government to legislate against the segregation, he has committed an illegal act, despite the subsequent change in the law.)

The institution of judicial review, in which the acts of governmental authorities are tested in the light of the higher law of the Constitution, provides for a kind of tamed or civilized "civil disobedience." One of the practical consequences of this institution is to divert disobedience and even revolution into the channel of law. Judicial review mediates between the positive claims of the legislature or official of initial jurisdiction and the universal claims of justice, through the higher positive law of the Constitution. But it is only a mediation; and the distinction remains between "breaking" a "law" that is invalid under the Constitution, which involves no unlawful behavior, and breaking a valid law because it is claimed to be unjust, which does of course involve unlawful behavior—even if the claim of injustice is sound and even if it is recognized as sound by a subsequent amendment of the law.

According to King, the Negro found in the doctrine of nonviolent resistance a practical and a moral answer to his centuries-old cry for justice. Decades of patient submission had produced no acceptable results; yet a resort to violence was practically and morally out of the question. Direct nonviolent resistance permits the Negro to move positively to foster a crisis and thus to expose a cleavage which his former passivity had helped to conceal.[1] By actively refusing to cooperate with an unjust system—the injustice, say, of segregated lunch counters—and at the same time by turning the other cheek to the violence that his resistance stimulates, the Negro wields a sword far more effective than violence could ever be. Large-scale noncooperation calls attention to the unjust system and strains its facilities. The demonstrators' failure to resist the billy club and the fire hose underlines the difference between oppressor and oppressed. Nonviolent resistance is the sword that heals. It ennobles its user and cuts without wounding. Loving the oppressor while standing nonviolently against the unjust system of segregation, the demonstrator turns his enemy into a friend, thus doubly contributing to the ultimate end, integration, which is "genuine intergroup and interpersonal living" or "total interrelatedness."[2]

One of the sharpest and most penetrating attacks on King's nonviolent resistance was made by Malcolm X: "Just as the slavemaster of that day used Tom, the house Negro, to keep the field Negroes in check, the same old slavemaster today has Negroes who are nothing but modern Uncle Toms, twentieth-century Uncle Toms, to

---

1. Martin Luther King, Jr., *Stride toward Freedom* (New York: Harper & Brothers, 1958), pp. 193–94; *Why We Can't Wait* (New York: New American Library Signet Book, 1964), p. 79.

2. King, *Stride toward Freedom*, p. 220; *Why We Can't Wait*, p. 152.

keep you and me in check, to keep us under control, keep us passive and peaceful and nonviolent. That's Tom making you nonviolent." It's like the dentist deadening the pain with novocaine: "Blood running all down your jaw, and you don't know what's happening. Because someone has taught you to suffer—peacefully."[3] "I don't mean go out and get violent; but at the same time you should never be nonviolent unless you run into some nonviolence. I'm nonviolent with those who are nonviolent with me. But when you drop that violence on me, then you've made me go insane, and I'm not responsible for what I do. And that's the way every Negro should get."[4]

Many moderates in the civil rights movement, while rejecting the most extreme statements of men like Malcolm X and Stokely Carmichael, also find themselves increasingly unwilling to defend the doctrine of nonviolent resistance. There has consequently been much discussion lately—often rather shallow discussion—about the limits of nonviolence and the forms, effectiveness, and justifiability of violence. But at a deeper level the tendency to reject the nonviolent part of King's teaching derives from a taking seriously of the revolutionary part of that teaching.

King frequently spoke of the Negro Revolution, the third American revolution; and in former times, at least, he adopted the revolutionary's uncompromising rejection of politics as usual. Scorning "moderate" contentions that the Negro demonstrations in Birmingham in 1963 were ill-timed, King asserted "that it was ridiculous to speak of timing when the clock of history showed that the Negro had already suffered one hundred years of delay." "Gradualism and moderation are not the answer to the great moral indictment which, in the Revolution of 1963, finally came to stand in the center of our national stage." The Negro wants "absolute and immediate freedom and equality . . . right here in this land today. . . . Negroes no longer are tolerant of or interested in compromise. . . . In the bursting mood that has overtaken the Negro in 1963, the word 'compromise' is profane and pernicious."[5] In the words of the Student Nonviolent Coordinating Committee (SNCC) chairman, John Lewis, in 1963, "the revolution is at hand, and we must free ourselves of the chains of political and economic slavery. . . . To those who have said,

---

3. George Breitman, ed., *Malcolm X Speaks* (New York: Grove Press, Inc., 1966), p. 12.

4. Ibid., pp. 33–34.

5. King, *Why We Can't Wait*, pp. 66, 128, 131.

'Be Patient and Wait,' we must say that, 'Patience is a dirty and nasty word.' "[6]

Perhaps all this is only the exaggeration of the partisan, legitimate in times when "gradualism" and "moderation" have been soiled by use as disguises for repression and injustice. Uncompromising talk is not necessarily incompatible with prudent action. A relatively small group of followers may be more or less successfully turned from righteous indignation to political prudence, as conditions require. But King spoke not to the few but to the many; and a mass is much less easily maneuvered, much more likely to crush its leaders' prudence with its leaders' extremism. King said of cautious moderates in 1964 that "the breath of the new movement chilled them."[7] Very soon King felt the full storm he had helped to create.

Malcolm X rejected nonviolence in the name of the truly revolutionary character of the Negro movement: "There's no such thing as a nonviolent revolution. . . ." "Revolution is bloody, revolution is hostile, revolution knows no compromise, revolution overturns and destroys everything that gets in its way." "These Negroes aren't asking for any nation—they're trying to crawl back on the plantation." "Revolution is always based on land. Revolution is never based on begging somebody for an integrated cup of coffee. Revolutions are never fought by turning the other cheek. Revolutions are never based upon love-your-enemy and pray-for-those-who-spitefully-use-you. And revolutions are never waged singing 'We Shall Overcome.' Revolutions are based upon bloodshed. Revolutions are never compromising. Revolutions are never based upon negotiations. Revolutions are never based upon any kind of tokenism whatsoever. Revolutions are never based upon that which is begging a corrupt society or a corrupt system to accept us into it. Revolutions overturn systems. And there is no system on this earth which has proven itself more corrupt, more criminal, than this system that in 1964 still colonizes 22 million African-Americans, still enslaves 22 million Africo-Americans."[8]

Malcolm urged that Negroes take seriously the idea of revolution, so loosely used by King. He tested King's moderation against King's extremism; and he found that moderation weak, false, and untenable. Although the assassin's bullet prevented Malcolm from

---

6. John Lewis, "Speech at March on Washington, 1963," Staughton Lynd, ed., *Nonviolence in America: A Documentary History* (Indianapolis: Bobbs-Merrill Co., 1966), p. 484.

7. King, *Why We Can't Wait*, p. 119.

8. Breitman, *Malcolm X Speaks*, pp. 9–10, 50.

concluding his reflections on the character of the Negro revolution and on the means open to the Negro to overturn the American system or abandon it, he was remarkably successful in exposing the revolutionary side—the system-overturning, violent side—of nonviolent resistance. It will be part of the business of the immediate future to explore the fundamental questions raised by the radical versions of black power and black nationalism.

There are questions of ends. Is the problem simply that whites have power and blacks do not? Or is there some fundamental and ineradicable injustice in the American system? If the latter, is that injustice essentially the "racism" now officially acknowledged, or is it a deeper defect, such as a preoccupation with material comfort and a lessening of concern for the "human values"? What are the valued and valuable characteristics of the Negro? Have they grown out of his heroic resistance to and survival under oppression? Are they of African derivation? What will be the character of the new society?

There are also questions of means. Is the future to be sought in separation? In some form of internal "separation"? What are the possible modes and outcomes of revolutionary action by Negroes within the United States? Of violent confrontation? There are many fundamental questions raised if a Negro revolution is taken seriously, but civil disobedience is not one of them. If what is called for is revolution, civil disobedience is at most a mere tactic, of no more independent significance as a principle and of no greater moral or political stature than the tactics of guerrilla warfare, boycott, and sabotage.

Granting, however, that the most strident voices of the Negro movement today reject the American system radically and thus reject civil disobedience as anything but a mere tactic, is there not another view which remains fundamentally committed to the American system, which seeks to hold that system to its avowed principles so far as its behavior toward Negroes is concerned? And is this not the true ground of justification of the espousal and practice of civil disobedience by American Negroes? Is there not a fundamental distinction to be made between the reform of a political system that is fundamentally sound, although unjust in some very important particulars, and the overturning of one that is corrupt at heart?

One of the striking characteristics of Martin Luther King's doctrine, a characteristic that it seems to share with other versions of civil disobedience, is the extent to which this crucial distinction is obscured. In *Stride toward Freedom*, King described his concern when the impending 1955 boycott against segregated buses in Montgomery, Alabama, was likened to the White Citizens' Councils' resistance

241

to school desegregation. Reflecting on the differences between these cases and on the teachings of Thoreau, King said, "Something began to say to me, 'He who passively accepts evil is as much involved in it as he who helps to perpetrate it. He who accepts evil without protesting against it is really cooperating with it.' "[9]

King's major statement of civil disobedience is his famous "Letter from the Birmingham Jail," written in 1963, in which he replies to those who ask how Negroes can urge others to obey the 1954 school desegregation decision while themselves breaking laws.[10] "The answer lies in the fact that there are two types of laws; just and unjust. I would be the first to advocate obeying just laws." King goes on to provide some rules of thumb for distinguishing just from unjust laws (to which we shall return), and he concedes that some respect is due to law *per se*. "In no sense do I advocate evading or defying the law, as would the rabid segregationist. That would lead to anarchy. One who breaks an unjust law must do so openly, lovingly, and with a willingness to accept the penalty." He argues "that an individual who breaks a law that conscience tells him is unjust, and who willingly accepts the penalty of imprisonment in order to arouse the conscience of the community over its injustice, is in reality expressing the highest respect for law." Indeed, such behavior is not only permitted but demanded. "We must learn that passively to accept an unjust system is to cooperate with that system, and thereby to become a participant in its evil." "To cooperate passively with an unjust system makes the oppressed as evil as the oppressor."[11]

There are several issues here that deserve to be sorted out and considered. First is the problem of discovering justice, which is the aim and the test of law. King, unlike some other advocates of nonviolent resistance, adheres to the view that there *are* just and unjust laws, and that this distinction is not merely a matter of personal preference. Individual "conscience" is, for him, not merely personal but directed by a cosmic guide towards the truly just. The foundation of civil disobedience must be, in King's view, not mere "feeling" or "commitment," but justice.

Yet King's discussion of justice is exceedingly loose. The heart of his definition is that "Any law that uplifts human personality is just.

9. King, *Stride toward Freedom*, p. 51; compare p. 212.

10. The "Letter from the Birmingham Jail" is printed in King, *Why We Can't Wait*, pp. 76–95.

11. Ibid., pp. 61–77; Martin Luther King, *Strength to Love* (New York: Harper & Row, 1963), pp. 6, 83; compare with King, *Stride toward Freedom*, p. 212.

Any law that degrades human personality is unjust. All segregation statutes are unjust because segregation distorts the soul and damages the personality."[12] As John Lewis said, "segregation is evil and . . . it must be destroyed in all forms."[13] Now it is becoming increasingly clear to growing numbers of people that segregation is not always and under all circumstances unjust, that the assimilationist test by which King judged race relations is inadequate if not false, and that the questions of what it *means* to "uplift the human personality" and how that can be done are a good deal more complicated than they appeared to King in the context of legally segregated Southern cities. The growing reaction against nonviolent resistance includes a more or less emphatic rejection of the assimilationist *end*. For our present purpose, however, the important point is that to the extent that the demands of justice are obscure the ground for civil disobedience is weakened and the need for political deliberation and political working out of the answers is strengthened.

A second issue is whether even an open and loving breaking of the law with a willingness to accept the penalty does not constitute or lead to a defiance of the law and whether it would not on any substantial scale lead to anarchy.[14] An open refusal to obey an unjust law shows the highest respect for law in the same way that an open insult to a degraded woman, with a willingness to be slapped for the insult, shows the highest respect for womanhood.

Our usual view, however, is that we owe respect to the law as law, to women as women, even when they do *not* in fact exhibit the

---

12. In his "Letter from the Birmingham Jail," King suggests two other "examples" of unjust laws—when a majority inflicts on a minority a code that is not binding on itself, or when a code is inflicted on a minority which the minority had no part in enacting because not permitted to vote. The latter is important but insufficient, since King would not confine unjust laws to those adopted without the participation of some minority. The former is a simple statement of the extremely complex "equal protection" problem that has so vexed the courts and takes on substance only when seen in the light of King's view of the injustice of racial segregation.

13. Lynd, ed., *Nonviolence in America*, p. 483.

14. Consider the reasonable, if perhaps rather strict, rule of the Congress of Racial Equality (CORE): "When in an action project, a CORE member will obey the order issued by the authorized leader or spokesman of the project, whether these orders please him or not. If he does not approve of such orders, he shall later refer the criticism back to the group or to the committee which was the source of the project plan." Francis Broderick and August Meier, eds., *Negro Protest Thought in the Twentieth Century* (Indianapolis: Bobbs-Merrill Co., 1965), p. 302.

traits we respect them for. We think that those traits are strengthened by our acting on the presumption of their presence, even when they are not present. This is not the whole story, obviously, and there are circumstances where the rule does not apply. But do we not treat the respectable qualities as the rule because we want to maintain them as the rule, and do we not carefully identify and circumscribe the exceptions in order to help maintain their exceptional character? Do we not, as beneficiaries of the law, have an interest in having the law obeyed even where there is disagreement about its justice? Do we not benefit from a community of law-abiding men? Are we seriously prepared to say, with Thoreau, "For my own part, I should not like to think that I ever rely on the protection of the State"?[15] The advocates of civil disobedience contend that we are protected from these dangers to the law by the practical and moral consequences of the rule that the lawbreaker must act openly and with a willingness to accept the punishment. But are we so sure that we can enforce this rule, as the teaching of disobedience extends through the populace, especially the desperately poor, the degraded, and the bitter? Despite some outstanding successes in limited areas under special circumstances, I think it is now clear—as it should have been from the beginning—that the broad result of the propagation of civil disobedience is disobedience. The question then becomes whether the encouragement of disobedience endangers law and civil society, and the answer seems clear enough today, if it was ever in doubt, that it does.

Indeed, why *should* the breaker of an unjust law do so "openly, lovingly and with a willingness to accept the penalty?" The reason, King suggests, is to show his respect for law. It is not clear, in the first place, why if he need not obey the law to show respect for law, he needs to accept the punishment to show respect for law. It is not surprising that the subtlety of this distinction tends to get lost in its application. Moreover, accepting the punishment for breaking an unjust law is not always necessary to show respect for law. Revolution need not be in disrespect of law, as the American Revolution surely was not. Nor, on the other hand, is civil disobedience—open and loving breaking of law with a willingness to accept the punishment—always the way to show respect for law. King says:

> We should never forget that everything Adolf Hitler did in Germany was "legal" and everything the Hungarian freedom fighters did in Hungary was "illegal." It was "illegal" to aid and comfort a Jew in Hitler's Germany. Even so, I am

---

15. Henry David Thoreau, "Civil Disobedience."

sure that, had I lived in Germany at the time, I would have aided and comforted my Jewish brothers. If today I lived in a Communist country where certain principles dear to the Christian faith are suppressed, I would openly advocate disobeying that country's antireligious laws.[16]

But would King have openly aided and comforted Jews in Hitler's Germany? Precious few Jews he would have aided! Would he openly advocate disobeying the antireligious laws of a Communist country at the price of leaving his and other Christian flocks untended? And would he—ought he to?—disobey the laws of Hitler's Germany lovingly? Is he obliged to show his respect for "law" in general by willingly accepting the punishment imposed by the "laws" of that regime? The extension of the principles of civil disobedience to such cases makes a mockery of law and justice.

A more tenable argument would be that the breaking of an unjust law *in a fundamentally just regime* must be done in an open, loving manner and with a willingness to accept the punishment, not to show respect for law in the abstract but to show respect for and concede the legitimacy of this system of law, of which this unjust law is a part. The laws of segregation deserve to be broken, this argument runs; but their breaking ought to be done in a way that shows respect for and helps to support the broader legal principles of the American government which, unlike the segregation laws, deserve the respect of a just man. The distinction, which King fails to make, between regimes like that of the United States and regimes like that of Nazi Germany is at the foundation of the political action of all decent, to say nothing of just, men, precisely because it is the distinction between those political systems to which decent men can and cannot lend their cooperation. Obviously this does not settle questions of political action. It is only the beginning. If the regime is fundamentally unjust it must be changed, brought down, endured, or deserted—whichever seems most likely to result in something better. If the regime is fundamentally just, there remains the substance of politics, involving all of the heavy and difficult judgments about where justice can be done and injustice avoided consistently with the overall aim of maintaining and strengthening the capacity of the system to act well.

There is another side of this issue to which King also appears to have given little attention. Sometimes he speaks of just and unjust laws, sometimes of just and unjust systems. Where does the duty not to cooperate with injustice end? Must the conscientious man refuse

---

16. King, "Letter from the Birmingham Jail."

his cooperation with every unjust law? with every system of which an unjust law is a part? The preeminence of the issue of legally sanctioned or supported racial discrimination in the South provided a focus for civil disobedience there which did not force questions like this to the surface, but they quickly arise as less clear-cut injustices are confronted. It seems likely that King would have accepted the well-known rule provided by Thoreau:

> If the injustice is part of the necessary friction of the machine of government, let it go, let it go: perchance it will wear smooth,—certainly the machine will wear out. If the injustice has a spring, or a pulley, or a rope, or a crank, exclusively for itself, then perhaps you may consider whether the remedy will not be worse than the evil; but if it is of such a nature that it requires you to be the agent of injustice to another, then, I say, break the law. Let your life be a counter friction to stop the machine. What I have to do is to see, at any rate, that I do not lend myself to the wrong which I condemn.[17]

But the distinction manifestly breaks down (as Thoreau virtually concedes later in the essay)[18] once one recognizes the obvious fact of the interdependence of the parts of a political system. The nexus of taxes, the specific ground of Thoreau's disobedience, connects every man with every wrong (as well as every right) done by the state. And if a man pays no tax—and is so consistent as to permit no one to pay it for him—he would still be connected by commerce or civil intercourse. If the lesson of civil disobedience is to become *in nowise* the agent of injustice, the result is revolution against this government, both in Thoreau's time and ours, and against every government I have read of or heard of. That does indeed seem to be the drift of this hero of civil disobedience, who milked so much out of one night in jail. "Under a government which imprisons any unjustly, the true place for a just man is also in prison." King never expressed himself quite so foolishly. But if, on the other hand, the advocates of civil disobedience are to be understood to say not that one must never in any way contribute to injustice but that one should consider whether he is, through his cooperation or compromise with a given political system, the instrument of *too much* injustice in comparison with the

---

17. Thoreau, "Civil Disobedience."

18. "In fact, I quietly declare war with the State, after my fashion, though I will still make what use and get what advantage of her as I can, as is usual in such cases."

good that his cooperation does, then he has begun—barely begun—to think and act *politically*, which is to say, beyond civil disobedience.

Civil disobedience attempts to substitute doctrine for political judgment, but the doctrine is empty. If the Negro proponents of civil disobedience would not teach revolution, they must learn politics. They could not wish a better teacher than Frederick Douglass, one of the greatest Negro leaders the United States has (in its paradoxical way) produced. I would emphasize that a comparison of men like King with Douglass is legitimate because we are comparing like things. Douglass was in fact one of the original sitters-in; and the forceful dignity with which he conducted himself on these occasions cannot but endear him to his descendants on the firing line today, particularly when they recall that Douglass had considerably less public opinion at his back than they have. Like King, Douglass was primarily a Negro leader, aggressive in his assertion of Negro rights and relentless in his resistance to segregation and color prejudice. Nor was Douglass timid about the consequences of his agitation. "Those who profess to favor freedom and yet deprecate agitation," he said, "are men who want crops without plowing up the ground, they want rain without thunder and lightning. They want the ocean without the awful roar of its many waters."[19]

As a slave, Douglass knew the brutal depths and the sharp frustrations of the human chattel in a free land. As an escaped slave, legally subject to seizure and return to bondage, he knew what it was to live in a society of enemies. As an abolitionist writer and agitator, he knew the alienation of the freed Negro and the despair of finding redress under the American Constitution. It is not surprising that Douglass early took up a hard, uncompromising abolitionism, the antecedent of today's civil disobedience. Yet within a very few years he learned the severe limits of civil disobedience. While not one whit relaxing his claim for the Negro, he learned that justice must be served through politics and that the hand that refuses to touch politics for fear of being soiled becomes useless and corrupt.

Where Martin Luther King has stood in the last decade, Frederick Douglass stood when, escaping from slavery in 1838 and making his way north, he became a Garrisonian abolitionist. Like King, the Garrisonians thought that to participate in an unjust system is to participate in its evil. "No union with slaveholders" was their moral foundation, "no political participation" their political principle. In Douglass's early words, "we utterly abhor and repudiate this govern-

---

19. Philip S. Foner, *The Life and Writings of Frederick Douglass* (New York: International Publishers, 1950), vol. 2, p. 437.

ment and the Constitution as a dark and damning conspiracy against all the purposes of government." "I welcome the bolt, either from the North or the South, which shall shatter this Union. . . ." Down with both the Constitution and the government, he said, "for it is not fit that either should exist!" "If there is one Christian principle more firmly fixed in our heart than another, it is this, that it is wrong to do evil that good may come; and if there is one heresy more to be guarded against than another, it is the doctrine that the end justifies the means." The oath to support the Constitution "requires that which is morally impossible," and therefore "the platform for us to occupy, is outside that piece of parchment."[20]

In 1851 Douglass broke with the Garrisonians. The break was ostensibly over the interpretation of the Constitution, Douglass arriving at the conviction that, properly interpreted, the Constitution did not sanction slavery. More fundamentally, Douglass revised his opinion about the duty of the Negro reformer in the face of legally sanctioned injustice. He adhered to the opinion that slavery existed because it was reputable and that the abolition of slavery would require the restoration in the United States of the moral power to abolish it. But how? Here is where the Garrisonians fell down. "As a mere expression of abhorrence of slavery, the sentiment [no union with slaveholders] is a good one; but it expresses no intelligible principle of action, and throws no light on the pathway of duty. Defined, as its authors define it, it leads to false doctrines, and mischievous results."[21] Douglass perceived the advantage of arguing on the side of the law rather than against it, and he found in the Constitution support for his antislavery arguments. His doctrine was that slavery was "a system of lawless violence; that it *never was lawful, and never can be made so*"; and his program was that "it is the first duty of every American citizen, whose conscience permits so to do, to use his *political* as well as his *moral* power for its overthrow."[22] Thus Douglass's new position altered both his rhetoric and his practical policies. The Negro could now speak fully the language of law, the language of defense of the Constitution. He could now call the country to return, not only to the fundamental political principles of the republic as expressed in the Declaration of Independence, but to its fundamental legal principles as expressed in the Constitution.

So far as the practical policies were concerned, Douglass embarked upon a course of political activity that sought to maintain the

20. Ibid., vol. 1, pp. 375, 270, 379, 378; vol. 2, pp. 117, 119.
21. Ibid., vol. 2, p. 351.
22. Ibid., p. 156.

moral purity and therefore the moral power of abolition, while at the same time finding ways of making it politically effective. To the man who said that he wanted his vote to represent *all* of his moral convictions, Douglass replied that "the fallacy here is the assumption that what is *morally* right is, at all times, equally politically possible."[23] Defending his support of the Free Soil candidate in 1852, Douglass stated the following rule of political action:

> It is evident that all reforms have their beginning with ideas, and that for a time they have to rely solely on the tongue and pen for progress, until they gain a sufficient number of adherents to make themselves felt at the ballot-box. . . . We ask no man to lose sight of any of his aims and objects. We only ask that they be allowed to serve out their natural probation. Our rule of political action is this: the voter ought to see to it that his vote shall secure the highest good possible, at the same time that it does no harm.[24]

With his tongue and pen Douglass continued to fight for uncompromising abolition; but when the time came to go to the polls, when the opportunity arose for political action, he focused on the good that he could do in the immediate future rather than on the good he was aiming at in the long run. Douglass' problems well illustrate the apparent dilemma of the reformer in politics. In 1856, for example, writing on "What Is My Duty as an Anti-Slavery Voter?" Douglass argued that "the purity of the cause is the success of the cause." While he might participate in politics, "the first duty of the Reformer is to be right. If right, he may go forward; but if wrong, or partly wrong, he is as an house divided against itself, and will fall." Since the Republican party did "not occupy this high Anti-Slavery ground, (and what is worse, does not mean to occupy it)," Douglass urged his readers to vote for the presidential candidate of the Radical Abolitionists, even at the risk of throwing the election to the Democrats and losing Kansas to slavery. "We deliberately prefer the loss of Kansas to the loss of our Anti-Slavery integrity."[25] Yet four months later, in August 1856, Douglass abandoned the Abolitionist candidate, Gerrit Smith, and announced his support of Republicans John Charles Fremont and William Lewis Dayton. The purity of the cause was subordinate, even for the partisan reformer, to a higher morality.

> The time has passed for an honest man to attempt any defence of a right to change his opinion as to political

---

23. Ibid., vol. 2, p. 213.
24. Ibid., vol. 2, pp. 213–14.
25. Ibid., pp. 393–94.

methods of opposing Slavery. Anti-Slavery consistency itself, in our view, requires of the Anti-Slavery voter that disposition of his vote and his influence, which, in all the circumstances and likelihoods of the case tend most to the triumph of Free Principles in the Councils and Government of the nation. It is not to be consistent to pursue a course politically this year, merely because that course seemed the best last year, or at any previous time. Right Anti-Slavery action is that which deals the severest deadliest blow upon Slavery that can be given at that particular time. Such action is always consistent, however different may be the forms through which it expresses itself.[26]

On this basis, Douglass later supported Lincoln, although often with grave doubts and usually with impatience and exasperation. As circumstances drew the Negro leader and the white statesman closer together, Douglass grew in his understanding of Lincoln. This is not to say that their relations were ever smooth or that Douglass saw matters as Lincoln saw them. Regarding the use by the Union of colored troops, for example, they were constantly at odds, although for a reason that will sound strange to many today. After months of urging that Negro troops should be used and long negotiations about how they would be used, Douglass reluctantly agreed to support a system that was in some respects unfair to Negro troops, because he thought that the cause of Negro freedom was served by cooperation even on such terms. The point is that he did not think that justice for the Negro could be achieved simply by withdrawing or withholding his cooperation from a system that did any injustice to the Negro. Moreover, Douglass saw not merely the political necessities of putting together alliances—important as that was—but also the higher political morality of the genuine statesman. Harris Wofford, Jr., says that "the abolitionists awakened the conscience of the nation and set the stage for Lincoln. . . ."[27] Granting that the abolitionists were indispensable stage hands, yet Lincoln was the actor. (And, to carry the metaphor one step further, the founders wrote the plot.)

Douglass met in Lincoln true statesmanship and came to understand his own and his people's place in relation to it. While Charles Sumner was "to me and to my oppressed race," "higher than the highest, better than the best of all our statesmen," Lincoln was simply "the greatest statesman that ever presided over the destinies

---

26. Ibid., p. 397.

27. Harris Wofford, Jr., "Non-Violence and the Law: The Law Needs Help," *The Journal of Religious Thought,* vol. 15, no. 1, Autumn-Winter, 1957–58, p. 30.

of this Republic."[28] Douglass gave expression to this understanding in 1876 on the occasion of the unveiling of the Freedmen's Monument in Washington, D.C. Lincoln was not, he said, "in the fullest sense of the word, either our man or our model. In his interests, in his associations, in his habits of thought, and in his prejudices, he was a white man." Yet, "while Abraham Lincoln saved for you a country, he delivered us from a bondage, according to Jefferson, one hour of which was worse than ages of the oppression your fathers rose in rebellion to oppose." Douglass described the Negro's faith in and understanding of Lincoln during the war, despite acts and words that tried the faith and taxed the understanding. He conceded that Lincoln's very prejudices were an element of his success in preparing the American people for the great conflict and bringing them safely through it. "Viewed from the genuine abolition ground, Mr. Lincoln seemed tardy, cold, dull, and indifferent; but measuring him by the sentiment of his country, a sentiment he was bound as a statesman to consult, he was swift, zealous, radical, and determined."[29]

This speech was meant by Douglass as the rhetorical end of the great struggle of his long career against Negro expatriation or colonization, whether proposed by whites or Negroes. At the bottom of that resistance was his recognition that, for all their oppression, the American Negroes had a hold on a civil society of extraordinary excellence, within which the Negro—once he secured admission— could pursue his happiness better than anywhere else on earth. What Douglass said of Lincoln on this occasion he meant to apply to the country at whose head Lincoln had stood. Lincoln was, Douglass said,

> pre-eminently the white man's President, entirely devoted to the welfare of white men. He was ready and willing at any time during the first years of his administration to deny, postpone, and sacrifice the rights of humanity in the colored people to promote the welfare of the white people of this country. In all his education and feeling he was an American of the Americans. . . . The race to which we belong were not the special objects of his consideration. . . . We are at best only his step-children; children by adoption, children by forces of circumstances and necessity.

The monument stood for the Negroes' praise of Lincoln but also for their title to praise him—stepchildren, indeed, but at last his and the country's children:

---

28. Foner, *Life and Writings of Frederick Douglass*, vol. 4, pp. 239, 368.
29. Ibid., pp. 309ff.

Fellow-citizens, I end, as I began, with congratulations. We have done a good work for our race today. In doing honor to the memory of our friend and liberator, we have been doing highest honors to ourselves and those who come after us; we have been fastening ourselves to a name and fame imperishable and immortal. . . .

The Negro did not inherit the gift of American citizenship; he had to fight to secure it. The different positions of the Negro with respect to American civil society at different points in time were always carefully reflected in Douglass's powerful and precise rhetoric. When thundering in the 1840s and 1850s against the Fugitive Slave law, he attempted to show that the Constitution authorized no such law, but he also suggested defiance and violence:

The man who takes the office of a bloodhound ought to be treated as a bloodhound; and I believe that the lines of eternal justice are sometimes so obliterated by a course of long continued oppression that it is necessary to revive them by deepening their traces with the blood of a tyrant.[30]

Douglass could never compromise on that point—however much a Lincoln might do so and even be right in doing so—for in this matter the slave was fighting for his very life and liberty. Douglass's language is hardly less strong—although the invitation to violence is lacking—in his denunciation of the *Dred Scott* decision in 1857; for in this decision Chief Justice Taney held that the Constitution forever prevented the Negro from becoming part of the American polity and, indeed, acknowledged him only as property. The decision was "infamous," "devilish," "this judicial incarnation of wolfishness," "an open, glaring, and scandalous tissue of lies." Douglass appealed against "this hell-black judgment of the Supreme Court, to the court of common sense and common humanity." He declared that "all that is merciful and just, on earth and in Heaven, will execrate and despise this edict of Taney."[31] The Court's decision in *Dred Scott* thrust the Negro out of any participation in the American political community. Thus Douglass confessed in his autobiography to a feeling allied to satisfaction at the prospect of a war between North and South:

Standing outside the pale of American humanity, denied citizenship, unable to call the land of my birth my country, and adjudged by the Supreme Court of the United States to have no rights which white men were bound to respect, and

---

30. Ibid., vol. 2, p. 207.
31. Ibid., pp. 410–12.

longing for the end of the bondage of my people, I was ready for any political upheaval which should bring about a change in the existing condition of things.[32]

It is instructive to compare Douglass's speech on the *Dred Scott* decision with his speech in 1883 on the *Civil Rights* cases, striking down federal legislation prohibiting discrimination against Negroes.[33] The war was over, for the country and for the Negro, and the character of the speech is determined by that great fact. This is not to suggest that the *Civil Rights* decision was not a serious blow. Douglass saw it as standing in a line that included the forcing of slavery into Kansas, the enactment of the Fugitive Slave Bill, the repeal of the Missouri Compromise, and the *Dred Scott* decision. "We have been, as a class, grievously wounded, wounded in the house of our friends, and this wound is too deep and too painful for ordinary measured speech," he said at the mass meeting called to protest the *Civil Rights* decision. But Douglass's speech, although not ordinary, was measured, precisely because the *Civil Rights* case, although wounding the Negro in the house of his friends, did not threaten to turn him out of that house, as *Dred Scott* had. Here there was none of the violence of the rejection of the Fugitive Slave Act or the uncompromising denunciation of the attack on the Taney decision. Douglass began by noting that he had taken pains to write out his speech, that perhaps indeed the time called for silence rather than speech. He spoke as strongly in defense of American law and legal institutions as in opposition to its injustice in this case. Indeed he asserted that the evil in the land, "which most threatens to undermine and destroy the foundations of our free institutions," was (not race prejudice or injustice to Negroes, serious as he thought those evils to be, but) "the great and apparently increasing want of respect entertained for those to whom are committed the responsibility and the duty of administering our government." Douglass urged his partisan audience never to forget that "whatever may be the incidental mistakes or misconduct of rulers, government is better than anarchy, and patient reform is better than violent revolution." While not interfering with fair criticism, he would give "the emphasis of a voice from heaven" to the repugnance felt by all good citizens to any disrespect for governors. Coming "a little nearer to the case now before us," he began his criticism, but again interrupted.

---

32. *Life and Times of Frederick Douglass, The Complete Autobiography* (New York: Collier Books, 1962), p. 329.

33. Foner, *Life and Writings of Frederick Douglass*, vol. 4, pp. 392–403.

Now let me say here, before I go on a step further in this discussion, if any man has come here to-night with his breast heaving with passion, his heart flooded with acrimony, wishing and expecting to hear violent denunciation of the Supreme Court, on account of this decision, he has mistaken the object of this meeting, and the character of the men by whom it is called.

Finally Douglass moved to the body of his criticism, but he did so only after having introduced the subject with the greatest circumspection and concern for maintaining the dignity and authority of the Court. This was now the Negroes' court as well as the whites'. Better to have a court that does serious harm to Negroes than to have none at all. Negroes today reap what Douglass helped to sow.

There is one further argument that needs to be considered, which is that, contrary to what I have contended, civil disobedience is not only a mode of politics but a subtle and profound support of law. The argument is an extension of the command that the unjust law be disobeyed openly and lovingly and with a willingness to accept the punishment. Civil disobedience implies, in this view, not merely a passive respect for law but an active participation with the law in a dialogue about justice. Harris Wofford, Jr., for example, takes one of the arguments often made by opponents of civil disobedience and turns it to a defense of civil disobedience. The law does not merely regulate; it also teaches. But whereas it is often argued that the teaching function of law is weakened by disobedience, Wofford contends that "the law will play its full role as a teacher only when we look upon it as a question." The law is "the voice of our body politic with which we must remain in dialogue." Each law should be looked upon by the free man "not as a command but as a question, for implicit in each law is the alternative of obedience or of respectful civil disobedience and full acceptance of the consequences."[34] Once each man is freed from the belief that he must obey the law just because it is law, he will ask, shall I obey this law? Is it just? Wofford suggests that it is this choice that makes men free and also that this choice will lead to a fruitful dialogue, the result of which will be an improved understanding of the ends of law. "I am presenting civil disobedience as a natural and necessary part of the great Due Process of our law, that process of persuasion through which we govern ourselves."[35]

34. *The Journal of Religious Thought*, Autumn–Winter, 1957–58, p. 31.

35. Harris Wofford, Jr., "The Law and Civil Disobedience," *The Presbyterian Outlook*, vol. 142, no. 34, p. 5.

While the free-choice argument does not appear to be basic, its tendency is suggested by the following. Wofford says that while we all engage in such

This is obviously an attractive idea. Civil disobedience may at last find solid ground if it can be shown to be part of our great "due process" of law, the dialogue through which the law teaches and thereby learns. There are, however, some problems. Wofford seems to think of civil society as a great seminar on justice, with the law as discussion leader. This is not an altogether false view, but it passes over too quickly the primary functions of law. This is not the place for any extended discussion of this matter, but if the law teaches, surely it also commands, punishes, and habituates.

Law—our law at any rate—is not merely command, but is it not that in the first place? Wofford argues that "implicit in each law is the alternative of obedience or of respectful civil disobedience and full acceptance of the consequences."[36] It is difficult to take seriously the suggestion that the law *intends* to offer the "option" of civil disobedience. The law does not present itself in the form of an either-or proposition. It is in the form of a command that men behave in a certain way, with a penalty attached as punishment if the command is disobeyed. If, on the other hand, Wofford means merely to describe the alternatives that are "implicit" in the sense of logically consistent, then the statement is too narrow, for secretive disobedience, avoidance, and violent rejection are also implicit in this sense. So far as enforcement is concerned, we may recall that the American founders had experienced, under the Articles of Confederation, a system of law that attempted to dispense with sanctions, penalties, or punishments for disobedience; and they learned that such laws amount in fact "to nothing more than advice or recommendation." Law does not address itself merely to the reason. It is precisely "because the passions of men will not conform to the dictates of reason and justice without constraint" that government is necessary.[37] Moreover, the law rests on and encourages habitual law-abidingness, the "taking for granted" of the justice of the law and its title to obedience. If mere habituation threatens freedom, sound habituation provides its necessary foundation. The man who seeks his freedom in a resistance

---

forms of "civil disobedience" as jaywalking or speeding, we hesitate to resist unjust laws. "Instead of taking Socrates straight, we seem to prefer the comic version. I am referring to Aristophanes' portrayal in *The Clouds,* where the student of Socrates says, 'But I wish to succeed, just enough for my need, and to slip through the clutches of law.' But there again we are free to choose which Socrates—which inner light or higher law—to follow, and it is the choice that makes us free." Better, it would seem, to disobey a just law than to disobey no law at all.

36. *Journal of Religious Thought,* p. 31.
37. *Federalist* 15.

to law as law will find instead anarchy or, more likely, paralysis. It is only through command, enforcement, and habituation that the law of the liberal regime performs one of its most admired functions, to provide the basis for political deliberation and political education.

Unquestionably the law does teach. It gives reasons and thereby invites an inspection of the validity of these reasons. Thoreau was wrong when he denied that the state ever "intentionally confronts a man's sense, intellectual or moral." The state confronts men's intellectual and moral sense every day in the public deliberations and addresses of the officers of the state, in the law courts, and in the laws themselves, with their preambles, "whereas" clauses, and explanatory notes and provisions. But while it is true that the giving of reasons implies a willingness to have those reasons and thus the foundation of the law questioned, the primary teaching lies in the reasons, not in the response. Admit that the reason of law may be regarded as a question to its subjects; admit that this is an invitation to a dialogue; admit that the subject takes a necessary part; admit that there is mutual instruction in the dialogue. Yet it is, after all, Socrates, who asks the questions, who teaches. The "education" that is involved in civil disobedience is, in the very best case, the responsive, subordinate, learning part of the dialogue. The guiding question of political education is, after all, not, shall I obey? but, what shall be done?

Civil disobedience is part of the subject's view, as distinguished from the citizen's view, of law and government. It is the subject for whom the first question is obedience or disobedience. It is the subject who is restricted in his political participation to those modes that are connected with his power to obey or not obey. It is the subject whose question is not, what shall be done? but, shall I obey? For people whose only role is that of subject, civil disobedience may indeed be the only available form of political participation. It may sometimes help to secure an excluded people a place among the governors of this self-governing community. But it is always a feeble instrument; because its principles are contradictory, its effects are dubious, it tends to undermine respect for the law, and above all its foundation is the role and point of view of the recipient of law, the subject. Civil disobedience is not rule, and it will be the resort of those who cannot or will not share in rule. Civil disobedience may be necessary and at least partly successful in removing restrictions on the registration of Negro voters in the South. It is neither necessary nor successful in dealing with the problems of northern slums—as Martin Luther King seemed to learn. Civil disobedience is a response to initiatives from elsewhere, an appeal to someone else to do something—or, more often, to stop doing something. It is inherently subordinate, responsive, dependent, and—for the citizen of a democracy—degrading.

There is a good deal of evidence that many Negro leaders today, having, like Frederick Douglass, pursued civil disobedience through its false morality to its political dead end, and rejecting the revolutionary demands of separation or destruction, are turning to a sober assessment of their political alternatives and political tasks. Bayard Rustin has described the beginning of this change in his well-known essay, "From Protest to Politics": "What began as a protest movement is being challenged to translate itself into a political movement."[38] In his last book, King, while defending nonviolent resistance against radical attack, conceded its inadequacy. "We found a method in nonviolent protest that worked, and we employed it enthusiastically. We did not have leisure to probe for a deeper understanding of its laws and lines of development."[39] We shall never know how far this probing might have gone, but it is clear that King looked increasingly to political power. Negroes need, he wrote in 1967, "to generate the kind of power that shapes basic decisions." There is a need to develop leaders and to enroll Negroes, formerly confined to the school of protest, in the school of citizenship.

> How shall we turn the ghettos into a vast school? How shall
> we make every street corner a forum, not a lounging place
> for trivial gossip and petty gambling, where life is wasted
> and human experience withers to trivial sensations? How
> shall we make every houseworker and every laborer a demonstrator, a voter, a canvasser and a student? The dignity
> their jobs may deny them is waiting for them in political
> social action.[40]

This political and social action by the Negro will be, in the first place, in pursuit of his own immediate needs and interests. "We can no longer rely on pressuring and cajoling political units toward desired actions," James Farmer has said. "We must be in a position of power, a position to change these political units when they are not responsive. The only way to achieve political objectives is through power, political power."[41] This is the beginning of democratic politics.

38. *Commentary*, February 1965; in Broderick and Meier, eds., *Negro Protest Thought in the Twentieth Century*, p. 407.

39. Martin Luther King, *Where Do We Go from Here, Chaos or Community?* (Boston: Beacon Press, 1967), p. 137.

40. Ibid., pp. 138, 156.

41. James Farmer, "Annual Report to the CORE National Convention," July 1, 1965; Broderick and Meier, *Negro Protest Thought in the Twentieth Century*, p. 425.

There is not yet much evidence among major Negro leaders of the understanding that a Frederick Douglass had of an Abraham Lincoln. (There may, it must be conceded, be more than one reason for that.) The emphasis that even the moderates place upon power is a sign, not only of their rhetorical problem in the face of a radical challenge, but also of the relatively narrow view they take of citizenship and political leadership. But the decent pursuit of self-interest through politics is, in the American system of ruling and being ruled, the beginning from which the subject of the law is stimulated and guided, through alliances and bargaining and compromises, to something like the comprehensive view of the true citizen. In such citizenship, as King suggests, lies not only a power but a dignity surpassing anything accessible through the mere subject's tactics of civil disobedience.

The circumstances of the Negro in America, under slavery and after the Civil War, taught Frederick Douglass a lesson which many whites at that time and many whites and blacks today have forgotten: that a fundamentally decent and just civil society, in which men are protected and encouraged in the pursuit of happiness, is a rare and precious thing. Not so rare and precious that it cannot be vigorously used, changed, and improved. American civil society is robust enough to take a good deal of mauling—that is one of its rare and precious qualities. The advocates of civil disobedience are surely right in asserting that American society can tolerate and be improved by vigorous criticism and dissent. Accepting the fundamental soundness of the American political system, its *capacity* to do justice, does not require any lessening in the energy directed toward the huge imperfections that this system suffers. It does require that that soundness, that capacity to do justice, be taken as the first principle of political reason and political action. No action can be well taken, no words wisely spoken, except in reference to that first principle.

Let it be granted that the injunction to "obey the law merely because it is a law" is not a sufficient principle of political action or of political duty—though, in all conscience, it seems to come closer than an injunction *not* to obey the law merely because it is a law. Injustice can be protested and private conscience gratified from a protest march or a jail cell, but the positive demands of justice cannot be served there. What Frederick Douglass once said of the uncompromising abolitionism of men like Garrison and Thoreau may be said today of civil disobedience: "As a mere expression of abhorrence" of injustice, "the sentiment is a good one; but it expresses no intelligible principle of action, and throws no light on the pathway of duty."[42]

---

42. Foner, *Life and Writings of Frederick Douglass*, vol. 2, p. 351.

12
Interest Groups and the Public Interest

Our intention in this chapter is to consider the "partnership" between the state and the farmer in the light of the public interest. There is a strong tendency in the literature on interest groups to regard any such attempt as altogether quixotic, and it is therefore necessary to consider briefly the grounds of such an evaluation as we here propose. Before considering the "public interest," however, we should examine the notion of interest itself. In this section we present, not a theory of interest or the public interest, but some elementary, if often overlooked, reflections about the meaning of these words as they are used in political life.

Generally writers in this field try to define *interest* objectively. Thus for S. E. Finer, interest groups are those with "a social or economic 'stake' in society," and for Harry Eckstein they are distinguished "chiefly by objective characteristics" such as income or occupation. In contrast, both writers refer to a different type of group whose values are subjective. Finer calls these "promotional bodies" which are concerned with some cause, and Eckstein talks of "attitude groups" whose goals reflect "purely subjective values."[1] The main point of these distinctions is to draw a line between groups seeking some hard material advantage on the basis of a common objective interest and groups which are held together only by common ideals or policies.

This essay, written with Peter Self and originally entitled "Agriculture and the Public Interest," was first published as a chapter in *The State and the Farmer: British Agricultural Policies and Politics* (Berkeley: University of California Press, 1963; London: George Allen and Unwin, 1963), pp. 212–220. It is reprinted with permission from the University of California Press. Although the piece was written specifically to show how agricultural advocacy groups influence British politics, the authors' observations are relevant to the role of advocacy groups in general in democratic governments.

1. S. E. Finer, *Anonymous Empire*, pp. 3–4; Harry Eckstein, *Pressure Group Politics* (George Allen and Unwin, 1960), pp. 9–10.

This distinction certainly has some utility, but it may be misleading. It suggests that interest groups are wholly or mainly guided by considerations of gain (generally material gain) of a sort that can be deduced from their circumstances. In fact, however, most such groups are also concerned with something wider than such private advantage. Finer concedes that the National Union of Teachers "has a genuine faith in Education."[2] But is this, as Finer implies, the exception, or is it not rather the rule? The National Farmers' Union certainly has a genuine faith in agriculture, and so, one supposes, has the Federation of British Industries in free enterprise and the British Medical Association in health. The faith or concern of these bodies in their respective fields is of course closely connected with (and sometimes only a cover for) the advantage of their members; but it is certainly part of their "interest." The point is that their interest is ambiguous, and one function of interest group studies, it seems to us, is to attempt to elucidate and understand that ambiguity, not to define it away.

Moreover, an objective interest is not just given by the facts. It has to be recognized, and unless society is viewed as wholly deterministic, the questions of what mutual interests men recognize and to which ones they give priority are themselves important questions of choice. For example, small farmers in Britain might have formed a separate organization or joined with farm workers; or large farmers might have made common cause with landowners; or tenant farmers might have separated themselves from owner-occupiers. While economic facts may make some choices of organization more likely, they do not automatically exclude other alternatives.[3]

---

2. S. E. Finer, "Interest Groups and the Political Process in Great Britain," Henry W. Ehrmann, ed., *Interest Groups on Four Continents* (University of Pittsburgh Press, 1958), p. 117.

3. Thus Eckstein says that "in interest groups there exists a high probability that political purposes will be pursued collectively, and normally this is the case in groups sharing objective characteristics" (*Pressure Group Politics*, p. 9). But at most this is "normally" the case only in groups sharing certain *kinds* of objective characteristics, such as (to use Eckstein's examples) income and occupation. It is not normally true of children, redheads, thirty-seven-year-olds, etc., all of whom share objective characteristics. The crucial point is that the distinction between those objective characteristics that are politically relevant and those that are not is based on what Eckstein would have to call "subjective" or "value" grounds. It was partly in recognition of this difficulty that David Truman reduced "interest" to "attitude," thus obliterating altogether the distinction under consideration here. See his *The Governmental Process* (New York: Alfred A. Knopf, 1953), pp. 33ff.

Nor, once a group has organized, can its policies and activities simply be deduced from the common objective characteristics of the members. It is for this reason that we find too restrictive the term, *pressure group*, which is now in rather general use in Britain.[4] *Pressure group* stresses the methods of these groups to the exclusion of their ends. These methods are certainly important, and the use of the term is reasonable in this limited context. However, organized interest groups do more than promote their interests; they also have to discover and define what their interests are.

This is not so easy a task as is sometimes assumed. In the first place, interests cannot be viewed simply as the wants or appetites of individuals or groups. Groups do not usually advance claims which they know to be completely unreasonable or socially unacceptable, even though they often engage in special pleading. As Plamenatz puts it, "What they [men] ask for and insist upon having is partly determined by their conceptions of justice."[5] It is for this reason that the notion of interest, as used in ordinary language, tends to be ambiguous. It refers partly to the actual articulated demands which individuals or groups put forward; but it also refers to the social principles which they invoke to support their claims. Shorn of the second factor, an interest would be lacking any reason for social acceptability. This is not to presume a complete correspondence of group interest and general interest. On the contrary, in modern democratic societies it is recognized that interests clash and that up to a point it is reasonable to fight for the distinctive interest of one's own group. We can say that it is even the duty of group leaders to advance the distinctive interests of their groups, so long as this is accompanied by an adequate recognition of the wider social interests within which their claims ought to be defined. This is the meaning of the distinction in ordinary speech between statesmanship and politics, a distinction which has the same significance at the group as at the national level.

In the second place, however cunning or stupid special interest

---

4. S. E. Finer does not like either *interest group* or *pressure group* and suggests instead *The Lobby*. This has the disadvantage, among others, of suggesting activities aimed at the *legislature* which, in Britain at least, seriously misplaces the emphasis. It is also of some importance that the representatives of influential organizations such as the National Farmers' Union spend very little time waiting in anyone's lobby.

5. John Plamenatz, "Interests," *Political Studies* (February 1954). See also the interesting analysis by S. I. Benn, "Interests in Politics," *Proceedings of the Aristotelian Society* (January 1960).

261

groups may be, they almost invariably recognize the elementary fact of their own partiality—as we do when we called them "special" interests or "sectional" interests. They are parts of some whole, and their conception and promotion of their own interest must be based on *some* view of that whole. This is the reason why interest groups do not simply make demands, but frequently also put forward arguments about the public interest. Very often these arguments are not taken seriously by students of politics because it is assumed that they are only "rationalizations" of private or sectional interests (or "attitudes"). It is certainly true that these arguments will overstate the importance of the special interest to the interest of the community, and that they will often be motivated less by a genuine concern for the public interest than by a shrewd awareness of the need to secure general support. Any schoolboy knows that—and government officials and the representatives of interest groups themselves certainly know it—but it is a superficial kind of "realism" that stops here. It is as unrealistic to assume that the process of government consists of nothing but political pressure as it would be to assume that it consists of nothing but pure reason.

The National Farmers' Union stresses repeatedly its concern for the general or public interest. Sometimes its claims are so exaggerated as to raise a smile. "We are met here," said its president on one occasion, "to defend not an industry but a nation."[6] More soberly, its journal described postwar union policy in the following terms:

> The Union set about conveying the urgency of its vision to the Government and to the nation, placing before the people the need for a full employment of our land and its resources as the solid foundation of economic security. Had the Union been actuated in this by no motive other than that of benefiting the farmers of this country it need not have been ashamed. In fact, however, the Union was moved by considerations far wider than the interests, however valid, of any single section of our community; the future of the whole nation, not of our farmers only, was, as it still is, at stake in this issue.[7]

Exaggerated and one-sided as it is, this statement certainly reflects the beliefs of union leaders. They are sure that the development and economic security of agriculture serve the interests of the nation as well as of farmers; and they are not unwilling to abate

---

6. *The British Farmer*, January 31, 1952.
7. Ibid., August, 1952.

their claims if an injury to the public interest can be persuasively demonstrated.

It is often asserted, however, that it is not meaningful to talk about the public interest, since there is no way of giving it a clear definition or one to which general assent will be given. Curiously the denial that there is a public interest typically goes along with an assumption that there certainly are special interests. But the former is at least as real as the latter. One trouble with the argument that apparently demolishes the public interest is that it likewise demolishes the group interest.

The special interest may be easier to perceive, but the difference in this respect should not be overemphasized. J. D. Stewart, for example, says that "the sectional interest, as represented by the group is clear,"[8] but that is by no means always the case. It is not clear where the farmers' interest lies with respect, say, to price supports versus direct grants. It is not easy for farm workers to see where their interests lie when they are pulled one way by their links with farmers and another way by their links with the Labour movement. It is not easy for landowners to see where their interests lie in a changing postwar Britain which seems to have no place for the old landowning tradition.

Moreover, the public interest is often at any rate as clear as that of any special interest. It was relatively easy to see that an increase in domestic food production was required after the war. Nor was it so difficult even for farmers to see the case for reducing the level of agricultural support in the late 1950s. Of course there are important questions about the public interest where there is much doubt and darkness. Few would venture to assert with unbounded confidence, for example, where the public interest lies with respect to the social value of small farms. But in principle such questions are no more obscure or difficult than those which have already been raised in relation to the interest of special groups. Indeed they are usually the same questions, asked from the viewpoint of society as a whole instead of from the viewpoint of farmers or farm workers.

Yet there does seem to be one important sense in which the interests of the parts are more obvious than those of the whole. Under conditions in which the state is prepared to dispense economic support and other favors, such groups as farmers are in a position to band together to demand benefits without having to accept equiva-

---

8. J. D. Stewart, *British Pressure Groups*, OUP, 1958, p. 244. It should be noted, however, that in other respects Stewart's conclusions are not unlike those presented here.

lent costs. The citizens of a state possess no such unilaterally advantageous direction of interest. Each citizen's interest as a taxpayer, for example, is balanced in various ways by his interest as a consumer of state services, with the equation working out differently for every individual. It is of course this situation which creates the distinctive character of "pressure group politics" where clearly defined special interests compete for special privileges. Even in terms of sectional advantage, however, the interests of a group are not necessarily well served by a single-minded pursuit of the favors of the state. The result may be not only to leave the group dangerously exposed if those favors are modified or withdrawn, but to inhibit voluntary measures and mutual cooperation which might well prove of more lasting benefit than state assistance.

The concept of the public interest raises broad questions of political philosophy which cannot be adequately treated in this chapter. It is, however, necessary to state at least the broad problems that arise with respect to the relationship between a modern democratic state and the special or sectional interests within it. These problems are of two kinds. There is first the need to relate the claims of special interests to the general welfare of the community. Second, there is the state's concern with the equitable adjudication of conflicts between and within groups.

It is well to be explicit about the implications of our statement of the first of these problems. First, it implies, as already suggested, that there are numerous overlapping, more or less well-organized interests in modern societies and that they are not per se illegitimate. We take it that there would be little disagreement with the proposition that, given their present conditions, the health of political societies like Britain is not to be found in the elimination of special interest groups but in their reconciliation with one another and with the public interest.[9] The statement implies, in the second place, that the special interest and the public interest are, as a general rule, reconcilable but that there is no automatic natural harmony; the reconciliation is the product of art as well as nature. Finally the statement implies

---

9. Whether they are desirable in principle is a question which it is impossible to consider here. Fortunately, that is not necessary for our limited purposes. Special interest groups are one of the conditions of modern life; this condition may be modified but not fundamentally altered. It is a mistake, we think, to move too quickly to the theories of, say, Rousseau in a discussion such as this. Relevant as Rousseau certainly is to a full treatment of interest group theory, it is important to recognize (as he did) that his ideal state depended upon certain special, and rare, conditions.

that in case of conflict, the public interest must prevail. This is not to adopt a simple "monistic" as against a "pluralistic" view, for the priority of the whole does not preclude a very considerable amount of vigorous, self-directed activity in the parts; indeed, the public interest lies partly in just such vitality.

The prevalence in the United States of a school of group theory, which attempts to reduce the whole process of government to the interaction of special groups, can be explained partly by a historical absence of pressing national problems. When A. F. Bentley wrote the first important study of modern group pressures,[10] the American people as a whole seemed to have little need to concern themselves with collective problems of defense, foreign policy, world trade, or the conservation of natural resources. Today, the American position is wholly different, although the group theorists do not seem to have realized it yet. In British political life, nobody doubts the existence of a public interest in such matters as physical security, foreign trade, financial solvency, economic growth, and other matters. This point would hardly need making, were it not that some writers on the political process, influenced by American group theory, seem to forget that public interests, although much broader, are fully as "objective" and discernible as those of special groups.

Public interest in this sense refers to the needs, rather than to the wants, of a particular community. In a democracy the wishes of a majority may be accepted as providing a prima facie indication of the public interest, but they do not provide a final or unqualified verdict. Nor is the public interest adequately defined as an accommodation of special interests. This is generally understood in Britain, where political institutions and conventions foster the screening of sectional claims by reference to notions of the general interest. In our view, however, the basic soundness of British political life has misled some observers into undue complacency about the character and consequences of group pressures upon government.[11]

---

10. A. F. Bentley, *The Process of Government* (Evanston, Illinois: The Principia Press, 1949; first published in 1908). For an excellent brief essay on American group theory see W. J. M. Mackenzie, "Pressure Groups: The 'Conceptual Framework,' " *Political Studies* (October 1955).

11. For example *The Political Quarterly*'s special number, "Pressure Groups in Britain" (January–March 1958), contains interesting material on the workings of groups, but most of the authors simply assume that these groups can be satisfactorily assimilated into the workings of the British constitution, without producing any special problems. Harry Eckstein (*Pressure Group Politics*, chap. 7) concludes that if the private negotiations between the government and the British Medical Association had led to undesirable

Since the strength of special interests has developed *pari passu* with a growth in the range and importance of public interests, the defense of the latter against the former becomes both more important and more difficult, while the transference of much of the process of adjustment of interests from the political to the administrative level reduces public awareness of the issues at stake. These developments throw an increasing burden of responsibility upon the guardians of the public interest, the ministers of the Crown and the senior civil servants who advise them. Neither their capacity to exercise this responsibility wisely nor the public's willingness to support them can be taken for granted. Moreover, that view of politics which ignores or subordinates the government's custody of the general interest is not confined entirely to American students. Harold Laski's comment that "the making of policy . . . is the more successful the larger the number of affected interests consulted in its construction,"[12] is closely related to American group theory, both in its theoretical foundation and in its effect on political life.

Especially important for the treatment of sectional economic groups is the public interest in economic growth and welfare. Thus the claims of farmers are generally reviewed in terms of two standards: that of utility (for example, their contribution to the national economy) and that of equity (for example, their right to a fair share in the wealth of the community). The standard of utility rests upon the presumption that the maximization of real or "consumable" wealth is inherently desirable and that it is the state's business to further this goal. Leaving aside the formidable difficulties which arise in measuring the wealth of a community, it is enough to note that the desirability of raising the total wealth and average living standards of the community is rarely questioned and that this objective constitutes a general standard by which sectional claims must expect to be tested.

There is of course no necessary reason why this should be so. A society might quite reasonably attach greater weight to other values and less to the value of material wealth. While Britain's vulnerable trading position does limit the extent to which the public interest can be defined in nonmaterial terms, this emphasis upon economics

---

decisions on important matters, the public would have heard about it and action would have been taken. We see no reason for this conclusion. S. E. Finer (*Anonymous Empire*, chap. 9) ends on the other hand with an appeal for "more light" on group activities, without however explaining what kind of action might need to follow.

12. Harold Laski, *A Grammar of Politics*, 4th ed. (Allen and Unwin, 1941), p. 375.

should not obscure the importance or validity of other types of standard. The public interest is often invoked to defend or to promote certain cultural values. A good example is the protection given to green belts, national parks, and areas of "outstanding scenic beauty" under town and country planning legislation. Such action generally involves a considerable frustration of individual wishes, and often adds to the costs of economic development. It is by no means certain that it would be supported by majority opinion, nor is it usually justified in those terms. The justification is that certain aspects of human experience and cultural heritage ought to be safeguarded against permanent destruction or injury. This opinion is of course open to challenge, both in principle and (still more) in application; but the idea that there is a public interest involved in such matters is very widely understood and accepted.

In addition to the problem of reconciling group with public interest, the state is also concerned with the equitable adjudication of conflicting claims between and within groups. While the government's responsibility is less active in the latter case, it is scarcely necessary to say that there is no sharp line dividing these two spheres. Indeed, the most important point is that the relations between particular groups are a matter of public interest. There are, it is true, some very limited matters in which this interest is negligible, except in the sense that the public is always interested in fairness between parties. Such, for example, is the question as to whether and under what conditions farmers should be permitted to pay their workers by check rather than in cash. The weak bargaining position of the individual worker and the inconvenience to him of having to negotiate a check has led to a requirement by government that he be paid in cash. But if representatives of farmers and workers can agree to some modification of this rule, the public may reasonably leave it to the parties immediately concerned. And if they cannot agree, the public interest requires no more than that the inconveniences on both sides be fairly balanced.

Similar considerations apply to the choice by groups of their representatives, although here the public interest is more immediate. If the government accepts the claim of a single organization, such as the National Farmers' Union, to speak for an entire industry, the ability of lesser organizations to recruit support or to press their views will be severely handicapped. The dominance of one main organization may also cause politicians and administrators to attach excessive importance to the views of its leaders. These drawbacks do not necessarily outweigh the advantages of the arrangement, but they do illustrate the public interest in equitable representation.

Generally, however, the public interest is directly involved even in what presents itself as wholly a dispute between sectional interests. The claim for equal treatment or for "fair shares" has a kind of limited prima facie validity, especially where the state makes extensive use of economic regulation and aid. But when such a claim is made the question immediately arises whether, under given circumstances, equal treatment is equivalent to *fair* treatment, and this question requires recourse to the public interest. For example, it might be accepted as in the general interest that no section of the community should fall below a certain minimum level of economic welfare, just as a similar rule is accepted in the case of individuals. This might then justify the provision of minimum guaranteed prices for farmers, and minimum wages for farm workers, even if this necessitated a degree of state aid not extended to other industries.

To take a somewhat different kind of case which presents itself as merely a dispute between parties, we might consider the question of how much security of tenure should be given to agricultural tenants. This is a question in which the public has a direct interest, bearing as it does upon farming standards, the cost of support, and the ability of newcomers to enter farming. Under such circumstances, agreement between the parties immediately concerned is an insufficient guide. One of the dangers of the weight that is now placed upon consultation with affected parties, an emphasis which is especially prominent in agricultural policy, is that politicians and civil servants are likely to regard their tasks as completed when accommodation between the parties has been reached. They tend to lose sight of their broader obligation, which is not only to accommodate the interests of conflicting parties but to search out and to promote the broader public interest.

13
The Crucial Link: Public Administration, Responsibility, and the Public Interest

Where men once said "the common good," we now say "the public interest"; where men once said "duty," we now say "responsibility." In these shifts of terminology lie much of the meaning and the problem of modern political thought, and therefore of thought about public administration.

The three volumes under consideration, containing together more than fifty essays clustered around some very general (and important) themes, provide a rich sample of contemporary opinion on what is widely regarded as the "soft" side of political science and public administration. The two volumes edited by Carl Friedrich, *Responsibility (Nomos III)* and *The Public Interest (Nomos V)*, are yearbooks of the American Society of Political and Legal Philosophy, of which Friedrich is founder and elder statesman, and are based on the papers and discussions at the society's 1958 and 1960 annual meetings. The papers in the Harlan Cleveland–Harold Lasswell collection were prepared for a 1960 Conference on Science, Philosophy, and Religion in Their Relation to the Democratic Way of Life. The breathtaking range of this volume—*Ethics and Bigness: Scientific, Academic,*

This essay was originally published in *Public Administration Review*, vol. 24, March 1964. Reprinted with permission from Public Administration Review, copyright by the American Society for Public Administration (ASPA), 1120 G Street, NW, Suite 700, Washington, D.C. 20005. All rights reserved.

It is a review of three books: Carl J. Friedrich, ed., *Nomos III: Responsibility* (Yearbook of the American Society of Political and Legal Philosophy) (The Liberal Arts Press, 1960); Carl J. Friedrich, ed., *Nomos V: The Public Interest* (Yearbook of the American Society of Political and Legal Philosophy) (Atherton Press, 1962); and Harlan Cleveland and Harold D. Lasswell, eds., *Ethics and Bigness: Scientific, Academic, Religious, Political, and Military*, Conference on Science, Philosophy and Religion in Their Relation to the Democratic Way of Life, Inc. (Harper & Brothers, 1962).

Religious, Political, and Military—requires a preface and three introductions to get it properly launched; but the subject becomes somewhat less formidable as the student of public administration discovers that most of the essays are concerned with familiar problems of bureaucracy and responsibility. Obviously it is almost impossible to give an overall view of such volumes; moreover, the *Review's* policy leaves the commentator with a wide discretion in the exercise of his duty and encourages him to state and reflect a bit upon what seem to him to be the major issues. The result inevitably is that some essays—including some good ones—are not treated adequately or at all.

Perhaps the best place to begin is with the public interest and particularly with Glendon Schubert's and Frank Sorauf's attacks on it. These essays merit special consideration both because earlier articles by these authors helped to foster the current round of discussion of the public interest and because of the vigor and, one gathers, the influence of their remarks.[1] There is, Schubert asserts, "no public-interest theory worthy of the name."[2] "Perhaps," concludes Sorauf, "the academicians ought to take the lead in drawing up a list of ambiguous words and phrases 'which never would be missed.' For such a list I would have several candidates, but it should suffice here to nominate the 'public interest.' "[3]

Conceptual Criticisms of "Public Interest"

Generally speaking, there are three major parts of the criticism of the meaningfulness and usefulness of "public interest": that the idea is undemocratic, that it is vague, and that it is unscientific. The belief that the idea of the public interest is undemocratic helps to agitate

---

1. See Frank Sorauf, "The Public Interest Reconsidered," *Journal of Politics*, vol. 19, pp. 616–39 (November 1957) and Glendon Schubert, " 'The Public Interest' in Administrative Decision-Making," *American Political Science Review*, vol. 51, pp. 346–68 (June 1957). These two articles were taken as starting points by Charner M. Perry and Wayne A. R. Leys in a 1958–1959 survey of the literature on the public interest done under the auspices of the American Philosophical Association. The conclusions were reported in *Philosophy and the Public Interest* (Committee to Advance Original Work in Philosophy, 1959) and are summarized in *Nomos V* in an essay by Leys. Schubert published his full study as *The Public Interest: A Critique of the Theory of a Political Concept* (Glencoe, Illinois: Free Press, 1960), from which his article in the *Nomos* volume is drawn.

2. Friedrich, *The Public Interest*, p. 175.

3. Ibid., p. 190.

Schubert to impassioned scorn against what he calls the "idealists."[4] The argument is not very sophisticated. "According to idealist thought, congressmen are responsible neither to political parties nor to their constituencies; they have a higher obligation to God and to their own consciences."[5] The argument at this level is sufficiently met by C. W. Cassinelli, who points out that "the immediate and normally overriding responsibility of every official is to exercise his authority [allocated by the Constitution] to the best of his ability; but the public interest is still the final justification for this authority and for the constitution that confers it." The official "cannot avoid exercising discretion, and in doing so he often must act according to his own interpretation of the public interest."[6] Obviously this does not dispose of the problem; there *is* a question whether "public interest" is reconcilable with "democracy"—a question that a genuine exploration of "public interest" would have to take up. The absence from this volume of anything but oblique or superficial discussion of this central question, by either critics or defenders, testifies to the character and quality of much contemporary discussion of the public interest.[7] The fact is that its allegedly undemocratic character is the least important argument made by the critics of "public interest"—thus perhaps the willingness to stop at caricature. This is still a political question (and as such it comes into prominence when the theme shifts to responsibility); and academic discussions of "public interest" these days have a strikingly unpolitical character.

The second allegation against "public interest" is that it is hopelessly vague. "[W]e are widely reassured," says Sorauf, "that politics (and its study) is an art rather than a science, and that a certain genteel fuzziness—often masquerading as literary elegance—would

---

4. To enter into the questionable character of Schubert's approach and of his categories would require a detailed examination of his book, which would leave no space for anything else. Illustrative, perhaps, is the fact that although Schubert sets out in his book to deal with writing about the public interest during the last three decades, he finds it necessary to cast his net back some eighteen decades for his first "idealist"—a group known in one of his earlier formulations as "Platonists"—and that his catch turns out to be James Madison.

5. Ibid., p. 166.

6. Ibid., pp. 52–53.

7. William S. Minor argues, for example: "The shared responsibility necessary to the development and maintenance of democratic relations within and among publics depends basically upon man's sincere search for evidence, because it is evidence rather than mere opinion which is useful in resolving conflicts of interest." Compare with *Federalist* 10.

not be out of place."[8] There are grounds, in this volume and the others here considered, for such impatience, although it should be said that literary inelegance does not necessarily result in clarity and precision.

To dissipate the vagueness of "public interest," its fundamental grounds and implications would have to be explored, which Schubert and Sorauf scarcely begin to do. One might begin by observing that the most interesting and revealing quality of the term is precisely the quality that the critics wish to throw out: its implication of a good. As a man's interest is what is good for him, so the public interest is what is good for the public; and we distinguish, therefore, as Hamilton does in *Federalist* 71, between the interests and the inclinations of the people.[9] However, the analogy between individual interest and public interest is problematical. While interest implies a good, it implies a relatively low or narrow good; it implies, moreover, an individual good. The first definition of interest in the Oxford dictionary is "objectively concerned by having a *right* or title," and rights are primarily the possession of individuals. The foundation of the public interest, it appears, is individual rights. The beginning and the end of political life is the individual with his interest in and right to physical security and comfort; and the public interest is the maintenance of the conditions necessary for the enjoyment of those individual rights. One might at this point recall Madison's reference to "the permanent and aggregate interests of the community" and raise the question whether the public interest is a mere aggregate of individual interests or whether something else has to be added, and, if the latter, what that something else can be and where it comes from.[10] These are serious difficulties and any fundamental discussion of

---

8. Friedrich, *The Public Interest*, p. 183.

9. Compare with Ludwig Freund in Friedrich, *Responsibility* (The Liberal Arts Press, 1960), p. 35: "The problem of responsible leadership in a democracy begins here with the seemingly subtle, in reality rather definite distinctions between wants, desires, and needs as synonyms of interest."

10. See Edgar Bodenheimer's exploration of this question in Friedrich, *The Public Interest*. Here also Gerhard Colm suggests the interesting analogy of a play, in which producers, actors, and audience, all motivated by self-interest, "find a common ground under the spell of the play as a work of art" (p. 127); but he does not raise the question whether "common ground" might be found—for example, in commercial television—under a spell that no one would think of calling a work of art and what the consequences of different grounds might be for the quality and level of self-interest as well as the public interest.

"public interest" must face them; but (and this is the immediate point here) they are not difficulties arising out of *vagueness*.

Regarding more recent writers, it must be confessed that the charge of vagueness has more plausibility. To the rights enumerated in the Declaration of Independence we find writers here adding those of the Charter on Human Rights. Added to physical security and comfort we find a right to individual development. Edgar Bodenheimer, expressing a general view, states the goal as "a well-ordered and productive community in which everybody has an opportunity to develop his capabilities to the fullest."[11] "Individual development" no doubt makes a better starting point than quibbling, as George Nakhnikian does, about whether Lasswell's assumption of the desirability of preserving human dignity is any good, since it would not be useful to those who are not in favor of human dignity.

Yet is there not some reason to doubt what Bodenheimer thinks no reasonable man will censure, namely, the aim of providing "the widest possible opportunities for the activation of all human energies and talents. . . ."?[12] Admirable as this aim may be in most cases, Bodenheimer himself recognizes that there are human energies and talents that ought not to be activated, for the sake of the further development of the individual himself as well as the community at large. Yet in the end there does not seem to be any basis in this widespread view, which Bodenheimer represents well, for saying what "development" consists in; there is therefore no basis for saying what kinds of activities and talents ought to be encouraged and what discouraged.

Accompanying this emphasis on individual development is a concern in these essays with procedures, the rules of the game by means of which the open society prevents itself from falling apart.[13] There is a good deal of sensible discussion along these well-worn lines, with little disposition to inquire whether it is possible to give any meaningful and lasting procedural definition of the public interest when there is disagreement about the most important things. So far as the question is raised at all, the reply tends to be a formal one, as illustrated by Charner Perry's observation in *Ethics and Bigness:* ". . . the utilization of sources of agreement depends in large part on there being appropriate institutions for maximizing the results of

---

11. Ibid., p. 212.

12. Ibid., p. 213.

13. See for example the essays by Gerhard Colm and Schubert in Friedrich, *The Public Interest,* Herbert J. Spiro in Friedrich, *Responsibility,* and Charner Perry and Richard McKeon in Cleveland and Lasswell, *Ethics and Bigness.*

limited agreement and for minimizing the disruptive effects of dis-agreement."[14]

Another way of attempting to dissipate the vagueness of "public interest" is to explore its meaning, not in the abstract, but in the context of a set of concrete circumstances and problems. This is the aim, for example, of Stephen K. Bailey's essay in *The Public Interest* and of his, James MacGregor Burns's, and Paul N. Ylvisaker's essays in *Ethics and Bigness*. Yet although Ylvisaker's sharp, tight description of two cases of metropolitan decision making eschews any "genteel fuzziness" and all the essays are obviously motivated by a genuine perplexity about the public interest, in general and particular, a kind of tired cynicism is never far from the surface. What are we to make, for example, of Bailey's defense of the public interest as a "myth," which must nevertheless be given "rational content," and the value of which, it seems, lies in its very moralistic vagueness?[15] Bailey seems to echo Pendleton Herring, who defined the public interest as a "verbal symbol" whose "value is psychological and does not extend beyond the significance that each responsible civil servant must find in the phrase for himself," and who yet saw the public interest as a *standard* for judging between one contending group and another: "Without this standard for judgment between contenders, the scales would simply be weighted in favor of victory for the strongest."[16] So on the one hand, there must be a standard if the law of the jungle is to be avoided; on the other hand, there is no standard but rather an indefinite number of psychological, subjective feelings. The fruit of this tree is cynicism. The art of government or prudence, which these men seek to practice and to describe, is on their own principles groundless. Prudence cannot defend itself, as it once could, as being rooted in an understanding of the ends served because it is conceded that those ends are beyond or beneath rational understanding. Pru-dence cannot, therefore, defend itself against the attack that, far from

---

14. Ibid., p. lx. Perry continues, "I think I have stated the main require-ment regarding institutions in a pluralistic society: the requirement, namely, that they should be such as to extend cooperation beyond the limits of achieved doctrinal agreement and that they should be capable of utilizing for limited agreement the points of coincidence among the multiple strands of diverse myths and ideologies, and that they should be such as to minimize the bad effects of disagreement."

15. Friedrich, *The Public Interest*, p. 97.

16. E. Pendelton Herring, *Public Administration and the Public Interest* (Mc-Graw-Hill Co., 1936), pp. 23–24, 377.

being the legitimate pride of the practical man, it is but a poor substitute for the theory or science of instrumental decision making.[17]

These criticisms of its alleged undemocratic character and vagueness are, however, only a preface to the case against "public interest." At the heart of the case lies the third criticism, that it is unscientific. Schubert's root assumption is that if the concept of the public interest is to have any value, either as a guide to behavior or as a description of it, it must be capable of being made "operational," which, according to Schubert, "public interest" is not. This basic test is made more explicit by Sorauf. "Public interest," he explains, is one of the chief offenders in mixing together the "ought" and the "is," in confusing "the normative and the real." What is needed is, if not a completely "value-free" study of politics (because that is impracticable), "a maximum degree of separation of the two."[18] The purpose of this separation is to enable political scientists to get on with their scientific study of the "facts."

It is not clear what Schubert and Sorauf would have political scientists or politicians or citizens do with the "value" questions, if anything. There are some attempts in *The Public Interest,* the most interesting being that of William Minor, to show the beneficial effects of such a separation for politics as well as science; but the benefits remain shadowy—at least as vague, indeed, as anything that can be laid at the door of traditional talk about the public interest. There is a good deal of truth in Cassinelli's remark that "the critics often say, in effect, that since we have difficulty in deciding what is most desirable in politics, we should stop discussing the issue."[19] The happy situation of the economist, in this respect, has long attracted political scientists, but the economist can defend the partiality of his science by pointing out that there are others to deal with the whole—such as political scientists. As R. A. Musgrave says in *The Public Interest,*

> economic analysis has traditionally stopped short of certain noneconomic implications of economic processes. Thus it might be argued that a continuous increase in the standard of living may be demoralizing, that pursuit of the profit motive harms the trader's soul, and so forth. Economists will not deny that the concept of the public interest must be

---

17. See the exchange between Edward Banfield and Herbert A. Simon in *Public Administration Review,* Autumn 1957, and Winter 1958.

18. Friedrich, *The Public Interest,* p. 186.

19. Ibid., p. 47.

broadened at some point to include such matters, but they would hold this to be outside their province.[20]

In view of their strong commitment to a "value-free" social science, it is interesting to observe that Sorauf uses the phrase "legitimate differences of interests" in the very essay in which he attacks the vague, nonoperational, value-laden term, "public interest,"[21] and that Schubert uses a similar term, "legitimate interests," in his book.[22] Even without the evaluating adjective, the term "interest" is full of difficulties from this scientific point of view. As Charner Perry points out, " 'interest' does not denote an observable fact and is not operationally definable."[23] Any argument directed against the meaningfulness of "public interest" is equally applicable to "group interest," and most of the arguments in common use throw doubt on the concept of "interest" itself. A whole family of favorite babies will be thrown out with this bath.

Even more significant than Schubert's and Sorauf's unself-conscious use of "interest" and "legitimate interest" is the former's use of "responsibility." The first chapter of Schubert's book, *The Public Interest*, is entitled, "The Quest for Responsibility," and it begins with the observation that "the search for forms of government conducive to *responsible decision making* is as old as political philosophy" (italics added). To have said "conducive to decision making in the public interest" would have carried roughly the same meaning; it would surely have been no more vague, no more incapable of operationalization, no more unscientific. "Responsibility" is used throughout by Schubert in the same old general unscientific way that we used "public interest" in the past, until Schubert and other stern scientific patriarchs told us to stop. Schubert concludes his essay in the *Nomos* volume, as he concludes his book, with the argument that "if the public interest concept makes no operational sense . . . then political scientists might better spend their time nurturing concepts that offer greater promise of becoming useful tools in the *scientific study of political responsibility*" (italics added). One could again reverse the terms, talk about the lack of operational sense in political responsibility, and urge the development of better tools for the scientific study of the public interest. If it were not for the common knowledge that our most vocal scientific students of politics rarely subject them-

---

20. Ibid., pp. 113–14.
21. Ibid., p. 189.
22. Schubert, *The Public Interest*, p. 184.
23. Friedrich, *The Public Interest*, p. 245.

selves to a strict practice of what they preach, one might suspect the operation of a fairly simple shell game.

Responsibility as the Link

"Responsibility" is in even more frequent use today than "public interest." It is, moreover, more generally accepted as a respectable term, as Schubert's usage illustrates, perhaps because its "value" implications are a bit further from the surface. In any case, there is less emphasis here on attacking and defending the term and more concern with understanding it. One of the reasons for its popularity is that responsibility is, or appears to be, essentially a procedural criterion. Harlan Cleveland, for example, in his introduction to *Ethics and Bigness*, contends that ethical standards are "ultimately subjective, personal, individual" and that "each of us has both the freedom and the obligation to fashion his own ethical standards. . . ."[24] Cleveland says that he cannot suggest an affirmative code of ethics for the government official (although in fact he does so), but he suggests a guiding question: "If I am publicly criticized, will I still feel that this is what I should have done, and the way I should have decided to do it?"[25] This is not a bad first step in the quest for responsibility, but it is surely no more than that. Cleveland takes for granted the desirability of the official making his public face the same as his private face, a simple view of the relation between the public and private that is understandably questioned in several of these essays. He fails to consider what Friedrich for example does take some notice of, the different audiences by whom the official's action might be criticized and to whom he might have to make explanation. He relies finally on the "feelings" of the official whose behavior may be questioned.

That is by no means unimportant; it is even sufficient for many practical purposes, but it is not fundamentally sufficient. Decent feelings require training and support. They require at least the support of a general opinion that there *are* standards of better and worse behavior. Yet, as Senator Eugene McCarthy points out in this same volume, that support tends to be lacking in contemporary American society: "When a leading scholar declares that 'the seat of ethics is in the heart'; when it is acceptable to assert that the only absolute is that there are no absolutes; when religious and philosophical leaders lend their names to a declaration of their faith in man's

---

24. Cleveland and Lasswell, *Ethics and Bigness*, p. xlv.
25. Ibid.

ability 'to make his way by his own means to the truth which is true to him'; we should not be surprised to find some government officials making up rules which may be convenient to their own purposes."[26]

Roland Pennock's provocative opening essay in *Responsibility* explores more fully the meaning of responsibility.

> It is easy to get into muddles in connection with this term ["responsible government"], simply because we use it, often at the same time, in varying applications. We mean that the government is responsible to the electorate. . . ; it is accountable, in some not completely arbitrary fashion, for the exercise of its trust. But we also mean that it is morally responsible; that is, that it acts in a fashion that would be morally approved by disinterested observers (or by ourselves). It holds itself to account to high standards of duty, justice, and public welfare.[27]

Responsibility has, according to Pennock, two primary meanings: "(a) accountability and (b) the rational and moral exercise of discretionary power (or the capacity or disposition for such exercise), and . . . each of these notions tends to flavor the other."[28] Responsibility is a liability to answer, to give an account, to give reasons; the last is not identical to the first but implicit in it. Thus, responsibility is a procedural liability, but, as Pennock's discussion suggests, an obligation to give reasons implies the distinction between good and bad reasons; the truly responsible man is one who can give good reasons for his behavior.

Regarding the popularity that the term "responsibility" enjoys today, Pennock makes this interesting suggestion:

> "Rugged" individualism stressed rights; the [totalitarian] reaction against this philosophy emphasized duties; we may today, I believe, be seeing the emergence of a new individualism in which responsibility is the central theme. . . . "Responsibility," then, is a term for use in a complicated, dynamic, quasi-organic society. In criminal law and in morals, increased attention to this notion reflects a growing belief that relations between "individual" and "society" are too complicated and involve too much dynamic reciprocity or "feedback" to be dealt with adequately by the concept of "rights" and "duties," "guilt" and "innocence." In politics, too, the term "responsibility" is useful for a period when simple concepts like "will of the people" are recognized as

---

26. Ibid., p. 46.
27. Friedrich, *Responsibility*, p. 10.
28. Ibid., p. 13.

inadequate, and when "responsible" government is distinguished from "responsive" government and even from public accountability, although it includes the latter.[29]

Whether the old concepts, such as "rights" and "duties," "guilt" and "innocence," are so inadequate as Pennock argues may be questioned. In particular, it may be doubted whether "duty" is necessarily so narrow and rigid and so devoid of the exercise of judgment and discretion as he suggests. It may be that Pennock is misled in this crucial respect by his narrow view of the history of ideas. The totalitarian notion of duty, which, according to Pennock, came as a reaction against rugged individualism, was a *false* notion of duty, as is now universally agreed and juridically settled, in the Western world at least; and totalitarianism may not be the best place to look for the meaning of duty. Nevertheless, the increased concern with responsibility to which Pennock points is significant as emphasizing—if in a broad and general way—a dissatisfaction with what he calls rugged individualism, a concern for the development of a "sense of responsibility" for broader interests than those of one's self or immediate groups, and a belief that man's "full development" requires, after all, some participation in a common good beyond a general interest in being left alone.

Perhaps nothing is more widely agreed upon by the writers of the essays in *Responsibility* and *Ethics and Bigness* than the vital need for an increased and more widespread "sense of responsibility" in the United States. But how is this to be achieved? How, indeed, even to begin? The faith in the efficacy for good of increased popular participation in government, so much a part of the discipline of public administration in its early days, is now shaken—and for good reason. We are not less democrats but less simple-minded democrats.

"There was a time," Roland Egger says in *Ethics and Bigness*

when the enhancement of popular sovereignty—the maximization of public participation in decision making—was an effective counterweight to almost any excess in the concentration of political power, but none would today suppose that public participation could significantly improve the quality of the decision making process or relieve the President of the consequences of decisions. The extension of the franchise . . . is always a good thing, but it has nothing to contribute to the amelioration of the unbearable responsibility.[30]

---

29. Ibid., pp. 18, 19.
30. Cleveland and Lasswell, *Ethics and Bigness*, pp. 285–86.

The notion of the "will of the people" seems inadequate to us, as Pennock remarks, because we begin to see what the best theorists and practitioners of democracy have always known, that the problem is the *quality* of the will of the people, its "sense of responsibility." And we are on the way to understanding what our ablest democrats have also always known, that with the full emancipation of the many it is especially important to look to the place of the few—not the hereditary few or the privileged few or the wealthy few, but the few of capacity and devotion to the common good, on whom the growth of civic responsibility largely depends.

Leadership in a Democracy

Norton Long, always provocative and often wise, is perhaps less successful in his essay in *Responsibility* in bringing into focus his hopeful picture of the responsible metropolitan citizen of the future than in sketching the too-familiar city dweller of today—"Like a Goth in the Roman Empire with his vote for a weapon, he may conceive himself as plundering an alien edifice."[31] But Long draws out the essential point:

> Democracy, as Irving Babbitt pointed out, even more than other regimes depends on the quality of its leadership. It depends on the self devotion of a natural aristocracy to the precarious leadership roles of a mass society. In fact the eliciting of the efforts of this natural aristocracy, its education for the responsible conduct of affairs and the provision of a significant and accessible *cursus honorum* are major requisites for institutionalizing responsible citizenship.[32]

American students of politics, whose nation's leaders include Washington, Hamilton, Lincoln, and the Roosevelts, have strikingly little to say about leadership in a democracy. Students of public administration have scarcely been willing even to consider the issue except when it can be confined within some technical prison. Philip Selznick has, it is true, pushed vigorously beyond the technical limits and made a preliminary foray into the land of genuine leadership. But Selznick, who is not represented in these volumes, is still far less influential or reflective of general opinion among students of government and public administration than, for example, Carl Friedrich. It is of course impossible here to do justice to the learning and wisdom which Friedrich has brought to this subject in his numerous

---

31. Friedrich, *Responsibility*, p. 234.
32. Ibid., pp. 230–31.

writings, to which there are copious references in his essay in *Responsibility*. But when Friedrich suggests that "the responsible administrator is responsive to these two dominant factors, technical knowledge as well as popular sentiment,"[33] he differs in detail and sophistication but not in principle from the administrative writings of Woodrow Wilson and Frank Goodnow.

It is significant that Roland Egger and Don K. Price, in their valuable essays in *Ethics and Bigness*, turn to American political history—as did Leonard D. White—for the deeper instruction that the doctrines of management have failed to provide. It is significant too that, while they ably discuss administrative organization and management, both are led to pursue the question of political leadership. "[W]e have not quite accepted," Price argues, "in some of the important segments of our society, the primary assumption which is the foundation of responsibility for policy—that the most respected citizens of the nation will themselves consider political leadership their most important calling."[34] Unquestionably we require, as Price points out, "the dedication of a higher order of ability to both the political and the administrative responsibilities of government";[35] and we will get no more than we are willing to pay for. But there is a further consideration, which is the theme of the one-page comment by David Truman that ends *Ethics and Bigness*. Short as it is, this comment contains perhaps the wisest observations in this very long and often very good volume. While acknowledging the force and quality of the Egger and Price essays, Truman makes a qualification or reservation which has, and is no doubt intended to have, deep implications.

> How [the ethical dilemmas of government] are faced, however, is not primarily dependent on whether "the most respected citizens of the nation will themselves consider political leadership their most important calling," as Price argues. Whether they assume leadership in this way or not may be of less consequence, given the apparent limits on the utility of the amateur in such affairs, than that the most respected citizens regard those who do accept the burden of political leadership as being engaged in *the society's* most important calling. This, it seems to me, is "the foundation of responsibility for policy," to use Price's phrase, the indispensable obligation of the chief beneficiaries of the system if it, and they, are to survive.[36]

---

33. Friedrich, *Responsibility*, p. 199.
34. Cleveland and Lasswell, *Ethics and Bigness*, p. 447.
35. Ibid., p. 466.
36. Ibid., p. 468.

The high turnover of our political executives, for example, is harmful not merely because it interferes with the business of government, but because of its effect on general opinion about what the business of government is and where it stands in comparison with other businesses. The lesson is all too evident. Having obeyed the call to public duty, the political executive scarcely learns to find his way to his office without asking directions before he is planning to leave it. It may be that not much can be done about the transient character of the political executive; certainly suggestions for reform seem typically to be loose and superficial. It may be, indeed, that a large part of their work cannot be done well by amateurs. In any case, the difficulties at the level of the political executive make it all the more important to look to the quality, the education, and the self understanding of the permanent civil service.

The education of the civil servant is most deficient in its most important respect, and this includes not only his formal education but all of the instruction and advice aimed at him by the various representatives of the discipline of administration. The question of his responsibility—his duty, he may still say, especially if he is in military service—is that question about which the civil servant receives least instruction from his teachers and which is typically shrugged off with smug toleration or superficial relativism. He is in fact taught irresponsibility in the most important cases. He is taught to look to two standards: technical competence and popular will; beyond these he has no business to venture—and there are no higher standards anyway.

Yet it is where these standards are unavailable, or contradictory, or insufficient that he meets his most difficult and highest tests. How does he respond? If he can, he may try to avoid confronting such problems by securing himself in a narrow, comfortable haven of technical specialization and refusing to leave it. Or, he may emulate the world of private affairs, where questions of responsibility are less complex. He may conclude that the fundamental implication of his training in "management" is that the civil service, like all other forms of social life, is organized on the principle of dog-eat-dog and that his problem is to divert as much as he can of the available resources—material, honorific, psychological—to the satisfaction of his own private desires. Better-hearted, or less touched by his administrative training, he may conscientiously try to do his duty. What is significant is that in this last case he will stand very much alone. Of course there are many other individuals trying to do the same thing; but their institutional backing is, to say the least, slim.

The conventions of American public life, general opinions about what is respectable and permissible, tend to draw the civil servant back from his highest public duties rather than to guide him toward them. Obviously there is no question here of solving the problem by legislating a code of ethics and brainwashing civil servants with it. Nor can it be ignored that the character of an educational system is profoundly affected by the character of the society; but the relation is a mutual one. Those who teach and write about administration and those who practice it help to form the character of the civil service and, through the civil service, of the community at large. It is due to his constraining education, as well as the powerful pull in American life of the private and the technical, that the civil servant has least understanding of his own doings when he is exercising his highest responsibilities.

The question of responsibility is the link between the civil servant's particular business in government and that government's business. It is the link between his particular problem of whether, for example, at his own risk to fight hard for a project he believes to be in the public interest and the basic ambiguity in the notion of "the public interest": the tension between public wants and the public good. The understanding and practice of public administration begin in a willingness to confront that ambiguity. If, as Truman suggests, our society requires, "especially in its more privileged segments, a respect for and an understanding of the arts of governing"[37] as society's most important calling, that respect and that understanding will have to grow first among men who practice and study those arts. Perhaps then, even in the United States, the executive of the private corporation might come to emulate the man who serves the common good, rather than the other way around.

---

37. Ibid.

PART FOUR

Public Administration, Bureaucracy, and Big Government

14
The Problem of Big Government

"Big government" is widely considered to be one of the most serious threats to the preservation of cherished American institutions and values. Government constantly takes on new functions and scarcely ever abandons an old one; it grows increasingly centralized, complex, and remote. Somewhere the old idea of a limited government of limited powers seems to have been lost sight of, and the loss seems to have to do with two diseases infecting political life in the United States today: the stifling of the states by the imperialistic expansion of the national government and the growth of an enormous, irresponsible bureaucracy.

Deploring the tendency "to further centralize problems and their attempted solutions in the National Government rather than to leave them to proper State and local treatment," the president of the Chamber of Commerce told a committee of the House of Representatives in 1957 that "there is hardly anyone who will not agree that the basic intent of the founders of the Constitution regarding federalism has been distorted over the years."[1] The "basic intent of the founders" is indeed the place to begin, although we may find it necessary to go beyond their intent regarding federalism in order to understand federalism itself. That is not to say that we must accept uncritically the opinions of the founders or that we should expect to find in them the whole solution to present problems. We shall need to investigate not only the intention of the founders but also the reasons that lay behind that intention; we shall need to examine not only the machinery of government which they devised but also the principles upon which that machinery was based. Those principles give our government its enduring character, and it is with them that an understanding of our modern problem of big government must begin.

This essay is reprinted from Robert A. Goldwin, ed., *A Nation of States: Essays on the American Federal System*, 2nd ed. (Chicago: Rand McNally & Co., 1974).

1. Hearings before a Subcommittee of the Committee on Government Operations, *Federal-State-Local Relations*, 85th Congress, 1st session, 1958, pp. 52–53.

As we consider the intention of the framers of the Constitution, it is of the greatest importance to understand that they deliberately chose a strong national government. The most persistent argument of those who opposed the Constitution was directed against that great decision; and even some of the defenders of "big government" accepted it reluctantly and fearfully and urged that the powers of the national government be cautiously granted and prudently hedged. Consequently much of the discussion at the time of the framing and ratification of the Constitution was about whether the national government should be a little more or a little less powerful, whether the line between it and the state governments should be drawn a little higher here, a little lower there. No man could then, or can today, ignore the multitude of contingencies that must affect the apportionment of powers in particular cases or fail to recognize that these are judgments about which even sober and wise men may disagree; but wise men will try to form their judgments in the light of enduring principle. What were the principles underlying the decision for a strong national government? By examining briefly the views of some of those founders who distinguished themselves by their share in the decision and their understanding of its significance, we can perceive several distinct but connected levels of the argument that found expression in the Constitution, each of which retains an immediate relevance to federalism today.

All past history seemed to many Americans in 1787 to show that no republican government could cover an area as large as the thirteen states and their adjacent territories. Only in a very small country, many contended, is it possible to foster that self-sacrificing devotion to the public interest, that pervasive patriotic spirit, and that close scrutiny of government officials by the people which are essential to the maintenance of freedom. It is the states, Luther Martin argued in the Constitutional Convention, to which the people look "for the security of their lives, liberties and properties"; the federal government was formed for the limited purpose of defending the whole against foreign enemies and the smaller states against the greater.[2] This view of the American Union suffered from at least one obvious defect. Most of the American states were already considerably larger than the small republics to which the defenders of state authority alluded. Referring to Montesquieu's influential argument that popular government can exist only in a small territory, Alexander Hamilton pointed out that

---

2. Max Farrand, ed., *The Records of the Federal Convention* (rev. ed.; New Haven: Yale University Press, 1937), vol. 1, pp. 340–41 (June 20).

the standards he had in view were of dimensions, far short of the limits of almost every one of these States. . . . If we therefore take his ideas on this point, as the criterion of truth, we shall be driven to the alternative, either of taking refuge at once in the arms of monarchy, or of splitting ourselves into an infinity of little jealous, clashing, tumultuous commonwealths, the wretched nurseries of unceasing discord and the miserable objects of universal pity or contempt.[3]

Even in their own states Americans were committed to a form of popular government on a far larger scale than the small republics of theory or of classical antiquity.

Hamilton also attacked the accepted view of confederation, and the inferences drawn from it, from the other side. The Articles of Confederation, in one view, constituted a league principally concerned with the most primitive of political objectives: defense. A substantial part of Hamilton's argument in *The Federalist* (where safety against foreign arms and influence is the first subject treated) is devoted to showing that even that very limited but primary and universally accepted end requires a real government with very substantial powers. "States," Patrick Henry told the Virginia Ratifying Convention, "are the characteristics and the soul of a confederation."[4] Hamilton showed (and Henry agreed) that the Constitution was based on a decisive rejection of that first principle of confederation. Under the Articles of Confederation, whose Congress depended on the states both for its sustenance and for the execution of its commands, we had "neither troops nor treasury nor government."[5] The articles were an attempt to provide the benefits of government through the instrumentality of a league; but only government, an effective controlling authority, can provide the benefits of government. Moreover, the needs of defense and diplomacy cannot be predicted in advance, because they will be largely determined by other nations: "The circumstances that endanger the safety of nations are infinite; and for this reason no constitutional shackles can wisely be imposed on the power to which the care of it is committed."[6] If out of cowardice or parsimony such shackles are imposed, either

---

3. *Federalist* 9. Quotations are taken from the edition of Jacob E. Cooke (Middletown, Conn.: Wesleyan University Press, 1961).

4. Jonathan Elliot, *The Debates in the Several State Conventions on the Adoption of the Federal Constitution*, 2d ed. (Washington, D.C., 1836), vol. 3, p. 22.

5. *Federalist* 15.

6. Ibid. 23; compare 30, 31, 34.

they will prove fatal to the defense of the Union against unscrupulous enemies or they will be violently broken under the strain of necessity.

Define the powers of the national government and apportion the different objects of government between the nation and the states "as far as it can be done," Hamilton said; but let us have no mean cheeseparing in giving the national government its powers. The limited character of the national government established by the Constitution, important as that is, is subordinate to the fact that it *is* a national government:

> For the absurdity must continually stare us in the face of confiding to a government, the direction of the most essential national interests, without daring to trust it with the authorities which are indispensable to their proper and efficient management. Let us not attempt to reconcile contradictions, but firmly embrace a rational alternative.[7]

The congenital and fatal contradiction in the argument of the Anti-Federalists (and of their heirs throughout American history) lay in their unwillingness either to abandon a national government to protect national interests (to adopt, that is to say, a purely federal arrangement) or to entrust that national government with the authority necessary to accomplish its ends.

To this it might be replied that an illogical argument is not necessarily an impolitic one. Some of the opponents of the Constitution, like Patrick Henry, feared, not without reason, that the tendency of Hamilton's cold logic was to expand the primary objective of defense into something of a less modest character. "You are not to inquire how your trade may be increased," Henry thundered to the Virginia Ratifying Convention, "nor how you are to become a great and powerful people, but how your liberties can be secured; for liberty ought to be the direct end of your government." "If we admit this consolidated government, it will be because we like a great, splendid one."[8] Some form of federation is indeed necessary, it was admitted, but the emphasis ought to be on the small republican units, where liberty is at home. If there is a tension between the safety of the Union and individual liberty, it is at least arguable (although, not surprisingly, it is seldom argued openly) that it is preferable to risk the former rather than the latter. If the Anti-Federalists neither resolved what was very widely seen as the dilemma of the American confederation nor accepted Hamilton's reso-

---

7. Ibid. 23.
8. Elliot, *Debates*, vol. 3, pp. 44–45, 53.

lution, at least they continued to cling, as hard as they could, to the other horn.

James Madison's great contribution to the defense of the Constitution, during and after the convention, was his powerful and influential effort to resolve this dilemma by transcending it, by showing the inadequacy of the Anti-Federalists' argument, not only on the ground of the needs of the Union, but on their own chosen ground of the preservation of individual liberty.[9] Madison was of course committed to popular government as the surest means to that end which all Americans regarded, with Jefferson, as the end of government, to secure the inalienable rights of men. But he argued (what would also have been widely accepted) that popular government faces one great danger to which all popular governments of former times had succumbed, namely, the tendency of the mass of the people to form unjust combinations against the few. Within the cramped confines of a small state, where economic opportunities are narrow and the number of different interests small, the line between rich and poor is likely to become sharply defined and ominously rigid—and when the many combine, the liberties of all are in peril. Only a large and rich territory under a single government can provide that diversity and opportunity by means of which the elemental conflict of rich and poor may be softened and diffused.

What is significant about this argument for our present purposes is that the states do not in principle play any necessary part in it. (*Federalist* 10 is a discussion of the principle of the enlargement of the orbit of republican government in its application to a single unit of government.) Madison does not accept the view that the American Union is fundamentally a kind of tension or balance between the general and the particular governments. The federal features of the system established by the Constitution, including the federal features of the central government itself, were indeed a practical necessity; and, providing they do not get out of hand, they contribute a useful additional basis of fragmentation and mutual check. But they are not

---

9. See especially Farrand, *Records*, vol. 1, pp. 134–36, 421–23 (June 6, June 26); Letter to Thomas Jefferson, October 24, 1787; and *Federalist Papers* 10.

In view of a popular opinion that the multiple authorship of *The Federalist Papers* resulted in an argument which has a "split personality," it should be said that, although the authors are identified separately in this essay and although they sometimes make *different* arguments, there is no *inconsistency* in their arguments presented here. Specifically, whatever their differences on other questions and at other times, there was no substantial difference between Hamilton and Madison on the subject of federalism, or the relation of the nation and the states, at the time of the founding.

essential. And because they are not essential, their necessity and usefulness depend on a wide variety of changeable circumstances.

Madison's argument rests on a doubt about the efficacy of securing liberty by relying on the moral, religious, and patriotic sentiments which were supposed to characterize the small republic. A better, or more reliable, base is a wide community of industrious men with much opportunity to gratify their private desires and little opportunity to combine unjustly with others. But even Madison's intricate net of calculation rests upon a deeper conviction about the nature of American life, a perception of the moral unity of the United States of America and, before that, of the united colonies. Madison clearly assumes, although he does not always stress, that the platform for the release of men's private energies is some degree of public-spiritedness or patriotism, expressed at least as veneration of the Constitution. The conviction of a more than expediential foundation of the Union underlies even the expediential arguments themselves. It provides the theme of the opening *Federalist* papers, as well as one necessary condition of Madison's extended republic; it was the deepest ground touched (if not fully explored) in the Constitutional Convention and is the foundation of the nationalist position. Many times challenged, often only dimly understood and articulated, this national unity—not states' rights, localism, or "territorial democracy"—is the frame of American life.

The Federalist opens with an elaborate defense of Union and only later proceeds to criticize the Articles of Confederation. No doubt the authors were reluctant to begin their argument with a frontal attack on what was, after all, the established government (to the extent that it was a government) of the United States; and they were conscious of the rhetorical advantage of beginning their defense of the new Constitution with a suggestion that there was a whispering campaign under way against the old Union, which almost all Americans valued. But their strategy also has a deeper significance. The Constitution aimed to form, not a new Union, but "a more perfect Union"; and in the second *Federalist* paper, John Jay sought to give expression to the common understanding of that Union. He observed "one connected, fertile, wide spreading country" which

> Providence has been pleased to give . . . to one united people, a people descended from the same ancestors, speaking the same language, professing the same religion, attached to the same principles of government, very similar in their manners and customs, and who, by their joint counsels, arms and efforts, fighting side by side throughout

a long and bloody war, have nobly established their general Liberty and Independence.

This was no League of Nations, no alliance of separate, independent communities, but a country and a people made for each other. The argument of *The Federalist,* and of the founders generally, proceeds from and depends on a conviction that, in Jay's words, "an inheritance so proper and convenient for a band of brethren, united to each other by the strongest ties, should never be split into a number of unsocial, jealous and alien sovereignties." As this theme opens, so also it closes *The Federalist's* defense of Union. In the fourteenth paper, it is Madison who warns:

> Hearken not to the unnatural voice which tells you that the people of America, knit together as they are by so many cords of affection, can no longer live together as members of the same family; can no longer continue the mutual guardians of their mutual happiness; can no longer be fellow citizens of one great respectable and flourishing empire. . . . No my countrymen, shut your ears against this unhallowed language. Shut your hearts against the poison which it conveys; the kindred blood which flows in the veins of American citizens, the mingled blood which they have shed in defence of their sacred rights, consecrate their union, and excite horror at the idea of their becoming aliens, rivals, enemies.

The debates in the Constitutional Convention turned, at one of their most interesting and crucial points, on the same view of the nature of the Union. Discussing the legal status of the states and their representatives at the convention, Luther Martin of Maryland (later a prominent Anti-Federalist) contended that the separation from Great Britain had placed the thirteen former colonies in a state of nature toward each other, and that they would have thus remained except for the Articles of Confederation, which they had entered on a footing of equality. This was promptly denied by James Wilson of Pennsylvania, who read to the convention the language of the Declaration of Independence, observing "that the *United Colonies* were declared to be free and independent States." This language is not unambiguous, but Wilson inferred (as, incidentally, did Orestes Brownson later) that the states were independent not individually but unitedly, and that therefore they had never been independent of one another.[10] According to Martin, then, the only relations between

---

10. Farrand, *Records,* vol. 1, pp. 323–24 (June 19); compare Orestes A. Brownson, *The American Republic* (New York: P. O'Shea, 1866), p. 210.

the states had been those of free and equal sovereigns, whether at the time of the Revolution or under the Articles of Confederation. The states were the only real governments, and the Union was their creature. Wilson, on the other hand, argued that the states had never been independent sovereigns. The American Union was forged during the War of Independence and constituted by the Declaration of Independence. The articles, far from creating the Union, were only a temporary instrument of a preexisting Union. This instrument was defective in many respects, the most important being the admission of all states to equal suffrage; there was never an American *federation* in the old and strict sense. Wilson had stated the grounds of this argument early in the debates:

> Among the first sentiments expressed in the first Congress one was that Virginia is no more. That Massachusetts is no [more], that Pennsylvania is no more, etc. We are now one nation of brethren. We must bury all local interests and distinctions. This language continued for some time. The tables at length began to turn. No sooner were the State Governments formed than their jealousy and ambition began to display themselves. Each endeavoured to cut a slice from the common loaf, to add to its own morsel, till at length the confederation became frittered down to the impotent condition in which it now stands. . . . To correct its vices is the business of this convention. One of its vices is the want of an effectual controul in the whole over its parts. What danger is there that the whole will unnecessarily sacrifice a part? But reverse the case, and leave the whole at the mercy of each part, and will not the general interest be continually sacrificed to local interests?[11]

As is clear from the opening words of the Constitution, the issue was resolved in favor of the whole. As is also clear, the issue was not resolved without compromise. At each of the great crises of American history, and most of the minor ones, the issue has been raised again; each time it has been settled more decisively and with less compromise. What Tocqueville called an "incomplete national government" is, it seems, nearly completed. Yet there is a significant ambiguity in Tocqueville's characterization. Neither the original decision for Union—and this Union did not—after all, avoid its civil war—nor the numerous reaffirmations of this decision ensured the completion of the nation. The Constitution was imperfect, as any work of man must be; but the legal and institutional framework that

---

11. Farrand, *Records*, vol. 1, pp. 166–67 (June 8).

it provided did point in the direction of the completion of the nation precisely because it was, as John Adams said so well, "admirably calculated" to unite the "interests and affections" of the United States, to bring them "to an uniformity of principles and sentiments," and to unite "their wills and forces as a single nation."[12] The circumstances of the birth and colonial organization of the United States led to the consequence that its great political debates have taken the form (or sometimes the guise) of debates about federalism. Perhaps federalism is no longer so relevant as it once was to the question of the completion of the American nation, as a whole and in its parts; but the issue is not whether federalism is obsolete, because the debate was never fundamentally a debate about federalism.

What has this to do with "territorial democracy," or what has "territorial democracy" to do with this? Not much. It is true that Orestes Brownson's book *The American Republic* is centrally concerned with "the constitution of the people [of the United States] as one people, and the distinction at the same time of this one people into particular States. . . ."[13] Brownson conducts an elaborate exploration of the problem of unity and diversity in political life and, specifically, the problem of the one and the many in American political life. American democracy he describes as "territorial democracy," an expression of "the political truth that, though the people are sovereign, it is the organic, not the inorganic people, the territorial people, not the people as simple population. . . ."[14] "Territorial democracy" stands between two extreme or corrupt forms of democracy, pure individualism, on the one hand, and pure humanitarianism or socialism, on the other hand. "Territorial democracy" also stands between two extreme and mistaken notions of the American Republic, the one stressing its fundamental diversity, the other its fundamental unity.

Now to understand Brownson's notion of "territorial democracy" would require a careful examination of his whole system of political and theological principles. No such examination is provided anywhere in this volume. [Editor's note: see source note for this essay, above.] Russell Kirk, while repeating the incantation "territorial democracy," and commending certain ideas loosely associated with this phrase, apparently does not accept the whole of Brownson's theory. Yet he does not say which parts of his chief authority are retained and which cast out, or how anything that can be identified

---

12. John Adams, *A Defence of the Constitutions of Government of the United States of America* (London, 1794), vol. 3, pp. 505–6.

13. Brownson, *The American Republic*, p. 245.

14. Ibid., pp. 10–11.

with Brownson remains, once "territorial democracy" is emptied of principles that Brownson thought essential to it. Consider: Brownson's study is explicitly based, as Professor Kirk's is not, upon the theological foundations of Roman Catholicism and is directed especially, although not exclusively, to Catholics. Brownson rejects, what Professor Kirk seems to accept, the political philosophy of the Founding Fathers. Brownson denies, what both the founders and Professor Kirk assert, that the American system is one of checks and balances. Brownson denies, what the founders and apparently also Professor Kirk assert, the conventional origin of the government; Brownson's notion of territorial democracy is an inseparable part of his theory (going far beyond anything dreamed by Jay, for example) of the providential constitution of the United States. When to all this is added the fact that Brownson joins the founders in denying, what Professor Kirk asserts, that the parts of the American Union have priority over the whole and that the Constitution was an act of voluntary association of territorial democracies, it becomes evident that the meaning of "territorial democracy" as it is used in the present discussion cannot and apparently is not even intended to be found in the thought of Orestes Brownson.[15]

Yet Brownson's vision of the American Republic does contain a rule that is relevant to the present discussion. Brownson states the principle upon which authority is (or ought to be) divided between the general and the particular governments as follows: "The line that distinguishes the two governments is that which distinguishes the general relations and interests from the particular relations and interests of the people of the United States."[16] On the basis of this principle, Brownson takes a very narrow view of the powers of the general government, holding, for example, that it had no constitutional power to pass the Missouri Compromise or to establish the United States Bank, and that it cannot constitutionally naturalize foreigners or impose a protective tariff. If we follow the deductions that Brownson makes from his general principle, we are bound to hold that most of the domestic activities of the national government today are unconstitutional. And the significance of such a holding would be that the question we face is not whether to preserve "territorial democracy," but whether to try to restore it, thereby overthrowing at least a century's history in an attempt to revive what,

---

15. See ibid., chaps. 1, 7, 9, 10, 11, 15, *passim*; Orestes Brownson, *Selected Essays*, introduction by Russell Kirk (Gateway Editions; Chicago: Henry Regnery Co., 1955), pp. 128–30, 161–90.

16. Brownson, *The American Republic*, p. 255.

on this line of argument, cannot seriously be thought still to have the breath of life.

There is another possibility, however, and that is to accept Brownson's principle, to recognize the elusive and contingent character of any practical expression of the distinction between the general and the particular and the public and the private, and to make our own judgments as wisely and prudently as we can. If a need for civil defense reaching into every state, community, and family is not a matter that affects alike the relations and interests of all the states; if the problems of protecting rights of individual expression, rights of privacy, and decent standards of public communication are not questions of general interest; if the quality of public education is a matter that affects individuals or citizens only in their private and domestic relations—if these are not matters of common concern, then the national government has no business meddling with them. But there is nothing in the Constitution, or in the principles of American federalism, or in the history of American government that predetermines the answer to questions such as these. In this respect Alexander Hamilton is distinctive only in the force and clarity with which he gives expression to the authentic voice of the founders and of every responsible American statesman since that time: it is impossible to define and confine in advance the matters that may be of national concern, and the American Constitution provides, as any viable constitution must, for the exercise of national power commensurate with national exigency. The burden of proof does not lie with the advocates of strong national government but with its opponents.

That the states are not in any fundamental sense the small intimate communities of self-governing men, beloved of the heirs of Jeffersonian democracy, is surely even clearer today than it was when Hamilton pointed it out. It is difficult to see in the state governments of Tennessee or New York or Michigan much of those qualities of "local liberty," "self-government," and "democracy" with which, in the lore of federalism, the states are supposed to be associated. Tocqueville's much cited description of local government and administration[17] referred to *state* governments, where centralization has gone about as far as it has in Washington; so that school boards, for example, are much less numerous than they once were, as a result of consolidation by state governments, and are severely restricted in their discretion over curriculum, personnel, and finance, as a result of growing regulation by state departments of education. And if it is the local and municipal governments that are to be fostered as the

---

17. Alexis de Tocqueville, *Democracy in America*, vol. 1, chap. 5.

locus of participation and intelligent concern for the public good, then, in the first place, that is not a problem of federalism or "territorial democracy," and, in the second place, there is nothing wrong in principle, if it is desirable on other grounds, if the national government deals directly with the local units and uses them as administrative instruments, as the states do.

Obviously the American decision for Union had and still has its risks, required and still requires prudent implementation. To decide that a problem is one of national concern and requires national action is not necessarily to centralize the whole business of formulating and administering a program in Washington, even ignoring, as we ought not ignore, that while "Washington" is not merely the sum of its parts, neither is it a place where the states and localities are without influence. It may be conceded that a certain price was paid for Union, that there are some genuine values associated with the small community, and that one of the problems of modern American political life is to find ways of strengthening those values under conditions that are sometimes unfavorable. This does not require, or even permit, a doctrinaire commitment to a species of localism or states' rights that is even less relevant to the conditions of Union now than when it was first rejected as its governing principle. Tocqueville characterized the American system, let it be remembered, as one of centralized *government* and decentralized *administration*. It is by no means clear whether in this respect there has been any fundamental change since Tocqueville's time, although in response to new circumstances the means of government and administration have certainly changed. In many new (as well as the old) relationships between the established governments and in a wide variety of new instruments, serious and responsible attempts have been made to bring the values of decentralized administration into centralized government. If the countless devices of consultation that cluster around every national agency of government are sometimes ineffective or deficient and their value exaggerated—as doubtless they are—do they really compare so unfavorably with the more traditional forms of local participation as means of collecting information, securing consent, providing schools of citizenship, and checking central government? Even the much-criticized TVA "grass-roots democracy" and the "self-governing" committees in the agricultural program are scarcely open to a single objection that cannot equally well be directed against township, county, and state units of government and administration.

It is, moreover, important to beware of the excesses too often associated with a merely sentimental or ideological attachment to local democracy. When Madison argues that a democracy "will be confined to a small spot," while "a republic may be extended over a large region,"[18] he is not, to repeat, defending pure or simple democracy (and then trying to reconcile it with national interests): rather, he is pointing to the fundamental defect of local democracy and the way to its avoidance. Even if we did not have Madison's powerful assistance in warning us of the narrow, mean, and tyrannical aspects of the small units of republican government, we could scarcely ignore the examples that can be found in every state of the Union. Let it be conceded that it would be a national disaster if the educational system were wholly in the hands of the professional educators centered in Washington (or for that matter in the state capitals where they are now strongly entrenched), but the consequences would perhaps be only slightly less serious if the system were wholly in the hands of local school boards. The founders emphatically did not accept the idea that the best government is the government closest to the people. Their argument was almost the reverse: that one of the great defects of popular government up to that time, including many of the American states, had been that they were too close to the people, too easily infected with popular moods and fancies, too little equipped to guide the people and to resist them when the common good so demanded.

What then of the risks of strong central government? What of the dangers of "democratic centralism" of "Jacobinism" or "plebiscitary democracy"? What of the argument that today's resistance to a strong and increasingly popular national government is an extension of the original and laudable conservative defense against majority tyranny? This argument does indeed proceed from one of the main concerns of the founders and demands serious consideration.

Let us first remind ourselves of some fundamentals. The need for government, the founders thought, arises out of the impossibility of any real freedom without it. Under conditions of anarchy where every man is perfectly at liberty to do as he likes, every man is subject to constant fear of everyone else; and this is the meanest kind of slavery. Yet because of the tendency for any man to tyrannize over others if he gets the chance, government itself may become the source of another kind of slavery where men live in fear, not of all other men, but of that one man or small group of men who hold them in thralldom. The problem of government for the founders, one could almost say, is to steer a course between these extremes. That is the meaning of the remark:

---

18. *Federalist* 14.

> If men were angels, no government would be necessary. If angels were to govern men, neither external nor internal controuls on government would be necessary. In framing a government which is to be administered by men over men, the great difficulty lies in this: You must first enable the government to controul the governed: and in the next place, oblige it to controul itself.[19]

One way of controlling the government is to establish a federal system in which the powers of government are distributed between two levels of government, but it was by no means only Alexander Hamilton who feared that too strong a draught of the federal remedy was likely to prove as bad as the tyrannical disease. In any case the founders did not commit the absurdity of trying to control the national government by withholding from it powers necessary to the accomplishment of vital national objectives. The safeguard against tyranny and injustice was sought in a powerful national government with an *internal* composition and structure such as to render it a fit and trustworthy depository of the national interest.[20] The general principle, of course, was that it is prudent to let one governor check another. More particularly, the machinery of government should be so ordered as to provide a check against the tendency for the most popular branch of the government to concentrate power into its own hands and to become the engine of that tyranny of the majority which is fatal to liberty.

In devising a system of checks and balances, the founders confronted two major difficulties. First, merely dividing governmental powers was not likely to provide any effective restraint if each of the separate parts were animated by the same spirit. Yet the classic English solution—a government composed of king, nobles, and commons, whose authority rested, at least partly, on different princi-

---

19. *Federalist* 51.

20. Compare Tocqueville, *Democracy in America*, vol. 1, chap. 5, "Administration in New England."

John Adams' famous *Defence of the Constitutions of Government of the United States of America*, with its attack on Turgot's thesis of collecting "all authority into one center, the nation," was not a defense of federalism, has nothing to do with federalism, and was first published before the Constitutional Convention met. Convinced that "the mistakes of great men, and even the absurdities of fools" cannot be too fully refuted when they strengthen false prejudices, Adams did provide an elaborate defense of the organization of the American *state* governments and of the system of internal checks and balances on which they, and later the national government, were based. See vol. 1, letter 2.

ples—was clearly unavailable to Americans, even if they had desired to utilize it. The problem was how to inform some parts of a government that was *basically* popular with a spirit that would not be *simply* popular. The second difficulty was how to prevent a government of checks and balances from reaching such a perfect equilibrium that it could not act at all. The founders' response to both of these difficulties culminates in the presidency, an institution that, far more than federalism, represents the founders' achievement and their challenge.

The president was to be part of the system of checks and balances and the chief counterweight to the legislative branch. But he was also to be the primary source of energy and direction for the government as a whole. To select the president, the founders invented the electoral college system, and it is more important for the present to consider what this invention was supposed to do than to see that it did not work as expected. It was arranged to allow "the sense of the people" to operate, while leaving the immediate selection of the president to an ad hoc body of judicious and wise men. Under this system, Hamilton argued, "there will be a constant probability of seeing the station filled by characters pre-eminent for ability and virtue."[21] In addition, the system was designed to leave the president free from a dependence on any other branch of the government; for this was to be no subservient administrator, no timeserver, no mere doer of the will of Congress or the people. On the wisdom and courage of the president, on his capacity to guide the people when they were confused, encourage them when they were right, and stand against them—at least to demand that they think again—when they were wrong, would depend the excellence of the American government, the effectiveness of its protection of liberty, and the greatness to which it might aspire. The presidency was the crucial feature of the Constitution, and in spite of many changes it remains so, because the duty of the holder of this office is the most difficult in any popular government: to reconcile the wants of the people and the needs of the Republic.

While this reconciliation was to be above all the duty of the president, the founders provided subordinate institutions designed to the same end. Of these the Senate is especially relevant here. A smaller body than the other house of the legislature, composed of older men, and elected by the state legislatures, it was expected to be less inclined to yield to sudden and violent passions and thus to add stability and moderation to the national councils. The senators' longer

---

21. *Federalist* 68.

terms of office would enable them to acquire a greater understanding of "the objects and principles of legislation" and encourage them to think in terms of the long-range interest and reputation of the country. They could, when necessary, resist the excesses of the popular branch of the legislature and of the people themselves.

> As the cool and deliberate sense of the community ought in all governments, and actually will in all free governments ultimately prevail over the views of its rulers; so there are particular moments in public affairs, when the people stimulated by some irregular passion, or some illicit advantage, or misled by the artful misrepresentations of interested men, may call for measures which they themselves will afterwards be the most ready to lament and condemn. In these critical moments, how salutary will be the interference of some temperate and respectable body of citizens, in order to check the misguided career, and to suspend the blow meditated by the people against themselves, until reason, justice and truth, can regain their authority over the public mind?[22]

Today, of course, the Senate is elected directly by the people, and it is but a faint reflection of its original self. It is far more popular, far more susceptible to the passing fancies of the people, than the founders intended. Yet the people are still sometimes ignorant, fickle, and unjust; and it remains the problem of popular government not only to protect the people against betrayal by their representatives but also to protect them, in Madison's words, "against the transient impressions into which they themselves might be led."[23] If the Senate today is less well adapted to this end than it was expected by the founders to be, is there any institution in the national government that fills (or might fill) a role like that of the original Senate? I suggest that we consider—strange as it may seem—the national bureaucracy.

It is not for its "senatorial" qualities that the national bureaucracy is mainly known today, but rather for its size, complexity, unresponsiveness, and impenetrability. Hamilton, like Madison, thought that one of the advantages of the central government over the state governments was its being "more out of the reach of those occasional ill humors or temporary prejudices and propensities" which tend to infect public opinion.[24] The central government today is much less "out of reach," but the bureaucracy does to a very considerable extent

---

22. *Federalist* 63.
23. Farrand, *Records,* vol. 1, p. 421 (June 26).
24. *Federalist* 27.

(and might to a much greater extent) exercise a steady pressure upon our political leaders to transcend passing desires and prejudices. Obviously the bureaucracy is not a senate; but it may well be one of the most effective approximations to a senate that we have available today. That it has not performed its "senatorial" functions as well as it might is due in no small part to the thoughtless, irresponsible, and sometimes violent attacks to which it is so often subjected, even by those groups whose natural ally it is.

This does not mean that the bureaucracy ought to be above criticism. There is no disposition here to deny the existence of inefficiency, ignorance, cowardice, indecision, narrowness, irresponsibility, and petty tyranny in the national bureaucracy, although whether these evils are more prevalent there than in the states and localities is perhaps doubtful. Perhaps the most serious difficulty of our huge administration, as George Kennan points out in the powerful criticism to which Professor Kirk refers, is its tendency toward "fragmentation and diffusion of power."[25] Kennan's criticism, whatever else it is, is not an argument for decentralization of *government*, of deliberation about national requirements, of responsible decisions. Quite the reverse. It is significant, moreover, that the Department of State is selected by Professor Kirk as the outstanding example of the evils of the federal bureaucracy. The administrative difficulties in this first department of the national government were not created by national usurpation of local functions and are not to be overcome by any adjustment of the federal system or any revival of "territorial democracy." As for the bureaucracy generally, let us keep a sense of proportion; its difficulties, great as they are, would be only very marginally affected by any conceivable responsible program of reducing the size of the national government.

It may be, as Kennan suggests, that the problem of bureaucracy is insoluble, barring some major upheaval. This need not lead to an apathetic abandonment of attempts at improvement, although it may remind us of the sound maxim of moderation, that criticism and reform based on a blind determination to wipe away all the evils of the world—even of the bureaucracy—are likely to do more harm than good, whatever the ideological underpinnings.[26] Improvement is

25. George F. Kennan, "America's Administrative Response to Its World Problems," *Daedalus*, vol. 87 (Spring 1958), p. 13.

26. An approach to the problems of contemporary government that can criticize the transfer of many matters from the regular courts of law to administrative tribunals on the astounding ground that the latter are not governed by the "democratic process"—as if the former are—does not augur well for responsible and relevant criticism.

possible. The recommendation by the commission under former president Hoover of the establishment of a senior civil service rests on a sober recognition of the major role that the bureaucracy plays in the formulation as well as the execution of national policy, and it is a significant attempt to improve its organization and character.[27] Unquestionably, if our nation requires leadership, including administrative leadership, we had better give more and deeper consideration to the education of our leaders than we have done, in which quest we shall again return to the ways of the Fathers. Nor is training in "management," supplemented by short courses in "executive development," going to be enough. What is required is a higher civil service provided with not only the skills but also the political understanding and the moral character demanded by the duties thrust upon it by the modern republic. Perhaps the most serious shortcoming of the American civil service lies in its primarily technical competence and character. But random carping or wholesale condemnation of the bureaucracy has only the effect (when it has any effect) of diverting attention from the need to nurture and strengthen its capacity for administrative statesmanship and of weakening what is a prime source of intelligence as well as a major stabilizing and moderating force in American government today.

The bureaucracy is today's manifestation of the original decision for big government. Whether it is to be more a force for good than for evil depends, in the first place, on a recognition and acceptance of the fact that it is, in any case, a major force in American political life. It will not melt under the heat of fulmination or blow away on the wind of wish.

Viewed from the standpoint of the founders, American government today seems to have been turned on its head. Generally speaking, and contrary to the founders' expectation, it is in the state governments that the conservative and propertied interests find their main influence and support. It is the national government that seems most susceptible to pressures from the people at large and least concerned to protect the interests of the few. There lies the irony of the use by the president of the Chamber of Commerce of the Jeffersonian argument that "that government which is best for the people

---

27. Commission on the Organization of the Executive Branch of the Government, *Personnel and Civil Service* and *Task Force Report on Personnel and Civil Service* (Washington: U.S. Government Printing Office, 1955). See also my essay "Political Parties and the Bureaucracy," in Robert A. Goldwin, ed., *Political Parties in the United States* (Chicago: Rand McNally & Company, 1964) [chapter 15 in this book].

is that which is closest to them."[28] The state governments may be closer to the Chambers of Commerce, but today it is the national government that in all fundamental respects is closer to the people. Indeed the national government, including the Senate and the Supreme Court, seems to have been infused with the popular spirit. And although the president is still obliged to reconcile popular wants and national needs, he has to do so today as a great popular leader rather than as one chosen by a small group of judicious men.

Some argue, therefore, that when conservatives depart from the conception of American government held by their forebears they are only adjusting themselves to new circumstances while remaining true to the traditional end, namely, to support and defend those institutions of government most closely connected with the "temperate and respectable" elements. If the Democracy has occupied the national government and the Presidency, perhaps the party of the Republic must make its stand in the states and, when it can, in Congress.

This argument is untenable for two reasons. First, in seeking to strengthen state governments at the expense of the national, it demands an attitude toward American government that is not only contrary to the best conservative tradition but also hopelessly unrealistic. It amounts to a permanent commitment to a series of rear-guard actions in which there is room only for retreat. Only yesterday many men insisted that social security, agricultural policy, and labor relations were purely local matters, and they sought to enforce this opinion with constitutional shackles on the national government. The effect was only to deprive those men of any influence in deciding how the nation would meet what were manifestly national problems. A rigid insistence today that such matters as unemployment, education, and the condition of our cities are not national problems will have the same kind of consequence. Our modern advocates of localism, under whatever name, may well ponder Hamilton's warning that "nations pay little regard to rules and maxims calculated in their very nature to run counter to the necessities of society. Wise politicians will be cautious about fettering the government with restrictions, that cannot be observed. . . ."[29] To strengthen, on the other hand, those qualities of the bureaucracy that contribute knowledge and moderation to government and set an example of devotion to the public good is to defend an old position with a new institution and one that runs in harmony with the "necessities of society" today.

---

28. Hearings, *Federal-State-Local Relations*, 1958, p. 53.
29. *Federalist* 25.

Second, this argument in favor of weakening the national government fails to recognize that, while a government ought to be ordered so that it will not act badly, it must also and preeminently have the capacity to act well. Just as the dangers that the nation may face are illimitable, so are its opportunities. Hamilton always kept in mind (nor did Jefferson ignore) those moments in the life of every nation when it faces great crises and great opportunities, when its course and character may be decisively influenced. And while the decent operation of government from day to day is served by a plurality of interests, by divided government, and by checks on ambition, the times of crisis and greatness demand unity and power and leadership. A constitution should so far as possible provide for both. Checks and balances are still important, and let there be no misunderstanding: decentralization of administration, a continued and even increased emphasis on state and local government where that is possible, and internal checks on ill-conceived action are legitimate and necessary. But conservatives defeat their own purposes when they set themselves against an adequate national government and a strong president and administration just because the popular elements are for them. They do no service to themselves or to the Republic when they adopt a policy of strengthening those elements of the American governmental system whose tendency is to emphasize the separateness of the parts at the expense of those in whose hands it lies to maintain the unity of the whole.

15

Political Parties and the Bureaucracy

I

Following a conference at Morningside Heights in September 1952, Senator Robert Taft announced that the Republican candidate for the presidency, General Dwight D. Eisenhower, had "stated without qualification that in the making of appointments at high levels or low levels there will be no discrimination against anyone because he or she has supported me, and that he is determined to maintain the unity of the entire party by taking counsel with all factions and points of view."[1] Thus in the event of a Republican victory, the Taft supporters were to be given a share in the formulation and administration of government policy; and government offices, high and low, were not to be distributed in such a way as to punish the Taft group or to weaken its influence within the Republican party. This was one of the few relatively specific terms of the famous accommodation at Morningside Heights, and it illustrates the persistent and well-known concern of American political parties with government offices. Traditionally the parties have depended upon public offices to sustain themselves as organizations and to give effect to their policies; the civil service is both the trough at which they feed and the instrument by which they govern. In this paper we shall be concerned primarily with the latter part of the relationship.[2]

If the Eisenhower-Taft agreement illustrates the continued con-

---

This essay was originally published in Robert A. Goldwin, ed., *Political Parties, U.S.A.* (Chicago, Rand McNally & Co., 1964).

1. *New York Times*, September 13, p. 6.

2. For a valuable discussion emphasizing questions arising out of the traditional organizational dependence of parties on patronage, see Harvey C. Mansfield, "Political Parties, Patronage, and the Federal Government Service," *The Federal Government Service* (New York: The American Assembly, Columbia University, 1954), pp. 81–112.

cern of political parties with public offices, the experience of the Eisenhower administration with patronage illustrates (among other things) the extent to which the political party today is limited in its direct access to federal offices for any purpose. In 1952 about 85 percent of the federal service was under the merit system, and much of the remainder was practically unavailable for party purposes, either because the incumbents were needed or because the jobs were, for one reason or another, unattractive. Although the Republicans were accused of raiding the merit system in search of spoils, the steps taken to provide more places for Republicans were in fact very limited. By 1954 the proportion of the service under the merit system had dropped by only 2 or 3 percent. There was, it is true, a certain amount of party "clearance" even for positions filled by examination, but as one historian of the civil service has said, "The pickings for the National Committee have . . . been the leanest in history."[3] There is still some patronage available to the political party, especially at the beginning of a new administration, and the old tree will still produce an occasional plum (such as the 73 federal judgeships created in 1961); but the trend in the direction of the merit system is not likely to be reversed.

This exclusion of the political party from the vast majority of federal offices has not, of course, come about by accident or thoughtless adaptation to changed circumstances. It resulted from a deliberate reform of the American political system which found expression primarily in the Pendleton Act of 1883. As is well known, this act established a bipartisan Civil Service Commission charged, among other things, to provide open competitive examinations for entry into the "classified" federal service. Originally only about 10 percent of the 140,000 positions in the federal service were covered, but provision was made for extensions by executive order. Except for the provision that no person should be removed for failure to contribute time or money to a political party, the act imposed no limitations on removal from office; but limitations were imposed later, especially with respect to veterans. Later legislation also sought to complete the "neutralization" of the public administration by severely limiting the political activities of civil servants.

The post–Civil War reform movement which led to this legislation was directed immediately at the civil service, but its more fundamental objective was the reform of political parties. While the reformers did not seek to eradicate parties, they were, like the

---

3. Paul P. Van Riper, *History of the United States Civil Service* (Evanston, Ill.: Row, Peterson and Co., 1958), p. 491.

American founders, keenly aware that "party spirit, from the first, has been the terror of republics."[4] It is, George Curtis said, "the one fire that needs no fanning. The first duty of patriotism is to keep that fire low."[5] Specifically, the reformers were trying to rid the country of the spoils system, in which they saw three evils:

1. By distributing public office as the booty of party warfare, the spoils system introduced gross inefficiency and corruption into the public administration.

2. By basing political parties on a network of selfish private relationships, the spoils system distorted and frustrated the expression of the popular will.

3. By channeling men's minds along the lines of private and narrow group interest and away from a concern with the public interest, the spoils system corrupted American political life and character.

Unlike their successors, the early reformers—such men as George Curtis, Dorman Eaton, and Carl Schurz—thought that administrative inefficiency was the least of these evils. "[T]he question whether the Departments at Washington are managed well or badly," said Carl Schurz, "is, in proportion to the whole problem, an insignificant question after all. . . . The most important point to my mind is, how we can remove that element of demoralization which the now prevailing mode of distributing office has introduced into the body-politic."[6] Similarly Dorman Eaton wrote that "civil service reform is not merely a mode of procedure and an economy, but has become a vital question of principle and public morality, involving the counterpoise and in no small degree the stability of the government itself."[7] In an important statement of the object of civil service reform in an editorial for *Harper's Weekly* Schurz conceded that one aim was "an improved conduct of the public business."

> But the ultimate end of civil service reform is something far more important than a mere improvement in the machinery of administration. It is to elevate the character of our political

4. "The Relation between Morals and Politics," in Charles E. Norton, ed., *Orations and Addresses of George William Curtis* (New York: Harper & Brothers, 1894), vol. 2, p. 124.

5. "The Reason and the Result of Civil Service Reform," ibid., vol. 2, p. 387.

6. Speech in the Senate, January 27, 1871, in Frederic Bancroft, ed., *Speeches, Correspondence and Political Papers of Carl Schurz* (New York: G. P. Putnam's Sons, 1913), vol. 2, p. 123.

7. *Civil Service in Great Britain* (New York: Harper & Brothers, 1880), p. 438.

life by eliminating from it as much as possible the demoralizing elements of favoritism and of mercenary motives which under the spoils system have become the moving powers in our politics. It is to rescue our political parties, and in a great measure the management of our public affairs, from the control of men whose whole statesmanship consists in the low arts of office-mongering, and many of whom would never have risen to power had not the spoils system furnished them the means and opportunities for organizing gangs of political followers as mercenary as themselves. It is to restore ability, high character, and true public spirit once more to their legitimate spheres in our public life, and to make active politics once more attractive to men of self-respect and high patriotic aspirations.[8]

Many of the reformers were abolitionists in the controversy over slavery and regarded civil service reform as an extension of the same movement. Having freed the Negro slaves, they argued, it was time to free the civil service from its slavery to political parties. Like the system of chattel slavery, the spoils system corrupts slave, master, and the community that gives it countenance. The reformers' righteous indignation was founded on their conviction that the only two political questions of their time about which reasonable and patriotic men could not differ were Negro slavery and civil service reform. "Since the movement against personal slavery there has been nothing more truly American than this absolutely unselfish and patriotic demand for the emancipation of the Civil Service."[9] In consequence of their abundant and rather rigid morality, the civil service reformers were often scorned as idealistic dreamers, blind to the realities of American politics. But they did more than preach that good government is good. They had a specific, hardheaded program by means of which they proposed to purify American parties and elevate American politics.

---

8. *Harper's Weekly*, vol. 37 (July 1, 1893), p. 614.

9. "The Administration and Reform," in Norton, *Orations and Addresses of George William Curtis*, vol. 2, p. 359. Another reformer asserted, "no other public issue since the agitation against slavery has been so clearly and incontestably proved as Civil Service Reform. Every other question has two sides and a conclusion must be formed by balancing the advantages and disadvantages of each. . . . But the necessity of abolishing the evils which have accompanied the spoils system seems so clear and the methods proposed so perfectly adapted to the purpose that I find it hard to understand how any unprejudiced mind, after careful study of the subject, can oppose the competitive system." William Dudley Foulke, *Fighting the Spoilsmen* (New York: G. P. Putnam's Sons, 1919), p. 3.

This program and the reasoning on which it was based were given remarkably clear expression by William Dudley Foulke, who was active in the reform movement both nationally and in his own state of Indiana. Foulke explained that there are three major remedies that can be applied to corruption: penal legislation, which is necessary but effective only for the graver crimes; appeal to the moral sense of the community, which is desirable but often ineffective; and removal of the temptation, which is the principle of civil service reform.

> The great purpose of [civil service reform] is not so much to provide an efficient civil service (although it does this) as to remove the temptation to use the offices of the government for personal or party ends, in other words, to remove the incentive to that kind of political corruption which is nourished by the hope of office. It does this by something akin to a mechanical contrivance, making it automatically impossible for the politician seeking the control of patronage to appoint the particular man he wants. It was the concurrence of personal discretion with party government which brought in the spoils system, and rules requiring appointments by competitive examinations destroy this personal discretion.[10]

Thus while the problem was fundamentally a moral and political one, the solution was found in "something akin to a mechanical contrivance." Without attempting to plumb philosophical depths, the reformers reasoned that the immediate cause of political corruption was the spoils system; the spoils system, in turn, depended upon the discretion of appointing officers in choosing their subordinates. Abolish that discretion and you abolish the spoils system and the corruption flowing from it.

Although this chain of reasoning is not simply wrong, it is certainly insufficient. Civil service reform was not so efficacious as the reformers had expected in purifying politics and raising the moral tone of the community, and it brought new and unanticipated problems. Yet corruption *was* very considerably reduced, and politics *did* become less a matter of sheer self-seeking; most people would regard these as gains. One might imagine a moderate reformer asking us to imagine a situation where, not half, but all of the people were moved by nothing but selfish interests and where the political system positively fostered this tendency. Conceive the utter degradation and disaster to which such a system must inevitably lead. These are the

---

10. Ibid., pp. 9–10.

results which, but for civil service reform, the spoils system might well have produced.

It is undeniable, however, that the reformers grossly oversimplified the problem of popular government. They were inclined to think that, once the spoils system was out of the way, citizens would become pure, leaders noble, and politics patriotic. "[B]y making election, not a fight for plunder, but a contest of principle," civil service reform would make "the honest will of the people the actual government of the country."[11] Although the reformers often described their movement as a return to the original principles of the American republic, they paid too little heed to the founders' warning that a government fit for angels is not fit for men. Confronted with the need to rid American politics of selfishness run riot, they underestimated the enduring force of selfish interests, and consequently they failed to recognize sufficiently the permanent need to take account of such interests. They forgot the wisdom that lay in the founders' "policy of supplying by opposite and rival interests, the defect of better motives. . . ." It is an indication of the extent to which the reformers' ideas still dominate our political thinking that we have to rediscover the lesson that political stability may be found in a politics of interests. And it is ironical that this primary principle of the first American planners and reformers, the Founding Fathers, should now appear in the guise of an argument against planning and reform.

II

With the passage of the Pendleton Act and the steady extension of the merit system in the federal service, the immediate objectives of the reformers were largely accomplished. Although the question of civil service reform erupted periodically, it ceased to be a major political issue. The reform movement did not die, but it moved from the political arena to the universities. The men associated with the second phase of reform were not primarily agitators, pamphleteers, and politicians, like Schurz and Curtis, but university professors, like Frank Goodnow, or professor-politicians, like Woodrow Wilson.

This second generation of reformer–political scientists sought to state systematically the theory of government implicit in the reform movement and to elaborate in more detail its practical consequences. In so doing they established the main lines from which most contem-

---

11. "The Administration and Reform," in Norton, *Orations and Addresses of George William Curtis*, vol. 2, p. 359.

porary thinking about political parties and public administration derives. The key words are "responsible parties" and "efficient administration." As these men generally saw it, the ideal democracy consists, as it were, of two pyramids joined at the top. The will of the people flows up through the pyramid of politics, where it is collected by political parties and formed into programs of legislation. The programs of the majority party then flow down through the administrative pyramid, where they are implemented in the most efficient manner. According to this theory the prime requisites of a civil service are political neutrality and technical competence. The civil servant is not supposed to make policy. He decides, according to scientifically established technical criteria, the best, that is, most efficient, way to accomplish any given ends. Those ends are set by his political superiors, who are responsible through the party to the people.

In spite of some fairly obvious difficulties, this theory proved to be extremely durable, because it seems to state simply and clearly the whole problem of democratic government: to ensure the free expression and the efficient implementation of the popular will. With customary diligence and thoroughness the academicians set about investigating and explaining how the pyramid of politics and the pyramid of administration ought to be governed, each according to its proper principle. Proposals for the reform of political parties as such are dealt with in other papers in this series [see source note above], but it is significant that these proposals have fared much worse than proposals for the reform of administration. Thus while the report of the American Political Science Association *A More Responsible Two-Party System* has produced little but mild academic controversy, its predecessor and intellectual companion, the 1937 report of the President's Committee on Administrative Management, was widely accepted and largely implemented. A new and vigorous discipline of administration has grown up within the universities, and it trains and fosters a huge corps of professional administrators. Public administration today is subjected to continuous and exhaustive analysis, and a stream of proposals for improvement flows out of universities, research bureaus, and government offices. Administrative theorists and practitioners seem to have moved steadily forward in their understanding, improvement, and conduct of public administration.

So successful is this movement that there has been a tendency to ignore the crucial question of the proper *connection* between administration and politics. The stock answer is that of course the political master gives the orders, but he should not meddle in the activities of his administrative servants; if he does he will only get in the way of the efficient implementation of his own orders. "Administrative questions are not political questions," Wilson said. "Although politics sets the tasks for administration, it should not be suffered to manipulate its offices."[12] It is true that even the most ardent proponents of a neutral civil service rarely went so far as to assert that the intermediate and lower levels of public administration could be altogether free of direct political influence. There were even some doubts whether political control at the top could ever be sufficient to keep the administration politically responsible; but generally students and reformers of administration were too busy extending the merit system, neutralizing the civil service, and devising principles of administration to concern themselves much with the "external" problem of political control. In any case, the logic of the two pyramids, joined somehow at their respective peaks, seemed to settle the question in principle, whatever the practical difficulties.

In addition to its beguiling symmetry, this theory of government seemed to find powerful support in that country to which Americans have always looked for political instruction. One of the first shots in the early battle for civil service reform was Dorman Eaton's book on the civil service in Britain; and later Woodrow Wilson saw in the British system "perfected party government."[13] In Britain, the reformers explained, responsible, disciplined, centralized, programmatic parties compete for public favor. In Parliament the party programs are formed into legislation which is then handed to an efficient, unbiased, politically neutral civil service for execution. The link between the political and the administrative pyramids is provided by the cabinet and, above all, the prime minister: leader of the House of Commons, chief of his political party, and head of the administration.

III

While many administrators and students of administration are still content to work quietly in the cloister of the neutral–civil-service idea, others have discovered that the world is not so reasonable or so simple as they were taught in the "reform" school; and, like small boys in similar circumstances, they find a good deal of naughty pleasure in telling everyone about it. In spite of the extension of the

---

12. Woodrow Wilson, "The Study of Administration," *Political Science Quarterly*, vol. 56 (December 1941), p. 494.

13. Woodrow Wilson, *Congressional Government* (New York: Meridian Books, 1956), p. 91.

merit system and the application of ever more sophisticated principles of administration, there seems to be as much "politics" in federal administration as there ever was. Administration is not, it appears, simply a matter of drawing logical deductions from a general statement of policy. No general statement can be so exhaustive as to permit the civil servant to act on the basis of a series of purely technical calculations, even if he were willing to do so. He is inevitably left with some discretion; he has to exercise his judgment; he has to participate in the making of policy. This is, of course, especially true at the higher levels, but the same principle applies, often in very significant ways, at lower levels as well.

If, then, we need a vast administration staffed largely by permanent officials and if they cannot be confined to merely technical decisions, the result of the attempt to neutralize the civil service is likely to be not a perfectly efficient and responsive executive machine, but a bureaucratic monster. A civil service free of detailed political control, trained in a purely instrumental science of administration, and insulated from the political life of the community will not be nonpolitical; but it will be politically irresponsible. The spoils system, whatever its other effects, did at least ensure that the bureaucracy shared the political character of the community at large. There is not much serious consideration of going back to the spoils system, but it is argued very strongly that the civil service, being a political institution, must be *representative* of the political community that it serves if it is to be responsible. To the extent that the interests, opinions, and values of civil servants are intimately bound up with those of the community as a whole, any separate "bureaucratic" will or spirit will be out of the question.

Fortunately, in this view, the American civil service does represent the American society with a fair degree of faithfulness. Government offices are not reserved for any favored class or group, and educational prerequisites are usually modest. Appointment depends mainly on an individual's capacity to "do the job," thus permitting representation within the civil service of the diverse political, racial, ethnic, and religious groups which make up the American community. Moreover, entry is not restricted to the bottom rungs of the administrative ladder or to persons just out of school, so there is a constant and healthy infusion of new blood at all levels and a considerable movement between private life and the civil service. The proponents of a "representative bureaucracy" tend to be suspicious of "closed" career systems where there is little or no entry except at the bottom level and where the members ordinarily expect to spend their whole professional lives. The military services have, of course, long been open to suspicion on these grounds. Another favorite object of attack has been the foreign service, where long periods of residence outside the United States, the filling of higher positions exclusively from within the service, and a highly developed esprit de corps are seen to carry a threat of a rigid "inbred" bureaucracy, indifferent or hostile to American democratic values.

It seems, then, that the civil service reform movement has been turned on its head. The early reformers sought, as we have seen, to take the civil service out of politics and politics out of the civil service. A neutral civil service, properly organized and trained, was supposed to serve one party or to implement one policy just as willingly as any other. More than that, such a civil service could in principle be transplanted from one political environment to a totally different one, because there was thought to be, as Woodrow Wilson said, "but one rule of good administration for all governments alike."[14] In recent years the idea of a neutral civil service has lost ground. It is now widely recognized that politics and administration are not capable of such a strict separation and that, in fact, all interesting administrative questions are political questions. It is seen to be futile and dangerous to attempt to deprive the civil service of a political function and a political character. The problem, rather, is to see that the civil service has a political character that will cause it to perform its political function well. That has been thought to require in the United States a thoroughly democratic or representative civil service. What began as a movement to neutralize the civil service has become a movement to democratize it.

IV

Different as this view of a thoroughly democratized civil service is from the older one of a thoroughly neutralized civil service, they have one fundamental feature in common. Both assume that the civil service is an agency which ought to be responsive to the will or "values" of the people; both deny that the civil service should exercise a political will of its own. Only by questioning this common assumption is it possible to grasp the fundamental significance of the political role of the modern civil service. In the remainder of this paper we must consider the modern civil service not simply as an instrument of elected officials or as a reflector of widespread values, but as a political agency in its own right, endowed with certain qualities which give it a reasonable and legitimate claim to share in

---

14. *Political Science Quarterly*, vol. 56, December 1941, p. 502.

rule.[15] We may begin with the 1955 Hoover Commission's proposal to establish in the federal government a "senior civil service."[16]

Although the Hoover Commission made a wide range of suggestions for improvement, it would have left the bulk of the federal service substantially unchanged in character. The civil service would have remained heavily specialized, open to entry at all levels, and as thoroughly "representative" of American life as before. But at the very top level, the commission proposed to form the best civil servants into an elite corps. The commission warned against a blanket inclusion of all top civil servants into the new cadre, for this would defeat the purpose of establishing a small, necessarily exclusive corps of public servants of the very highest quality. These senior civil servants would be expected to exercise a strict political neutrality; they would refrain from defending controversial policies before Congress and from making other public statements which might taint them with partisanship and thus undermine their usefulness as civil servants. Indeed, the commission was criticized for trying to revive the old idea of a perfectly neutral civil service along British lines. It is true that the Hoover Commission, like the old civil service reformers, drew heavily (though in this case silently) on British experience; but the evidence suggests that its understanding of how British government works was considerably better.

The British civil service was not, is not, and could not be "neutral" in the sense in which the early reformers understood that term: a well-tuned machine responding automatically to whatever political instructions are fed into it. The official conduct of the British civil servant is certainly characterized by a scrupulous neutrality as between political parties. Even his private opinions are unlikely to be strongly partisan, though there are less severe formal restrictions on his political activities than on those of his American counterpart. But, far from resting on a purely technical concern with administration, this nonpartisanship rests on the agreement between the civil service and the political parties on political fundamentals. The civil servant knows that he can serve faithfully even a party with which he has serious disagreement, because in these party matters reasonable and honorable Britons may differ. Somewhat remote from the most active

---

15. For a comparative and typological study along these lines, see Fritz Morstein Marx, *The Administrative State* (Chicago: University of Chicago Press, 1957).

16. Commission on Organization of the Executive Branch of the Government, *Personnel and Civil Service* and *Task Force Report on Personnel and Civil Service* (Washington: U.S. Government Printing Office, 1955).

sphere of political life, he is likely to acquire a habitual moderation, avoiding extremes and reminding himself that his disagreements with his political superior about the issues of the day are insignificant compared with the deep agreement on which they rest. The British civil servant is "neutral," not because he is above all a civil servant but because he is above all British.

Thus the British civil servant's neutrality or, more precisely, nonpartisanship, has a political base. He can stand aloof from disputes between parts of the body politic precisely because he shares so thoroughly in the consensus about the character of the whole. But he also has a positive political role. While he carries out party programs with which he may disagree, he also helps to modify the partisanship of his political superiors. To give but one example, Labour partisans often expressed, prior to 1945, a doubt whether the predominantly middle-class civil service would loyally and effectively carry out the programs of a Labour government. When the test came, not only did the civil service not sabotage Labour programs, but there was surprisingly little evidence of bureaucratic dragging of feet. According to Labour's prime minister, "There were certainly some people in the Labour Party who doubted whether the civil servants would give fair play to a socialist government, but all doubts disappeared with experience."[17]

It is true that the responsiveness of the civil service to Labour programs was helped by the changed social and political composition of the service, though there was least change in the crucial top ranks. But it is also true that the Labour government proved to be much less of a threat to the fundamental political consensus than many, including many Labourites, had expected. Quite a different situation would have existed had Labour really tried to engineer a socialist revolution and had it cast aside the traditional institutions and conventions that contain British political life—and a different civil service would have been required. As it was, the old civil service dog certainly learned and loyally performed some new Labour tricks, but the Labour ministers also learned something from the civil service. As one of those ministers, Herbert Morrison, described it:

> The relationship between the Minister and the civil servants should be—and usually is—that of colleagues working together in a team, co-operative partners seeking to advance the public interest and the efficiency of the Department. . . .

17. The Right Hon. The Earl Attlee, "Civil Servants, Ministers, Parliament and the Public," in William A. Robson, ed., *The Civil Service in Britain and France* (London: The Hogarth Press, 1956), p. 16.

The partnership should be alive and virile, rival ideas and opinions should be fairly considered, and the relationship of all should be one of mutual respect—on the understanding, of course, that the Minister's decision is final and must be loyally and helpfully carried out, and that he requires efficient and energetic service.[18]

But does this kind of partnership have any meaningful or legitimate application in the United States? Obviously there are difficulties standing in the way of a transfer of British institutions to American shores. Thus for example, although the call of the Hoover Commission for strict "political neutrality" by the senior civil service did not (contrary to the views of some critics) imply acceptance of the old idea of a merely technical civil service, it was open to the criticism that it took too little account of the complex internal articulation of the American political system. Granting the validity of this criticism does not, however, necessarily mean that the notion of a partnership between political party leaders and civil servants is inapplicable in the United States, although it does point to the different and more complex form that an American partnership must take.

This question of the kind of political neutrality that can be expected or desired of American civil servants is closely connected with a feature of the American Constitution that has long embarrassed party and civil service reformers, namely the system of checks and balances. The reformers, firmly persuaded by the logic of the two pyramids (that elaboration of a misunderstanding of British government), tended to regard the separation of powers as a "defect" in the American system, to be remedied either by drastic constitutional change or through the informal agency of reformed parties in control of a reformed administration. Even in their most generous and patriotic mood, they could scarcely see in this central feature of the American Constitution anything but a curiosity of the eighteenth-century mind—a once harmless nuisance grown under modern conditions into an intolerable obstacle to responsible and efficient government. The very fact that the civil service is constitutionally not simply subordinate to either the president or the Congress tends to obscure lines of command and, incidentally, to increase the political influence of the civil service. It is easy to see why the reformers, with their idea of a neutral civil service, thought that such a system could produce nothing but confusion and irresponsibility.

If, however, the civil service is regarded not as a neutral instru-

---

18. Herbert Morrison, *Government and Parliament* (London: Oxford University Press, 1954), pp. 318–19.

ment but as a political institution, then the constitutional system of checks and balances appears in a different light. While the framers of the Constitution doubtless failed to anticipate the full significance of the administrative state, there is nevertheless a close harmony between the original intention of the system of checks and balances and the political role of the modern civil service. Without entering fully into this subject, we may say that the system of checks and balances was an attempt to institutionalize moderation; and one of the important ways it does this in modern American government is by adding to the political weight of the civil service which, more than any of the other active agencies of government, stands for moderation. Of course the founders recognized that their "inventions of prudence" were not a sufficient condition of good government and might sometimes prove a positive handicap, and we must recognize the same about a politically influential civil service. But if the civil service is a political institution with a political function, it does not appear unreasonable that it should have some political power. In what follows we shall consider what the bureaucracy, in partnership with political parties, can and does contribute to American government.[19]

V

One manifestation of the basic problem of government by political parties is the fact that politicians who run for office in their capacity as leaders of organized parts, or parties, of the body politic are expected to assume a responsibility for the government of the whole. This formulation is obviously incomplete. American political parties themselves undertake to form particular individuals, groups, interests, and opinions into some kind of whole. This is not the place to discuss this broad responsibility or the various means by which American parties discharge it. It may be observed, however, that one means is the appointment of men who are not distinctively party men to fill even high political positions, to say nothing of the appointment of members of the opposite party. Rexford Tugwell was not a Democrat in the same sense as James Farley; Charles Wilson was not a Republican in the same sense as Arthur Summerfield. And Harvard professors, it may be assumed, are not Democrats in the same sense as persons whose whole career is associated with that party. Yet in spite of this and other qualifications, the fact remains that in a

---

19. Of what follows it may be said, with Sir William Blackstone, "This is the spirit of our constitution: not that I assert it is in fact quite so perfect as I have here endeavoured to describe it. . . ." *Commentaries*, vol. 1, p. 172.

very important sense our system of government gives to a part the responsibility for governing the whole.

It is notorious that party politicians tend to learn moderation and responsibility when in office; but it is perhaps less generally recognized that one of their main teachers is the civil service. The common contrast between the politician, as the "practical man" experienced in "real life" and in touch with the wants and needs of the people, and the bureaucrat, as the remote, paper-shuffling office boy, is grossly overdrawn. In the first place, many civil servants have, in their particular fields, a kind of direct contact with the people and experience of the problems of government which even the politician whose ear never leaves the ground cannot possibly match. Moreover, modern government is to a large extent conducted by "shuffling papers," and it is of vital importance that they be shuffled well. Finally, a large part of the proposals for new policies and legislation come up through the civil service. Not only do civil servants exercise discretion in interpreting and applying the commands of their political superiors; they participate intimately in the formulation of those commands. They make proposals of their own and fight for them; they comment on the proposals of their political superiors—and may fight against them. They make a vital contribution to the process of deciding what is to be done. Government would come to a standstill if our "closet statesmen" in the civil service suddenly started doing only what they were told.

In the United States, of course, due partly to the constitutional system of checks and balances, the civil servant does not and perhaps cannot be expected to confine his statesmanship to the closet. Indeed, one of the peculiarities of American public administration is the fact that the civil servant may have more political knowledge and skill, even in the rather narrow sense, than his "political" superior. And he is almost certain to have, at least at first, more familiarity with the politics involved in actually running the government. A new secretary or assistant secretary will normally find himself heavily dependent upon his experienced civil servants to facilitate not only the internal management of the agency but also its relations with Congress, interested organizations, other agencies of government, and even the White House itself. Compared with his counterpart in England, the American political executive has, generally speaking, to steer through political waters that are more cloudy and turbulent and to do it with less training and experience. Little wonder that he has to place extensive trust in the political judgment of experienced pilots in the civil service.

It is true that much of the contribution of the civil service to the art of government, even in the United States, is of a restraining and even negative kind. The civil servant, especially at the higher levels, has seen many programs tried, and many failures; even the successful innovations have usually fallen short of their makers' hopes. His experience has caused him to be sensitive to difficulties; he is an expert in seeking out unanticipated consequences. Even after a new policy has been decided upon, the civil servant is likely to explain, perhaps at exasperating length, why it cannot possibly be carried out the way his political chief wants. The civil servant is full of procedures, rules, and regulations, and he will (if he is performing properly) instruct his chief in the reasons for them. Orderly administration is not the most important quality of good government and it may sometimes have to be sacrificed to higher ends, but it is, generally speaking, indispensable. The cautious prudence and orderliness which tend to characterize the civil service are precisely that part of practical wisdom in which the party politician is likely to be deficient. The political leader in the United States is at least as much in need of the "prudent counsel and efficient aid" of "able and judicious men" as was the English statesman of the nineteenth century addressed by Sir Henry Taylor;[20] and he will find many of them in the civil service.

The special kind of practical wisdom that characterizes the civil servant points to a more fundamental political function of the bureaucracy, namely to bring to bear on public policy its distinctive view of the common good or its way of looking at questions about the common good. The preoccupation of the civil service with rules and regulations, for example, is not aimed merely at orderly administration, important as that is. The rules and regulations, and the principle that there should *be* rules and regulations, represent a certain principle of justice, if only the principle of treating equals equally. Similar considerations apply to the civil servant's predilection for the way things have been done in the past. Generally speaking, to follow precedents is orderly, reasonable, and fair. One of the basic principles of American government is that governmental action should ordinarily be taken on the basis of established rules, however irritating that may sometimes be to a politician with a substantive program to put through. Like judges, civil servants have a special responsibility to preserve the rule of law.

Civil servants also bear a similarity to judges in their possession of what is, for most practical purposes, permanent tenure in office. Of course, like judges, they are influenced by the election returns— and it would be dangerous if they were not; but they have a degree

---

20. *The Statesman* (New York: Mentor Books, 1958), p. 108.

of insulation from shifting political breezes. The rhythm of their official lives and thoughts is not governed so strictly as is that of the political executive by periodic elections. Their position enables them to mitigate the partisanship of party politics, and it gives them some protection from the powerful temptation, to which the party politician is always subject, to serve the people's inclinations rather than their interests.

Clement Attlee described the higher civil servant in Britain as having, in addition to long personal experience, "that mysterious tradition of the office wherein is somehow embalmed the wisdom of past generations."[21] The civil service in the United States is of course far less time-encrusted, but here too the higher civil servant will ordinarily have long experience in government, nearly always longer than his political chiefs. Moreover the duties of the civil servant and the way he works—his concern for written records, for example—tend to make him conscious of the "long-termness" of political decisions to a degree that is unusual for transient party politicians. At its best, the civil service is a kind of democratic approximation to a hereditary aristocracy whose members are conscious of representing an institution of government which extends into the past and into the future beyond the life of any individual member. In our mobile democracy, the civil service is one of the few institutions we have for bringing the accumulated wisdom of the past to bear upon political decisions.

Perhaps the most important political contribution that a civil service can make is, of all those we have considered, the one the American civil service makes least. Neither the bureaucracy nor political parties merely "represent" or reflect the American polity; they also help to shape and guide that polity, and they perform this function by what they are as well as by what they do. The character of a country's public servants is one of the determinants of the character of its people. When George Washington sought honest, honorable, and loyal gentlemen to fill the public offices of the new country, he was concerned not only with getting the work of government done but also with distributing the patronage of government in such a way as to set the public stamp of approval on certain human qualities. When Andrew Jackson established the system of rotation in public office, he had the same broad objective in mind, but he sought to elevate the common man in the place of the gentleman. And what the civil service reformers feared most about the spoils system was the effect on the political character of the people of the

---

21. Robson, *The Civil Service in Britain and France*, p. 17.

example set by the kind of men which the spoils system tended to elevate. "Politics cannot be made a mere trade," George Curtis argued, "without dangerously relaxing the moral character of the country."[22] In the words of Dorman Eaton,

> It is in the struggles for office, and the opportunities for gain in the exercise of official power, that selfishness, deception, and partisan zeal have their everlasting contest with virtue, patriotism, and duty. It is in that contest that statesmen and demagogues, patriots and intriguers, the good citizen and the venal office seeker, all the high and all the low influences of political life, meet face to face, and by the balance of power, for good or for evil, give character to politics and determine the morality of nations.[23]

Except for the removal of corruption, however, the reformers gave little thought to the kind of character and morality which their neutral, merely technical civil service would exemplify. One indication of the result is the fact that American civil servants themselves, though they may be thoroughly devoted to serving the common good, ordinarily prefer to identify themselves by their profession or occupation or "job" rather than by their public service. It is thought more respectable to be an agricultural economist or a personnel specialist than to be a civil servant. Not the least of the merits of the Hoover Commission proposal for a senior civil service is the influence such a corps of public servants might have on American life and character by restoring to a place of honor and respect the title of "civil servant."

The civil service is, then, in possession of certain institutional qualities which give it a title to share with elected officials in rule. It has a distinctive competence in the art of government and a unique knowledge of the problems of government, without which stable and intelligent government under modern conditions would be literally impossible. It has, moreover, a distinctive view of the common good which can guide and supplement the view likely to be taken by elected party politicians. On the foundation of its procedures, its rules, its institutional memory and foresight, its traditions, its skepticism of political panaceas, and its protection from the whims of popularity, the civil service stands for the continuity and wholeness of American government.

---

22. Dorman Eaton, "The Reform of the Civil Service," in *Orations and Addresses*, vol. 2, p. 43.

23. Robson, *Civil Service in Great Britain*, pp. 423–24.

VI

It is not to be denied that bureaucracy suffers characteristic limitations and defects. Neither the party politician nor the bureaucrat has an unqualified claim to rule; neither is unqualifiedly competent or entitled to act on behalf of the whole people. Under ordinary circumstances the actual conduct of American government is in the charge of a partnership between them. We have emphasized the contributions of the bureaucratic part of this partnership, because they are less generally understood. But as the civil servant teaches, so also he is taught by the party politician. The civil servant is likely, for example, to overdo his concern with procedures and rules. He may be blind to the fact that procedural justice can do substantive injustice. It may be necessary for his political chief to show him that procedures have become so complex as to defeat their purpose or that the original reason for a rule has disappeared. While the civil servant may take a longer view of the common good, his view may also be distorted by a preoccupation with one program or a rather narrow range of programs. The broader range of responsibilities of the political chief may provide a corrective.[24] Moreover, although the civil servant bears the immediate responsibility for government because he does (or is closer to) the actual governing, he does not bear the final responsibility. He may instruct his political chief, he may advise him, guide him, even manage him—but he does not have the last word. This means that he may be overruled, for good reasons or bad; but it also means that his way of thinking and acting is molded in part by the fact of his formal subordination. Even at his best he is not a political captain but a faithful, wise, and influential counselor and servant.[25]

---

24. As one civil service bureau chief explained, "The assistant secretary and I deal with the same people and do many of the same sorts of things, but the task of the assistant secretary is to keep me from losing touch with the mass of the people, from becoming too ingrown. The political executive provides that sensitivity to the public pulse. He and I approach our similar jobs from different angles. If we can learn to talk each other's language, we make a good team." Marver H. Bernstein, *The Job of the Federal Executive* (Washington: The Brookings Institution, 1958), p. 49.

25. "I remember that I went to my new secretary and said: 'I think a man coming into your job should have his own men around him. I am a career employee, but if you should decide to have your own man in this job, I hope you will first give me a trial because I think I can help you. But if you decide to have your own man, there will be no difficulty about it. All you need to do is tell me. If you want to try me first, I will attempt to give you all the facts bearing on your particular problem, and I will give them to you as accurately and impartially as I can. You will have to have faith in me until you learn to know me better. If you want me to make a recommendation, I

This is connected with a final limitation of bureaucracy. Although a good civil service is one of the guardians of the traditional political wisdom of a regime, "sometimes it is necessary," as Attlee says, "to react violently against the tradition which was formed for a different state of society."[26] While it is difficult to imagine Lord Attlee reacting violently against anything, it is clear that traditional bureaucratic wisdom may not suit changed circumstances. The very tradition which it is the responsibility of the bureaucrat to carry forward may require fundamental redefinition, and that is a task for which his duties, training, and experience disqualify him. During such times of crisis, "administration" does become radically subordinate to "politics"; the institution of the civil service does become to a much greater extent than usual an instrument of the man who is president.

The peak of the spoils system is generally regarded as having come during Lincoln's first administration, and Lincoln removed the incumbents of almost all offices under his immediate control. He used the spoils of office to help bind together the Republican party, the North, and thereby the Union. So much was this the paramount aim that, according to one historian, Lincoln "made no attempt to obtain the men best fitted to perform the functions of the various offices, except in case of the very highest; for minor places he did not even insist that a man be fit."[27] The Civil War is an extreme example, but it is not the only one. The transformation which the civil service underwent at the hands of Franklin Roosevelt is well known. Roosevelt gave a new meaning to the civil service and to the Democratic party in the course of giving a new meaning to American political life as a whole. During such critical times, the question of bureaucracy as such is almost entirely subordinated to the more fundamental question of political reconstruction. It is not unfair to say of the bureaucracy (and perhaps of political parties too) that it contributes least to government in the most important cases, provided it is remembered that a government requires a capacity for everyday competence, prudence, and public-spiritedness, as well as a capacity for greatness.

---

will do so. If we get to the point where I cannot live with your decisions, I will get out. I will fight you outside the government, but I won't do so in the government. I won't make any end runs on you. Now, you don't know me from Adam, and you never heard of me before in all likelihood. You don't know whether I am going to live up to that statement or not. You will have to take it on faith.' The secretary really needed me, but he didn't know it yet. As it turned out, we got along very well." Ibid., p. 191.

26. Robson, *The Civil Service in Britain and France*, p. 17.

27. Carl Russell Fish, *The Civil Service and the Patronage* (Cambridge: Harvard University Press, 1920), p. 170.

16
Leonard D. White and the Study of Public Administration

Leonard D. White did not plant the seeds from which the field of public administration grew; but for four decades he tended that garden with unexcelled devotion. Carefully cultivating, pruning, and transplanting, he sought to understand and to make clear to others the plan of the whole and to articulate the details of the several parts. The vast majority of students of public administration today were shaped at least in part by their exposure to White. Many have seen no need to leave the paths that he laid out or improved. Others have found White's landscape too restrictive. Yet all must, in one way or another, come to terms with it as a vital part of coming to terms with their field of study.

Introduction

This chapter is designed to assist and deepen that confrontation. No reference is made to White's universally acknowledged qualities as administrator, teacher, and gentleman, or to his numerous specific contributions to the study and practice of public administration.[1] Our concern is with his attempts to give definition to the whole. It will be argued here that throughout his career White was concerned with a fundamental contradiction that lay and still lies at the heart of the study of public administration, and that in the work of his later years he provided his best advice on the approach to that study. The focus will be on White's *Introduction to the Study of Public Administration*, the

This essay was originally published in *Public Administration Review*, vol. 25, March 1965. Reprinted with permission from Public Administration Review, copyright by the American Society for Public Administration (ASPA), 1120 G Street NW, Suite 700, Washington, D.C. 20005. All rights reserved.

1. See John M. Gaus, "Leonard Dupee White—1891–1958," *Public Administration Review* (Summer 1958).

four editions of which appeared in 1926, 1939, 1948, and 1955, and particularly the introductory and more theoretical chapters.[2]

The first comprehensive text in public administration, the *Introduction* stood supreme even while an increasing number of texts appeared; it is still widely considered to be in a class by itself. To a degree unusual for a text, it was the focus and expressed the range and depth of its author's scholarly interests.[3] Admittedly, the *Introduction* has been criticized, at least in private, to an extent not entirely attributable to the hazards of preeminence. The generation of students after the Second World War, when memory of the reasons for the founding of the discipline had faded, often thought that White's conception of public administration avoided or obscured many of the important questions. In the third and fourth editions, it often seemed that problems had been cloaked in definition; vigorous criticism and prescription replaced by bland description; the driving force of reform transformed into a slow, methodical process of reorganization and re-reorganization; and the confident and restless pursuit of scientific principles of administration encrusted with qualification and reservation. In this as in other respects White faithfully represented his discipline. Dissatisfaction with White's approach is dissatisfaction with the study of public administration itself, as it is still widely understood.

White's Basic Assumptions

Administration Is a Single Process. In the preface to the first edition of the *Introduction* White wrote:

> The book rests upon at least four assumptions. It assumes that administration is a single process, substantially uniform in its essential characteristics wherever observed, and therefore avoids the study of municipal administration, state administration, or federal administration as such. It assumes that the study of administration should start from the base of management rather than the foundation of law, and is therefore more absorbed in the affairs of the American Management Association than in the decisions of the courts. It assumes that administration is still primarily an art but

---

2. Published by the Macmillan Company, New York.

3. While an elaborate discussion of this contention is unnecessary, an attempt has been made to provide sufficient references at appropriate points for the convenience of the reader who may wish to satisfy himself, as the writer has done, that the thesis presented here finds support in White's other writings.

attaches importance to the significant tendency to transform it into a science. It assumes that administration has become, and will continue to be the heart of the problem of modern government.[4]

These assumptions are still perhaps the best concise statement of the foundations of the discipline of public administration, despite the extraordinary development that the discipline has enjoyed since the words were written in 1926.

The most striking characteristic of these assumptions is that they all refer to *administration,* although the book is an introduction to *public* administration. Thus the positive part of the first assumption— "that administration is a single process, substantially uniform in its essential characteristics wherever observed"—emphasizes the uniformity of administration; but the negative part warns against an unrealistic division, not of administration, but of public administration. White begins his first chapter with an emphatic statement of this point:

> There is an essential unity in the process of administration, whether it be observed in city, state or federal governments, that precludes a "stratified" classification of the subject. To treat it in terms of municipal administration, state administration, or national administration, is to imply a distinction that in reality does not exist. The fundamental problems such as the development of personal initiative, the assurance of individual competence and integrity, responsibility, coordination, fiscal supervision, leadership, morale are in fact the same; and most of the subjects of administration defy the political boundaries of local and state government.[5]

This inevitably suggests the question whether the essential unity in the process of administration also precludes a "stratified" classification of *public* administration and *private* administration. Is that also a distinction "that in reality does not exist"? White seems to be led, in principle, to answer this question affirmatively; but the very title and subject matter of his book imply a negative answer. He seeks to leave the question open. Public administration, he says, is "the management of men and materials in the accomplishment of the purposes of the state"; its objective is "the most efficient utilization of the resources at the disposal of officials and employees."[6] This

---

4. First edition, pp. vii–viii; the preface is reprinted in all editions.

5. First edition, p. 1; compare the second edition, p. 7; the third edition, p. 3; the fourth edition, p. 1.

6. First edition, p. 2; second edition, p. 7.

definition "relates the conduct of government business to the conduct of the affairs of any other social organization . . . in all of which good management is recognized as an element essential to success"; but it "leaves open the question to what extent the administration itself participates in formulating the purposes of the state, and avoids any controversy as to the precise nature of administrative action."[7] White avoids this controversy partly by providing no definition of administration, despite his emphasis on its essential homogeneity.[8]

In the second edition, public administration in its broadest sense is said to consist "of all those operations having for their purpose the fulfillment or enforcement of public policy as declared by the competent authorities."[9] It is a special case of the larger category of administration, "a process which is common to all organized human effort" or (in the third and fourth editions) "a process common to all group effort, public or private, civil or military, large scale or small scale."[10] "The art of administration is the direction, coordination, and control of many persons to achieve some purpose or objective." An administrator is one who exercises that art, and "there are administrators in all human activities except those capable of being executed by one person."[11]

It is possible to construct a definition of administration from the elements that White provides, and the result may suggest the reason for this curious omission: administration consists of all those operations aiming at the achievement of some purpose or objective shared by two or more people. It excludes, then, only those "operations" that are nonpurposive and those that concern only one person.

Administration Has Its Base in Management. "Despite great differ-

---

7. First edition, p. 2.

8. In later editions White does define "the art of administration" and "an administrator." He also quotes in passing a well-known definition of administration by Brooks Adams in the third edition, p. 4, and the fourth edition, p. 2, as well as a comment by Paul Appleby that might be called a definition in the third edition, p. 8.

9. Second edition, p. 3. In italics in the original. Consistently with his broader, more "political" understanding of public administration in recent years, White repeats this definition in the third and fourth editions but omits "as declared by competent authorities," presumably in recognition of the participation of public administration in deciding, as well as fulfilling or enforcing, public policy. Third edition, p. 3; fourth edition, p. 1.

10. Second edition, pp. 3–4; third edition, p. 3; fourth edition, p. 1.

11. Third edition, p. 4; fourth edition, p. 2; the definition of the art of administration is in italics in the original.

ences in culture and technology, the process of management throughout the centuries was inherently the same as that which now makes feasible great business enterprises, continental systems of government, and the beginnings of a world order."[12] Yet only comparatively recently has the process of management as such been subjected to systematic study. In the case of public administration, the late start can be attributed to an excessive preoccupation with law.

White's second assumption is "that the study of administration should start from the base of management rather than the foundation of law, and is therefore more absorbed in the affairs of the American Management Association than in the decisions of the courts." This confirms what seemed to be an implication of the first assumption, that the unity in the process of administration precludes a distinction between public and private administration, as it precludes a distinction between federal, state, and municipal administration. However, this proposition is the end of one of the paths along which White proceeded; the beginning was a declaration of independence from law.

Goodnow and the relation to law. White would have agreed with Frank Goodnow's statement written in 1905:

> The most striking if not the most important questions of public law and the first to demand solution are those to which the name "constitutional" is applied. To their solution the wisdom and political activity of the past have been devoted. The present age, however, is devoting itself primarily to questions which are generally referred to as "administrative." A function of government called "administration" is being differentiated from the general sphere of governmental activity, and the term "administrative law" is applied to the rules of law which regulate its discharge.[13]

White argues, however, that Goodnow's writings "do not make a clear distinction between administration and administrative law. This distinction is only now emerging in fact."[14] He adopts Goodnow's definition of administrative law: "that part of the public law

---

12. Third edition, p. 3; fourth edition, p. 1.

13. Frank J. Goodnow, *The Principles of the Administrative Law of the United States* (New York: G. P. Putnam's Sons, 1905), p. 1.

14. First edition, note 2. White refers here to Goodnow's writings on administrative law and not to his *Politics and Administration* (New York: Macmillan Co., 1900), which, although cited in the first edition, appears to have made little impression on White until later; compare the second edition, p. 12.

which fixes the organization and determines the competence of the administrative authorities, and indicates to the individual remedies for the violation of his rights." This definition, White says, rightly emphasizes the major objective of administrative law, which is the protection of private rights. The objective of public administration, in contrast, is the efficient conduct of public business. "These two goals are not only different, but may at times conflict. Administration is of course bound by the rules of administrative law, as well as by the prescriptions of constitutional law; but within the boundaries thus set, it seeks the most effective accomplishment of public purposes."[15] What Goodnow did not sufficiently recognize was that public administration and administrative law are related but distinct fields, governed by internal principles of their own. Thus White does not focus, as Goodnow does, on the rules of law regulating the discharge of the emerging function of "administration," but on the internal rules of the function. This helps to explain both the similarity and the differences between White's *Introduction* and Goodnow's *The Principles of the Administrative Law of the United States*. Viewed in a half-century perspective, the similarity is perhaps the more surprising. In every respect but one[16] the main outlines of White's book follow those of Goodnow's, occasionally chapter by chapter and even section by section. The frequency with which White's discussion parallels Goodnow's is almost as striking as the fact that White exhibits a very considerable concern with the decisions of the courts and scarcely any concern with the affairs of the American Management Association.

Several explanations can be suggested for this similarity between the first comprehensive statement of the new field of public administration and the then major work in the field from which public administration issued. Goodnow, while a teacher and scholar in the field of administrative law, was at the same time deliberately laying the ground for the study of public administration and is one of its acknowledged founders. It is not startling that White patterned himself after Goodnow, even after having set out on his independent way. Although White's second edition contains a new section on fiscal management (which finds no parallel in Goodnow), and further changes occur in subsequent editions, the basic organization remains

---

15. First edition, pp. 4–5, quoting Goodnow, *Comparative Administrative Law*, vol. 1, pp. 8–9.

16. One of Goodnow's major sections deals with "Local Administration" to which there is nothing comparable in White. Many of White's individual chapters are, however, arranged on the basis of the federal-state-municipal distinction.

the same. Goodnow and White were, after all, examining the same subject, if from different points of view. Thus, for example, while Goodnow treats "offices and officers," White deals with "the personnel problem"; for Goodnow the central problem is the law governing the official relation, for White it is morale.

This is more than a difference in point of view. For White, it was the difference between looking at the "boundaries" of a thing, and looking at the thing itself. However, in order to press deeper into White's conception of the study of public administration, it is important to see why this statement of the difference is problematical. The thing looked at, administration, is said to be a process. As process, it does not contain its own definition; it does not set its own boundaries or the end toward which it moves. Indeed, as process, administration seems to comprehend all human activity, except that which is entirely solitary. What, then, gives public administration its definition? It is law, as White admits. Law provides both the ends and the means of public administration.

White's definition of public administration does not deny its dependence on law, but "emphasizes the managerial phase of administration and minimizes its legalistic and formal aspect."[17] This is not sufficiently precise, however, for White emphasizes the managerial phase of *public* administration. This adjective again introduces "the foundation of law" as starting point for the study of public administration—contrary to White's second assumption. White attempts to surmount this difficulty by arguing that, while the ends and boundaries of public administration are set by law, public administration *is* management and, as such, no different from any other kind of administration. In that case, why study *public* administration at all? Is such study a purely arbitrary selection of a part of the ubiquitous process of administration, or is it based on some fundamental distinction that cuts through "process as process"?

Wilson and subordination to law. The question of the basis of the study of public administration is most directly considered in the second edition, the only one to contain a chapter called "Scope and Nature of Public Administration," and the only one to make use of Woodrow Wilson's definition of public administration as "detailed and systematic execution of public law."[18] "Law," White says, "provides the immediate framework within which public administration

17. First edition, p. 2.
18. Second edition, p. 4. The definition is given in a footnote in the first edition, p. 2, and is taken from Wilson's essay "The Study of Administration," *Political Science Quarterly* (June 1887).

operates," defining its tasks, establishing its major structure, providing it with funds, and setting forth rules or procedure. "Public administration is embedded in law, and the student of the subject will often be with the statutes."[19] Nevertheless, White contends that an almost exclusive concern with law has blinded American students and civil servants to the essential unity of the process of administration and the internal nonlegal principles governing it. One practical result is that American public administration displays "an exaggeration of legal correctness, and in consequence an accentuation of the lawyer in administration. . . ."[20]

By Wilson's definition of public administration, "every particular application of general law is an act of administration." To deal with administration in such terms, White says, "would require analysis of the military as well as the judicial and civil arms of the government, and would lead into each of the many activities supported by the modern state. . . ." He proposes to deal with "only a part of the entire field" and proceeds to set some limits.[21]

White is not concerned with "operations peculiar to the special fields of administration," such as techniques of preventing soil erosion or identifying suspected criminals. These are highly particularized procedures, best left to specialists. "They are, however, the primary substantive functions of administration and from one point of view it is artificial to describe public administration apart from these major functions." It would be "feasible" to approach public

---

19. Second edition, p. 11.

20. Second edition, p. 32. "Legality therefore becomes a primary consideration of administrators, and legal advisers acquire an importance which far outweighs their strictly administrative contribution." Second edition, p. 11. For White's views on lawyers as administrators, see his *Government Career Service* (Chicago: University of Chicago Press, 1935), pp. 45–47; and his essay "The Public Service of the Future" in the volume of essays in honor of Charles E. Merriam, which White edited, *The Future of Government in the United States* (Chicago: University of Chicago Press, 1942), pp. 205–6.

21. Second edition, p. 4; the quotations in the following three paragraphs are taken from the second edition, pp. 5–7. It is unnecessary to deal with White's discussion of the exclusion of military administration. It appears, indeed, to be a misapprehension to think that Wilson's definition of public administration requires the inclusion of military administration, which does not have as its end the detailed and systematic execution of public law. The army is not characteristically a law enforcement agency but acts in an area and seeks to accomplish ends that the law cannot reach. Whatever the difficulty in excluding military administration, it arises from White's definition of public administration, not Wilson's.

administration "starting from the substantive activities toward which all official work is directed," but "for practical as well as technical reasons . . . it is necessary to stop short of describing all human problems and public policies in an effort to clear one path through the field of public administration." Clearing "one path" is possible and desirable, because, underlying the particular substantive functions, "there are certain common procedures and problems characteristic of modern administration under any political system and in any field of government activity. . . . These aspects of administration are broadly managerial in nature. They comprise the content of this volume."

These "managerial" procedures and problems are not, evidently, merely "aspects" of administration, for White goes on to say that his study "concentrates on the *central core* of the total complex of administration."[22] He is concerned with "process as process," and he seeks to expose and to treat the "essential unity in the process of administration." It is unnecessary to restate the whole series of questions and counter-questions to which this argument gives rise; but it is notable that while White concludes that "the study of the content of public policy, on which all administration depends, is not necessary to the technical study of administrative procedures as such," he does not retract his earlier warning that a description of public administration apart from its substantive functions is somehow "artificial."

Judicial administration is also excluded from the *Introduction*, even though "the major purpose of the court is the same as that of the administration: to enforce and to implement public policy as declared in law."[23] It is "due to the specialized nature of law enforcement by judicial decision [that] the judges as administrators will not be given systematic consideration in this volume." What is it about this particular specialization that supports the exclusion of judicial administration from a text in public administration? Wilson's definition seems to imply that what the courts do is public administration par excellence; thus, the study of public administration would seem to be centrally, although not exclusively, concerned with what is called the administration of justice. But one of White's major objectives was to replace the judge as the central figure in public administration with, say, the city manager.[24] Wilson's definition, which leads

22. Italics supplied.

23. Compare the first edition, p. 40.

24. White's book on the city manager was published the year after the first edition of the *Introduction* and gave expression to White's conviction of the significance of this "emerging technical-professional official" in the development of a "new ideal of officialdom." The city manager, White

back to the radical subordination of public administration to law, is abandoned in White's subsequent editions.[25]

Administration—An Art, in Transformation to a Science. The functioning of a modern administrative department "is a far cry from the Egyptian scribe who laboriously copied accounts on his roll of papyrus, but the natural history of administration connects its ancient and modern forms in an unbroken sequence of development. . . . What differentiates the modern public official from the scribe of antiquity is the marvelous material equipment with which he works, and the contribution which science has made, and continues to make, to his profession."[26] Thus, White's third assumption is that, while administration is still an art, there is a "significant tendency to transform it into a science." Besides furnishing the tools with which modern administration works, science "is transforming the methods of administration (in the sense of management) from rule of thumb empiricism to ascertained principle." Scientific management, with its quest for the "one best way," has been the leader in this movement. Sufficient progress has been made so that "we are wholly justified in asserting that a science of management appears to be immediately before us."[27]

However, each succeeding edition of the *Introduction* contains fewer scientific "principles" of organization and management and more qualifications about those remaining. For example, discussing the allocation of responsibility and authority, White says in the first edition: "The principle to be observed here is simple enough; to define responsibility so precisely that each official will be specifically charged with definite duties, under such conditions that success or failure will depend upon his own diligence and wisdom, or the contrary." A "necessary corollary" is that each official should be vested with "adequate authority, both legal and financial, to enable

thought, was "a forerunner of the type of official who must become the pattern of the next generation if the American government is to achieve its purpose, or even maintain its self-respect." *The City Manager* (Chicago: University of Chicago Press, 1927), p. 287. In later years the city manager was replaced as the central figure in White's view of public administration by the Hamiltonian Chief Executive and the federal senior civil servant. But see below, n. 57.

25. It should be said that White nevertheless follows, to a very considerable degree, the lines set out in Wilson's essay as a whole. Indeed, White's difficulty here reflects a difficulty in Wilson's essay itself.

26. First edition, p. 4.

27. Ibid., pp. 15–16; compare *The City Manager*, pp. 257–58.

him to discharge efficiently the duties pertaining to his office." White concedes that "the application of these principles is full of difficulty," but the principles themselves are clear.[28] In the second edition he adds "the rule of unity of command," to which he attaches "cardinal importance," and which "emphasizes the desirability of a single source of final authority in any organization, a reminder of the old saw, 'No man can serve two masters.' " He repeats that "the location of authority, given unity of command, must be in the clearest terms" and that "power must be commensurate with responsibility."[29]

In the third edition, these principles appear in a much more qualified form.[30] In a new section called "The Search for Principles" White says that "in the strictest sense of the term, principles in administration are still largely to be formulated. In the meaning of 'principles' that suggests only working rules of conduct which wide experience seems to have validated, a number can be stated."[31] He then shows, following Herbert Simon, that the traditional principles are often in conflict and invariably imprecise. White retains as "a sound working rule" the notion that authority should be allocated in clear and precise terms, especially at the bottom of the hierarchy; at the top, such allocation is difficult and perhaps even damaging. That authority must be commensurate with responsibility is now said to contain "an essential kernel of truth"; but it is a maxim "rarely if ever attained in practice, and ought perhaps to be reformulated in reverse: responsibility does not exceed the most effective use of authority and resources actually available."

Reevaluating scientific management. White never abandoned the pursuit of principles of administration,[32] but he came to the view that what had formerly seemed to be solid principles (however difficult their application) were, rather, prudential rules of thumb, useful but far from genuinely scientific. He came also to the view that the goal was something less than the "transformation" of administration into a science.

This was no radical revision of opinion. Moderate in everything, White had always reserved his opinion as to how far the "transforma-

---

28. Ibid., pp. 59–60. See White's brief informative essay "The Meaning of Principles in Public Administration," in the volume that he, Marshall E. Dimock, and John M. Gaus wrote in 1936, *The Frontiers of Public Administration* (Chicago: University of Chicago Press, 1936), esp. pp. 18, 22, 24–25.

29. Second edition, pp. 45–46.

30. Third edition, pp. 35–36.

31. Ibid., pp. 37–39.

32. Ibid., p. 39; fourth edition, p. 42.

tion" might go. The very formulation of his third assumption indicates a reservation. So, also, for example, does the discussion, in the first edition, of methods to measure the efficiency of public administration. White warns that the measurement of so complex and elusive a subject will be the work of many years if, indeed, it can ever be achieved. "But practically we are constantly making judgments as to the success or failure of our institutions and their methods, and it is certainly in point to attempt to refine those judgments so far as possible. . . . From the scientific point of view, the search for tangible standards is of fundamental importance; and brief experience indicates that it has a practical value as well."[33]

White did not in his early years unreservedly assert that administrative practice could be wholly comprehended under scientific administrative theory, as he did not in his later years altogether abandon the search for scientific principles. But there was a cooling of his confidence in the scientific way, as may be seen in the later editions of the *Introduction* and in the direction of his later research interests. Even as late as the third edition of the *Introduction*, White wrote that "scientific management in principle is applicable to government as well as to industry."[34] But, in the last edition scientific management is assessed in different and more modest terms. White argues that the influence of the "underlying ideas of Taylorism" was not destroyed by "a more sophisticated skepticism" about the possibility of discovering "the one best way."

> The very great influence of the scientific management movement in government has been due, not to its specialized procedures, but to the ideas that administration is subject to constant improvement, that some ways of organizing and operating are better than others, and that it is the duty of top management to find the best way for a given staff under given conditions of operation—all of which may change unpredictably.[35]

---

33. First edition, p. 76. In the same place White speaks of a technique of rating city services devised by the Colorado League of Municipalities. The technique would now be regarded as extremely crude, and White saw the difficulties; but at the same time he did not wish to discourage this kind of attempt. His criticism is a delightful model of his characteristic circumspection: "Consideration of this plan will reveal a number of assumptions which require careful consideration before too great reliance can be placed on results. In general it may be said that it is easier to secure statistical material than to give it a sound interpretation in evaluating the efficiency of city government."

34. Third edition, p. 18.

35. Fourth edition, p. 21.

There is little, according to this description, that is "scientific" in the contribution of scientific management. If White is correct, the main force of Taylorism appears to have been dissipated into the most general notions of continuous self-improvement.

In the last two editions, White chose to emphasize the problematical character of administrative science by calling the introductory chapter "The Art of Administration."[36] In the last edition this chapter contains a section called "Administration—Science or Art" in which White much qualifies the earlier expectation of a "transformation" of administration from an art into a science.

> Whether these promising attempts to reduce some part of the field of administration to propositions of general, if not universal, validity will transform the study and practice of administration is still an open question. The effort is eminently worth making. . . . Since administration is certainly in part an art, non-scientific writing will continue to hold an important place. It may, however, progressively become a science, or a science bounded by cultural differences. . . .[37]

"A science bounded by cultural differences"—bounded by what White calls "the form and spirit of public administration in the United States." These words reflect a significant change in emphasis or, perhaps more exactly, in perspective.

Each edition of the *Introduction* contains a chapter dealing with "technical problems of large-scale organization and management" or "pure theory" of organization—the subject matter of the science of administration, as White generally understood it.[38] In the last three editions this chapter deals systematically and more or less abstractly with such matters as the individual and his position, the formation of administrative units, hierarchy, authority, and coordination.[39] It

---

36. The title in the first edition was "Administration and the Modern State" and in the second edition, "Scope and Nature of Public Administration."

37. Fourth edition, p. 9.

38. Second edition, p. 38; third edition, p. 27; fourth edition, p. 27. This chapter introduces the section of the book dealing with "structure and organization." In the last edition White attempts to recast the whole discussion in terms of "Hamilton's doctrine of executive unity." Fourth edition, p. 44. Thus what began in the first edition as a discussion of "The Forms and Methods of Integration" became in the second and third editions a discussion of "The Chief Executive as General Manager" and in the fourth edition a discussion of "The Quest for Unity: The Chief Executive."

39. In the fourth edition, however, White proceeds "from the top of the hierarchy down through its principal levels" (p. 29) rather than, as in the former editions, from the bottom up.

presents "some of the characteristic elements of large and complex organizations, viewed for the moment merely as huge aggregations of people at work."[40] By the last edition, this chapter is "bounded," literally, by "cultural differences." It opens with the distinctly political and constitutional question of the authority to determine organization.[41] And, to the otherwise unchanged conclusion, White adds this sentence:

> These generalities become more meaningful in the pages that follow, as they are translated in terms of the living experience of Presidents, Secretaries, staff advisers, and field agents, into what President John Tyler once described as "the complex, but at the same time beautiful, machinery of our system of government."[42]

Thus, generalities about organization become more meaningful as they are seen in terms of the living experience of American public administration. This statement stands in significant contrast to the main thrust of White's original intention, which was to give meaning to American public administration by seeing it in terms of generalizations about administration as a universal process.

Administration—the Central Problem of Modern Government. The fourth assumption is "that administration has become, and will continue to be the heart of the problem of modern government." White begins the first edition, as writings on American government had ordinarily begun, with a discussion of the constitutional separation of powers or functions, but he insists that the traditional assertion of the centrality of the legislative function misses the main characteristic of modern government.

> In an earlier and simpler age, legislative bodies had the time to deal with the major issues, the character of which was suited to the deliberations of the lay mind; they were primarily problems involving judgments on important questions of political ethics, such as the enfranchisement of citizens by abolishing property qualifications, the disposition of the public land, the disestablishment of the Anglican Church, or the liberalization of a Monarchist state. The problems

---

40. Ibid., p. 26.

41. This subject had also opened the comparable chapter in the first edition but had been dropped from the intervening ones, presumably on the ground that it was not appropriately dealt with in a chapter on the "pure theory" of organization.

42. Fourth edition, p. 43.

which crowd upon legislative bodies today are often entangled with, or become exclusively technical questions which the layman can handle only by utilizing the services of the expert. . . . These [experts] are not merely useful to legislators overwhelmed by the increasing flood of bills; they are simply indispensable. They are the government. One may indeed suggest that the traditional assignment of the legislature as the pivotal agency in the governmental triumvirate is destined at no distant date to be replaced by a more realistic analysis which will establish government as the task of administration, operating within such areas as may be circumscribed by legislatures and courts.[43]

Nor is this merely a matter of the administration doing what legislatures (and courts) formerly did.[44] The work of government has changed, so that the experts now "are the government." More is involved here than an enormous increase in the complexity and technicality of the problems of modern government; for however indispensable the technician or the expert might become, he would remain, as technician, subordinate to those dealing with the nontechnical, political problems. The point is that the political sphere, to which the technician is in principle subordinate, is no longer the place where the real problems arise. The great political questions are settled, and a form of government and distribution of powers appropriate when these questions were still unanswered is appropriate no longer.[45] This is the explanation of White's comment that, though the role of administration "in the logic of our governmental system is distinctly subordinate," yet "this should not conceal the fact . . . that the business of government in the twentieth century is

---

43. First edition, p. 6.

44. But see below, "The Role of Administration in the United States."

45. "Governmental problems have become intricate and ever more insistent. They call for solution with the aid of science, not with the wisdom of a ward politician." *The City Manager*, p. 295; compare *Introduction*, the first edition, p. 13, where White says that "science has revealed the objects to be achieved. . . ." In another study during this early period, White says of the old disputes over the dominance of power in the federal system that "the advent of a new society . . . took the issue boldly away from the constitutional lawyers and the orators, settled it in broad outline by the pressure of events and vested the *modus vivendi* largely in the hands of the administrators." *Trends in Public Administration* (New York: McGraw-Hill, 1933), p. 8; and see pp. 11, 235–56, 330–31; see in the same connection White's more recent essay "The Public Service of the Future" in *The Future of Government in the United States*.

fundamentally the business of administration."[46] On this ground it is possible to understand the culmination of White's four assumptions: that administration, itself essentially nonpolitical, is the heart of the problem of modern government.

The development of American administration. Especially in the first edition, White takes care to describe how administration came to occupy this central position in modern government. The source is a new social philosophy, growing out of "the industrial revolution and its many social, economic, and political implications. . . ."

> The industrial revolution has necessitated . . . a degree of social cooperation in which *laissez faire* has become impossible; and gradually the new environment is building up in men's minds a conception of the role of the state which approximates the function assigned it by the conditions of modern life. These new ideas involve the acceptance of the state as a great agency of social cooperation, as well as an agency of social regulation.[47]

Again there is the implication that the fundamental political questions are closed.

This analysis is carried forward, in the second edition, in a chapter entitled "Trends in the American Administrative System," in which White traces the development of the American administrative system—and by implication other advanced systems—from that appropriate to a simple rural civilization demanding little from government to that required by an urban, industrialized civilization dependent on government at every turn. As industrialization developed, "the relative equality of life in early America began to fade. . . and the line of separation between those who had much and those who had little became clearer and clearer." But political inequality had been largely extinguished; and the government, "responsive to the voting power of the masses," began to protect those harmed by unregulated industrial competition and to prevent the steady concentration of wealth in a few hands. "Here is one of the basic social changes which supports much modern administration."[48]

White did not press on with this broad inquiry, perhaps because the historical understanding from which it was derived came to seem doubtful, or, more likely, because by 1939 it seemed that what

---

46. First edition, p. 24. "The legislature, although of all organs of government the most representative, is forced by its own methods to stand at the greatest distance from the real business of governing." Ibid., p. 399.

47. Ibid., p. 8; compare ibid., pp. 463–66.

48. Second edition, p. 22.

distinguished American government and administration from other modern administrative states was more significant than what it had in common with them—to say nothing of nongovernmental administration.[49]

The form and spirit of American administration. As early as the second edition, White anticipates his later use of history less as a way of understanding the rise of administration and administrative science than as a way of understanding the political conditions and ends that give American public administration its special character. "As the result of well over a hundred years' uninterrupted development, an administrative structure has been evolved with characteristics peculiar to it. It is different from the Dutch, the Japanese, the Argentinean or the English civil service; it is peculiarly American."[50]

The title of the comparable chapter in the third and fourth editions indicates a clarification of intention; the discussion now centers not upon "trends" but upon "The Form and Spirit of Public Administration in the United States" and consists of a more extensive and systematic statement of the foundations of the American system. Its significance lies in the effort to describe what distinguishes American public administration, not only from administration in general, but from systems of public administration elsewhere—to give the study of public administration that meaningfulness that comes from its connection with "the complex, but at the same time beautiful, machinery of our system of government."

> The complex organization that carries on the common business of the American people bears today the unmistakable marks of its evolution: the initial Federalist conception emphasizing energy and responsibility, the Jacksonian insistence upon democracy in administration, the appeal for integrity and decency launched by the moral reformers after the Civil War, and the influence of technology and management in a later day.
>
> The catastrophic forces of depression and war, the international tensions since 1945, and the mere magnitude of the

---

49. See the prefaces to the third and fourth editions. There are in the later editions expressions of the early view of the great march of history toward the modern administrative state where the problems are technical ones; but it is of some significance that more stress is laid on the political as distinguished from the economic and technological causes. See third edition, pp. 5–6; fourth edition, pp. 3–4. Moreover, this view lost its former importance in White's overall understanding.

50. Second edition, p. 32.

administrative machine, at home and overseas, tend toward the dominance of the ideas of Alexander Hamilton rather than those of Andrew Jackson. The first half of the present century may indeed be called the new Hamiltonianism. The democratic ideal, nevertheless, has not lost strength even though the rule of rotation is circumscribed; and the power of moral standards in the public service is magnified, not lessened, by occasional personal failures.[51]

Originally, White's problem seemed to be to dispose of the political aspect of public administration, while acknowledging its importance, in order to get down to the real work of studying administration proper.[52] This was thought to be consistent with the historical trend thrusting administration into preeminence. White never entirely abandoned this view, but increasingly a different one made a strong claim upon his understanding. This was the view that the "political" element of public administration cannot be disposed of by the student of public administration, because it affects "administration" at every turn and is, therefore, an intrinsic, even fundamental, part of the study of public administration.[53]

White could still write in the fourth edition that "one day a philosopher-practitioner with a global experience may write a book that has as much meaning for Mexico as for Sweden, for the Indonesian Republic as for Israel."[54] But it is difficult to imagine, on the basis of this last edition, what such a book would include and even

---

51. Fourth edition, pp. 22–23; compare the first edition, pp. 475–76; third edition, p. 7.

52. "It ought to be possible in this country to separate politics from administration. Sound administration can develop and continue only if this separation can be achieved. For a century they have been confused, with evil results beyond measure. The [city] managers have an unparalleled opportunity and a deep obligation to teach the American people by their precept and conduct that their job is to administer the affairs of the city with integrity and efficiency and loyalty to the council, without participating in or allowing their work to be affected by contending programs or partisans." *The City Manager*, p. 301. See generally the important discussion here in chaps. 10, 11, 14. On politics and administration, compare *Introduction*, second edition, pp. 12–13; fourth edition, pp. 6–8.

53. See for example White's shifting interests as indicated by the chapter headings in the section of the *Introduction* dealing with public personnel administration. White's study of *Whitley Councils in the British Civil Service* (Chicago: University of Chicago Press, 1933) represents an early exploration of the kind of "personnel" question with which White was always (but especially in later years) concerned. See below, n. 65.

54. Fourth edition, p. 11; compare the fourth edition, p. viii.

whether it would be a book about public administration; it is even more difficult to imagine White pursuing, or seriously urging the pursuit, of the common denominator among, not only these nations, but also, say, the Red Cross, General Motors, Dartmouth College, and the Egyptian scribe.

The Role of Administration in the United States

Inevitably, White's growing concern with the form and spirit of public administration in the United States, and his declining confidence in a science of administration, affected his view of the role of public administration and public administrators in the United States and other similar governments.

In the early years, he had argued that modern government is characterized by the replacement of the great old constitutional and political questions by what are essentially technical questions of administration or management—thus the paradox that the central problem of modern times is not a political problem. But in spite of all the emphasis on "management," there was always some reservation concerning the supposedly nonpolitical nature of administration. In the first edition, White writes that the work of the administrative branch of the government involves judicial and legislative functions, as well as the executive functions to which the theory of the separation of powers would seem to confine it. As he put it in the next edition, "the essence of modern government is an obstinate intermingling of functions theoretically separate."[55] Much of the work formerly done by legislatures and courts is now performed by officials in that part of the government called "administration." In itself, this means only that certain legislative and judicial functions are performed by new agencies. Assuredly, this raises problems unsettled by the old separation of powers theory; but it does not necessarily follow that these new functions of the administration are any the less legislative or judicial, or that they should be performed according to any but the traditional legislative and judicial standards. Following this line of reasoning, it could be argued that administration is the heart of modern government in the sense that age-old political and constitutional problems now present themselves as problems of (or in) public administration.[56]

55. First edition, p. 5; second edition, p. 9.

56. It is of some interest to note, bearing in mind White's second assumption, that this is the theme around which the discipline of administrative law turns, so far as it is concerned with more than legal technicalities.

More explicitly, this argument might be taken to imply that administration is the heart of modern government precisely to the extent that public administration in modern government is not mere administration, but the main field within which political and constitutional problems now move. This is, in fact, a secondary and subdued theme of White's *Introduction*; and although it never entirely displaces the emphasis on administrative management, it receives more emphatic statement in the later editions.[57]

> The initiation of public policy has escaped legislative halls and now rests principally with official agencies and with citizen groups. The latter necessarily represent special segments of opinion and interest. The former have the moral obligation to represent the interest of all, to seek the public good. Being somewhat less vulnerable to outside pressures, public servants may cultivate the general welfare with greater detachment, with a surer reliance on rational analysis, with a clearer appreciation of long-run consequences, than representative bodies. This is not to say that their opinions should supersede the preferences of elected, representative bodies; it is merely to indicate the special values that are involved in the role which administration has now achieved.
>
> This point of view suggests that statesmen are needed in the higher ranks of administration rather than technicians.[58]

On the one hand, then, "administration is a process common to all group effort, public or private, civil or military, large scale or small scale."[59] On the other, "the role which administration has now achieved" in American government is *not* common to all groups or to all governments; and it seems to be in that uncommon role, not in the common process, that the heart of the problem of modern government is to be found. "The need, incessant and urgent, is for

---

57. Both themes are present in White's well-known and still valuable *Government Career Service* (1935); see especially pp. 23, 60–61, 89ff. Some readers may find interesting White's dialogue with politician T. V. Smith, in their *Politics and the Public Service* (New York: Harper and Brothers, 1939). See *The Future of Government in the United States*, pp. 209–15. Finally should be mentioned White's undoubtedly influential membership on the committee that drew up the 1955 Hoover Commission Task Force *Report on Personnel and Civil Service*, with its proposal for a senior civil service of a more than technical competence and responsibility.

58. Third edition, pp. 7–8; compare the second edition, pp. 12–13; fourth edition, pp. 6–8.

59. Third edition, p. 3; fourth edition, p. 1.

the administrative mind that can hold fast to the public interest and bind conflicting special interests to it by skillful contrivance, based on knowledge but exceeding mere *expertise.*" Exceeding, that is to say, mere administration or management. "In the highest reaches the administrative art touches the political, but it grows out of different soil."[60]

White did not undertake the further reconstruction of the *Introduction* that this wise remark might be thought to call for. He did not consider whether a soil consisting of mere managerial expertise could nurture the highest form of the administrative art, or whether his original view of the way to study public administration—to search for principles of the uniform process of administration—was compatible with his later view of the governing reason for studying it—the urgent and incessant need for administrative statesmanship.

The True Foundations

White was confronted with two different guides to his subject. One urged the need to penetrate beneath the superficial differences between administrative systems and political orders to an investigation of the universal process of administration. The other persistently maintained the overriding importance of the difference between public and private administration and between the political conditions and ends of one administrative system and those of another.

In the early editions, the tension between these two guides is evident in White's struggle to define public administration and to set future lines of study. However often he fell back on the political guide to make the boundaries of his subject, he still thought that the subject itself was the uniform process of administration. However, the theoretical problem—whether a mere process is worth studying and can be studied apart from what directs it—persisted. The conviction that such a study is possible and worthwhile was never abandoned, but it became much less marked. By the third edition, the conflicting claims of the "political" and the "administrative" guides to the study of public administration had been muted. The introductory chapter, considerably compressed, and with the theoretical problem smoothed over as far as possible, was followed by a pair of chapters in which the form and spirit of public administration in the United States and the pure theory of organization were given separate treatment. These warring approaches were not reconciled; but, under

---

60. Third edition, p. 8; compare the fourth edition, p. 521.

White's judicious superintendence, they were made to march together, quietly if not harmoniously, throughout the book.

The comment should be made, however, that the third and fourth editions represent less fully than the first two, White's conception of public administration at the time he wrote them. In the third edition there is found a distinct indication that White had come to regard the *Introduction* as having been built on only a partial view of public administration.

> The study of public administration has advanced to an extraordinary degree since 1920. As an intellectual discipline the field of public administration still lacks much, including an account of its historical development, a comprehensive statement in general terms of its underlying principles, an exact definition of its central concepts, a penetrating analysis of its foundations in psychology and sociology, and an interpretative account of its role in the structure of government and of life. Further, it needs to be related to the broad generalizations of political theory concerned with such matters as justice, liberty, obedience, and the role of the state in human affairs.[61]

According to this statement, the discipline of public administration still lacked (among other important things) an account of its historical development and a comprehensive statement of its theoretical and political foundations. White's last works deal with the history. Why did he not choose what seems to be the greater of these tasks? Part of the answer may be that, while White saw the need, he found himself unable to perceive the line of inquiry by which the true foundations might be exposed. He saw the merits, but also the limitations, of many different approaches. Characteristically, the suggestion for fundamental probing quoted above is replaced, in the fourth edition, by a list of useful approaches.

> There are many ways to study the phenomena of public administration. The first systematic American approach was through law and was devoted to the legal organization of public authorities, their legal forms of action, and the limits of their powers. . . . Subsequently came systematic writing primarily concerned with the nature of administrative institutions viewed as agencies of management, an approach related to the scientific management movement and reflecting the criterion of efficiency. More recently attention has been given to historical and biographical materials that re-

---

61. Third edition, p. 10.

veal the evolution of administrative systems and trends in thinking about administration. The nature of administration has also been explored by sociologists, as one among many significant social structures. Most recently the sociological-psychological school of behaviorists has made important contributions to the understanding of why officials and public employees act as they do. All of these approaches are relevant and from all of them come wisdom and understanding.[62]

Missing here is an expression of White's earlier concern for a comprehensive theoretical examination, or reexamination, of the study of public administration.[63] Indeed, White seems to express that complacent, undiscriminating eclecticism which is all too common in this field—the view that public administration consists, somehow, of an aggregate of an almost infinite number of "perspectives," institutional, political, sociological, psychological, technical, historical. Yet this judgment is insufficient when the work that occupied White's last years is taken into account.

It is interesting to consider the order in which White presents these ways of studying public administration. It appears at first glance to be a simple progression—and so perhaps the behaviorists would argue; but there is reason to believe that White did not so regard it. Although he had a genuine respect for the contributions of sociology and the social-psychological school of behaviorists, and had made some early contributions himself along these lines,[64] he was not altogether comfortable with the ways in which they led. He observed a brash young science drive assumptions and principles, which he had been one of the first to state systematically, to extremes that were foreign and distasteful to him. He saw this science carry the pursuit of an underlying process to the point where it seemed to abandon a concern with public administration altogether—a direction in which he had also been pressed but which he had resisted, in practice if not always in principle. As the rest of the discipline became more scientific and more concerned with process as process, White

---

62. Fourth edition, p. 11.

63. But see fourth edition, p. viii.

64. *The Prestige Value of Public Employment in Chicago: An Experimental Study* (Chicago: University of Chicago Press, 1929); *Further Contributions to the Prestige Value of Public Employment* (Chicago: University of Chicago Press, 1932). These were preceded by *Conditions of Municipal Employment in Chicago* (City of Chicago, 1925), which yields insight into the methodological assumptions of White's very early work and provides valuable information about Chicago city government in the 1920s.

became less so. As the most vigorous movements within the discipline shunted the political environment and ends of public administration more and more to the periphery, White brought them back to a prominent place.

It is misleading to regard White as having sought haven in the quiet eddy of history, while the rest of the discipline rushed by. Following what was in his case always a strong and sound instinct, he put aside as far as possible inherited theoretical apparatus and simply looked at public administration in the United States. He looked, it is true, at the public administration of yesterday, not today. The skill with which he described and the wisdom with which he interpreted what he saw have been almost universally acclaimed; and it is both likely and appropriate that his historical studies will be the most enduring products of a long and fruitful career. But the full significance of these books is missed if they are taken merely as history.

A thorough investigation of the importance of White's histories for the study of public administration would require another lengthy essay, but the essential point has been anticipated, and can be stated briefly. White entitled the histories: *The Federalists, The Jeffersonians, The Jacksonians*, and *The Republican Era*.[65] What was most important about public administration in the early years of the United States was not what it shared with all administration everywhere, but its character as *Federalist* administration. Federalist administrative theory and practice—best expressed in Hamilton's views of executive energy, Washington's conception of competence, and the notion of administration by gentlemen—were intrinsically connected with and subordinate to Federalist political and constitutional theory; and that, in the main, is the way White treats them.

White did not choose arbitrarily, as one perspective among many, the middle way of historical study for his mature years. It was

---

65. Published in New York by the Macmillan Company in 1948, 1951, 1954, and 1958, respectively. White's reconsideration of federalism in *The States and the Nation* (Baton Rouge: Louisiana State University Press, 1953) is consistent with the interpretation here and should be compared with the earlier discussions in the first edition of the *Introduction* (chap. 4 and pp. 469–70) and in *Trends in Public Administration* (part 1, esp. chap. 11). It is significant that during his last decade White chose as the subjects of his articles in the field of public administration: "Strikes in the Public Service" (*Public Personnel Review*, January 1949); "The Loyalty Program of the United States Government" (*Bulletin of the Atomic Scientists*, December 1951); and "The Senior Civil Service" (*Public Administration Review*, Autumn 1955; *Personnel Administration*, January–February 1956).

his way of looking at the field of public administration afresh, of seeking not merely one perspective, but the true perspective within which other partial perspectives find their focus. White's histories may be taken as an object lesson in the study of public administration: which aspects are primary and which secondary; which perspectives are narrow and which broad; which ways lead to the heart and which to some nonessential limb.

This vital lesson in the discipline's standards of relevance and significance was taught, as White taught best, by example rather than by systematic theoretical exposition. Some of the original assumption—and the difficulties to which they give rise—are still present in the histories.[66] Theoretical precision is not to be expected. Although concerned with the theoretical problems of his discipline for most of his life, White's was not fundamentally a theoretical mind. His true compass was his uncommonly good common sense, which enabled him to make substantial contributions to the study of public administration, even while leaving unresolved some of its most basic questions.

This quality also led him to choose administrative history as his way of beginning to relate the study to what he called, in the third edition of the *Introduction*, "the broad generalizations of political theory concerned with such matters as justice, liberty, obedience, and the role of the state in human affairs."[67] White would have been the first to insist that his histories do not constitute a comprehensive "interpretative account" of the role of American public administration "in the structure of government and of life." But it is precisely White's breadth of concern—his concern with the relation between public administration and matters such as justice, liberty, obedience, and the role of the state in human affairs—that gives these books their special excellence and a great part of their value to present-day students of public administration.

---

66. Thus providing some ground for Dwight Waldo's criticism that "the dominant perspective in these volumes plainly is the POSDCORB perspective." *Perspectives on Administration* (University, Ala.: University of Alabama Press, 1956), p. 59. That the POSDCORB, or pure theory of organization, "perspective" is present is, indeed, plain, for example in White's numerous remarks on the state of the "administrative art" at different times. Whether, contrary to the argument here, this perspective is dominant, whether it provides the overall orientation, the standards of relevance and importance, the reader will have to judge for himself by reading the histories and reflecting on the relations between their parts and their whole.

67. Third edition, p. 10.

17

The Role of Government in Society

Big Government, we are likely to think, is a rather recent problem of American life. It is striking, therefore, to discover the extent to which the problems that so concern us today in this vast country—our huge governmental establishments, our various programs of public activity, our enormous national defense establishments, our sprawling federal bureaucracy—were anticipated in the debates surrounding the formation of our American nation. We Americans have not merely grown into Big Government; we were born as Big Government.

I want to give a brief account of the issues involved in the debates over the Constitution so far as they bear upon the question of Big Government and then to say something about what seem to me the five critical issues of American political history and their implications for the role of government in society. My theme throughout will be the fundamental American commitment to the large republic and to Big Government and the problems involved in this commitment.

I

Many Americans in the 1770s and the 1780s were doubtful whether any free government could exist over so large a territory as the whole United States of America. Even though the United States were at that time strung out along the eastern seaboard and contained only some 3 million people, Americans knew that the country they saw around them was only the beginning of a great new enterprise. Whether such an enterprise could be successfully conducted on the principles of free democratic government seemed to many of them profoundly doubtful. Reason, experience, and the opinions of the greatest thinkers about government seemed to agree that, whereas strong monarchical government might extend over a large territory, a self-governing republican community could only extend over a relatively small

---

This previously unpublished essay comes from a speech delivered at the University of North Carolina on February 25, 1967.

area. For whereas the monarch can infuse his energy and direction through his agents even into distant provinces, the strength and vigor of a republican government depend on the voluntary obedience and attachment of self-governing citizens; and that can only be secured in a small, homogeneous community where men can know one another, feel a mutual sense of respect and obligation, and share a common patriotism. In a large state, they thought, there are likely to be too many differences of wealth, social position, and private interests for the citizens to have a strong sense of community responsibility.

Therefore, these men thought along the following lines. Let the real governments of the United States be the state governments, where something like the small republics of the olden times were approximated. Let these governments be combined into a federation or league, designed for the limited aims of protecting the small governments from foreign dangers which they could not meet adequately themselves and securing certain minimal common commercial advantages. The United States were not one great nation, in this view, but numerous small ones, confederated together for certain very limited purposes.

It is difficult for us today to understand the enormous significance of the rejection of this then widely held opinion—that free republican government can only survive in a small territory. It was the great achievement of the framers and defenders of the Constitution of 1787 to persuade Americans to reject this idea and to build one great, self-governing nation. This achievement was based on two arguments, which remain the basic justifications of our big society and its Big Government today.

First, it was contended that a mere league or confederation of the very kind that many proposed would inevitably be too weak even for common defense. It was unrealistic to try to establish a central authority, responsible for national defense, without giving it the structure and the powers of a genuine government. If Americans wanted basically to trust their fate to numerous petty, squabbling republics, let them do so, men like Alexander Hamilton argued; but if they determined to have a government of the Union, then let that be a government capable of performing the tasks any government must perform. The opponents to the Constitution—the defenders of the small republics—were trying to have their cake and eat it too. Hamilton, and the other Federalists, drummed home the implications of this argument. If you are going to have a Union, you need a government to protect it, and that means a government with the *power* to protect it. And since no nation can determine what its enemies may do, so no nation, Hamilton insisted, can afford to limit in advance the acts that it may need to commit and the power that it may need to mobilize.

This argument seems to me massively persuasive. It is difficult, for example, for a politician to argue with any show of consistency both that the nation should be strong enough to confront any possible foreign danger and that the nation should never involve itself, say, in the educational system of the country. For such an involvement might well, under some circumstances, be necessary to meet foreign danger. And the same argument applies wherever a means-end connection can be shown between some aspect of our country's life, no matter how local it seems, and the great end of national defense.

Yet this Federalist argument also brings us to a massive dilemma. What happens to our cherished idea of *limited government* under this argument? Can a government that is capable of meeting illimitable demands be a limited government in any meaningful sense? This dilemma—our commitment to limited government and at the same time our commitment to a government of unlimited power in the pursuit of national security—is one of the great themes of American political history.

The second basic argument in favor of the Constitution was that, not only was a real national government necessary for national security, but that it was necessary for domestic purposes as well. The wisest of the Federalists thought that the small, homogeneous republics, so much admired by the Anti-Federalists, were in fact poor preservers of good government and individual liberties. They thought that these petty democracies were not only weak abroad but tumultuous and tyrannical at home. While wholly committed to popular government, the defenders of the Constitution thought that popular government faces one great danger to which all popular governments of former times succumbed, namely, the tendency of the mass of the people to form unjust combinations against the few. This danger was likely to be magnified within the cramped confines of a small state, where economic opportunities are narrow and the number of different interests small. The line between rich and poor, many and few, is likely to become sharply defined and ominously rigid—and when the many combine, the liberties of all are in peril. Only a large and rich territory under a single government can provide that diversity and opportunity by means of which the elementary conflict of rich and poor, many and few, majority and minorities, may be softened and diffused.

Now the implication of this Federalist argument is that the way to guarantee individual freedom is not to preach good behavior, not

354

to try to instill patriotism, not to try to foster homogeneous opinions. The Anti-Federalists argued that these things could only be done in the small community; but the Federalists replied that these preachings simply do not work in *any* kind of community. Men's private desires and private passions are too strong. Rather than to try to suppress, or transform, the self-seeking desires of men, the American founders proposed to channel and guide those desires, through the instrumentality of the Constitution, so that the results would be, even despite the intentions of the men themselves, publicly beneficial. For this purpose, the big, booming, commercial republic is ideally suited, providing as it does lots of elbow space, lots of interests, lots of differences, and lots of opportunity, out of which a genuinely free republic (or democracy) could be formed.

Thus the solution to the great problem of republican government—how to prevent the majority from tyrannizing over minorities—was to be found in releasing and channeling private interests and desires rather than in trying to promote a commitment to a general interest. But the problem is that even the Federalists had to concede finally that the system rests on some kind of public commitment, some kind of moral community, some respect and obedience at least to the Constitution. And yet, the difficulties of achieving such a public-spiritedness in a huge country come again to the fore. Indeed, there is the further question whether the qualities of citizenship needed to support the Constitution are in fact undermined by the sanction and stimulation that the great commercial republic gives to the private interests and the private life. This fundamental objection raised by the Anti-Federalists against the Constitution was never wholly laid to rest. It remains as a question about our government. Do we not require, to put it in its most elementary terms, patriotism, devotion to a common good, a moral community, in order that our political system shall survive and be worth surviving? But can we find a capacity for commitment to a common good in this big society that seems to be devoted wholly to the glorification of the private life and the private interest? This is the second great theme of American political history.

The original American decision for Big Society and Big Government left succeeding generations, then, to grapple with the two great themes of limited government and the moral community.

Moving beyond the founding, the American regime has confronted five great issues, which were to a very large extent framed but not solved by the initial decision for Big Government that I have been discussing. These issues have to do with (1) national defense, (2) national supremacy versus states' rights, (3) the regulation of the economy, (4) the welfare state, and (5) the relations between the races. I want to say something about each of these, linking them with the two great themes that I have described.

II

One of the chief criticisms of the Constitution of 1787 was the absence, in the critics' view, of any adequate protection against the dangers of a standing army. The dangers to individual liberty of armies, of the extraordinary powers of government in wartime, and of the transcendent demands of total mobilization are commonplace. One only has to think of Lincoln's suspension of the writ of habeas corpus, the relocation of Japanese-Americans during World War II, President Dwight Eisenhower's warning of the influence of the military establishment, and the enormous proportion of the national budget devoted to defense.

In this sphere we see with harsh clarity the unlimited implication of a governmental capacity to provide for the national defense. The very government that is formed to protect individual liberty can demand the most precious liberty, life itself. The Anti-Federalists were emphatic about the dangers, but they provided little in the way of solution. Their reliance on a citizen militia was wholly unrealistic even in those times, unless it was to be assumed—what no country can afford to assume—that there simply would be no substantial need to defend the country against foreign enemies.

It is a sign of the health of our republican institutions that they have been so well able to yield to the unlimited needs of total mobilization and yet to snap back pretty well to their normal limited character when the emergency has passed. How we have managed to do this is an important and fascinating subject, but I can make here only four observations that are especially important for our present purposes.

First, it bears repeating—though it is often said—that we Americans must learn not merely to respond to emergency and then relax to our earlier peaceful condition, but to live more or less permanently with the demands of an active part in international affairs, with tension and limited wars. We require more than we now have in the way of intellectual, moral, and institutional capacities for more or less indefinite cold war.

Second, the military establishment is not so monolithic as we sometimes think. One of the sources of limitation is the differences and even the squabbling within the military establishment, among the services, between the civilian and the military services, between the Pentagon and the State Department. These differences are not always dignified and they are usually confusing, but they are one of our major devices of limited government in this area today.

Third, as the Federalists pointed out in this connection, the basic safeguard is to be found in the good sense, the manly independence, and the patriotism of the people. The institutions of governmental power and the devices of restraint and limitation depend ultimately on their foundation in a sound moral community.

Fourth, although the demands of war and national emergency are dangerous, they can also be salutary. National emergencies tend to foster a sense of devotion to the common good and thus to offset, to some extent, our extreme individualism. Obviously this does not mean that we should invite national emergency in order to foster patriotism. But it does put the issue in a broader and better perspective. And it has important implications for more or less normal times. The army, for example, is not merely a necessary threat to individual liberty. It is also—or it can be—a powerful force in educating young men in our common values and in promoting a commitment to the common good. National service more broadly conceived—including for example the foreign and domestic peace corps and a national teacher corps—can help to weld our young people together into a common citizenry—into a community that, while still rich and diverse, is something more than an aggregate of self-seeking individuals.

III

The issue of common defense has of course been a perennial one, running from the War of the Revolution through the war in Vietnam. The other four issues that I listed have also been perennial: all of them in some way were present at the beginning and none of them has been wholly disposed of. But the four domestic issues reached their peaks at different times and fall into a rough chronology, which provides a sketch of American political history.

The first of these great domestic issues was, as I have said, the great constitutional question about the character of the Union—the supremacy of the Union versus states' rights.

When in April 1861 Abraham Lincoln called forth the militia of the United States, authorized an immediate increase in the regular military force, and instituted a blockade of the Southern ports, he was, in his view, enforcing the national laws against illegal local resistance. In the view of the seceding states, on the other hand,

357

Lincoln's actions amounted to a "declaration of war made against this Confederacy."[1]

The Southern constitutional argument is well known: The Union was formed by the states and given limited powers. When the government of the Union exceeded its powers, the states were entitled to withdraw from the Union; and this right was not a revolutionary right but strictly legal and constitutional.

This argument was an extension of the "confederal" argument that was made at the time of the founding and that was, in the main, rejected. But there had been compromise; there was some ambiguity; there was some ground (although I do not think it was very strong) for the secessionists' position. In any case, Lincoln put the force of arms behind the principle that the United States was fundamentally one great nation and not a confederacy of many small ones.

Back of the constitutional argument was a version of the limited government argument. The Confederacy stood on what it conceived to be the ground of limited government, that is to say, on the ground of the limited character of the federal government. Lincoln, on the other hand, took the Hamiltonian position that the federal government was limited only by the needs of the nation.

> This relative matter of National power, and State rights, as a principle, is no other than the principle of *generality*, and *locality*. Whatever concerns the whole, should be confided to the whole—to the general government; while, whatever concerns *only* the State, should be left exclusively, to the State. This is all there is of original principle about it.[2]

The difficulty of course—the problem of federalism—is that there seems to be a tendency for matters, once merely local, to become of national concern—education comes to mind as a good example today. And this tendency makes us wonder whether gradually all of the powers and rights of the states will, on Lincoln's argument, be absorbed by the national government. This must be allowed to be a genuine and legitimate question. In the face of this question, three responses seem to me essential.

First, I think that Lincoln's basic point must be conceded. We can see the force of this by asking whether anyone could argue for a national government that does *not* have a capacity to deal with questions of genuinely national concern?

---

1. Jefferson Davis, Message to Congress, April 29, 1861.

2. Abraham Lincoln, Message to Congress in Special Session, July 4, 1861, in Roy P. Basler, ed., *The Collected Works of Abraham Lincoln* (New Brunswick, N.J.: Rutgers University Press, 1953), vol. 4, p. 435.

Second, while we need to be careful about letting matters be drawn into the jurisdiction of the national government that do not need to be there, even the greatest and most intelligent care of this kind will not change and could not have changed the situation very much. The basic reason for the centralization has not been carelessness or federal grasping, but the nationalization of our lives—the largely inevitable working out of our destiny as a great republic requiring a Big Government to run it.

Third, it is more fruitful to think of federalism in broader terms than "states' rights versus national power." What we are really concerned about is not states' rights. The Federalists were certainly right in saying that the general government was not established for the sake of the states but for the sake of the *people* of the states. Our federalism is valued because it is one of our institutions of limited government. Federalism is a way of dispersing political authority, of setting up checks, of opening up the political process to the examination of affected localities and groups and individuals.

And when we look at our government in this way, we will learn that federalism is much more alive than it sometimes seems to be if we think only about states' rights. Not only are the states doing more and spending more than ever before, but there has been a healthy and dynamic partnership between nation and states, involving grants in aid, decentralization of various kinds, consultation with local and state authorities, and cooperative federalism. Moreover, the impact of local checks and influence may be seen in our system, not merely in what the states do, but in the very significant local and state influence in our political parties, in the Congress, and in the national administration.

This is not to say that there are not serious problems and perhaps dangerous centralization; but it does suggest that the picture is not so black as it is often painted and far more complicated, both for good and for ill.

Arguments over federalism always involve more fundamental questions about the character of the American union. In the Civil War the root issue was of course slavery and, more particularly, the implications of slavery for the American regime. Connected with the "state" side of the constitutional argument were the argument that the states ought to be left to deal with the question of slavery in their own ways and a growing tolerance for the idea of slavery as not merely an unfortunate necessity but a positive good. Lincoln, on the other hand, while accepting the constitutional settlement which required leaving the institution of slavery undisturbed where it existed, would do nothing to sanction it in principle.

In his words and thoughts on this great issue Lincoln confronted perhaps more profoundly than ever before or since what I have described as the second great theme of Big Government—the connection between the private, self-seeking individual and the community and its good. It was Lincoln's great aim to combine the Anti-Federalists' sense of moral community with the Federalists' emphasis on the nobility and greatness of the whole American nation. Although no shallow abolitionist, no easy moralizer, no quick idealist, Lincoln saw that the health and the integrity of the American political community depended upon a willingness to confront and to affirm the great principle that all men are created equal. That principle permits of much disagreement and of many variations in practice. It may even tolerate, at some times and for the sake of other goods, the gross abuse and injustice of chattel slavery. But it cannot tolerate any *principled* defense of the enslaving of one man by another, or even a refusal to deny the injustice of such enslavement. As the great black abolitionist, Frederick Douglass, saw very well, Lincoln's most profound object was not so much to free blacks as to free whites from a corruption of the principles on which their own community and therefore their own lives as individuals were based.

IV

Once the great constitutional question of the American nation was settled, that nation began to confront the implications of the private economic energies thereby released. Developing the continent, often with government encouragement and aid, men and corporations accumulated vast fortunes and, along with them, vast social and political, as well as economic, power. It became increasingly clear that liberty was threatened less by the government or by the majority than by the economically powerful few. The Big Economy threw down a challenge that only Big Government could meet. In the late nineteenth century, therefore, and on into the twentieth century, government undertook to regulate and control and check the harmful consequences of those economic strivings. These activities began in the days of the Granger laws, of trustbusting, of the interstate commerce commissions; and they extend into our own days of massive economic regulation and planning.

Generally, there seem to have been three (overlapping) stages in this matter: (1) trustbusting—breaking up economic concentration; (2) regulation—guiding and controlling the bad aspects of economic concentration; and (3) planning—taking a positive and more or less comprehensive responsibility for the economic health of the community. A few major points should be made here.

Obviously there is much room for disagreement over the role of the government in the economic life of the country. But it is hard to see how the story could have been much different in fundamental respects, once the decision for one nation and one national economy had been made.

We might disagree, for example, about whether the government ought to try to bust the trusts or to regulate them; but we could scarcely deny the need for the national government somehow to take a responsibility for checking the harmful consequences of tremendous concentrations of economic power.

We might disagree about whether the government should undertake the development of peaceful uses of atomic energy or leave it to be done by private developers; but we can scarcely deny the overwhelming national interest in this development and the responsibility of government to protect that interest.

We might disagree with the Wagner Act restrictions on employers or the Taft-Hartley reciprocal restrictions on unions; but it is hard to imagine a serious argument that the national government should stay out of the field of labor relations altogether.

Yet here again one wonders what has happened to limited government. There seems to be no economic enterprise free of governmental inspection, controls, regulation, and check—to say nothing of taxation. And since the economic life is involved in almost all we do, so there seems to be nothing free of the prying eye and grasping or regulating hand of government.

It may not help much to know that this is nothing new, but that is the fact. The Anti-Federalists objected to the new Constitution precisely on this ground—that taking the taxing power of the national government alone, nothing would be safe from the claws of this new Big Government.

Again, the Hamiltonian argument seems hard to refute. If you want a government to undertake the protection of vital national interests, then that government must be given whatever power may be necessary—and that means that there is nothing that the government may not have to do under some circumstances.

This dangerous conclusion is mitigated in various ways; and Hamilton and his friends pointed to the constitutional system of checks and balances as a great defense of limited government under circumstances where the *powers* of government must be very extensive. But it has been precisely in the area of economic regulation that grave questions have arisen regarding our traditional constitutional checks and balances. The characteristic features of the regulatory agency, for example—a chief instrument of economic regulation—are (1) very large discretion of a kind formerly exercised by legislative authorities; (2) mixtures of legislative, executive, and judicial powers; and therefore (3) enormous powers over private economic life that are, to a considerable extent, final. So there is enormous discretionary power and the old checks and balances seem much weakened.

However, there are some substantial mitigations. First, there are internal checks. Like the military establishment, these agencies are not so monolithic as they seem, and individual liberty is protected by the internal jostling. Internal checks and procedural protections can improve this. This is a chief concern of administrative law. Second, the bureaucracy itself can be a check with its tendency toward system, fair procedure, and conservatism. Third, there are new forms of public-private relationships. If the government sometimes goes into business—for example, the TVA—so private businesses are increasingly used to perform functions of government: military contracts of all kinds, research and development in many fields, and manpower training and economic opportunity programs.

In addition to the questions that economic regulation raises about limited government, there are the questions it raises about the other of my two themes, the moral basis of the American community.

Any form of economic regulation carries two absolutely inevitable implications. The first is that the unregulated economic activity of individuals is somehow deficient. This is an obvious point—it is at the bottom of our need for government in the first place. But it deserves emphasis, and it is directly connected with the Anti-Federalist criticism—that the commercial system increasingly demands public regulation, while undermining those qualities in the people and their leaders that can provide and support such regulation.

The second implication is that there is need of some standard or principle beyond the immediate self-interest of those being regulated. Sometimes this general principle can be defended narrowly as necessary to the individual interests of all—for example, enforcing contracts, the general law-preserving function. But this is already a leap from the individual, for it is *not* always in the interest of the individual to keep a contract or to obey the law. More interestingly, economic regulation leads us to consider the quality of our common life. When we have to distribute radio and television frequencies, for example—which their sheer scarcity almost forces government to do—we have to give some thought to the standard according to which they are to be distributed and, therefore, to the community interest in this area. Or when we decide how to distribute the burden of income tax we have to consider, not only some technical economic issues, but also the broad question of what is fair and just, which takes us beyond economics.

Thus economic regulation is so critical precisely because it presses us to consider the quality of our lives, individually and in common, and the government's inevitable and powerful effects on those lives.

V

With the great constitutional questions settled and concentration of economic power checked and regulated, if not altogether eliminated, the government faced—notably in some of the legislation of the New Deal and in our own time in the "welfare state"—the problem of ameliorating the conditions of life of individuals harmed or threatened or cast off by our industrial society. Some labor legislation, unemployment compensation, social security, welfare programs, Medicare, programs for the protection of consumers—in dozens, indeed hundreds, of ways, the government seeks to protect the weak individual confronted and threatened in one way or another by the enormous apparatus of modern life with which he can scarcely deal as an individual.

The general principle here is clear enough—and it is a direct consequence of our commitment to Big Society, Big Economy, and Big Government. Our huge, sprawling, impersonal industrial and commercial society casts some individuals off, or harms them, or puts them in jeopardy, or deprives them of reasonable security—all this under conditions where the individuals cannot do much to protect themselves. Thus, the extent of this defenselessness is of course a consequence of Big Society and Big Economy; but the way this need is met is also an aspect of Big Government. This kind of "welfare" function—so far as necessary (and it is always necessary to some extent)—would have been dealt with in more "natural" ways in smaller, less impersonal systems by family and local authorities.

Here again, there is a problem of what seems to be an unlimited involvement of government in all aspects of life—a problem of the weak individual at the mercy of a paternalistic but still huge and impersonal and sometimes unjust government. This *is* a problem— but again the alternative is not the autonomous individual or the individual in the small, precommercial society, but the individual faced with the less just and less friendly forces of the industrial society.

Here again there are internal checks: the representation of affected persons, state involvement in welfare programs and the checks they provide, and the bureaucracy's tendency toward system and fairness.

On the moral side there are several questions: (1) the question of the demoralizing effects of the large, industrial republic, to which the welfare state is a kind of response; (2) the question of demoralization caused by these welfare programs—the undermining of independence, enterprise, and self-respect; and (3) the whole question of the extent and nature of governmental responsibility in this area that we call, with such significant ambiguity, "welfare."

This leads, in turn, to the broader question of education and the responsibilities of Big Government in that vital field. Perhaps we are entering another great stage in our domestic political history.

VI

Finally we turn to the last of the issues I listed. In 1954 the Supreme Court of the United States handed down its famous opinion in *Brown v. Board of Education*, holding that separate educational facilities for blacks are inherently unequal and therefore unconstitutional under the Fourteenth Amendment prohibition on any state against denying any person the equal protection of the laws. The Court thereby stimulated, if it did not set off, a movement that is far too complex for me to deal with here. I will just try to link it with my general discussion.

An important aspect of the limited government question arises in connection with another important Supreme Court case in this area which, in a way, puts the issue in its clearest terms. In *Shelley v. Kraemer* (1948) the Court held that while restrictive covenants voluntarily entered into by white property holders to prevent the sale or rental of their property to nonwhites are not in themselves unconstitutional, such covenants cannot be enforced by state courts without violating the Fourteenth Amendment. This has implications for the private sphere because of the ultimate dependence of the private sphere on the protection of the law. We seem to have two conflicting principles. On the one side is the private sphere, including even the right to discriminate. This has implications for housing, education, and social relations. On the other side is the public doctrine—no discrimination on the basis of race.

How can these two principles be reconciled? One possibility is that the public principle is compatible with a good deal of flexibility—for example, open housing laws, going along with a good deal of self-selection. (But consider the Civil Rights Commission's recent report on school segregation in all parts of the country.) Another possibility is that maybe this area is of such overwhelming importance to the common life of the American community that here, in the area of race discrimination, there is no legitimate private sphere.

Regarding race relations and the second theme of Big Government, the question of the moral basis of the community, the main point is, I suppose, pretty clear. There is still much legitimate disagreement about both constitutional and prudential questions in the sphere of race relations—and I, for one, take these very seriously and don't find them easy to answer. But there can surely be no disagreement about the necessity of full participation, on equal terms in every significant respect, of blacks in the common life of our country. As in the days of slavery, this principle is as much demanded for the sake of the whites and their own self-understanding and self-respect as for the sake of the blacks. James Baldwin is not merely being bitter-clever when he refers to the "white problem." The most damaging effect of blind race hate and injustice is on the bigot and oppressor, North or South; and the most serious political danger is that this corruption might destroy our community, not mainly through the harm the white community can do to the black part of the community, but through the harm that that majority can do to itself by undermining its own moral and political integrity.

VII

To conclude, we are committed to an emphatically national government with a capacity to do whatever is necessary for national security, whether that involves total mobilization or limited diplomatic and military activity over a long period of time. We are committed to national solutions of national problems. We are committed specifically to national economic planning on a massive scale. We are committed to a national guarantee of a welfare floor to provide minimum standards of physical security, health, and education for all. And we are committed to national action to ensure racial justice and the full and equal participation of all races in the common life of the country, whatever exactly that may mean and whatever it may require. It is hard to see how any responsible American would wish us to withdraw these commitments even if we could.

Involved in these commitments, however, are many of the things we tend to dislike about Big Government in the United States today: extensive governmental programs of all kinds; centralization of at least major decisions and programs; the huge scale; the destruction of the small, human-sized community; bureaucratization, with its impersonalization and red tape; high taxes and other demands from government, especially in the military sphere; in sum, Big Government, Big Stakes, Big Demands, Big Risks, and Big Opportunities.

It is pointless merely to object to these things, but it does make sense to be conscious of difficulties and dangers and always alert to what can be done to avoid the bad and promote the good that our circumstances make possible.

There are no easy solutions, but I can suggest four base lines for further thinking and study.

First, in thinking about limited government, the basic limitation cannot be found in governmental powers—in what the government can do—but must be found in the way the government is organized and the way it acts.

Second, there is a need to look in new places for the institutional and procedural checks and balances that contribute to our modern limited government—for example, so-called creative [or cooperative] federalism, internal checks in government, the political functions of the bureaucracy, and the development of new and significant relations between the public and the private spheres.

Third, there is a need to look for approximations to the small republic in the midst of Big Government—for subordinate communities that can serve some of the functions that men like the Anti-Federalists saw were possible only in relatively small, "human-sized" communities. These can only mitigate the hugeness of Big Society and Big Government, but they can help.

Finally, there is a need to concern ourselves more than we often do with the moral foundations of Big Government. We need to inquire into the extremely difficult question of how to make a common good out of individual interests. If we find that we cannot have and do not want a country of "every man for himself," then we need to give some hard thought to the institutional, educational, and other ways of strengthening the commitment of each American to the community of all Americans.

PART FIVE

The Presidency and Statesmanship

18
The Creation of the Presidency

"There is an idea," Alexander Hamilton wrote in *The Federalist*, "which is not without its advocates, that a vigorous executive is inconsistent with the genius of republican government." So well did our founders build that the power and implications of that idea are now largely forgotten. Yet Hamilton did not go on to deny, as his reader might expect, that there is an inherent inconsistency between the executive principle and the republican principle. He asserted, rather, that the advocates of republican government had better *hope* that there is no such inconsistency, because executive energy is a requisite in any case: "Energy in the executive is a leading character in the definition of good government" (*Federalist* 70).

On the first of June, 1787, nine and a half months before Hamilton wrote these words, the delegates of the Philadelphia convention reached the Virginia proposal dealing with the executive.[1] James Wilson proposed that the executive consist of a single person, whereupon, according to James Madison's notes, "a considerable pause" ensued. It was as if the delegates were reluctant to enter into what they knew was the enormously difficult, perhaps insoluble, problem of establishing an adequate executive that would be consistent with the principles of republican government. Benjamin Franklin—on this occasion as on others the conscience of the convention—urged the delegates on to do their duty, observing, when the chairman asked if the members were ready to vote, "that it was a point of great importance and [he] wished the gentlemen would deliver their sentiments on it before the question was put."

The ensuing discussions and decisions regarding the executive are the central subject of this "excellent volume," as Edward S.

This essay was originally published as the introduction to Charles C. Thach, Jr., *The Creation of the Presidency, 1775–1789* (Baltimore: The Johns Hopkins Press, 1969). It is reprinted with permission from The Johns Hopkins University Press.

1. Max Farrand, ed., *The Records of the Federal Convention of 1787*, 4 vols. (New Haven: Yale University Press, 1937), vol. 1, p. 65.

Corwin has justly called it.[2] Charles Thach lucidly analyzes the experience with inadequate executives in the states and in Congress. He traces with care and judgment the Philadelphia deliberations, explaining the different roles of the main participants, following the gradual building of the presidency, and describing its place in the emerging constitutional scheme. Extending his view to the first Congress, he takes up the debate on the power of removal of executive officers, arguing persuasively that the modern view of presidential responsibility for administration is not an innovation, but an implication of the institutions and principles laid down by the founders. For the reader who is interested in following the creation of the presidency as it was seen by the men involved, Thach's book is so useful and so sound as to be indispensable. It is a pleasure to observe how well good scholarship directed to important questions holds up over the years.

The reader not primarily concerned with American history may tend to assume that there will be little to interest him in Thach's chapters on the state and national executives prior to 1787 (chapters 2 and 3). That would be a mistake, for in these chapters the author explores the two great themes that always have run through any substantial consideration of the presidency—the themes, in the version of Richard Neustadt, of "clerkship" and "leadership."[3] As Thach shows, there were two distinct lines of development that found expression in the strong, independent executive of the Constitution. In the state governments, experience with the instability, imprudence, and injustice caused by legislative dominance led to an awareness of the need to provide institutional support for the paper boundaries of limited government and, to this end, to strengthen and ensure the independence of the executive. As Madison put it in Philadelphia, "Experience had proved a tendency in our governments to throw all power into the Legislative vortex. The Executives of the States are in general little more than Cyphers; the legislatures omnipotent. If no effectual check be devised for restraining the instability & encroachments of the latter, a revolution of some kind or other would be inevitable."[4] The state governments generally lacked any principle, in the somewhat sharper language of John Marshall, "which could resist the wild projects of the moment, give

---

2. Edward S. Corwin, *The President, Office and Powers* (New York: New York University Press, 1957), p. 316.

3. Richard Neustadt, *Presidential Power* (New York: John Wiley & Sons, 1960), chap. 1.

4. Farrand, *Records*, vol. 2, p. 35.

the people an opportunity to reflect, and allow the good sense of the nation time for exertion."[5] That executive strength was such a principle, Thach shows, was a major lesson of the state experience. Of course, some of the states were relatively free of these deficiencies. New York, in particular, had a well-organized, independent executive, capable of weighty political participation and leadership; and Thach shows how important the model of the New York executive was to the American founders.

In Congress the problem was different. Experience with the difficulties of congressional and committee administration, and with the lack of system and vigor in carrying out the resolves of the developing nation, led to a growing awareness of the need for an effective administrative instrument distinct from the Congress. The movement toward an independent executive here was not to check the Congress, but to serve it. The views were similar to those of a later generation of civil service reformers who advocated an independent, but emphatically subordinate, administration. The eighteenth-century arguments have a distinctly contemporary ring. Washington argued for "more responsibility and permanency in the executive bodies." Hamilton complained of the "want of method and energy in the administration" and the "want of a proper executive." "Congress is, properly, a deliberative corps, and it forgets itself when it attempts to play the executive." Robert Morris insisted, in his bluff way, that Congress "must pay good executive men to do their business as it ought to be done, and not lavish millions away by their own mismanagement." Thomas Jefferson himself—one of the main proponents of an adequate national executive—insisted that "nothing is so embarrassing as the details of execution." "I have ever viewed the executive details as the greatest cause of evil to us, because they in fact place us as if we had no federal head, by diverting the attention of that head from great to small objects. . . ."[6]

While these two developments combined in a rather general opinion by 1787 in favor of a vigorous and independent executive, some significant differences remained, and it was by no means clear how they would be resolved. In particular, the administrative principle, while calling for the executive's independence, implies executive subordination to the legislature; the political principle, on the other hand, implies an equality (if not, indeed, a superiority) of the executive in the constitutional scheme. The beginning of wisdom about the American presidency is to see that it contains both princi-

5. Thach, *Creation of the Presidency*, p. 51.
6. Ibid., pp. 62–71.

ples and to reflect on their complex and subtle relation. And one of the best ways to begin that enterprise is with Thach's discussion of the early state and national experience.

Moving forward to Philadelphia, Thach shows the delegates taking up the problem of the republican executive, reluctantly at first, often haltingly, but finally with confidence and wisdom. These deliberations are somewhat difficult to follow in Madison's notes and the other records. The preeminence of the delegates' concern with the question of federalism tended to delay and scatter and sometimes skew their discussion of other matters, even one so important as the executive. Then, too, the enormous practical difficulties in devising a suitable plan for electing the president remained in the forefront throughout almost the whole discussion, pushing the more fundamental question of the role or function of the president into the background. This does not mean that the latter question was not considered; it was usually taken up somewhat obliquely in the course of discussion about election or organization. Finally, many of the most important decisions were made in committees toward the end of the convention. For all these reasons, the deliberations on the executive require a good deal of explanation and reconstruction. One needs a sure-footed, clear-eyed guide, and that is what Thach provides.

The reader will not agree, of course, with every judgment the author makes or every conclusion he reaches, but the book has the quality of being valuable even where it is questioned. Interest in the descriptions of the main builders of the presidency is enhanced, if anything, by the questions Thach leaves in his wake, stimulating the reader to return to the sources and to think again. James Madison's paternity of the Constitution does not extend, Thach shows convincingly, to Article II. Madison had not thought his way to the ground of the republican executive as he had to the ground of federalism and the extended republic. Moreover, as Thach very shrewdly suggests, "it may be that to Madison's contemplative, unassertive mind the executive problem was not particularly attractive."[7] Yet Madison learned quickly and well, and the author does not give him quite the credit he deserves for the exercise of that well-known capacity for political analysis even in this relatively unfamiliar and uncongenial area. It was James Wilson, however, who took the lead, pressing for a unitary executive derived directly from and responsible to the people. The reader who thinks that the founders were enemies of democracy, and that the notion of the American president as the

---

7. Ibid., p. 83.

man of the people was a later innovation, will have to revise his opinions. He will certainly be impressed by Wilson's clear view of the issues involved in providing for the organization and election of the president, though he may wonder whether his insight into the *functioning* of this popular representative in the constitutional system was quite as deep as Thach suggests. Here the intellectual powers of Gouverneur Morris come into action, giving him a strong claim to share paternity of the presidency. Here too the broad constitutional understandings of Madison and Hamilton come into their own.

Thach's focus on what he considered the chief problem confronting the founders—"to get a sufficiently strong executive"[8]—occasionally leads him to give less attention to some of the theoretical questions raised by men like Madison and Hamilton. It may—indeed, must—be conceded that there was a widespread conviction of the need for a vigorous, independent executive. One could go on, moreover, to observe that the Anti-Federalists showed a surprising willingness to admit the need for an independent executive and even to concede that the Constitution's provisions for the executive were not too bad. Yet there were some major reservations. A substantial body of opinion, formed out of experience and reflection and teaching, pulled the men of the founding generation back, even while most of them were moving toward a strong, independent, coequal executive. As Hamilton suggested, the erection of an effective executive on a republican base was thought to be deeply problematical, even by many of those thoroughly committed to the attempt.

Thach does not take up the most important argument against the emerging executive made during the convention, contained in a speech by George Mason on June 4.[9] In criticizing the proposal for a unitary executive, Mason sought to raise the whole question of the status of the executive or monarchical principle in a republican government. He admitted that secrecy, dispatch, and energy are great advantages and that they are possessed to a great degree by a monarchy, of which the unitary executive is a kind of imitation. "Yet perhaps a little reflection may incline us to doubt whether these advantages are not greater in theory than in practice, or lead us to enquire whether there is not some pervading principle in republican government which sets at naught and tramples upon this boasted superiority. . . ." Mason's suggestion is not merely that the executive principle must be reconciled with the republican principle; this the

---

8. Ibid., p. 171.

9. Mason's own draft of this speech has been preserved; Farrand, *Records*, vol. 1, pp. 110–14.

advocates of a vigorous executive readily admitted, and admitted to be a grave difficulty. His argument is that in a genuine republic—one that does not ape the great monarchies—there is a capacity to beat the executive at its own game of ensuring strong and effective action. "This invincible principle is to be found in the love, the affection, the attachment of the citizens to their laws, to their freedom, and to their country." Here lies not only the goodness of republican government, but its strength. "And who that reflects seriously upon the situation of America, in the beginning of the late war—without arms—without soldiers—without trade, money or credit, in a manner destitute of all resources, but must ascribe our success to this pervading, all-powerful principle?" Attempts to introduce the monarchical principle of executive vigor would, Mason suggests, tend to make America less strong by making her less free. Mason and other critics of the Constitution had considerable difficulty in maintaining this view and in reconciling it with their concession that a strong government and a strong executive were needed. Without pursuing that matter further here, the point is that Mason raised a major reservation about the very status in a free republic of the kind of executive provided by the Constitution. That reservation was widely shared, though in different proportions; and it raised then, as indeed it still raises, questions of the most profound kind about the character of the presidency and of the constitutional government of which it is a part.

Another kind of question was raised by Benjamin Franklin in a speech on the remuneration of the executive.[10] That Thach passes this by without comment is not surprising, since Franklin seems to be making one of his characteristically cheerful and impractical suggestions, namely, that the executive should not be paid. Yet the theoretically alert reader will want to reflect on the broad view of the presidency that Franklin presents, a view that has—as Franklin surely intended—implications going far beyond the immediate question.

One reply to George Mason's emphasis on the citizens' love of country is that reliance on that principle, far from saving the country, "had like to have lost us our independence" (*Federalist* 25). It was not civic virtue, the proponents of a strong national government contended, that won the war for American independence, but the leadership of George Washington. Washington was very much in the minds of the creators of the presidency, not only as the probable first occupant of the office, but also (and more fundamentally) as the very model of what a republican executive ought to be. However, it was at least as important that most presidents would not be George

---

10. Farrand, *Records*, vol. 1, pp. 81–85.

Washingtons as that the first one would be. Washington had taken no pay for his services as commander in chief, but how many men would serve on such a condition? Franklin pointed to the dangers of combining the passions of avarice and ambition. Such a combination would be likely to bring to the office not the "wise and moderate" but "the bold and violent, the men of strong passions, and indefatigable activity in their selfish pursuits." Could not enough men be found motivated by the honorable ambition of a Washington to make unnecessary the risky appeal to lower motives?

The convention tried to take into account both the desirability of attracting men like Washington to the presidency and its unlikelihood. The electoral college system, as Hamilton explained in *The Federalist*, "affords a moral certainty, that the office of president, will seldom fall to the lot of any man, who is not in an eminent degree endowed with the requisite qualifications" (*Federalist* 68). At the same time, the presidency, like the other offices under the Constitution, was organized with a view to directing the private passions of the men who would fill the office into channels that would serve the public good. Thus Gouverneur Morris argued in favor of reeligibility (anticipating Hamilton's classic argument in *Federalist* 72) as a way of rewarding public service and maintaining legitimate channels through which presidents could gratify their desires for wealth and glory.[11] Or, as Hamilton wrote in the spare, rich notes for his major speech at Philadelphia on June 18:

> . . . the govt. must be so constituted as to offer strong motives.
> In short, to interest all the *passions* of individuals.
> And turn them into that channel.[12]

Franklin's motion that the president should not be paid, seconded as a mark of respect by none other than Alexander Hamilton, went unsupported and undiscussed. The delegates no doubt considered Franklin's argument scarcely tenable as an everyday matter, even if they had been willing to accept its aristocratic implications. Franklin himself might have agreed, but he wanted to remind his fellow delegates of the character of the genuine article they were trying to approximate and of the dangers of going too far in the attempt, by mere constitution-making, to tie low private passions to high public service.

After reading Thach's *The Creation of the Presidency*, the reader

---

11. Farrand, *Records*, vol. 2, p. 53.
12. Ibid., p. 311; compare with *Federalists* 51 and 72.

would be well advised to examine Hamilton's discussion of the executive branch in *Federalists 67–77*. Not only does Hamilton provide the first and best general treatment of the American presidency but he follows to their end the very themes that Thach traces from their origins in the states and the Congress, through the debates at Philadelphia, and into the debate over the removal power. Hamilton makes the case for executive independence, unity, and vigor in a way that would be difficult to improve upon. He shows that administration is the beginning and end of government: "the true test of a good government is its aptitude and tendency to produce a good administration." He shows that the president's responsibility for administrative details implies a responsibility for the administration in the greatest and most comprehensive sense. He shows that the president's duty to check the legislature and even the people, when they are wrong, carries a duty, not merely to resist but to lead, to provide the direction that finally only he can provide.

Hamilton thus transcends the initial distinction between the executive as independent administrator and the executive as a counterweight to the legislature, but he does so by clarifying and carrying forward the very elements of that distinction. It is not going too far to say that in his treatment in *The Federalist* Hamilton brings the creation of the presidency to completion, so far as the founding generation was concerned.

The reader will be well advised, then, to carry his study of the creation of the presidency into Hamilton's discussion in *The Federalist*. He will find his way cleared and a remarkably solid foundation laid by this volume by Charles C. Thach.

19
The Presidency and the Constitution

Our topic is the presidency and the Constitution. The basic theme or problem is simple: the presidency is a creature of the Constitution, it is an office established by the Constitution; yet today's presidency is—or seems to many to be—a threat to that Constitution.

A curious consequence of the activities of the Nixon administration (and the response to them) has been a revival of concern with the Constitution.

Observers, including political scientists and lawyers, who had for years been telling us that the Constitution does not have a fixed meaning, that it is a "living document," and that its meaning changes as circumstances change and practices change, suddenly found established practice illegitimate, saw the "living constitution" as a cancer rather than a healthy growth, and looked for fixed standards and limits to that old Constitution, as Americans have so often done.

The revival of interest in and commitment to the rule of law, of the Constitution, is all to the good, in my judgment, however partisan its motives (and its motives *have* been partisan in many important cases). The United States is a constitutional democracy, a government of laws not men. That has to mean not, of course, that men do not exercise significant and decisive discretion, but that what government does, or more precisely what government may legitimately do, is determined or limited by a system of law, at the apex of which rests the Constitution.

There are three levels of questions that can be raised about the Presidency and the Constitution:

1. Have recent presidents claimed and exercised specific powers to which they have no constitutional right? Regarding the war power, for example, Congress has the power to declare war, to make appro-

---

This previously unpublished essay comes from a speech delivered at Beloit College in March 1974.

priations, and to provide for an army and navy; the president is commander in chief and is granted the "executive power." Given these constitutional provisions, may the president initiate hostilities? Or regarding the spending power, Congress appropriates money, and the president has authority to "take care that the laws are faithfully executed." Given these provisions, may the president decline to spend money appropriated by Congress?

Often we cannot give definitive answers to these questions. There is some ambiguity. Often there is a constitutional no man's land contested by the president and Congress. We have to try to make some judgments about the law, but we are also driven to a broader question:

2. Has there been so much presidential encroachment or congressional abdication that we have a basic change in our system of government—a change for the worse? Has "presidential government" escaped the limits that are supposed to characterize "constitutional government"? Has our government lost its capacity to rule *under law*?

3. Is there a fundamental contradiction or tension between a strong president—or more generally, the executive power—and the rule of law?

I will be talking mainly about the middle-level question, whether presidential government today has escaped from the limits of the Constitution and become what Arthur Schlesinger, Jr., calls "the imperial president."

First, the basic doctrine of American constitutional government:

Justice Hugo Black in *Reid v. Covert* (1957), a case dealing with the application of military law to military dependents overseas, said: "The United States is entirely a creature of the Constitution. Its powers and authority have no other source. It can only act in accordance with all the limitations imposed by the Constitution."

Justice Robert Jackson said in the Youngstown Steel case: "I did not suppose, and I am not persuaded that history leaves it open to question, at least in the courts, that the executive branch, like the federal government as a whole, possesses only delegated powers."

And Thomas Jefferson in his Notes on Virginia commented on the proposals in 1776 and 1781 to turn over power in Virginia to a dictator. He says that there is no such power in our Constitution: "Its fundamental principle is, that the State shall be governed as a commonwealth. It provides a republican organization, proscribes under the name of prerogative the exercise of all powers undefined by the laws; places on this basis the whole system of our laws; and by consolidating them together, chooses that they should be left to stand or fall together, never providing for any circumstances, nor admitting that such could arise, wherein either should be suspended; no, not for a moment."

This is the doctrine of constitutional government which recent (and not so recent) executive encroachments seem to many to have breached. "The presidency," says Arthur Schlesinger, Jr., "has got out of control and badly needs new definition and restraint." We need a strong president, but a strong president within the Constitution. There is a need to restore constitutionalism.

Yet it is striking that very early in the first chapter of his book Schlesinger finds it necessary to discuss and to accept the notion of what he calls emergency prerogative: executive action outside the law that is justified by necessity. There are times (such as the Cuban missile crisis) when the president is justified in acting illegally to meet an "emergency" situation.

Schlesinger concedes that the framers did not admit the need for executive prerogative and indeed that their view was that the Constitution was "equal to any emergency." "Yet there is reason to believe that the doctrine that crisis might require the executive to act outside the Constitution in order to save the Constitution remained in the back of their minds. Even in the *Federalist Papers* Hamilton wrote of 'that original right of self-defence which is paramount to all positive forms of government' and Madison thought it 'vain to oppose constitutional barriers to the impulse of self-preservation.' "

The basic point of prerogative is that there may be necessities (most commonly emergencies) that are not and cannot be anticipated by the law, which someone is going to have to deal with. That "someone" is going to be, in John Locke's phrase, he who "has the Executive Power in his hands"—in our case the president.

But in admitting emergency prerogative, does not Schlesinger vastly and dangerously extend the power of the presidency? But Schlesinger's strategy is to concede a sphere of emergency prerogative outside the Constitution as a way of restoring a *more strict* construction of the Constitution and of the president's constitutional powers. Thus, admit that the president can deal with the Cuban missile crisis by exercising a (nonconstitutional) prerogative power and you do not have to say he can do it as commander in chief.

This is the strategy of the strict constructionists. Consider Patrick Henry's reaction to Randolph's comment that Americans had established a dictator in 1781: "We never had an American President. In making a Dictator, we follow the example of the most glorious, magnanimous and skillful nations. In great dangers this power has been given.—Rome had furnished us with an illustrious example.—America found a person worthy of that trust: She looked to Virginia for him. We gave a dictatorial power to hands that used it gloriously; and which were rendered more glorious by surrendering it up. Where is there a breed of such Dictators? Shall we find a set of American Presidents of such a breed? Will the American President come and lay prostrate at the feet of Congress his laurels? I fear there are few men who can be trusted on that head."

Also, consider Jefferson's statement in 1807: "On great occasions every good officer must be willing to risk himself in going beyond the strict line of the law, when the public preservation requires it; his motives will be a justification. . . ."

This strategy in defense of constitutionalism has a powerful appeal. It bends to necessity without trying to constitutionalize it. Justice Jackson in *Korematsu v. U.S.* (1944):

> It would be impracticable and dangerous idealism to expect or insist that each specific military command in an area of probable operations will conform to conventional tests of constitutionality. . . . But if we cannot confine military expedients by the Constitution, neither would I distort the Constitution to approve all that the military may deem expedient. . . . [Even if the orders here were expedient military precautions,] I deny that it follows that they were constitutional. . . . [O]nce a judicial opinion rationalizes such an order to show that it conforms to the Constitution, or rather rationalizes the Constitution to show that the Constitution sanctions such an order, the Court for all times has validated the principle of racial discrimination in criminal procedure and of transplanting American citizens. The principle then lies about like a loaded pistol ready for the hand of any authority that can bring forward a plausible claim of an urgent need.

This is surely a powerful argument (although it did not happen here). An excellent example is the way the president's constitutional position as commander in chief, originally rather narrowly understood, has acquired a judicially sanctioned sweeping breadth under the force of a series of necessities. Jackson would not deny the necessity, but he would try to avoid letting it stretch the Constitution out of all recognizable shape.

The difficulty is that prerogative—even Arthur Schlesinger's "emergency prerogative"—is a loaded pistol too; and, all things considered, a more dangerous one. Do we want to save our Constitution by admitting that we must at times resort to nonconstitutional, plebiscitary dictatorship? The question would then be, shall we abide by the Constitution or not?

Schlesinger quoted Madison to the effect that "it is vain to oppose constitutional barriers to the impulse of self-preservation." But Madison was arguing that the Constitution must be broad enough to provide a place for the impulse of self-preservation. He went on to write in *Federalist* 41: "It is worse than in vain; because it plants in the Constitution itself necessary usurpations of power, every precedent of which is a germ of unnecessary and multiplied repetitions." And Hamilton writes, in *Federalist* 25,

> nations pay little regard to rules and maxims calculated in their nature to run counter to the necessities of society. Wise politicians will be cautious about fettering the government with restrictions that cannot be observed, because they know that every breach of the fundamental laws, though dictated by necessity, impairs that sacred reverence which ought to be maintained in the breast of rulers towards the constitution of a country, and forms a precedent for other breaches where the same plea of necessity does not exist at all, or is less urgent and palpable.

On the one hand, the resort from the Constitution to prerogative tends to undermine the Constitution. But, on the other hand, constitutional barriers will not be able to resist real necessity. So the conclusion the founders drew was that the Constitution must lie with the grain of nature; it must "constitutionalize" prerogative, so far as any law can do that.

That is what the Constitution meant to do: it meant to have room for whatever powers would be necessary. This is Justice David Davis's point in *Ex parte Milligan* (1866) in a much quoted (and now rather scorned) passage:

> The Constitution of the United States is a law for rulers and people, equally in war and peace, and covers with the shield of its protection all classes of men at all times, and under all circumstances. No doctrine, involving more pernicious consequences was ever invented by the wit of man than that any of its provisions can be suspended during any of the great exigencies of government. Such a doctrine leads directly to anarchy or despotism, but the theory of necessity on which it is based is false; for the government, within the Constitution, has all the powers granted to it which are necessary to preserve its existence, as has been happily proved by the result of the great effort to throw off its just authority.

Especially in the case of the executive, the framers provided constitutional powers with a noble spaciousness. Three provisions stand out: (1) "The executive Power shall be vested" in the president statement; (2) the "take care" clause; and (3) the presidential oath of office. Abraham Lincoln's contribution was to explore, explain, and use these three powers. This is especially exemplified in his use of the "war power," which flowed into the presidency particularly through his role as commander in chief. "This marked," Schlesinger says, "the beginning of a fateful evolution." (Or a flowering.)

Lincoln's defense of his suspension of the writ of habeas corpus in his speech of July 4, 1861, was a careful and deliberate combination of law and prerogative. Pointing out that critics said that he who is responsible for taking care that the laws be faithfully executed should not himself violate them, he had considered that

> The whole of the laws which were required to be faithfully executed were being resisted, and failing of execution in nearly one third of the States. Must they be allowed to finally fail of execution, even had it been perfectly clear that by the use of the means necessary to their execution some single law . . . should to a very limited extent be violated? To state the question more directly: are all the laws but one to go unexecuted, and the Government itself go to pieces, lest that one be violated? Even in such a case, would not the official oath be broken if the government should be overthrown, when it was believed that disregarding the single law would tend to preserve it? But it was not believed that this question was presented. It was not believed that any law was violated.

The Constitution must be read—was meant to be read—in light of necessity. The Constitution is law that opens up to the realm of necessity—and returns to the realm of law. The Constitution is meant to be commodious and elastic enough to meet the demands of necessity and yet retain its character as law. It has to be broad and ambiguous; yet that may enable a clever president to exercise dictatorial powers under cover of law. But there are some very important built-in checks that support constitutional restraints.

First, as long as the basic doctrine is adhered to that no action is legitimate unless authorized by the Constitution, that means that—broad as the Constitution may be and wide as the president may stretch it—the president has got to make a defense of his action in constitutional terms. This means (1) that if his constitutional argument is weak, that will weaken his authority; (2) that his claims are rebuttable—there is a constitutional tradition to draw upon, in terms of which the raw emergency question is debatable; (3) that this keeps the constitutional question primary even when the Constitution is being interpreted in the most ample manner, thus maintaining constitutional supremacy and comprehensiveness even in prerogative situations (like Lincoln's); and (4) that since presidents are generally reluctant to break laws because of inner restraints, this will foster that "sacred reverence" that rulers ought to have for their constitution.

Second, the presidential claim is, potentially at least, subject to judicial review. Once it was the fashion to say that this is meaningless at least in practice. The Supreme Court would not dare to stand against the presidency. But when a Court can order the president to return the steel mills, seized to maintain steel production during the Korean War; when a Court can order the House of Representatives to reinstate a member they had deemed unfit for office; and when a Court can order the president to produce in court tape recordings for which he claimed an absolute privilege—then one has to revise old ideas of what the Court will and will not do in "enforcing" the rule of law against the more popular departments of government.

Moreover, even when the Court is unwilling to stand in the president's way in the height of an emergency—as it usually (and prudently) is—it has ways of keeping the rule of law to the fore. Sometimes, for example, the issue can be avoided, thus tacitly admitting extraordinary powers without giving doctrinal sanction (so-called political questions). The Court can also postpone decisions and then restore or tighten up the rule of law when the pressure of necessity is off. Justice Davis wrote in the Milligan case:

> During the late wicked Rebellion the temper of the times did not allow that calmness in deliberation and discussion so necessary to a correct conclusion of a purely judicial question. Then, considerations of safety were mingled with the exercise of power, and feelings and interests prevailed which are happily terminated. Now that the public safety is assured, this question, as well as all others, can be discussed and decided without passion or the admixture of any element not required to form a legal judgment.

Finally, however, the framers saw that all this was not enough; mere "parchment barriers" against abuse of power, even when enforced by a vigorous judiciary, are not sufficient. The framers saw clearly the need to give the rule of law *muscle,* as it were; and they did that in the well known but not always well understood mechanism of separation of powers and checks and balances. I will not try to restate the whole argument (see *Federalist* 51), but authority is divided and balanced and checked.

I want to make two points here. First, the system of checks and balances is the *working* principle or the *enforcer* of the rule of law. The doctrine is important; the courts are important; but they ultimately depend on this hardheaded use of interest to check interest. Second, this system is misunderstood if it is seen as static. It is often seen that way—the language of "balance" tends to foster that. It seems like a house of cards—wobbling between paralysis and collapse. There is some truth in this, but it misses the main point or intention. The intention and the actual working of the system of checks and balances is one of dynamic tension: action, reaction, re-reaction, etc. You cannot take a cross section at a given time and understand the system; you have to look at it as it works, which means over a period of time.

This dynamic balance over time is what the founders relied on to make the rule of law work: "work" here means do the things that have to be done, while yet keeping government within the limits of law.

This still leaves the question whether modern presidents have caused a fundamental imbalance in this system and with it a fundamental breach in the rule of law. This is controversial. Arthur Schlesinger thinks there has been. You will have to judge.

But there are several ways this issue should not be approached: (1) It should not be judged through the narrow eye of Jeffersonian strict constructionism (and with its ultimately isolationist implications). (2) It should not be judged merely under the impression of a momentary impression of dangerous imbalance. (3) It should not be judged, of course, in the heat of anti-Nixon partisanship.

It should be judged as a somewhat rough-and-ready mechanism meant to achieve governmental vigor and governmental balance and governmental restraint *over time*. Judged in that way, the system seems to me to have performed remarkably well (even aside from Watergate—though that is part of it).

Consider war making. Vietnam was never merely the president's war; Congress was always more or less involved. During the Nixon administration Congress forced an agreement to stop bombing in Cambodia, placed restraints on expenditures, and passed the War Powers Act, which recognizes the president's right to commit troops overseas but requires information and tries to limit commitments without congressional authorization. This should not be seen as final, but as a resting place in a moving balance.

Consider also the impoundment controversy: Congress appropriates money and the president must "take care" that the laws are faithfully executed. Does this mean that presidents must spend *all* the money appropriated by Congress? This is an even more interesting case of the dynamics of separation of powers. President Nixon did impound appropriated funds to save money, for programmatic reasons, and to enforce budgetary responsibility in view of inflation. But he would be in political trouble if he persisted too long. The system allows him to do it, but he has to pay a price. And there is also pressure from the courts. Congress responded with the Budget and Impoundment Act of 1974, curtailing the power of impoundment. It allows a postponement of expenditures subject to a congressional veto, and it requires congressional approval for a permanent impoundment. This again recognizes the initial legitimacy of presidential action, subject to congressional review. Congress increased its own control and improved its responsibility.

The principle is: the law rules. But the law is meant to be commodious enough to allow the government to do whatever needs to be done; therefore the law must be very broad and that of course opens up the danger of such a broad interpretation that law in any meaningful sense slips away altogether.

The practical side (established by law, be it noted) is that government is shared among institutions and individuals who are in a dynamic relation of action and reaction with one another meant to make possible in practice government that is, on the whole and within reasonable limits, energetic, wise, and limited.

My own judgment is that the elastic in the old Constitution is still pretty supple and that the presidency—thanks to the vigor of the basic doctrine of American constitutionalism and through the working of the system of checks and balances of American institutions—is still a constitutional presidency. This is not the crabbed Constitution of Thomas Jefferson, James Buchanan, William Howard Taft, and Arthur Schlesinger, but the spacious yet nevertheless limiting Constitution of Alexander Hamilton, Abraham Lincoln, and Franklin Delano Roosevelt.

20
A Plan for Studying the Presidency

The following is a proposal submitted to President Gerald Ford in 1975.

A Proposal for a President's Commission on the
Conduct of the Government

Forty years ago President Franklin Roosevelt presented to the public the report of his Committee on Administrative Management, the most important and influential report of its kind ever produced in the United States. Written out of the tradition of administrative management, the president's committee recommended (1) overhauling the White House staff to give the president a number of personal assistants and to strengthen his managerial control of the administration, (2) strengthening the agencies of budget, personnel, and planning management, (3) extending the merit system, (4) reorganizing the myriad of executive agencies into twelve major departments, and (5) reorganizing the auditing procedures, giving the executive final responsibility for accounts, subject to an independent postaudit.

In almost every case these recommendations have been implemented. They led in particular to the establishment of the White House Office in 1939, with its flexible system of counsel and assistance to the president, which is the heart of modern presidential government. The report of the president's committee was highly controversial when it first appeared, but it quickly prevailed, and to a very large extent it set the pattern for thinking about the executive branch, especially the presidency, for several decades. It laid out, for example, the major lines of inquiry, the main questions, the guiding standards for the vast projects of the Hoover Commissions of 1947–1949 and, to a lesser extent, of 1953–1955. Even when, later, different views were expressed—for example in Richard Neustadt's influential study of presidential leadership—they were typically put forward in response to those of the president's committee.

The strength of the president's committee is the strength of ideas. It set the agenda for *thinking about* the executive and modern American government. Most such reports try to be as practical and concrete as possible, with the result that—however valuable the specific recommendations—they remain derivative from whatever or whomever is setting the questions. The president's committee showed the capacity of lucid, persuasive, well-conceived principles to guide practice.

The theoretical basis of the president's committee was, as the name suggests, the notion of administrative management and the body of ideas that had developed around that notion, drawing on the latter-day civil service reform movement, scientific management, and the developing field of public administration and management science. This was the committee's strength and its weakness. The basic conviction was that the great problems of modern government were not political problems—who should rule and what should be done?—but problems of management, problems of "how?" The president's committee argued that we need to "get down to business" and make government effective.

> Stated in simple terms these canons of efficiency require the establishment of a responsible and effective chief executive as the center of energy, direction, and administrative management; the systematic organization of activities in the hands of qualified personnel under the direction of the chief executive, and to aid him in this, the establishment of appropriate management and staff agencies. There must also be provision for planning, a complete fiscal system, and for holding the executive accountable for his program.

With this set of principles, the president's committee could and, for decades, did "make sense" out of the problem of government for theorists and practitioners alike.

The weakness of the president's committee was its shallow view of the political side of "executive management." While giving lip service to the president's role as political leader and head of nation, the president's committee clearly thought the role that mattered was "chief executive and administrator." The president's committee found in the Constitution and in the intention of the framers the goal of a unified, responsible executive capable of effectively administering the government. They did not see that that is, at most, only half the story.

The committee displayed a crude and superficial view of what the problem of democratic government is: "to make our Government an up-to-date efficient and effective instrument for carrying out the will of the nation." This view is misleadingly, even dangerously, superficial. Most thoughtful American thinkers and statesmen have seen what the president's committee did not see (but what, by the way, its sponsoring president did see), that democracy is right but that it is also problematical. Popular will can sometimes be badly informed, foolish, or despotic. Organizing and administrating government are not merely matters of securing efficiency in the implementation of some predetermined sovereign will, they must also be concerned with trying to make that will decent, wise, and moderate. Nor is this something somehow separate from running the government; it is part of the problem of administration.

As the Americans of the 1780s grappled with the problems of their state and general governments, there developed two distinct lines of thinking about the executive. In 1787 these lines of thinking merged in the president established in the U.S. Constitution. Under the Articles of Confederation there was of course no executive at all; whenever something had to be done, a method had to be found for doing it: individuals, standing committees, ad hoc groups, and departments were charged with specific administrative tasks. There was little central direction and the system was neither efficient nor responsible. It became clear that merely to have the will of the Congress executed effectively and efficiently, a strong unified executive was needed. This is the "administrative" strand of the American presidency that the president's committee saw and developed.

But in that same early period, in the states, a different problem developed. Most of the state constitutions had established strong legislatures and weak executives. With growing experience of legislative excess and injustice, it was seen that there was a need for some institution in government capable of resisting the legislature, capable of playing a part in a moderating and elevating scheme of checks and balances. And it was seen that the best candidate for such a role had to be the executive. Consequently there developed a large body of opinion favoring a strong and independent executive, capable of playing an active political role. This political role is largely ignored by the president's committee—at least so far as presidential administration is concerned—yet it is clear that everything the president does must somehow take account of these two distinct but connected duties.

Indeed, there is the yet more fundamental question of whether the American Constitution does not set for the president an even higher political task. Considering for example his unique oath and his duty to report on the state of the Union and to make recommendations, it seems clear that the president is given by the Constitution a fundamental and far-reaching task of leadership.

"Energy in the executive," Hamilton said, "is a leading character in the definition of good government." This maxim (which might well be the theme of a new President's Committee on the Conduct of the Government) has reference to three distinct kinds of levels of energy in the executive. The energetic executive has the main responsibility for the actual conduct of the government; he participates in the daily business of politics and in the constitutional scheme of checks and balances; and he must, finally, take the lead in clarifying questions and setting goals.

Against this background, there are many questions about the conduct of the government to be clarified and specific proposals to be considered. None of these is new—many of them have been the subject of endless reports and recommendations. No substantive attempt has ever been made, however, to integrate them into anything like the comprehensive view of presidential duties suggested above. Some sketchy suggestions follow.

1. The recently and thoroughly ventilated question of constitutional powers needs to be reconsidered in the light of the several roles described here. Two matters deserve special emphasis and consideration. First, most of the debate has been over the *powers* of the president, or the respective powers of the president and Congress. That is important, but it has thrown into the shadow a matter that the framers thought was more fundamental, namely the constitutional provisions for the structure and functioning of government. Limited government is to be found most fundamentally not in definitions of powers but in the care and skill with which the parts of government are organized and set in motion by the Constitution. Second, the whole system of divided powers and checks and balances needs to be seen not as a static "drawing of the lines" by the Constitution, but rather as a moving, dynamic system, in which it is to be expected that views will conflict. There can be, in the nature of the case, no fixed lines of powers between the departments—there is an inherent and deliberate tension, which is one of the major sources of both energy and moderation in our government. We have not generally *seen* the basic problem of our constitutional government clearly, because we have been taught to think that the solution to our problem is to be found in a clear *apportionment* of the *powers* of government.

2. Is the administration essentially the hands and fingers of the president—his instrument—as Jackson and most of our strong presidents have claimed? Or is it, as Webster and the Whig tradition have

insisted, the administration "of the country," not necessarily and simply under presidential control? This question has never been even adequately stated, far less explored, in any authoritative way in recent times.

The question of the relation between the White House staff and the departments has been the subject of considerable discussion and study, but there is a need to try to pull together the major considerations in the light of the broader scheme suggested here. That done, it may be possible to make some specific recommendations. A careful, unbiased study of the vigorous attempts by the Nixon White House to secure control of the machinery of government would be an important part of this study.

The relation between the president himself and his own "bureaucracy" in the White House office is another vital, modern question. On the one hand, the presidency seems to acquire new strength with every passing year; but on the other hand, it is claimed by many (though Richard Neustadt is now rather out of fashion) that the president tends to become the prisoner of that very administrative apparatus that was created (at the instigation of the president's committee) to help him.

An important issue here is the old but never adequately examined issue of presidential "control" over the administration through the leadership of ideas or principles, in contradistinction to control through administrative devices.

3. The issues of the presidency and Congress need to be seen in the light of the tension between the president's role as "chief administrator" and his role as participant in checks and balances. (a) A thoughtful examination is needed of the conflicting claims of the Congress and the president to control or influence or hold responsible the administration. While one should not expect any perfectly clear resolution of these conflicts, the beginning of wisdom is to recognize that both the president and Congress have legitimate claims in this area and that those claims need to be articulated and understood to provide a meaningful context for specific proposals. (b) The president's committee was concerned with the independent regulatory commissions, as a "headless fourth branch of government." This concern is a good example of both the strength and weakness of the committee. Clearly they did identify a critically important area in the conduct of the government of the United States. But they saw it merely in management terms. A broader view would raise the question of whether there is a constitutional necessity for administration to be somehow in the charge of the president. To what extent may Congress appoint administrators of its laws inde-

pendent of the president? There has been no adequate account of the constitutional, political, and administrative significance of the fact that the president is the constitutionally established and designated executor of the laws made by Congress. Even in his capacity as executor of the laws, the president is, paradoxically, independent and yet the servant of Congress. (c) The very old issue of what used to be called the "dispensing" power—the power of the executive to dispense with or make exceptions to the law in particular circumstances—has again come to the fore, especially in the impoundment controversy, and it needs exploration in the broader context provided by this scheme.

4. Finally, the president's role and duty as national agenda-setter needs to be considered as an intrinsic part of his responsibility for seeing to the conduct of the nation's business. The chief points that need to be made and explored here seem to be: (a) that the president's leadership role is not a usurpation or a recent development; it is intrinsic to the constitutional scheme; but (b) that the president leads, points the way, sets agendas—he does not command results. Both of these bear on the question of how the president carries on the business of his office and how he relates to the other parts of the government.

The original president's committee was small, containing three men: Louis Brownlow, a journalist, Charles Merriam, a political scientist, and Luther Gulick, a writer in the field of public administration. A larger body could not secure the kind of principled coherence that was the distinctive contribution of the president's committee. The committee had a reasonably large staff and conducted some studies of its own; but it did nothing on the order of the huge research enterprises carried out by the Hoover Commission. Again, this is the right principle. The Committee on the Conduct of the Government should have the staff necessary to collect and analyze materials from the existing literature (including both scholarly writings and official reports), to conduct extensive interviews, and to inaugurate new research where needed; but the goals should be the writing of a relatively short, tight, principled statement about the presidency and the conduct of the government in a way that would guide thinking for the remainder of the century.

The following is from a letter sent to Frederick E. Nolting, Jr., director of the White Burkett Miller Center for Public Affairs, University of Virginia, September 29, 1976.

A Plan for a Program on the Presidency

I think that it is sound to divide the subject into three basic parts: (1) the presidency as an institution (the administrative side); (2) the relations between the president and Congress (the political side); and (3) the president and the people (the issue of democracy and leadership). Underlying these themes is the fundamental question, popularized recently by Arthur Schlesinger, Jr., of the "imperial presidency"—the question of the constitutional role of the president and the alleged unconstitutional enlargement.

I think that the focus of a serious, large-scale examination of the presidency in our constitutional system should be a probing, balanced examination of precisely these common (and commonly unexplored) assumptions . . . that the presidency needs to be made more effective and more democratic.

Regarding effectiveness . . . I would begin with a basic and long-standing debate between the administrative views of the "Jacksonians" and the "Whigs." The former see the administration as the hands and fingers of the president; they conclude therefore that the problem of "effective" government is to give the president "control" over these instruments. The most notable modern product of this line of thinking has been the enormously influential Report of the President's Committee on Administrative Management of 1937, which laid the ground (only recently and ineffectively again brought into question) of the whole modern organization of the presidency. The second view was that taken by Daniel Webster and Henry Clay in opposition to Andrew Jackson, by the Republican opposition to the New Deal presidential centralization, by the advocates of independent regulatory commissions, and (uncomfortably) by liberal critics today of the "imperial presidency." The view here is that the administration does not belong to the president and should not necessarily be under the control of the president. "Effective" government, in this view, is not necessarily presidential government. Large patches of administration independent of the president are not only inevitable but healthy.

I would want to give a full articulation of this dichotomy, which I think illuminates as nothing else can what we *mean* when we talk about "effective" government. I would then want to explore the thesis that neither of these views is simply right, that each of them fits different times and different places. The kind of presidential supervision that is appropriate for the crisis days of the New Deal may be neither necessary nor desirable in, say, the relatively calm 1950s. I think this approach would lead to a sounder, because more dynamic, understanding of what "effective" government means and therefore to better practical recommendations.

Regarding the second . . . assumption . . . that the presidency needs to be made more "democratic," there are even more serious questions. The basic flaw here is the easy assumption that the presidency is or ought to be simply democratic. That was not the view of the framers of the Constitution, and this is one of several questions on which the framers can throw useful and highly relevant light. Many of the framers saw that the president would have to be the "man of the people," in James Wilson's words; but they also saw that the president would have to be a major element in government capable of restraining, checking, and guiding the people. It is this combination that makes the politics of the presidency so fascinating and difficult. Any serious exploration of the presidency, and of the relations between president and Congress, must rest on an understanding of this very complex responsibility. Such an understanding is very rare today, and I think a major contribution that could be made under the auspices of the Miller Center would be to recover this old but still sound view of what the presidency is all about. Even if it should turn out to be the case that today a more democratic presidency is needed, to ignore the nondemocratic responsibilities of the president as understood by our founders and by our best presidents will lead to missing or grossly oversimplifying most of the interesting questions here.

The subtle relation of the presidency to "democracy" leads to the question of presidential leadership. . . . Demythologizing the presidency, getting presidential activities out in the sunlight, eliminating secrecy are currently fashionable prescriptions, but they hardly touch the vital and deep issue of the need of even a democratic government for leadership—leadership with respect to policy, leadership with respect to common morality, and leadership with respect to the basic principles of our regime. The dangers of abuse of presidential powers must surely be faced and, so far as possible, avoided; but it is foolish and ultimately self-defeating to try to deal with the abuse of a necessary power by pretending that the power itself can be dispensed with.

So far as the imperial presidency is concerned, the problem is that we want (and we are right in wanting) both the rule of law and an energetic executive. We must have both, and yet they are, in practice and in principle, in tension. To say that we must get the presidency back under the Constitution (while there may be some truth in that) is to fail to understand how deep the problem lies—and also, incidentally, how wisely our founders dealt with it. The framers tried to draw up a constitution that would *grant* to government all power that might be necessary and yet *limit* power. That is, in a very real sense, impossible—and yet, they succeeded to an extraordinary degree. One of the first things I would like to do is to delineate this absolutely basic issue in theory and to show how it is *worked out* in our constitutional scheme in very practical terms. I want to initiate a study of the long dispute over the president's "impoundment" of appropriated funds, which I think will be seen (when traced over a course of time) to illustrate the practical working of a system well designed to provide both the possibility of extraordinary executive authority and rule of law.

[What is needed in the Miller Center's Program on the Presidency is a] solid grasp of the fundamental *orienting* issues of the American presidency that must guide and inform any serious examination, theoretical or practical. This was one of the strongest elements of the President's Committee on Administrative Management. However mistaken it may have been in some of its views (and I think it was mistaken in some of them), its practical effectiveness grew out of its theoretical depth, range, and clarity. I think that studies under the Miller Center should have a similar character.

21

In Defense of the Electoral College

Statement on Proposals for Direct Popular Election of the President of the United States.

The most worrisome aspect of the movement to adopt some form of direct popular election of the president of the United States is, in my view, the erroneous understanding of American government on which it is based. That erroneous understanding, which I shall call "simplistic democracy," has for our present purposes two main elements. Simplistic democracy assumes, first, that government is good so far as it is *responsive* to popular wishes: the business of democratic government is simply to do whatever the people want it to do. Not all advocates of direct popular election of the president hold this view in all its starkness, but it is the underlying premise. (I should also say that it is the premise of many opponents of direct popular election, which is one of the reasons why many of those opponents have had a hard time explaining their opposition.) The second element of simplistic democracy, and the one directly involved here, is the notion that in a democratic election the only thing that counts is that the person wanted by the most people should be elected to office. For any other consideration to affect the outcome is unfair, irrational, undemocratic.

Clearly there is a great deal to be said for these principles. Government *should* be responsive. And elections *do* rest on an assumption that the electors should choose whom they want for their representatives. Any gross departure from either of these principles would surely and properly be resisted by all Americans. The question, however, is not whether there is truth in these principles but

---

This was a statement Storing submitted to the Subcommittee on the Constitution of the Senate Judiciary Committee addressing a proposal to replace the electoral college with the direct popular election of presidents. Storing testified before the committee on July 22, 1977.

whether they are *sufficient*. And in fact the great architectural principle of the American government as it was conceived by its framers is precisely that responsiveness to public opinion is a necessary but *not* a sufficient condition of good government. The chief danger of the movement for direct popular election of the president is its tendency to weaken further our already loose grasp on this vital principle.

Mitigated Popular Government

To say that democratic responsiveness is necessary but not sufficient implies that government ought to be responsive to public opinion in general and over time but that it need not be—indeed that it should not be—merely responsive. A merely responsive government is likely to tend toward instability, ignorance, and indifference to individual and minority rights. The government the American framers built was erected on public opinion, but that opinion was to be checked, guided, and channeled when appropriate by the constitutional system and the officers serving under it. The aim was to provide for a government that would be competent, stable, and just, as well as responsive.

I want to make two points about this great design of the American framers, one a broad and very important background consideration and the other directly pertinent to the question of the method of presidential election. The background point is that this notion of a "mitigated" popular government, as James Madison called it, is itself altogether consistent with democracy: it is not something foisted on the people from outside. Just as any one of us is likely to arrange his own affairs so that circumstances will help him resist his own vices or deficiencies (like most of you, I suppose, I deliberately accept specific deadlines as ways of anticipating and dealing with my probable future laziness and procrastination), so a people, as Madison explained, might anticipate its own probable future flightiness or foolishness and try to build into its constitution institutions to counteract those tendencies. The "antidemocratic" or nondemocratic devices in our Constitution are democracy's own inventions of prudence to deal with its own harmful tendencies. These ideas are not very familiar to us today, so influenced are we all by doctrines of simplistic democracy. Yet my own experience (teaching undergraduates, for example) is that their good sense is obvious once they are explained.

Of course, these broad considerations do not settle the question of direct popular election of the president. They do suggest, however, that an institution or a procedure of government should not be judged merely in terms of its responsiveness or nonresponsiveness to public opinion. That is a very important point in the present context, because the beginning and the end of the case for direct popular election are the fact that under the present system a man might be elected president even though he had fewer popular votes than his opponent. That fact *in itself* is widely thought to demonstrate the evils of the present system. (That is precisely the initial assumption of my undergraduates until they begin to think through the question and see that it is a good deal more complicated than that.) Such a possibility should surely be carefully watched, especially if it seems likely to occur with some frequency (which it does not); it is not, however, the end of the story but the bare beginning.

The case *for* direct popular election of the president collapses, it seems to me, once the dangerous shallowness of the doctrine of simplistic democracy is exposed and understood. That in itself is reason enough to leave a working and reasonably satisfactory system in place; but is there really a case to be made *for* the electoral college system? There is, indeed; but it is a *complex* case, and for that reason alone it is distasteful to those who seek to solve our political problems with a single stroke of reform.

To see the case for the present constitutional system of electing the president requires a shift in point of view from that usually taken by the critics of the present system. They tend to view elections in terms of *input*—in terms of the right to vote, equal weight of votes, who in fact votes, and the like. The framers thought it at least as important to consider the *output* of any given electoral system. What kind of men does it bring to office? How will it affect the working of the political system? What is its bearing on the political character of the whole country?

There is much room for disagreement and uncertainty about the results for our political system of a change to direct popular election of the president. I would surely not pretend that my very brief sketch is comprehensive or conclusive. What I want to stress, however, is that no proposal for electoral reform can be intelligently considered by looking at only one end of the electoral process. Elections are means to some *ends*, and some attempt has to be made to establish what the ends are and to compare different methods of election in the light of those ends. The *output* of any given method of election is at least as important as the *input*.

The paradox of the constitutional system for electing the president is that while it does not work as the framers intended it to work, it nevertheless achieves to a remarkable extent the ends the framers wanted to achieve. Despite the framers' pride in their invention of the electoral college system—and it was one of the least criticized parts of the Constitution—it may have been a bit too clever and the first stage too loosely tied to popular elections. (If the state legislatures today were to start choosing electors themselves, or assigning that task to, say, college professors, as they might constitutionally do, I would start agitating for constitutional amendment.) But the framers surely saw very clearly what such a system of elections should do; and the system as it works today does those things rather well. It does them largely through our system of political parties; and it is another paradox that while the framers opposed parties as they knew them, the American party system today is one of their most remarkable achievements.

Once one turns to the question of output, to the ends that a method of election should aim for (and that requires putting aside the blinders of simplistic democracy), there is likely to be fairly wide, though not universal, agreement. The ends of any system for electing the president, as the framers saw them, were something like the following: (1) it should provide for significant participation by the people at large; (2) it should foster political stability and avoid the excesses of partisanship and factionalism which tend to form around important elections; (3) it should give some special place of influence to some individuals who are specially informed about and committed to the process of government; (4) it should recognize that this is a nation of states and give some weight to the interests of states as such; (5) it should leave the president independent of any other institution of the government; and (6) it should, of course, tend to produce presidents of respectable character and intelligence. It is striking how little concern there is among the proponents of direct popular elections with these objectives. These is little or no argument that the individuals chosen under a system of direct popular elections would be better presidents; that policies would be more intelligent; that presidential behavior would be more prudent or equitable; or that American politics as a whole would be improved in stability, moderation, competence, or justice.

And, on the other side, it is fairly obvious that our present system does secure these goals to a reasonable degree. This seems to be connected with our present two-party system, and it is generally agreed—even among advocates of direct popular election of the president—that the main elements of our present party system should be maintained. There are many issues here, but I pass them over to come to what seems to be the vital question, about which there is serious disagreement. That is whether the American two-party system, which underlies most of these benefits, is in any way dependent on the way we now elect our president.

The American Two-Party System

This crucial question is by no means easy to answer. It would take more space than I have to give even an adequate sketch of the issue. On the one side the argument is that by giving the popular vote-winner in any state all the electoral votes of that state (which is of course not constitutionally required but is and is likely to remain the almost universal practice), the electoral college system tends to freeze out minority parties (who cannot hope to win a state's whole electoral vote). The system effectively creates a powerful incentive to drive all interests into one of two great parties, each of which can realistically hope to win in the "all or nothing" electoral vote game if it makes a broad enough appeal. Without this practice, the argument goes, there would be much more incentive for minorities to strike out on their own and much less incentive for the two great parties to cast their nets very widely; and there would, in consequence, be a decay of the two-party system.

Proponents of direct popular election contend, on the other side, that the basic shape of American politics is determined by forces far more fundamental than the way we elect the president. They refer to the long tradition of two-party politics. They point out that the fact that the presidency is a single office itself tends to discourage the formation of minority parties in presidential politics; minorities could no more hope to win the presidency as independent parties under direct popular election than they can today—perhaps (remembering the George Wallace phenomenon) even less so.

It is not only difficult to weigh these and similar arguments. It is also difficult to know how various modes of direct popular election would affect the pattern of American politics. Presumably, for example, a major reason for requiring a 40 percent plurality of popular vote to win is to discourage minority parties. Yet it is not entirely clear whether this would in fact discourage minority parties (on the theory that they cannot hope to get 40 percent of the vote) or encourage them (on the theory that by remaining independent they may be able to influence a probable runoff election). It should also be observed that many other forces in the electoral system—public financing, for example—may be as important or more important than the electoral college versus direct popular election issue in determining the basic character of American politics in the next decade.

Yet one thing seems reasonably clear. To the extent that direct popular election does have an effect, it is likely to be in the *direction* of weakening or further weakening our traditional two-party system. The tendency of minority groups to go directly into presidential politics, either in hopes of influencing a runoff election, or with the intention of bargaining for other advantages, or even to provide an organizational focus for interest-group activity of a fundamentally nonelectoral kind, seems very likely to increase. Similarly, the role of the states, and specifically state party organizations, already weakened in various respects, seems likely to be further undermined. Direct popular election of the president would foster a more open, volatile system of national politics—one less rooted in state political organizations, less influenced by the party professionals or quasi-professionals, and dominated by shifting personal alliances of nationally oriented personalities, ideologues, interest-group spokesmen, and media specialists. We could anticipate a political system pulled, in the one direction toward fragmentation and, in the other direction, toward plebiscitary unity rooted not in party organization but in an individual president's personality and personal staff.

Governmental Legitimacy

All of this seems to most proponents of direct popular election to be largely beside the point. What we are dealing with, they contend, is not so much a question of achieving certain political ends but a question of *legitimacy*, a question of the principle that ties the people to their government and continues to persuade them that government is entitled to obedience and support, if not affection.

The trump card in the hand of the proponents of direct popular election of the president is the possibility that a man might receive a majority of the electoral votes who had nevertheless received fewer popular votes than an opponent. This has never happened in this century (leaving aside the arguable case of 1960), but it could happen, as it did in the nineteenth century. If the United States survives, and its system for electing the president remains intact, it probably will happen again.

It is worth reiterating at this point that the constitutional system for electing the president, as it was conceived and as it works today, is basically a system of popular election, though mitigated in various ways for various purposes. While it is very hard to know what effect direct popular election of the president would have had, or would have in the future, on the whole shape of American politics and on the candidates and the issues involved (itself a good reason for being skeptical about the proposed amendments), there is no doubt that the broad result of our present system of electing the president has in fact been to choose the man desired by most of the voters. Any solid exceptions to this—as Benjamin Harrison's choice over Grover Cleveland in 1888; any probable exceptions to it—as John F. Kennedy's choice over Richard Nixon in 1960; any future exceptions to it—of the kind warned against by the proponents of direct election—can be only that, *exceptions*. Indeed, these have been rare and will surely continue to be rare exceptions to an electoral system that has on the whole reflected and will continue to reflect the choice of the American people.

To the proponents of direct popular election, however, these exceptions are unacceptable. Part of the reason for this is the simplistic democrat's blindness to electoral considerations other than mere responsiveness. But another part is a fear that even a single occurrence of this exceptional result of the election of a president with fewer popular votes than his opponent would shake the whole system to its foundation, or at least introduce a crack in popular confidence that would be deeply harmful. I doubt it. Unless there were other reasons for widespread loss of confidence, I think the system would weather such a tremor without much trouble. I would expect a flurry of newspaper editorials, some revival of doctrines of simplistic democracy, another push for the (I trust) yet unpassed constitutional amendment for direct popular election of the president; but on the whole I think politics would continue much as usual. I would be surprised if the defeated candidate were to make any serious attempt to undermine his opponent's constitutional authority; I would imagine instead that he would use his popular plurality as a major weapon in his next campaign. I think it is shallow and misleading to portray such an event as the probable downfall of governmental legitimacy in the United States. Legitimacy is, as wise politicians and political thinkers have always known, a complex and mysterious force, not necessarily determined by electoral success, as the cases of Richard Nixon and Gerald Ford remind us.

Legitimacy is considerably more complex than numbers of votes. It depends on those qualities the founders tried to build into the American system and that we have on the whole enjoyed: stability, adequate representation of our diversity, a recognition of our federal character, a capacity to govern well, as well as popular responsiveness. In no one of these respects is the present system of electing the president perfect; the main reason for that is that they are to some extent in tension. We are trying to have the best of several worlds—the world of political stability, the world of social diversity, the world

401

of governmental confidence, as well as the world of democratic responsiveness. The proponents of direct popular election seem bent on resolving this complex set of worlds into the single one of numerical preponderance.

That world, the world of simplistic democracy, would be, I am confident, a good deal less satisfactory than what we have now. It would also turn out to be a good deal less simple than it seems to be on the surface. Would a series of extremely close popular votes, in contrast with our history of substantial electoral majorities, foster legitimacy? Will we have to institute compulsory voting to secure numerical legitimacy? Does the doctrine of numerical legitimacy have any adequate answer to the complaint of the voter who is always on the losing side? And does the doctrine of numerical legitimacy not logically imply majoritarianism? Yet I know of no serious proposal for direct popular election of the president that would require a majority. Does not any form of election by mere plurality, however, leave open the possibility—indeed under our circumstances the probability— that the victor will be someone who was *not* preferred by *most* of the voters? How solid, on numerical grounds, would be the legitimacy of such a president? And what of the vast problems of the inevitable runoff elections? Would the close results, the public bickering and bargaining, the decline in participation in runoff elections be likely to reconcile all parts of the public to the final result and to the whole political system better than does our present system of the electoral college, managed by our great, aggregating political parties? I doubt it.

The case against the present constitutional system for electing the president rests upon a simplistic view of American democracy that is contrary to our traditions and dangerously shallow. It tends to ignore or to downgrade all the characteristics other than popular responsiveness that our government needs. When viewed in terms of results, as well as in terms of capacity to attract the respect and loyalty of the American people, the existing system, while surely imperfect, appears to be far superior to any form of direct popular election of the president.

22
American Statesmanship:
Old and New

"Statesmanship" is almost un-American. The word has an elitist and obsolete ring. I will use it, nevertheless, both because it is serviceable enough to refer to the practice (and the theory of the practice) of government rather broadly understood, and because I want to try to rehabilitate, to some extent, an older view. I shall be concerned not so much with the practice of statesmanship as with the way Americans in significant public office, from the president down through at least the upper levels of the bureaucracy, understand their public roles (to use a much more fashionable term).

My beginning point is the observation that there is a strong tendency to resolve the role of the public official into two simple elements: populism, or radical democracy, and scientific management. Since I will be trying to follow some very accessible, though often vaguely understood and expressed, ideas to their roots, I shall not begin with any attempt at precise or elaborate definition—premature definition obscures the interesting questions. I refer to the broad sets of ideas these terms immediately call to mind. They are admittedly vague and they will need refinement and explanation, but they will turn out, as our common language so often does, to identify rather well the kernel of the principles involved. These elements not only tend to characterize American "statesmanship" (and it is precisely because they characterize it that the word "statesmanship" no longer seems to fit), they also are responsible for its characteristic narrowness.

I do not claim that American statesmen always *act* in terms of these principles. Indeed one of the facts of their lives is that they find that they cannot do so. They act in many ways as statesmen have traditionally acted, as leaders trying to deal with problems justly and prudently on their merits. But they have, to a very large extent, lost

This essay originally appeared in Robert A. Goldwin, ed., *Bureaucrats, Policy Analysts, Statesmen: Who Leads?* (Washington, D.C.: AEI Press, 1980).

the understanding of the legitimacy of nonpopulist, nonscientific-management decision making. They "do" statesmanship in the broader and more traditional sense, but they do not understand it. Therefore, they often do not do it very well. While there is much truth in the frequent criticism that our representatives and (especially) our officials are unfeeling and arrogant in their indifference to opinions and concerns other than their own, the more profound phenomenon, I think, is their lack of confidence in their own judgments.

They are rather good at articulating consensus. They are usually reasonably good at implementing clear-cut goals. Much of the time, however, there is no consensus to articulate, or it is foolish or unjust. Most of the time, the goals are not very clear or are in conflict, and their implementation has to be pursued under conditions that do not stand still for the principles of scientific management to be applied. Nonpopulist, nonscientific concerns seem even in American democracy to be at the heart of statesmanship; yet the American statesman is likely to believe that they are not really his proper business, even when he spends most of his time with them. The result is that these nonpopulist, nonscientific sides of American statesmanship tend to be done poorly and, even when done well, tend to be done under cover.

While I shall not here be much concerned specifically with presidential statesmanship, President Jimmy Carter does provide an instructive case in point. It has become almost a truism that Jimmy Carter, who once seemed such an exotic in presidential politics, is emphatically in the mainstream. His first presidential campaign was built around the two themes that I have suggested are the dominant themes of contemporary American statesmanship: populism and scientific management. The American government was to be brought up to the level of the American people by opening up that government and making it more responsive to the healthy good sense and compassion of the people. ("Make the government as good as the people.") Carter's second theme—the answer to the question of what the candidate would actually *do* when he had opened up the government to the popular impulse—was the promise to reorganize thoroughly the whole government, to reduce the great number of agencies, to cut away at excessive bureaucracy, to improve planning, and to eliminate vast inefficiencies. In short, the promise was to make the government an efficient instrument for doing what the people, now again in control of their own government, want done. Once we became accustomed to the style and the accent, we saw that what was distinctive about the Carter campaign rhetoric was precisely the clarity with which it expressed the distinctive themes of American statesmanship.

There are two qualifications to these observations. First, I have not referred to another strand of the Carter rhetoric, namely, a version of Protestant fundamentalism. In this he is, again, representative of American statesmanship as a whole. In leaving the religious strain of American statesmanship out of account, I admit the incompleteness of my sketch, while also indicating my opinion that this strain would not turn out to be bedrock. A second qualification is closer to my present concern. For better or worse (and opinion on that varies sharply), once in office President Carter did not behave the way his campaign rhetoric indicated that he would behave. True, the populist style was ably, even brilliantly, maintained, and the president pressed hard the theme of technical efficiency, in his reorganization plans, his energy proposals, his decision to drop the development of the B-1 bomber, and so forth. Yet, in substance, President Carter acted very much as other middle-of-the-road presidents have usually acted, attempting to respond to specific policy questions prudently and on their merits, within limits enclosed by popular opinion, but with a willingness to stand against popular opinion and to lead it when that seems wise and possible.

It is arguable that President Carter understood quite well the limits of populism and scientific management and built a rhetoric from them, in quite a clear-headed way, in order, first, to secure office, and then, once in office, to provide the shell for a much broader, more traditional statesmanship. The thrust of this paper is to doubt the feasibility, at least on any significant scale or over any considerable period of time, of a statesmanship in which there is such a sharp difference between style and substance.

At the level of scholarship or "theory," almost all political scientists understand American statesmanship in terms of some combination or variance of the two principles I have identified. Compared with this basic agreement, their disagreements, which seem so compelling in the discipline, are secondary. Scholars in public administration debate the principles of efficient management, the connection between efficiency and "responsibility" (which is understood as responsiveness ultimately to popular will), and the extent to which the science of administration can be divorced in theory and practice from the requirements of democratic responsiveness. Students of American politics debate how adequately the American system collects and orders and gives effect to public opinion. A human relations expert criticizes the formal organization tradition for inadequately perceiving the human requisites of true efficiency. A Richard Neustadt criticizes the President's Committee on Administrative Management for its preoccupation with administrative arrangements and its failure to see the importance of the president's task of persuasion and consensus building. The pluralists criticize the antielite theorists for their simplification of democracy and their failure to see the varied and subtle texture of American society. The differences among academic students of American politics are great and the debate is vigorous and often illuminating. Nonetheless, with very rare exceptions (including some parts of the fast-disappearing discipline of constitutional law), the bedrock of principle from which all else derives in American politics is seen to be popular opinion and scientific management. The articulation of these principles and their relation to one another are the whole substance of American politics.

These themes of populism and scientific management are pervasive and deep. They are not, I repeat, always the terms in which American statesman act; they are not always explicit in specific policy discussion; they are often ignored or overridden in specific decisions. But they are the general terms in which American statesmanship presents and understands itself and is understood both by the people at large and by those whose business it is to study and understand it.

The Decay of Democratic Statesmanship

That there has been a broad change since the beginnings of the American republic in both the theory and practice of what may loosely be called democratic statesmanship is widely agreed, and the rough outlines of that change are not in much dispute. American political society, and with it American statesmanship, has become much less elitist or, in the older term, aristocratic, and much more democratic or popular. The general view is that that is an improvement, a maturation, a sloughing-off of elements alien to American democracy properly understood. I will try to establish, on the contrary, that from the point of view of the founders this change represents a decay, and that that point of view makes sense. I will also try to give some account of the main elements of that decay before reflecting on its broad significance.

The indispensable beginning point is to take seriously the framers' commitment to popular government. This commitment stands out boldly in almost all they said and did; and yet it is seldom seen today for what it was. Part of the reason for this is our tendency to assume that men (and especially "elites") always act for reasons other than those they profess. Even if we overcome that paralyzing and self-defeating premise, we stumble on the framers' persistent and often sharp criticisms of democracy. They seem to be either hypocritical or half-hearted in their commitment to popular government.

The explanation at this level is simple and, it seems to me, altogether compelling. Martin Diamond spent much of his scholarly life trying to show that the framers' devotion to popular government was the devotion of a true friend, who sees the defects of his friend, studies them, and combats them so that they should not destroy the thing he loves. Popular government is good, but it is problematic. It is not, in this, different from any other kind of government, as Madison explained so well to Jefferson (who understood the point, though he understood it differently from Madison). Each government has an evil tendency that is connected to its own vital principle. In a monarchy it is the king who must be watched; in an oligarchy, the rich; in a popular government, the people. Democracy is a problem in the United States precisely because of the extent to which the people are made the ruler. The beginning point, then, is that popular government is good but problematic in its own way, the specific danger being majority foolishness or tyranny. Democratic statesmanship must be understood, above all, in the light of that great danger, which implies its great task.

At the time of the American founding, the traditional solution to this problem was to build into the government representation of social elements that could check one another, and particularly the *demos*, with the aim of securing the benefits of all and resisting the dangers of each. The American Constitution of 1787 rested on a rejection of this traditional solution. Part of the reason was the unavailability in the United States of the elements of the traditional mixed regime, and especially of a hereditary aristocracy. We do not, the American founders often said, have the materials for such a mixture. A deeper reason, and the reason most of the Americans thought their solution to the problem was superior even to the admirable and time-tested British regime, was that in the modern mixed regime there was inherent a degree of deception, of resting the working government on appearances rather than on fundamental truths. The traditional mixed regime, as the Americans knew it from Blackstone and Montesquieu, softened the truth of original human equality with the willingness of men to take their places in a natural-seeming hierarchy. It relied heavily on a traditional class of leaders disposed to public service and popularly accepted as entitled to it. The problem was how to secure the benefits of the traditional mixed government without the materials and without the myths and deceptions that such governments involve. The Constitution of 1787 was the founders' answer.

From the point of view of traditional mixed government, this Constitution looks "democratic"; from the point of view of simple democracy it looks "mixed." Both of these terms were sometimes used by the founders, but the more common and accurate designations were "popular" and "complex." James Wilson caught the essence, I think, in this characterization:

> In its principles, Sir, it is purely democratical; varying indeed, in its form, in order to admit all the advantages, and to exclude all the disadvantages which are incidental to the known and established constitutions of government. But when we take an extensive and accurate view of the streams of power that appear through this great and comprehensive plan, when we contemplate the variety of their directions, the force and dignity of their currents, when we behold them intersecting, embracing, and surrounding the vast possessions and interests of the continent, and when we see them distributing on all hands beauty, energy and riches, still, however numerous and wide their courses, however diversified and remote the blessings they diffuse, we shall be able to trace them all to one great and noble source, THE PEOPLE.[1]

This government is popular but not simply popular. It does not, however, rely on mystery or myth to check the fundamental popular impulse. "Nondemocratic" "elements" are at work (though not nondemocratic social entities, in Wilson's description), but they are out in the open. This government is like a glass-enclosed clock. Its "works" are visible to all and must be understood and accepted by all in order to function properly. Not many of the framers were quite as confident as Wilson of the reasonableness of the people, but the government they constructed was nevertheless understood by them all to be unusual in the relatively small demands it placed on a political aristocracy and in the relatively great demands it placed on the people. The Senate was to make its distinctive contribution, for example, not because it consists of people presumed to have some superior title to rule or people with huge social influence derived from family tradition or wealth, but mainly because the interest of the men in the Senate is constitutionally tied to certain "senatorial" duties and because the people would *see*, over a relatively short time, the benefits of such a nonpopular institution.

---

1. John Bach McMaster and Frederick D. Stone, eds., *Pennsylvania and the Federal Constitution, 1787–1788* (Lancaster: Historical Society of Pennsylvania, 1888), p. 11.

There were men of the founding generation who found this solution facile and feeble. Alexander Hamilton's reservations are the most pertinent for our present purpose. Hamilton feared that there would be nothing in the new government (and the new society) strong enough to check or channel the reigning popular impulse. Hamilton doubted the effectiveness of the Virginia plan (put forward in the Constitutional Convention by Madison, Randolph, and others) to check the excesses of democracy that had been experienced in many of the states. "A democratic assembly is to be checked by a democratic senate, and both these by a democratic chief magistrate," Hamilton wrote.[2] This looked to him like "pork still, with a little change of the sauce."[3]

While Hamilton labored brilliantly to explain and to defend and to operate this Constitution, his earlier reservations revived, as is well known, as he saw what he thought to be the weakness of the elements in the Constitution designed to check democratic foolishness and injustice. Tocqueville confirms this view, but at the same time presents a wider or at least a different horizon. Even more directly pertinent are the more modest administrative histories of Leonard D. White. It is striking that when White looked at the actual conduct of the government in the early years, including both the Federalist and Jeffersonian periods, it was characterized by what he called "administration by gentlemen." The federal government in its early years was operated by a relatively small group of men who were socially prominent and who took their bearings from English notions of the right and, more especially, the obligation of members of the class of gentlemen to serve their country by conducting its affairs, and to do that with wisdom, honesty, and public spirit. To the extent that White is correct, it appears the actual conduct of the government then depended crucially on the existence of the political influence of a class of gentlemen, with an ability and a commitment to prudent statesmanship for which the framers of the Constitution had made no provision. Once the residual, English-based gentry was used up, there was little to preserve or maintain it, and the underlying populism—Hamilton's "pork"—took full command.

I exaggerate, of course. The constitutional scheme of checks and balances continued to function (indeed, in a certain sense, came into its own) under the Jacksonians. If the gentry were swept aside, if demagoguery thrived, the results were still mixed. Jackson's claims

---

2. Max Farrand, ed., *The Records of the Federal Convention of 1787*, rev. ed. (New Haven: Yale University Press, 1966), vol. I, p. 310.

3. Ibid., p. 301.

for the democratic presidency (accompanied by a certain notion of administration) were challenged, deflected, blunted by men in the Senate and the courts acting much as Madison expected they would act. But I am here following one strand of American history and American political thinking. It is not the only strand; it may or may not turn out to be the strongest and most persistent one; but it does seem to be the one most clearly tied to the self-understanding of American statesmen. It became increasingly difficult as the nineteenth and twentieth centuries wore on for American statesmen to see themselves politically as anything more than mouthpieces of popular opinion.

The story we are recounting is completed, in the decisive sense, with civil-service reform, which is the end of democratic statesmanship and the beginning of the contemporary decay of practical statesmanship. The Jacksonian doctrine of rotation (and the Jacksonian program in general) was meant to take the government out of the hands of the few and give it to the many. As rotation declined into spoils, however, it seemed that the result had been to turn over the government from an honest and competent aristocracy to a dishonest and incompetent one. Indeed the concern of the civil-service reform movement that began to build after the Civil War was fundamentally with government dishonesty rather than with government incompetence. Like the Jacksonians, the civil-service reformers' concern was political and moral; and like the Jacksonians the civil-service reformers sought to remove an illegitimate and corrupting obstruction that had grown up in the way of the free, healthy, spontaneous expression of the political will of the American people. The civil-service reform movement is today often described as having been "elitist" and antidemocratic. It involved a "good-government" elite attempting to destroy the vulgar, corrupt, unsystematic, but democratic functioning of patronage-based political parties. This is not inconsistent with the civil-service reformers' view of themselves as returning to the principles of the founders. But what both this self-understanding and this sociological view of the civil-service reform movement missed is that the reformers had rejected, or forgotten, the central element in the founders' statesmanship, namely, a sense of the problematic character of democracy. In this fundamental respect they stood with the Jacksonians against the founders.

Even that, however, is not precise enough. Democracy was in a way still seen as problematic by the reformers, but the locus of the problem had shifted for them from politics to administration. They believed that democracy itself is not unproblematic (the problem here is clearing away the rubble of various kinds that obstructs it), but its implementation *is* unproblematic.

This prepared the way for the next and, as it were, final step in the development of American statesmanship, the science of administration or scientific management. Before turning to that, however, it may be useful to summarize and to reflect on the significance of this development. Leonard D. White described this whole development as a healthy working through of the basic principle of the American republic (again Tocqueville's similar but more critical account is pertinent). As White saw it, bringing into focus a very widespread view, the development ran as follows: first came the Federalist period, characterized by elitist politics plus sound administration; then the Jacksonian period, characterized by democratic politics and unsound administration; and now, a "new Hamiltonianism," characterized by the return, as a result of civil-service reform, to the sound administration of the founders but now in the service of democratic politics.[4] This view misses three major considerations: (1) The old Hamiltonianism was not antidemocratic, but it was concerned with the problematic character of democracy. (2) Democracy is still problematic; and in losing the sense of that problem (however much the framers may have missed solving it), the new Hamiltonianism is shallow in the decisive respect. (3) The administrative theory and practice of the old Hamiltonianism, although it was indeed related to scientific management, had a common-sense quality that may have given it more severe limits in some respects than modern administrative science but also a breadth and soundness that today's understanding of administration lacks. To that second aspect of the decay of American statesmanship I now turn.

The Decay of Rational Statesmanship

When Woodrow Wilson called in 1887 for a new science of administration he saw himself as building upon and to some extent restoring the work of the founders. With the decisive victory of liberal democratic theory, the making of the U.S. Constitution, and the repair of the major defect of that Constitution in the Civil War, the great task of regime building and constitution making was finished. There would still be a need to extend liberal democracy to other parts of the

---

4. See Leonard D. White's introduction to Lynton K. Caldwell's *The Administrative Theories of Hamilton and Jefferson,* as quoted in Louis C. Gawthrop, *The Administrative Process and Democratic Theory* (Boston: Houghton Mifflin, 1970), p. 5.

world and a continuing need to modify and repair its constitutional structure. Nonetheless, the locus of the decisive problems of government had shifted from questions of constitution making and high politics to questions of administration. Wilson sought, then, to turn attention from largely obsolete and fruitless political controversy to the pressing and still unsolved problems of running the Constitution. Political theory had had its day; the task for today and tomorrow was the development and application of administrative theory. Wilson proposed that the democracies look to the systematic development of administration that had taken place under more autocratic governments, with the view to developing and learning to use the science of administration, the fundamental premise of which is that there is "but one rule of good administration for all governments alike."[5]

In many important ways, Wilson's proposal and the project of administrative science and practice that followed from it were indeed extensions of the founders' own project. In the most crucial sense, it can be said that, for the founders, the problem of government is a matter of administration. Government was no longer seen as a grappling with various and conflicting claims to rule, claims to determine the ends and character of social life. Instead, they believed the legitimate end of government is fixed: the securing of individual rights. In question, in terms of both forms of government and their operation, are the arrangements and policies that under given circumstances would be the best means to that fixed end.

This is the reason that discussions by the founding generation of forms of government have the curiously shallow quality that has frustrated so many analysts. Monarchy no longer "rides tilt against democracy," as Woodrow Wilson put it.[6] There were still differences, and forms of government were still important (see *Federalist* 70), but they no longer carried anything like their traditional freight. Government was no longer seen as directing and shaping human existence, but as having the much narrower (though indispensable) function of facilitating the peaceful enjoyment of the private life. In this view, government and the whole public sphere are decisively instrumental; government is reduced to administration. Questions of forms of government, too, become instrumental. Much less is *at stake* in a dispute between "democracy" and "monarchy," for example. The question is merely what kind of governmental arrangements

---

5. Woodrow Wilson, "The Study of Administration," *Political Science Quarterly* (June 1887). An abridged version can be found in Gawthrop, *Administrative Process and Democratic Theory*, p. 20.

6. Gawthrop, *Administrative Process and Democratic Theory*, pp. 77–78.

will, under given conditions, be most likely to secure the aggregate of individual liberty, which it is the business of any government to secure. (This is why constitutional and administrative questions, in contrast to *political* questions, are closely related for Wilson.)

"Statesmanship" in such a government is diminished in proportion. It can reasonably be called administration, though it may be administration of a rather high and demanding kind. The moral demands on statesmen in such a government are reduced to a commitment to serve the "permanent and aggregate interests of the society," as Madison called them. The intellectual demands are reduced to the formulation and implementation of appropriate means to fairly limited ends. To the American founders, however, even these demands seemed too great. The moral demands on the statesman were further reduced by putting him in a constitutional position, so far as possible, where his private interests would coincide with his public duty. The whole complex system of checks and balances and related constitutional devices have this aim. The intellectual demands (our special concern here) would be reduced through the development of the sciences dealing with the main areas of the statesman's (now rather limited) concerns. Thus, to the founders, the science of economics—or rather political economy—is queen; derivative from this are the subordinate sciences of, for example, military administration, governmental budgeting and accounting, and the arrangement of public offices. The American statesman of the future would be not a George Washington but a Robert Morris, a man whose private interests were closely tied to his country's fortunes and whose statesmanship consisted of the knowledge that a merchant and financier has of the way society works.

In sum, then, the American founders' view of statesmanship could be described as follows. There is never needed that kind of statesmanship which had formerly been regarded as its essence: great, "way of life"-setting, character-forming political leadership. That kind of leadership was based upon a misapprehension of political life, a failure to understand its decisively instrumental function. There may be needed, however, rarely but occasionally, what might be called high American statesmanship, or high liberal statesmanship, comparable to that of the founders themselves. The requirements here are an extraordinary (and perhaps ultimately inexplicable) devotion to public duty and an understanding of the principles of governmental structure and operation of the broadest and deepest kind. Note that this statesmanship is still, in a fundamental sense, "administrative"; it ministers to the private sphere essentially by securing private rights. Most of the time, however, an even narrower statesmanship will be sufficient: the activities of reasonably decent and well-informed men, guided by the constitutional system and by moral and prudential maxims derived from widely understood principles of political economy, military science, public finance, and so forth.

Just as the popular principle became radicalized, so did the "science" of government or administration become radicalized. The founders' maxims of administrative statesmanship became Woodrow Wilson's "one rule of good administration for all governments alike," which in turn became Frederick Taylor's "one best method," and that in turn became the "maximizing" model (and all of its various elaborations and qualifications) of contemporary decision-making science.

Frederick Taylor is perhaps the crucial turning point. Taylor insisted that his techniques—such as time-and-motion studies—must never be separated from the broader "philosophy of scientific management." That philosophy was a simplification of modern liberalism. Taylor saw scientific management as the working principle of a whole social system in which there is ultimately social harmony among apparently competing groups and individuals. He believed that once the true principles of organized activity are discovered and applied through scientific management, political and social conflict, which is based upon ignorance and misunderstanding, will be dispelled. Compared with the founders' view of American statesmen, Taylor's administrative statesman is relatively narrow.

The context of the older statesmanship was still a political or constitutional order which was, indeed, expected to limit the statesman's horizon; but that horizon was, nevertheless, a political one, and that was reflected in his everyday judgments. For Taylor, on the other hand, the context is a presumed natural harmony. There is ultimately no need for politics—either as providing a broad political order within which economic activity is pursued or (therefore) as adjusting competing and (in terms of mere self-interest) irreconcilable demands. Taylor did not in fact entirely escape the need for the more traditional moral and political judgment. The increase in pay for Schmitt, the carrier of iron hogs, was not to be in proportion to his greater efficiency (which resulted merely from his willingness to accept the commands of the scientifically informed supervisor); it was to be enough to stimulate him to raise the level of his private life, but not so much as to demoralize him. It is not clear where the standard for such judgments comes from in Taylor's scheme (though it should be noted that it is not clear either where the standard for equivalent decisions by traditional liberal statesmen comes from). Nor is it clear why the scientific manager does not attempt to pay Schmitt as little as possible in order to keep an unfair share of the benefits of increased efficiency for himself. The whole problem of the fidelity of the statesman, with which the framers were so deeply and, on the whole, effectively concerned, was largely ignored by Taylor. Not surprisingly, Taylorism came to be, or at least was widely thought to be, an instrument of management. It became, after all, part of a broader political context, for which Taylorism itself could not account and to which it could not direct itself.

This "philosophy" of scientific management, which seemed to Taylor so fundamental, quickly dropped away, distorting Taylorism in ways that seemed to have been invited by Taylor (as Taylorism distorted the administrative thought of the founders). What was left was the pool of techniques of scientific management, the best known of which are time-and-motion studies, and the notion of the "one best method."

> Now, among the various methods and implements used in each element of each trade there is always one method and one implement which is quicker and better than any of the rest. And this one best method and best implement can only be discovered or developed through a scientific study and analysis of all of the methods and implements in use, together with accurate, minute, motion and time study. This involves the gradual substitution of science for rule of thumb throughout the mechanic arts.[7]

This notion, which is basic to scientific management and all its heirs, would have seemed strange to the founders with their more common-sense notions of administrative science. Yet, it could be argued that Taylor was merely making clear and explicit what the earlier science implied: that the theoretical challenge is to develop that science of "management" in the broadest sense that will ultimately or in principle utterly displace the ad hoc, muddled, and inefficient lore of the traditional craftsman, as well as the ad hoc, muddled, and inefficient judgment of the traditional statesman.

What I have called scientific management in the broadest sense has taken a further large step beyond Taylorism, but in the same direction. Taylor can be understood as radicalizing the founders' attempt to free the statesman from major concern with the broadest ends of his activities. The statesman provided for by the founders "works" the system without having to try to follow his decisions to

---

7. Frederick Winslow Taylor, *The Principles of Scientific Management* (New York: Harper and Brothers, 1911), p. 25.

their broadest ends; the Taylor manager similarly develops his science secure in the knowledge that better means will naturally lead to good ends. In these ways both the founders' statesman and Taylor's statesman are substantially relieved of responsibility for considering the highest or broadest ends. In the concrete situation, however, both are emphatically end-oriented. Taylorism is a science or means to given ends. The science was instrumental in the way administration had always been understood to be instrumental, as subordinate to given ends. The rationale of practical statesmanship became severely narrowed, but it was not transformed.

This traditional way of thinking about administration has the great advantage that the given ends guide and limit the search for means. That advantage, however, is purchased at a price that is scientifically unacceptable. The standard scientific formula becomes: Given a comprehensive measurable statement of ends, there is but one best means. It became increasingly clear that such a requirement is not only impossible in practice (that is not regarded as fatal), but also inadequate in principle. "Ends" are misleading reflections of prescientific judgmental statesmanship. What common sense calls "ends" are ultimately mere wants, and one cannot be expected to know what one wants until one knows what one might have and at what cost. The very language of means-ends is not merely imprecise or approximate, it is essentially misleading. The decisive break comes with its replacement by something like a "behavior-alternative" model (what are my possible courses of action and which do I want?) or a utility-maximization model freed from the teleological implications of the means-ends, but now at the price of crushing informational and calculational demands and utter subjection to essentially arbitrary preference.

This independence from ends, and its accompanying benefits and problems, is what characterized the most recent version of scientific management. While it is surely true, as earlier laborers in the vineyard of scientific management complained, that such fashionable schemes as "systems analysis" and Program Planning and Budgeting System (PPBS) are in many ways less new and original than they claim, there is today a rather widespread understanding of the fact that what scientific management has been moving toward is not statesmanship, and not even administration or management, but rather economizing in the true sense.

The contribution of "systems analysis" is to clarify and elaborate the proposition that all practical rationality, the rationality of administration, the rationality of choice, is economic rationality. "It should go without saying that all decision-making persons or groups attempt to economize, in the true sense of the word. That is, they try to make the 'most,' as they conceive of the 'most,' of whatever resources they have."[8]

With this understanding clearly in mind, the new science of choice can overcome the two great defects of traditional statesmanship, which even the earlier forms of scientific management had not altogether corrected: its preoccupation with ends and its inability or unwillingness to replace mere maxims of action with objective measurement. In his preoccupation with given ends—those that seem important at the moment or those he is administratively responsible for—the traditional statesman or even the fairly sophisticated "manager" has failed to see the essentially economic character of all decision making. Thus, one of the men who helped to apply the new understanding to the Department of Defense, where it has had its greatest (though still disputed) success, explained that in 1961 military planning was in "disarray" because of the separation of military planning and fiscal planning. Military plans were made more or less incrementally and in terms of certain presumed military needs and objectives, with the price tag tacked on afterward. With the help of PPBS, the economic character of the decisions was recognized; thus costs and national security objectives were linked at the outset, while systems analysis provided quantitative information on various possibilities.

Although it is not always easy to understand just how far the claims of systems analysis extend, in general it can be said that greater sophistication about the economic underpinnings and techniques of quantification has been accompanied by greater sophistication in claims about practical applicability. The proponents of systems analysis are, generally, considerably less expansive than Taylor, for example, in the extent of their claims to replace traditional common-sense judgment. They emphasize that quantitative analysis can clarify and make more intelligent, but cannot displace, the nonscientific decision of the responsible administrator. Both implicitly (for example, in the "end" implications of "program" budgeting) and explicitly (for example, in various models of what Herbert Simon called "satisficing"), the proposals of systems analysis concede and even grapple with the limits of their science. If the practical claim is muted, the theoretical claim is even sharper and more comprehensive. Systems analysis admits, indeed emphasizes, that it can never absorb completely the "practical" side of practical reason. At the same time, it

---

8. Richard N. McKean, "The Role of Analytical Aids," in Gawthrop, *Administrative Process and Democratic Theory*, p. 253.

clearly affirms that it does in principle comprehend the "rational" side of practical reason. Systems analysis (or the science of the economics of decision making) is not all that there is to practical reason in decision making, but it is all there is to the *reason* of practical reason.

Some Common-Sense Corrections

Does this more or less historical analysis help us to understand contemporary issues of American statesmanship? It seems to me that it does. It encourages us to revive for consideration some rather obvious, useful common-sense observations about American states-manship, what it is and what it ought to be. It also leads into some less obvious, more fundamental theoretical issues, the practical thrust of which is much more obscure, but which are probably determina-tive in the long run.

Populism. It is not difficult to grasp and to be persuaded by the need a democracy has of regulation and guidance in the face of some of its own tendencies toward foolishness and injustice. If we can add to our rather sharp consciousness of the dangers of "elites" a recollection of the dangers of majorities, our statesmanship will be better grounded. Indeed this lesson has never been forgotten in practice. What has been neglected is its understanding and justification in principle. Government still acts in opposition to simple democracy (when it secures the rights of minorities and individuals, for example), but mostly we talk as if the solution to the problems of democracy is more democracy. That is why there is a persistent *tendency* to resolve more or less complex notions of American democracy into some kind of simple populism.

This simplistic talk at the level of principle tends to undermine more prudent views at the level of practice. Even the modern Su-preme Court, the strongest bastion of nonpopulist principle, has an increasingly difficult time giving an account of itself. Nevertheless, in the courts there is still a self-conscious and principled capacity to resist mere majoritarianism, weakened as this may have become. In the other parts of the government, such a capacity is much less evident. One of the results is, I think, an undermining of the statesman's confidence in his own judgment, in the legitimacy of relying on his own judgment even in the face of popular disagree-ment. The further and even more harmful result is that the people at large are constantly taught by their statesmen's rhetoric that their opinion is the touchstone of politics. Because this is not the case in

418

practice, and cannot be the case in any respectable regime, the contradiction strains the system, driving true leadership underground and depriving the system of popular confidence. The whole doctrine of elitism, in both its popular and scholarly forms, owes much to the absence in our public rhetoric (and behind that in our scholarly understanding) of a justification of the role of an "elite," a not simply responsive statesmanship in American democracy.

The danger of populism to popular government has to be met, I think, at two levels. At the level of institutions, the problem is basically recovering (perhaps in different forms) the lessons of the framers. I have mentioned the Supreme Court, and it is surely vital to our whole constitutional system that the broad understanding and acceptance of the legitimacy of such a contrademocratic institution, as Alexander Bickel called it, not be lost; or if it has in principle been lost, that it be recovered.

Another institution that has seemed promising to me in this regard is the bureaucracy which, for all its limitations, does introduce into the political system elements of stability, intelligence, and equity that are not altogether dissimilar to the qualities intended to be provided by the original Senate. The advantage of the bureaucracy from this point of view is its very invincibility (a democracy has a much harder time dispensing with the bureaucracy than with the Senate, as Max Weber—with somewhat different intentions—has shown). The disadvantage is the bureaucracy's narrowness and its strong tendency toward the merely technical, a tendency strengthened under modern doctrines of scientific management. A properly schooled bureaucracy might, however, be a solidly based source of the intelligence, stability, equity, and public-spiritedness that a democracy needs.

But institutional arrangements are probably not sufficient, and the degree to which the founders relied on them may partly explain the power of the populist principle. For the institutions require what I have argued has been seriously lacking, namely public justification and, therefore, continued legitimacy in the eyes of the people, who are the ultimate rulers. What some of the founders neglected is that in a popular government, however much it is modified with various "sauces" (and the bureaucracy is a fairly penetrating one), the people have to be reasoned with by their statesmen. This means reasoning not only at the level of specific policies but also at the level of constitutional principle. Precisely because the American government is so transparent, relatively speaking, so little reliant on lords, kings, and priests, American statesmen must keep alive its basic rationale. At the least this means not playing the easy game of populist rhetoric, which cannot but undermine, in the long run, the capacity of the system to act well. At the most it means finding ways of reinforcing and deepening the people's common-sense understanding that government, even popular government, is more than a matter of registering and implementing dominant opinion.

This task of leadership is crucial, and it provides a kind of rough test of contemporary statesmen. Any American statesman whose public face is populistic is not performing his highest duty, no matter how prudent and successful his specific policies may be. This points us, however, to the deeper consideration to which I have made reference. The founding generation, people and leaders alike, could grasp the principles of checks on popular opinion and could make informed judgments about specific institutions and policies because they were persuaded of the truth of the foundation and end of that government. That there can be majority tyranny is a notion that makes sense to men who see government as designed to secure inalienable rights. If this truth is denied or lost sight of—as is surely the case today—it becomes exceedingly difficult to hold any ground against the populist impulse.

The loose relativism that today penetrates popular political and ethical understanding tends, of course, to support the kind of loose populism I have been examining and criticizing. Such relativism is the ultimate obstacle to any thoroughgoing mitigation (by which I do not mean some kind of aristocratic displacement) of simplistic democracy. The great popular—and final—challenge today is, "Who's to say?" The question implies not only that it is extremely difficult and dangerous to give anyone (or any governmental institution) the power to "say" what is right or what is to be done, but that there is in principle no way to "say" what is right or what should be done. Liberal government exists in a tension between popular control and individual rights. With the washing away of the ground of individual rights, consent in one form or another seems to be the only place for a statesman to stand.

If this describes the popular view, the scholarly view is fundamentally identical. Almost the whole range of dispute among scholars about how American democracy does and should work takes place within the "consent" arena. What is popular consent? How is it articulated, and how is it to be most accurately recorded and responded to by government? These are the agreed issues. There are occasional forays outside the field of populism, but their general feebleness tends to support my broad point. The "new public administration," for example, has been dissatisfied, mainly on political grounds, with the subordination of the old public administration to dominant public opinion. The *ground* on which the new public administration might resist popular opinion is a treacherous bog consisting of supposed silent or suppressed majorities (a path out of the bog and onto the safe ground of populism again), or an almost undefended commitment to socially disadvantaged people (as the definition of social equality and social consciousness), or a more or less simple existentialism, which the new public administration is not the first to see is the main alternative to democratism. If sheer preference or commitment is all there is, why not mine?

Scientific Management. Just as a serious examination of the insufficiency of populism yields a number of common-sense corrections, so does the serious examination of the insufficiencies of scientific management. But as contemporary populism points to the underlying issue of natural rights, so contemporary scientific management points to the underlying issue of the nature of human reason. In this case it may be more helpful to touch (with some apprehension) on this underlying issue before turning to some common-sense thoughts about statesmanship or practical reason. We are not going to be much helped here by the thought of the American founders. They were far less articulate and self-conscious in their thinking about practical reason, or decision making, or the science of government, than they were about the political side of government. Their thrust was in the direction of systematic science, but this science did not seem to be inconsistent with, or likely to replace, traditional prudence. We who live with the sometimes unintended results of their work and thought need to try to recover and reflect upon some of their more or less hidden assumptions.

Our problem is to understand practical reason or, in the contemporary term, "rational" decision making. The issue is well framed in Herbert Simon's forceful and influential attack on the maxims of so-called practical judgment. Simon's argument is that these maxims, which are supposed to guide practical reason and which are the glory of the "practical man," are in fact empty because they are self-contradictory. For every maxim there is a counter-maxim: look before you leap; he who hesitates is lost. The sum of practical rationality here is zero. If the practical man decides well (for example, if he maximizes his values), either he is lucky or he is proceeding according to a rationality more systematic and scientific than he knows, which it is the business of the science of decision making to elaborate and extend. (This is a theoretical elaboration of Frederick Taylor's scientific management.)

The issue here is, What *is* rational decision making? I think many

421

of the critics of scientific management have given up the game too easily, granting a Simonian understanding of what rational decision making is but contending that the sphere of rationality in decision making is much more limited than Simon and others suggest. Practical judgment turns out to be either an accommodation to practical political necessities or an unavoidable arbitrariness. (It is the current willingness of systems-analysis proponents to admit these limitations on practical rationality that has typically muddled the issue in the current literature.) I think the attack must be carried further.

I will not claim victory here, but I do want at least to open the question whether scientific management misunderstands the essence, if not the scope, of practical rationality. I will frame the issue as a proposition: the two critical principles of the current understanding of practical reason, or rational decision making—the notion of the "one best method" and the assumption that all practical reasoning is essentially economic reasoning—do not make good sense.

As already suggested, the crux of scientific management is the notion of "one best method." Does it not make more sense to say that practically there often *is* no one best method? The road to the one best method is not the road to rationality but to insanity. There are many cases where it just does not matter much which one of alternative choices is made (whether, for example, to ride elevator A or elevator B). It is not rational to worry or calculate much about something that does not matter much, even if one could conceive of and even perhaps discover some marginal benefit one way or the other (elevator A is closer to the entrance and thus more used and thus more worn—or is it therefore better maintained?). In other cases, the difference between alternative possible choices may matter very much, but there may be practically no way to know which one is better. It is likely that the outcomes cannot be known in crucial respects. There is, of course, a good deal of thinking and research on decision making under conditions of uncertainty, but again the premise of this thinking is that these conditions *limit* rationality. My suggestion is the common-sensical and, I think, practically indispensable notion that one of the most important elements of practical reason—or "rational" decision making—is precisely how well or poorly such limits are grappled with.

The man who insists on calculating, and constantly postpones decisions in order to get more information and make more predictions and calculations, is acting *irrationally* in any sensible view, though he is merely persisting in a rational pursuit according to the strict economizing model. Herbert Simon speaks of "bounded rationality," yet he more or less admits that it is only because of these irrational boundaries that any given exercise of rationality makes any sense at all.[9] Simon's main response to the insanity of the maximizing model is what he calls "satisficing," which is a much more common-sense (and, incidentally, traditional means-end) approach in which the decision maker is satisfied with the decision that is "good enough" instead of insisting on maximizing. That seems altogether, may we say, reasonable. But for Simon it is a necessary falling short of reason. We "satisfice" because we have not the wits to maximize. If we can maximize, we would be silly to "satisfice." On the contrary, I think we "satisfice" because we have the wits to know that we *cannot* maximize and that we would be insane to try to do so. The notion of the "one best method," that human rationality is the maximization of utility, is, as I have tried to show in an extended analysis of Herbert Simon, a fragile bridge suspended between two great fires, the arbitrariness of preference and the insanity of infinite calculation, by which it is consumed.[10]

The second side of the contemporary view of practical reason is the contention that all practical reasoning, all rational decision making, is essentially economic. That does not mean that there is any claim that all people do act as economizers—or even that anyone actually does it (it turns out to be quite impossible); but so far as they are rational they are economizers. The genius of "economic" rationality is that it is unqualifiably comprehensive and it is also a purely instrumental science. All "ends," "values," are reduced to "utility," which provides the ultimate test of the science of rational choice without threatening its purely instrumental character. Clearly, there is some truth in this whole understanding. To take the pre-viously given example of military planning, it is surely correct that for military planners utterly to ignore questions of cost does involve their avoiding the "hard management choices" that must be made. In government, at least, every decision (well, almost every decision) can be and at some point must be reduced to a decision about budget, about economizing. Clearly, economizing is involved in practical reasoning, is necessary to it; the question is whether that is all there is to it or whether that is truly its essence.

Consider the experience and the character of the Bureau of the Budget or, in its present form, the Office of Management and Budget

---

9. Herbert Simon, *Administrative Behavior: A Study of Decision Making Processes in Administrative Organization,* 2nd ed. (New York: Macmillan, 1957).

10. Herbert Storing, ed., *Essays on the Scientific Study of Politics* (New York: Holt, Rinehart and Winston, 1962), pp. 63–150.

(OMB). The centrality and independence of the OMB are undeniable. It is hard to imagine a government without such an institution performing such a function (though it is perhaps not quite as hard to imagine as we might today think, and the effort might be instructive). It is easy, moreover, to agree that the director of the OMB, whoever he may be, is the superior, despite his lack of cabinet position and his lower salary, of most heads of departments. But is it imaginable that the OMB should govern—would that be reasonable? My point is simple, but I think very pertinent to the present issue. It is surely important that generals be compelled to face the issue of cost/benefit, and the people who do that compelling are as vital in practice as that element of practical rationality is vital in principle. But must not generals remain generals? Could the OMB defend the country? Could it conduct foreign relations? Could it protect individual rights?

What we need to consider here is the effect of economic *thinking* and whether its claim to be practical rationality makes sense. Is not the beginning of military rationality some kind of understanding of an adequate defense, rather than some abstract notion of maximizing utility or even the rather less abstract notion of "more bang for the buck"? Are not similar understandings the essential basis for practical rationality in other spheres? The legitimate rights of minorities ought to be secured. Old people ought to be able to live decently. All of these raise or point to economic questions, but they are not "economizing" in themselves. The question is whether such end-oriented views are not independent, indispensable bases of practical rationality.

The crux in practice is what kind of decision results from one view or the other. Grant that a general will make bad decisions if he utterly ignores questions of cost (which the fact of limited resources makes it extremely difficult to do). But then consider what kind of decision the economist is likely to make. Is he not likely to be easily shifted from a "utility" that is costly to one that is less so? Is he not likely to prefer utilities and costs that are measurable over those that are not? I do not claim that the economists *necessarily* make such errors in practical reasoning—any more than it can be claimed that the general is necessarily irresponsible or indifferent to cost/bene-fit—but that is the tendency.

One of the common criticisms of scientific management in vari-ous forms, including systems analysis, is its indifference to structure and institutions and, at the same time, its thoughtless tendency to foster centralized institutions. The basis of this criticism is the tradi-tional fear that the centralization fostered by the pursuit of adminis-trative efficiency will threaten democracy. It should be noted that the claim that scientific management has a centralizing tendency is controversial. Some defenders of systems analysis have contended that it is neutral with regard to structure and indeed can foster decentralization. Taking advantage of an ambiguity that is unresolved in Max Weber's account of bureaucracy, they contend that the development of objectively rational bases of decision reduces the dependence on their authority and therefore on hierarchy. In Weberian terms, the stronger and more comprehensive the definition of jurisdiction, the weaker can be the lines of hierarchical authority (subject, of course, to the necessity of enforcing jurisdictional definitions which are relatively unexplored by scientific management). In practice, surely, and, as I have tried at least to suggest, in principle also, scientific management is centralizing. It is centralizing in the sense that Frederick Taylor understood perfectly well, that the crucial and governing activity is development of the science itself, which can only occur (except derivatively) at the top. It is centralizing, further, to the extent that gaps in the science make it necessary to resort to central *authority* to support the science itself. And it is centralizing to the extent that (presuming a comprehensive science) there remains a continuing need to *enforce* the rational design of the science.

Scientific management radicalizes the claim for "unity" in administration. When Andrew Jackson defended his removal of subordinates even contrary to congressional legislation, he presented a view of administration as well as a view of democracy. Administration was seen as residing crucially in the president, with the administration serving as his eyes and hands. The Whig view, on the other hand, rested not only on a different (more "pluralistic") view of American politics but also on a different view of administration. The Whigs saw public administration not as a closed hierarchy leading to the top but as pools of official discretion, loosely connected but largely independent. Jackson and the Whigs were primarily concerned with what today we would call the issue of responsibility—Jackson, to the president; the Whigs, to the law. But the implicit views of public administration are especially interesting here, and the Whig view in particular since it is the one that seems always to lose. This view emphasizes the importance of the exercise of experienced, informed, responsible discretion as the heart of administration. Sound discretion, not obedience to higher command, is the essence of good administration, though both, of course, are always involved. Administrative structures should be built to provide the right conditions for this informed good judgment—independent regulatory commissions are a case in point. The Whig view of administration is modeled, one might say, on the judge. (One could describe modern administrative

425

science as the decisive displacement of the judge as the model administrator by the administrative assistant—even, increasingly, in the courts themselves). A major aspect of the Whig model was the notion of the judge's responsibility, but I want to point to another side, the kind of practical reason the judge exercises. His judgment here is confined and guided by more or less severe limits of the law, but within these limits the judge is expected to secure a personal grasp on the whole and to exercise his best judgment. He is thus, characteristically, assisted by law clerks, whose very immaturity, transience, and small numbers reinforce the judge's personal responsibility and judgment.

It seems reasonably clear that any government, to be well administered, needs a judicious combination of these two principles—each may appropriately predominate in its own time and place. But what we need to recover is an understanding of the claim of what can be called the judicial model of *rationality*. Partly because of our failure to grasp the *reason* of that model, it always tends to lose out in a contest with centralized, hierarchical rationality.

Perhaps the most striking omission in scientific management is any concern with the moral side of decision making, especially of political decision making. There is some current renewed interest in the ethics of administration or decision making, but it tends to result either in (fringe) codes-of-ethics thinking, the assumption of which is that ethics surround practical decision making but do not really enter into it; or in (sterile) case studies of the confrontation of (arbitrary) public policies and (arbitrary) personal preferences.

What we can roughly but usefully call the moral side of public decision making was for the American founders the major concern; today the intellectual side has occupied almost the whole ground. Yet in any kind of practical situation the question of the fidelity of the decision maker is crucial. The question that Frederick Taylor could not answer (or could answer only by assuming a simplistic harmony)—Why will the scientific manager not try to exploit his workers?—was for the founders the vital issue of statesmanship.

Robert Hutchins once observed of university administration that the intellectual problems, adapting means to ends, are small compared with the moral problems. A fairly simple example: It is on the whole easier to know that someone does not deserve academic tenure than it is to decide not to give it to him. As I cast my mind back on the many administrative situations I have been involved in, I am struck by the importance of the moral character of the people in charge. I think of a small army unit that constantly threatened to come unhinged under the leadership of an intelligent and able but weak commander and which was held together only by the stern, mule-skinner army morality of an old, extremely inefficient master sergeant. I think of political science departments whose fortunes (so far as they are not determined from the outside) seem to wax and wane far more in rhythm with the integrity and moral stature of department heads than with their administrative ability in the usual sense. I do not mean to assert the simple-minded proposition that good men make good administrators, or even that good administrators need to be good men—although that is not a bad place to start. I think that one could defend the proposition that moral stature is vital to administration or statesmanship of any consequence. And that is precisely what is lacking in our statesmen trained in and oriented to scientific management. They are no more really bad men than really good ones; rather, they tend to be morally uninteresting children. That dimension—moral stature—is missing or severely truncated.

The reference to Robert Hutchins suggests another common-sense correction of the scientific-management view of statesmanship, namely that the good statesman has a good understanding of and commitment to the ends of his organization, whatever they are. University presidents these days tend to be bookkeepers and brokers among their various "constituencies." That may, often, be good enough, but such administrators work in the shadow of men who knew what universities are for and how any particular university fit into that broad function. Greatness in a president of the United States, in a president of a university, in a general of the army, or in a chief of a governmental bureau is determined among other things by the grasp he has of the *ends* of his organization. A fairly loose grasp may be sufficient most of the time, but even mundane statesmanship is rooted in some such understanding. If an ordinary public servant does not need the grasp of the American regime of a Lincoln, he does need, as John Rohr suggests, at least the grasp of a reasonably competent student of some parts of American constitutional law.[11]

A final common-sense observation, harder to explain and defend, and for that reason more directly pertinent to the underlying question of practical reason, is that the essence of statesmanship is to be found in the old distinction between line and staff. The curious thing about decision-making theory is that it is not about decisions but about getting ready to make decisions. The rationality of scientific management is the rationality of the staff, but it does not reach, it does not treat whatever it is that is finally *decisive*. Decisiveness is, after all, universally acknowledged to be central to good administra-

---

11. John A. Rohr, *Ethics for Bureaucrats* (New York: Marcel Dekker, 1978).

tion of any consequence, yet it has no place in decision-making theory.

EDITORIAL NOTE
Herbert Storing had not quite completed his work on this essay when he died, suddenly, on September 9, 1977. A comparison of this draft with his outline for the essay indicates that a final section, "Conclusion," was never written. The portion of the outline covering the "Conclusion" is presented below.

The reader is cautioned that Mr. Storing may have intended some changes as he developed the ideas from the outline into their final essay form; however, a careful comparison of the outline and the essay as a whole indicates that he followed the outline, as far as he went, quite closely.

Conclusion

Authentic American statesmanship has decayed, but it decayed (as it were) from within.

1. Premise: statesmanship is in the service of the private sphere. This means that the activity of statesmanship is not seen as "fulfilling" and tends to be held in low esteem.
2. This is magnified by the American founders' effort to rely even on this instrumental statesmanship as little as possible.
3. Radicalization of popular principle
4. Radicalization of science as government principle

Thus statesmanship is not much respected; doesn't much respect itself ("civil servants" want to be "professionals" or even "government employees" rather than "civil servants")

Statesmanship tends to narrow itself to the role of the respectable technician, leaving the big decisions to "politicians" who in turn have to find their justification in being spokesmen of the popular will.

There is an alternative tradition, growing out of what the framers did rather than what they said.

They were pulled between the private and public lives; usually they chose the public, and not merely out of duty (and anyway, what's the basis of that?)

There is also a strain of popular recognition of need for nontechnical leadership and of leaders who see that need and try to meet it; always a presumption against that—which has been radicalized.

(this will not, however, be the last point made)

PART SIX

Liberal Education and the Study of Politics

23
Liberal Education and the Common Man

It is said that there is a widespread loss of confidence in our schools, which can hardly be denied. The problem is, it is suggested, that education today is seen as the accumulation of knowledge, in contrast to the education of former times when it was more philosophical, in the sense that it was an education in the nature and order of things, or when it was at least based on a view of the nature and order of things.

I accept this general formulation—only suggesting in passing that the distinctive modern view of education is perhaps concerned not so much with accumulation of knowledge as with modes of inquiry. The notion that education ought to be more "philosophical" might be taken to mean, and often has been taken to mean, that what we need is more liberal education in the schools—I am thinking especially of high schools and college—and less narrow, technical, professional, and vocational education. We need less "training," as the distinction often goes, and more "education," and that usually means liberal education as that has been traditionally understood. To put the point yet more broadly, American democracy requires that citizens must be philosophers, as I heard a prominent educator say; and the way to make citizens philosophers is through universal liberal education.

That is the idea I want to investigate. I would contend, on the contrary, that one of the reasons for the loss of confidence in our schools is that this idea of universal liberal education is too prevalent already and that we are therefore asking our schools to do something that they should not be asked to do and that they cannot but do badly. My contention is that the common man is bad for liberal education and that liberal education is bad for the common man. Note that I am speaking about liberal education as it is conventionally

This previously unpublished essay was written for a conference at Hillsdale College, in Hillsdale, Michigan, February 1975.

understood. I will defend a liberalizing education for the common man, but I do not think that this is best found in liberal education as that is ordinarily understood.

I do not want to get involved, at this point, with the complex and ultimately profound questions about the meaning of "liberal education" or, indeed, of "the common man." I begin with the obvious, ordinary understandings, which are admittedly insufficient but which are usable and meaningful in the present context. By "liberal education" I mean an attempt to provide a significant exposure to and participation in the great cultural tradition of the West (at least); it is an education based upon reading the great books, studying the great men, viewing the great aspirations and achievements, exploring the great questions that represent the peaks of the art, literature, and thought of the West. By "the common man" I mean most people. I am thinking of the bulk of men, women, and children, perhaps 75 or 85 percent.

Obviously there can be many questions about where to draw the line and what subgradations might be appropriate; but we do not need to consider these questions here. One implication of the term "the common man" is of course that there are "uncommon men" and that there are many of the former and few of the latter. Men are not equal in all respects that are relevant for education. That does not, of course, in any way deny that the foundation of our educational system is, or ought to be if it is not, an equality of opportunity. But the educational superstructure is a series of distinctions and discriminations which respond to and develop the manifest inequalities that human beings display. One can say that the very end of liberal government is, as James Madison said, to protect the diverse and unequal faculties of men.

My first contention, then, is that liberal education in the traditional sense that I have referred to is not accessible to the bulk of mankind and that to try to make it accessible to them involves a tremendous watering down, with results that are bad for liberal education. Liberal education is education in the extraordinary. It is concerned with the heights of human achievement. Its materials are distinguished for their depth, learning, comprehensiveness, subtlety, and refinement—and these are not the characteristics of the ordinary mind. Woodrow Wilson once said that "the bulk of mankind is rigidly unphilosophical, and nowadays the bulk of mankind votes. A truth must become not only plain but also commonplace before it will be seen by the people who go to their work very early in the morning. . . ." But the extraordinary cannot be made commonplace without losing precisely whatever it is that made it extraordinary.

432

What worries me is that if your aim is Plato for the masses; if you shave down Aristotle to fit minds that are stretched by Walter Lippmann; if you treat Shakespeare as antique James Baldwin, then you will destroy the distinction between the ordinary (even when it is very good) and the heights and thereby the very ground of liberal education.

I think that the truth of the degradation that liberal education suffers when it is democratized is sufficiently obvious and needs little illustration. One can hardly imagine anything more damaging to liberal education in any meaningful sense than the travesties of it that are widely practiced in many of our high schools and so-called liberal arts colleges. A favorite example of mine, illustrating both the tendency and its danger, is a syndicated column once written by Mortimer Adler—I read it in the *Chicago Sun Times* in the early 1950s—on the Great Ideas, or some such title. Someone would write Adler a letter saying that he and his girlfriend discovered in the heat of a lovers' quarrel that they did not really know what "love" is, and could he help? Adler would then produce 750 words or so on the meaning of "love" as it had been understood by the Great Thinkers, scanning a half dozen writers from Plato to Freud. The writer of each letter selected for publication was sent a complete set of the Great Books; but it was never clear to me why anyone should bother reading those long and difficult books, when he could, apparently, get the gist of their thoughts in a daily newspaper column. This was liberal education in the time it takes to drink a glass of orange juice.

My point is not that liberal education is irrelevant to democracy— far from it—but that liberal education cannot itself be made democratic without losing those qualities that enable it to contribute to the elevation of taste and thought in a democracy. Some very interesting illustrations of this problem can be found in the activities of the National Endowment for the Humanities, for which I have great respect. In one of their programs a major effort is being made to bring the distinctive and relatively rare insights of "academic humanists" (the representatives of "liberal education" in our present sense) to bear on consideration of public policy in various forms of adult education. The idea seems altogether legitimate to me, and I was involved for a while in the program in Illinois. But what was striking was the pervasiveness of the view not merely that the humanists have something to contribute to discussions of public policy, but that the humanists really ought to get down out of their ivory towers altogether and spend their time in contact with the real people (mainly, it seems, in local taverns) and in solving the problems confronting society. To the extent that the guardians of liberal education and the humanities yield to this kind of pressure—and they do not on the whole resist very well—liberal education decays into some form of democratic social engineering. And of course in the process the humanities tend to lose that aristocratic connection with the Western tradition that led the democracy to call upon them in the first place.

My point is, then, that precisely because there is an enormous pressure in a democracy to bring down liberal education to the level of the common man and his daily problems, there is a need for a special sensitivity to the distinction between the extraordinary and the ordinary and to ways in which that distinction can be maintained.

One of the problems in maintaining this distinction is that liberal education was traditionally the province of the small group of people who enjoyed leisure, as distinguished from the much larger group of people who had to work. Liberal education is for leisure; vocational education, or training, is for work. Since in the United States, with insignificant exceptions, we all work, there is a serious question about the status of liberal education in the traditional sense. We are driven to distinguish not between those who must work and those who do not but between those who must go to their work very early in the morning and those who can go to their work somewhat later. Or we find ways of subsidizing leisure, as some foundations and some programs of the National Endowment for the Humanities—and Arts, and Sciences—do, and as we try to do on a wider scale for the faculties at our universities and liberal arts colleges. There are some very serious questions, as I hope these examples suggest, about the project of maintaining liberal education in American democracy at all. I do not intend to follow this line of thought here, except to reiterate that the problem is to maintain the healthy tension between liberal education and democracy and that in practice that means finding ways to protect liberal education against being overwhelmed by the democratic impulse.

Let us consider the other side of the distinction between the leisured (or relatively leisured) few and the working many. For my contention is not only that the common man is bad for liberal education, in the sense I have described, but that liberal education is bad for the common man. I suggest that the common man in the United States has two primary characteristics and that his education should be primarily directed to them: he works for a living and he is a citizen of a democracy.

One of the best and most thoughtful educators of the common man in the United States was Booker T. Washington; and his educational principles are directly relevant to our present question. (I am not here concerned with Washington's views about the relations between the races or about the politics of turn-of-the-century United States.) Washington called his educational scheme, learned at the Hampton Institute and fully developed at Tuskegee, "industrial education," education for work. He discouraged Negroes from taking up the "cultural" subjects, which were so appealing as evidence of "real" education, and urged them instead to begin with immediate needs, especially the need to earn a living. He was profoundly offended at the half-literate Negro preacher whose example was practically and morally debilitating to the people he was supposed to lead. He saw something grotesquely unfitting in the image of a slovenly young Negro man sitting in a weed-filled garden poring over a French grammar. Even apart from the strong probability that his French would never be good, such a youth was beginning, Washington insisted, at the wrong end. As the foundation of life for most people is work, so the foundation of education for most people should be industrial or vocational education.

This view seems to me altogether sound. Yet our high schools seem blindly committed to the notion that their primary goal is to teach the liberal arts. I know that there are outstandingly good vocational schools and courses in our high schools (and, ironically, that they are generally much harder to get into than the "liberal arts" schools); but on the whole, vocational education seems to be regarded as peripheral. Yet surely it is the schools in this case that are peripheral. One can hardly blame the ordinary teenage boy or girl for losing his respect for and interest in a school system that tries to teach him everything except what he most needs to know, that somehow implies that his desire to know how to do something that will enable him to earn his living is beneath the concern of his teachers. There is a widespread tendency in educational circles to denigrate vocational education as low, narrow, and merely technical, and to contrast it with the breadth and elevation of liberal education. But if, as I have suggested, it is vital to maintain liberal education and the possibility of liberal education in a democracy, it is also necessary to acknowledge the enormous role that education for work must play in any sensible scheme of universal education. Vocational education is the principal concern, I suggest, of education of the common man.

It is true, of course, that job training can be very narrow. But merely technical training is bad not because it is specialized and vocational but because it does not open up into anything broader or higher. That is not, however, an intrinsic defect. There is a perfectly natural way in which technical or vocational education can be broadening, and that is through reflection on the ends or aims to which it points. When W. E. B. Du Bois criticized Booker T. Washington for propagating a Gospel of Work and Money, he did not grasp that Washington's view was that work and money were indeed necessary in themselves but that they were also the first step in moral and civic and liberalizing education for the common man.

Thus while liberal education begins with leisure, vocational or industrial education begins with the need to work. Washington taught his students how to work, how to earn their living. There followed a series of lessons that raised the students beyond mere work. He taught the worth of a job well done. He taught the need for order and discipline. He taught the meaning of freedom. "Those are most truly free today who have passed through great discipline. Those persons in the United States who are most truly free in body, mind, morals, are those who have passed through the most severe training—are those who have exercised the most patience and, at the same time, the most dogged persistence and determination."

Washington wanted to make men independent, to instruct them in the life of a free man. He did it in a way that was more meaningful than traditional liberal education, not only for turn-of-the-century Negroes but, I suggest, for most people most of the time; because the teaching was drawn out of the kind of concerns that are primary and natural for most people most of the time. Vocational has the same basic aim as liberal education, though the student body, the circumstances, and thus the means are different: it is the education of free men.

Industrial education could also be, Washington thought, liberalizing in the sense of opening up to the students, not only a higher morality and self-understanding, but also broader horizons and deeper understanding of the world, both natural and human. Properly understood, vocational education can be a form of liberal education—the best form for most people—rather than in opposition to it. Describing a commencement oration on cabbages by one of his Tuskegee students, Washington said, "As a matter of fact, there is just as much that is interesting, strange, mysterious, and wonderful; just as much to be learned that is edifying, broadening, and refining in a cabbage as there is in a page of Latin." The difference is that education in "cabbages" is also useful.

There are edifying, broadening, and refining lessons to be found in every vocational area. The secretary's need to know how to spell can be extended into an interest in words—where they come from, what they mean, and what they imply about the nature of things—and their grammatical relation. The vocational training of the engineer can be directed out through architecture and the visual arts to

436

beauty, and through city planning to the principles and ends of the polity. The nurse can be encouraged to draw on her nurse's training to extend her understanding of human psychology, of the promise and limits of the biological sciences, of life and the good life. Here, it seems to me, lies one of the major educational tasks of today: to find ways of liberalizing vocational education. And that does not mean mainly adding courses on "cultural" subjects. It means discovering and teaching and extending the liberalizing potential of vocational training.

Whereas vocational education, including its moral and liberalizing side, is concerned primarily with the private or individual life, the common man is also a citizen. And the second kind of education I have suggested for the common man is civic education. This distinction between the private man and the public man—a distinction with profound and problematic implications—is not always clear-cut. For example, one of the chief subjects of civic education is the American hero, especially American public men. Admiration for these men and what they stand for is part of the social bond, and their study should surely be near the center of civic education. At the same time, these men often serve also as models of how to live, and particularly how free men ought to live. One thinks, for example, of the autobiographies of Theodore Roosevelt or Booker T. Washington, both quite explicitly directed to teaching the ordinary man how to make the most of himself as an individual and as a citizen. As models of individual life, as well as of high citizenship, these American heroes are more limited than some of the models available in the great Western tradition. But they are immediately relevant; they are harmonious with the principles of the American polity; and they are elevating and broadening.

The most common objection to civic education is that it involves indoctrination which, it is said, conflicts with the aim of real education, which is to teach people how to think. Is there a conflict between civic education, which aims to make a good citizen, and liberal education, which aims to make a free man with a free mind? Again I do not propose to consider this question in its most profound reaches. But at least in our present context I do not think that the usual distinction between "indoctrination in values" and "teaching how to think" is so sharp or contradictory as might appear.

Not only does any teaching involve a kind of indoctrination (every educational institution, curriculum, and teacher stands for something), but any indoctrination, or any kind of indoctrination at issue here, involves teaching. The simple but powerful point is that human beings cannot be indoctrinated without giving them some reasons, and reasons permit and even invite reasoning. What this suggests to me is not so much a sharp dichotomy between the inculcation of values and independent reasoning as a continuum or (better) a hierarchy. The problem of civic education is, surely, to inculcate healthy civic values, but to do so in a way that does not foreclose, that indeed encourages and assists, a questioning and thereby a deepened understanding of those values. In this way civic education too becomes liberalizing in what is essentially the same way that vocational education can be liberalizing. The Declaration of Independence, for example, must be a prime text of American civic education; it articulates the basis and the ends of the American polity. But the Declaration of Independence cannot be studied merely as an American document; it cannot be simply "received." It is grounded in reasonings based on what are said to be universal principles of human equality and human right. One cannot indoctrinate an American citizen without leading him to think about "nature and nature's god," "self-evident" truths, and "unalienable" rights.

I have said that the study of the American heroes ought to be near the center of American civic education. This means, in the first place, the propagation of what are usually called "myths" about great Americans. Happily, however, the American heroes *do* bear examination. Abraham Lincoln is the crucial example. The tendency today is to see Lincoln in terms of a rather sharp alternative, either as the Great Emancipator or as a self-seeking politician. Since the former is not simply true, we tend to assume that it is simply false. Thus arises the enthusiastic debunking of the myths of the old civics books that seems to be a favorite occupation of American historians.

But such a view is not only politically unhealthy—for a country without heroes is a country without principles or aspirations—it is also false. The truth about Lincoln consists in various levels or stages of understanding. At the first and simplest level there is the Lincoln who freed the slaves, the Great Emancipator. More study and understanding reveal that Lincoln was not altogether "above" ordinary politics: he was a shrewd and ambitious politician. At a still higher level, however, one learns about Lincoln's commitment to the preservation of the Union and his (startling) willingness to free or not to free slaves according to whether that would help or not help preserve the Union. Yet further, we learn why Lincoln wanted to preserve the Union, and discover that it was because of his well-reasoned conviction that Union was the best existing institution to protect and foster human freedom. Finally we may understand what Lincoln's defense of Union implied for Negro slavery and thus grasp the deeper truth that the original simple view of Lincoln as Great Emancipator embodies, that Lincoln had (as Frederick Douglass put it) put himself "at the head of a great movement, and was in living and earnest sympathy with that movement, which, in the nature of things, must go on until slavery should be utterly and forever abolished in the United States."

This process of deepening the understanding of the primary truths of civic education is what is involved in good civic education. It is also a form of liberal education. The study of Lincoln, properly conducted, makes good citizens at the same time that it extends their horizons. It is no accident that Booker T. Washington's model was Abraham Lincoln and that both Washington and Lincoln were concerned preeminently with the question of freedom. There may be times and places where the pressing problem is an excess of civic indoctrination at the expense of adequate opportunity for questioning and thinking. I do not think that that is the problem in American education today, at either the secondary or the college levels. Our distinctive problem seems rather to be a loss of confidence in the legitimacy and necessity of providing educational support for the political and moral principles on which the country is based.

My conclusion, then, is that vocational education and civic education are the kinds of education needed by and suited to most people. To depreciate vocational and civic education or to push them to the periphery tends, it seems to me, to have three unfortunate results: (1) it tends to weaken the society's grasp on and respect for liberal education proper; (2) it tends to ignore or downgrade the major legitimate educational needs of most people, which is education for work and for citizenship; and (3) it tends to overlook the most relevant and solid vehicles for liberalizing education for the vast majority of the American people.

24
The "Chicago School" of Political Science

I

I will try to talk about the department of political science at the University of Chicago as a whole and to say something about what I think is its particular excellence. This will involve what may seem an immodest praise. This attempt to look at the whole is appropriate here, but it may leave unsaid the most important things—that is, you may find that what is most important and most valuable about the department has to do with some part of it, rather than with anything that can be said about it as a whole.

It was in the days of Charles Merriam that the reputation of this department was established. The names associated with the Merriam department make an astounding roster. In addition to attracting to its faculty such men as Leonard White, Jerome Kerwin, Herman Finder, and Quincy Wright, the department turned out Harold Lasswell, Harold Gosnell, V. O. Key, C. Herman Pritchett, Gabriel Almond, David Truman, and Herbert Simon—many of whom have also taught here. This list represents many different interests and many differences of opinion; but it makes sense to talk about the Merriam "school," even though its character might not be easy to define precisely.

It would be quite impossible today to name any man or any approach to the study of government as representative of what the department stands for. That fact is my theme.

Before saying why I think this is a good thing, let me point out that there are some distinct advantages in a department that is clearly going one way. There is a certain kind of vigorous community spirit and intercommunication which is probably impossible in any other

This previously unpublished material comes from remarks addressed to incoming graduate students at the University of Chicago, probably in the early 1960s.

circumstances. There is (or at least seems to be) a very substantial saving of resources, both student and faculty. It is possible to concentrate energies. If all the members of the department pretty much agree where they are going, they can get on with it, they can fertilize one another's work, and there is likely to be a distinct *movement* when one views the work of the department as a whole. This increases the possibility of making a perceptible impact on the profession at large, because (although there will always be disagreements) relatively little time has to be spent along the way with methodological and philosophical skirmishes—in which different sections of the department seem to do little more than to cancel each other out. In such a department there can be a coherent curriculum; it is relatively easy for students to plan their program and for advice to be given to them. You begin, say, with a "scope and methods" course, required for everyone in the first year of graduate school, then to certain broad substantive areas (approached in a certain way), then into specific areas of research. I think Merriam was the first to set up such a course. It is significant to my theme that we are one of the few graduate departments without one such course of study. We have several under different names!

The department today does not share a common orientation like that of the Merriam department or, I understand, of the department at Northwestern University today, for example. On the other hand, neither do its divisions give rise to a faction-ridden environment in which the student has to make a shrewd estimate of the relative strength of the different cliques, choose his side during his first quarter, and remain loyal to it—at the peril of both his research grant or teaching assistantship and his degree. Yet finally, the department certainly does not present what is no doubt the worst (and unfortunately probably the most common) picture of all: the namby-pamby department where everyone agrees a little and disagrees a little, where everything is very gentle and dull, and no one says (or learns) much about anything.

What I am trying to suggest in this negative way is that the divisions here cut very deeply in a substantive way but, at the same time, they are not allowed to dismember the department as an institution. The latter is necessary to the corporate life which the faculty leads, and in which you share. The former is the department's particular excellence, and its end as a department.

I think there is probably no other department in the country where there is more penetrating debate and inquiry into the foundations of political science. There is no better place for you to achieve some clarity about what the *questions* of political science are. Most

political scientists never get themselves oriented even in this preliminary way. It is this advantage, I think, that generally distinguishes
the best of our graduates from the best graduates of other institutions. Ours are sometimes less comprehensively acquainted with the
literature as it rolls off the presses, less facile in academic name-
dropping, but they are likely to be better acquainted with basic issues.

I am perfectly well aware that, while I have referred to vigorous
and penetrating debate, I have talked around it. I have not laid out
the elements of the disagreement or summarized what the debate is
about. And I should be surprised if you did not wish for some clear
statement of the issue or issues. You may live with this wish for some
considerable time. But it would not be helpful for me to try to state in
a few sentences what the debate is about, because *that* is one of the
matters debated.

There often appears to students to be a failure of communication
between one faculty member and another. This is partly because
there is likely to be disagreement between them about what are the
fundamental questions. There are, in the students, 100 vehicles of
communication—you bear the major responsibility. You will not find
any corporate answer here to the question, What is political science?
but you will not be allowed to overlook the question.

These fundamental questions are most fully articulated and
thoroughly exposed in the field of political theory: hence, the central
place of theory in our curriculum. The formal expression of this is the
fact that the preliminary examination in political theory is the only
one that every Ph.D. candidate is required to take. Another manifestation is that one of the few propositions to which the department
would, I think, assent unanimously is the absolutely outstanding
caliber of our faculty in political theory.

This emphasis on theory colors the whole department. That is
not to say that the department is characterized by the merely theoretical or that we think that everyone ought to be a theorist. I know that
this is not the opinion of the teachers of theory themselves—and
even if it were, the rest of us have them outnumbered. The members
of the department spend their time in the field as well as in the
cloister—as you may discover when you try to find them in their
offices. As the work of virtually every member demonstrates, the
department does not shrink from the laborious and necessary task of
collecting the facts. Most of the theses and dissertations written by
our students are based on the same kind of empirical investigation.
A majority of our faculty and students are not concerned primarily
with theory but with understanding as well as they can one or
another aspect of government; but the department gives explicit

recognition and emphasis to the fact that research and study in any field of government inevitably both raises theoretical questions and is guided by some theory. That means of course that it may also be *misguided* by theory. The department as such cannot prevent that, because this is precisely where the most profound divisions lie. But by engaging the student in penetrating and vigorous theoretical discussion, it can enable him to ensure that his empirical research is at least not muddled because of a lack of awareness of the basic issues.

II

As a new student your question addressed to the department is: How shall I become a good political scientist?

The only answer that any spokesman for the whole department can give—whether our official written statements, or the chairman, or myself, or anyone else seeking to speak on behalf of the whole department—the only answer that the department can give is a formal or procedural one.

This procedural advice suffers all the weaknesses that such advice usually suffers; but it is aimed to help you go looking for the substantive answer to the question, and it does that by advising, encouraging, and sometimes requiring you to take serious account of the wide variety of approaches to the study of political phenomena.

We present as a department a variety of different and often incompatible views of what it means to be a good political scientist. In that fact lies our challenge as a department to you, and your opportunity as students of political science.

25
The Achievement of Leo Strauss

The political science profession that Leo Strauss entered when he came to Chicago in 1949 radiated confidence in the capacity of the scientific study of politics to advance the frontiers of knowledge and to contribute to the practice of politics and to social planning. No one denied that there was a huge gap between promise and performance, but this seemed to be the defect of a still-young enterprise and it served as stimulus rather than restraint. There were of course students of government who did not share the prevailing scientific ideology, but they were scattered and could be regarded as merely behind the times. The dominant spirit, especially in the leading institutions, was the brotherhood of modern science.

The political science profession that Strauss leaves behind, only twenty-odd years later, is far less self-confident. Its science seems pedestrian and its mastery of political life further away than ever. It suffers from diversity, not merely at its fringes but painfully close to the heart. Questions that the scientific orthodoxy thought it had excised have reemerged. One prominent professor of political science ends a survey of scientific approaches to the study of judicial process by calling for the serious study of values; another declares the poverty of academic liberalism; yet another, an excellent social scientist, insists that the question of the justice of capital punishment is more important and probably more answerable than the question of its deterrent effect. Without making exaggerated claims, it is undeniable, I think, that Strauss had a great deal to do with these changes. If he did not reform political science, he did administer a resounding jolt.

Three Characteristics

Strauss took his responsibilities as a political scientist seriously. He and his students had an obligation, he conceded, to show that

This essay originally appeared in the *National Review*, vol. 25, December 7, 1973. Copyright by *National Review*, Inc., 150 East 35th Street, New York, NY 10016. Reprinted by permission.

their activities (mostly reading and talking about old books) were legitimate things for political scientists to be doing. This concession led, however, to a thoroughgoing and aggressive criticism of that political science before whose bar he stood. In particular Strauss addressed himself to three prime characteristics of political science: its distinction between facts and values; its attempt to dissolve political things into their prepolitical elements; and its blind assumption that the world of liberal democracy is the world as it is and ought to be.

Scientific political science has been guided, not by what it knows about politics, but by what it knows about knowing. Its positivist epistemology requires that a basic distinction be made between facts, which can be subjected to empirical validation, and values, which cannot. Values are relegated to the academic limbo of the history of political philosophy or "normative theory" (whatever that can be), while political scientists get on with the real work of formulating hypotheses that can be empirically tested. Strauss's criticism of the fact-value distinction is often misunderstood as merely a claim in behalf of "values."

It is true that Strauss denied what scientific political science affirms, that value questions are outside the realm of rational discourse. But his argument was not primarily for values but against the distinction between facts and values. He did not scorn or oppose the factual study of political things as they are. He had learned his Hobbes and Machiavelli, to say nothing of his Plato and Aristotle, too well for that. He valued highly any sensible, informative political writing; and there were few keener-eyed or harder-headed observers of politics. Nor was his purpose to propagate some favorite "value" position. Rather, he taught that political things cannot be seen for what they are if they are viewed through the artificial distinction between facts and values. American slavery is not seen for what it is if it is not seen to be unjust. There can be no account of voting behavior that is not utterly dependent on and inseparable from some notion of what voting is for.

This does not deny the importance of carefully done empirical studies of the economics of slavery, for example, or of the working of large-scale organizations, or of voting behavior. But it does mean that such studies need to be informed and guided—as political life itself is informed and guided—by a concern with the ends of political life. At the least, the student should not allow himself to be arbitrarily cut off from such questions. Common sense knowledge (which is always "valuing" knowledge) is not sufficient, but it provides the only access to the world of politics that we have. If Strauss's students have sometimes displayed an unseemly self-assurance, the source is not so much pride of truth as relief that they have not allowed political science to make them more stupid than they need to be.

The second characteristic of political science subjected to Strauss's uncompromising analysis is its attempt to reduce political things to their economic, sociological, or psychological elements. While the political actors may say, and even think, that they are debating about the public interest, political science knows in advance that that is merely a façade. Public political discourse is not itself of much interest to the political scientist. What citizens and politicians say to one another about public issues is useful mainly in providing clues to the hidden, private, and often unconscious motives that really count. Political scientists thus make themselves into more or less adequate economists, sociologists, or psychologists, and diligently dig to undermine the study of politics.

Strauss revived an alternative: the view of politics as architectonic, as forming the human materials, including the subpolitical lives and motivations, to its ends. Instead of explaining American politics in terms of supermarkets and ethnic groups, he showed the deeper sense in which supermarkets and ethnic groups have to be explained in terms of American politics. Strauss pointed the student of politics back to the principles of the regime—to those rules and ends and standards of the human good that constitute the life of the community. He showed the formative importance of times of founding and crisis, the very times typically ignored by political scientists.

Despite its reductionism, American political science has had a political view, but it has remained largely unacknowledged and undefended. Strauss showed the profound parochialism of most of political science, its tendency to assume that the familiar world of liberal democracy is both natural and good. Because of this facile assumption, voting studies, opinion surveys, interest group studies, and the other favorites of political science seem less narrowly bounded by time and place than they are. Part of the reason for this parochialism, Strauss showed, is a harmony between scientific political science, with its methodological commitment to what is common, and crude democratism. Another part is its ignorance of past thought and therefore of the alternative to liberal democracy.

In an attempt to defend himself from the charge of unselfconscious parochialism, the political scientist sometimes nails his liberal democratic preference to the mast. He likes peaceful change better than violence. Admitting that such preferences are utterly irrational, he at least exposes them so that he can get on to the scientific work with a clean conscience. Obviously there is here no need, more precisely there is no possibility, of any serious examination of the case against liberal democracy. The predictable result is flabby politics and flabby scholarship. Struass made his students confront the enemies of liberal democracy—not only its modern enemies but also the more far-reaching criticism of the thinkers of classical antiquity who denied that men are equal in the crucial respects and who affirmed that the proper end of political life is virtue, not freedom. That such confrontation does not tend to produce unqualified admiration of liberal democracy is true. That it weakens liberal democracy would be true only if under present circumstances liberal democracy cannot be provided with a rational defense persuasive to thoughtful and well-informed men. That was not Strauss's view.

Strauss's constructive project was to recover sight of the ends of political life for a profession that had blinded itself to such considerations. He invited a fresh and serious examination of the American Declaration of Independence, not as a reflection of the times but as having a claim to truth. He explored in the writings of modern political philosophers the deeper grounds of the argument of the Declaration of Independence. And he opened up the great alternative of classical political philosophy. He turned to the great men and the great books of political philosophy as teachers, not sociological resources. He taught the reader to explore the author's intention, not to impose one of his own, and to open himself to the possibility that the author is right, that what he says is true.

Careful Reading

Strauss was not a methodologist, but he had a method. He sometimes described it as "content analysis." It is the method of careful reading. Assume that your writer may be telling the truth. Assume that he knows what he is doing. Read with the greatest care and alertness that you can muster. If your writer falls into a contradiction that you can see, assume that he could see it, and try to figure out his reason for arguing as he did. Remember (what we all know) that one does not say all one has to say to everyone, that for various reasons one may speak and write at different levels. A great deal of ill-informed controversy surges around Strauss's concern with esoteric writing. But the basic principles are simple and wholly plausible: What student or journalist has not hidden a weak argument between a strong beginning and a strong conclusion? Strauss showed that many writers invite the intelligent reader to dig beneath the surface for truths that it is dangerous or unfitting to leave in the open. Unquestionably this is heady stuff, and there has been a certain amount of puppylike frolicking in the esoteric garden. But to dismiss the whole enterprise as "obscurantism" is merely to confess an inability or unwillingness to learn something of the depth, precision, and subtlety of which the human mind addressing itself to political questions is capable.

Strauss did not intend that all students of politics should be mainly students of political philosophy. Much of his project was aimed at clearing away the barriers that stand in the way of a meaningful study of politics. Returning to the political arena, the student of politics can perform his proper role of articulating and comparing and clarifying the concerns of citizens and politicians. While the main and more visible thrust of Strauss's teaching is in the direction of political philosophy (itself understood as an extension of the debate of the public arena), there is a steadily growing number of students of government, many of them little concerned with political philosophy or with Strauss, whose paths will be less cumbered, whose studies will be more meaningful, and whose eyes for politics will be clearer because of the work Strauss did.

Greater Diversity

While there has been a significant opening up, however, there has been no transformation in the professional business of studying politics. Subjected to Strauss's persistent hammering from within, frustrated by the continuing gap between promise and performance, and bored (one supposes) with its own triviality, American political science was susceptible to the New Left indictment of irrelevancy and (still worse) institutional conservatism. The results have been solemn analyses of the "postbehavioral era," confessions that the science has not indeed been neutral but that it is now ready to go to work for the Left, and pronouncements by the leaders of the scientific establishment that "values" and "relevance" are after all terribly important. There is an acceptance of greater diversity in approaches to political study and of the legitimacy of criticism of narrow scientific orthodoxy. But for all the scrambling among the leaders of the profession for philosophical postures that can be said to deal with the "normative" questions and for all the claims that the "fact-value" controversy is obsolete, the old positivist and historicist foundations that were the objects of Strauss's attack remain in place—if not quite so firmly in place—beneath the turmoil. In 1962 Strauss wrote that scientific political science could be described as fiddling while Rome burned. "It is excused by two facts: It does not know that it fiddles, and it does not know that Rome burns." Ten years later, it may perhaps be said that political science is beginning to suspect that Rome is burning.

The following remarks were presented by Mr. Storing at a memorial service for Leo Strauss held at the University of Chicago on November 16, 1973, recorded and transcribed by Frank Kruesi.

Leo Strauss: In Memoriam

We are here today to remember and pay our respects to Leo Strauss, Robert Maynard Hutchins Distinguished Service Professor Emeritus of Political Science, University of Chicago.

There have been two commanding figures in the Department of Political Science at the University of Chicago: Charles Merriam and Leo Strauss. There are some important similarities between these two men, including their interest in political theory, their very wide scholarly impact, their unusual gifts as teachers, and the direct effect on others of their extraordinary intellectual and moral qualities. But the differences are perhaps even more significant.

I mention only one, which is superficial but which points to others. Whereas Merriam's effect on our department and on the political science profession was unifying, Strauss's effect was divisive. It is widely believed that our political science department during Strauss's days was torn by warring factions, and that that was somehow Strauss's doing. There is much truth in that belief, though it needs some qualification, or explanation.

The controversy was, on the whole, civil and substantive. And it went along with mutual affection and deep personal attachments which helped to maintain collegiality amidst controversy. And the factions were neither the incredibly complex and somewhat nostalgic factions of the émigrés at the New School for Social Research (in which Strauss had participated with a good deal of pleasure) nor the native-born petty academic factions of personalities and preferments. Indeed, petty factionalism was remarkably limited and unimportant. Most tendencies of that kind were displaced or absorbed by a vigorous substantive debate about what we as political scientists ought to be doing. Strauss was the main fermenter of and participant in that debate. He provoked controversy. He disturbed our personal and our departmental tranquility. But he divided us in ways that scholars ought to be divided: by challenging us to think more deeply and comprehensively than we had been accustomed to think about the scope and method of political science and the place in political science of political philosophy. . . .

449

Bibliography of the Writings of Herbert J. Storing

Chronological Listing of Previously Published Works

"The Farmers and the State." With Peter Self. *The Political Quarterly* (January–March 1958).

"The Birch in the Cupboard." With Peter Self. *Public Law* (Winter 1960).

The State and the Farmer. With Peter Self. Berkeley: University of California Press, 1963; paperback edition, 1971.

Essays on the Scientific Study of Politics, editor. Author of "The Science of Administration: Herbert A. Simon." New York: Holt, Rinehart and Winston, 1962.

"Replies to Wolin and Schaar." *American Political Science Review* 57 (March 1963).

"The Problem of Big Government." In *A Nation of States,* ed. Robert A. Goldwin. Chicago: Rand McNally, 1963.

"William Blackstone." In *History of Political Philosophy,* ed. Leo Strauss and Joseph Cropsey. Chicago: Rand McNally, 1963.

"Political Parties and the Bureaucracy." In *Political Parties, U.S.A.,* ed. Robert A. Goldwin. Chicago: Rand McNally, 1964.

"The School of Slavery: A Reconsideration of Booker T. Washington." In *One Hundred Years of Emancipation,* ed. Robert A. Goldwin. Chicago: Rand McNally, 1964.

"The Crucial Link: Public Administration, Responsibility, and the Public Interest." *Public Administration Review* 24 (March 1965).

"Leonard D. White and the Study of Public Administration." *Public Administration Review* 25 (March 1965).

"Foreword" to Paul Eidelberg, *The Philosophy of the American Constitution: A Reinterpretation of the Intentions of the Founding Fathers.* New York: The Free Press, 1968.

"The Case against Civil Disobedience." In *On Civil Disobedience,* ed. Robert A. Goldwin. Chicago: Rand McNally, 1969.

"Introduction" to the reissue of Charles C. Thach, Jr., *The Creation of*

451

the Presidency, 1775–1789. Baltimore: The Johns Hopkins Press, 1969.

What Country Have I? Political Writings by Black Americans, editor. New York: St. Martin's Press, 1970.

"Frederick Douglass." In *American Political Thought: The Philosophic Dimensions of American Statesmanship,* ed. Morton J. Frisch and Richard G. Stevens. New York: Charles Scribner's Sons, 1971.

"The Achievement of Leo Strauss." *National Review,* December 7, 1973.

"The 'Other' Federalist Papers: A Preliminary Sketch." *Political Science Reviewer* 6 (Fall 1976).

"Slavery and the Moral Foundations of the American Republic." In *The Moral Foundations of the American Republic,* ed. Robert H. Horwitz. Charlottesville: University Press of Virginia, 1977. Originally given as a lecture at St. John's College, Annapolis, Md., on March 5, 1976, and published as "The Founders and Slavery," in *The College* (St. John's College), July 1976.

"Martin Diamond." *PS* (Fall 1977).

"Foreword" to John Rohr, *Ethics for Bureaucrats: An Essay in Law and Values.* New York: Marcel Dekker, 1978.

"The Constitution and the Bill of Rights." In *Essays on the Constitution of the United States,* ed. M. Judd Harmon. Port Washington, N.Y.: Kennikat Press, 1978.

"American Statesmanship: Old and New." In *Bureaucrats, Policy Analysts, Statesmen: Who Leads?* ed. Robert A. Goldwin. Washington, D.C.: American Enterprise Institute, 1980.

The Complete Anti-Federalist, editor. 7 vols. Chicago: University of Chicago Press, 1981. Introductory essay also published separately, as *What the Anti-Federalists Were For.* Chicago: University of Chicago Press, 1981. Selections from the 7-volume edition were published in one volume as *The Anti-Federalist.* Chicago: University of Chicago Press, 1985.

"The Federal Constitution of 1787: Politics, Principles, and Statesmanship." In *The American Founding: Politics, Statesmanship, and the Constitution,* ed. Ralph A. Rossum and Gary L. McDowell. Port Washington, N.Y.: Kennikat Press, 1981. Reprinted in *American Political Thought: The Philosophic Dimension of American Statesmanship,* ed. Morton J. Frisch and Richard G. Stevens, 2nd ed. Itasca, Ill.: F. E. Peacock Publishers, Inc., 1983. Published in this volume with the title, "The Constitutional Convention: Toward a More Perfect Union."

Index

About the Author

HERBERT J. STORING was born on January 29, 1928, in Ames, Iowa. He served in the United States Army from 1946 to 1948, and received his A.B. degree from Colgate University in 1950. He then attended the University of Chicago, earning his A.M. in 1951 and Ph.D. in 1956. He was a Fulbright Scholar to the United Kingdom from 1953 to 1955 and also received research grants from the Rockefeller, Ford, and Relm Foundations and from the National Endowment for the Humanities.

Mr. Storing served as senior research assistant at the London School of Economics; as assistant, associate, and professor of political science at the University of Chicago (1956–1977); and as director of the Telluride summer program at the Hampton Institute in 1967. He was Visiting Charles Evans Hughes Professor of Jurisprudence at Colgate University from 1968 to 1969, and part-time professor of political science at Northern Illinois University from 1969 to 1975.

At the time of his death in September 1977, Mr. Storing was Robert Kent Gooch Professor of Government and Foreign Affairs at the University of Virginia, where he also served as director of the Study of the Presidency at the White Burkett Miller Center for Public Affairs. He was also a member of the President's Commission on White House Fellows.

He is coauthor of *The State and the Farmer*; editor and contributor to *Essays on the Scientific Study of Politics*; editor of *What Country Have I? Political Writings by Black Americans*; editor of the seven-volume *The Complete Anti-Federalist*; author of *What the Anti-Federalists Were For*; and author of numerous essays on the American founding, constitutional law, public administration, American political thought, and the American presidency.

About the Editor

JOSEPH M. BESSETTE has served as associate professor in the Alice Tweed Tuohy Chair of Government and Ethics at Claremont McKenna College since 1990. From 1985 to 1990, he served as deputy director for data analysis and as acting director of the Bureau of Justice Statistics in the U.S. Department of Justice, and from 1981 to 1985 he was director of Planning, Training, and Management of the Cook County (Illinois) State's Attorney's Office. He has held teaching positions at the University of Virginia, Catholic University of America, the University of Chicago, and Georgetown University. In 1983, he was issues coordinator for the Chicago mayoral campaign of Richard M. Daley.

In addition to other published writings on American government and politics, he is author of *The Mild Voice of Reason: Deliberative Democracy and American National Government*; coeditor and contributor to *The Presidency in the Constitutional Order*; and coauthor of *American Government: Origins, Institutions, and Public Policy*.

A NOTE ON THE BOOK

This book was edited by
Cheryl Weissman
of the staff of the AEI Press.
The text was set in Palatino, a typeface designed by
the twentieth-century Swiss designer Hermann Zapf.
Coghill Composition, of Richmond, Virginia,
set the type, and Data Reproductions Corporation,
of Rochester Hills, Michigan, printed and bound the book,
using permanent acid-free paper.

The AEI PRESS is the publisher for the American Enterprise Institute for Public Policy Research, 1150 17th Street, N.W., Washington, D.C. 20036; *Christopher C. DeMuth*, publisher; *Dana Lane*, director; *Ann Petty*, editor; *Leigh Tripoli*, editor; *Cheryl Weissman*, editor; *Lisa Roman*, editorial assistant (rights and permissions).

DATE DUE

GAYLORD			PRINTED IN U.S.A.